ECHOES OF ETERNITY

Also by Pavan K. Varma

Adi Shankaracharya: Hinduism's Greatest Thinker

The Great Hindu Civilisation: Achievement, Neglect, Bias and the Way Forward

The Greatest Ode to Lord Ram: Tulsidas's Ramcharitmanas

Ghalib: The Man, the Times

Krishna: The Playful Divine

Yudhishtar & Draupadi

The Great Indian Middle Class

Being Indian

Becoming Indian

Chanakya's View: India in Transition

PAVAN K. VARMA

ECHOES OF ETERNITY

A Journey Through Indian Thought from the Rigveda to the Present

Published by Westland Books, a division of Nasadiya Technologies Private Limited, in 2025

No. 269/2B, First Floor, 'Irai Arul', Vimalraj Street, Nethaji Nagar, Alapakkam Main Road, Maduravoyal, Chennai 600095

Westland and the Westland logo are the trademarks of Nasadiya Technologies Private Limited, or its affiliates.

ISBN: 9789360455194

10 9 8 7 6 5 4 3 2 1

The views and opinions expressed in this work are the author's own and the facts are as reported by him, and the publisher is in no way liable for the same.

Every possible effort has been made to identify and reach out to the respective copyright holders. In case you have any query regarding this, we welcome you to contact us. Any errors or omissions brought to our notice will be rectified in future editions.

Typeset by Mukul

Printed at Thomson Press (India) Ltd

Contents

Introduction

India is a civilisation of *moulik soch*—the power of original thought. This faculty has been the bedrock on which the Indian people have survived and flourished since the dawn of time. Other ancient civilisations, such as the Greek, Roman, Persian, Assyrian and even classical Chinese, have long since ceased to exist. What makes our civilisation different is a certain ability for cerebral interrogation, discovery and renewal that has bestowed the great stream of Indian ideas with antiquity, continuity, diversity, assimilation and peaks of refinement.

This compendium, or anthology, seeks to capture some of the magnitude of this vast ideational canvas. Its breadth covers a period of 7,000 years at the very least, from the Rigveda, dated circa 3500 to 3000 BCE, to the philosopher Osho, closer to the present. The subjects it includes range from philosophy, metaphysics, religion, values, politics, economics, arts, literature, poetry and aesthetics to social change and renewal. The geographical sweep is as wide, covering the whole of Bharatvarsha, from the Himalayas to Kanyakumari, and Dwaraka to Puri and the Northeast. The selection would have been even richer in content had the script of the great Indus Valley Civilisation been deciphered, and one can only hope that scholars will succeed one day.

As can be imagined, the greatest challenge in such a task was what to select and what to leave out. Our corpus of thought is so copious that some degree of judicious selectivity had to be exercised. It also required going through tons of literary material in order to decide what the final selection would be. Certainly, there was an element of subjectivity involved in the process and the final decision was mine. I am fully conscious that there will be some who feel that the contents are incomplete, or that certain texts have been excluded which, according to their thinking, need to be there, or that the material is disproportionately focused on some texts, or even on some historical periods, to the neglect of others. I plead guilty to these accusations, since I have already made the disclaimer that a process of selectivity was involved, and that is bound to lead to some exclusions. My only defence is that I was influenced by no extraneous or ulterior agenda, that my intent was entirely benevolent, and it was my genuine attempt to provide a fair sampling of the infinite sparkle of ideas that have gone into the making of our civilisational heritage.

To my mind, even this is a good beginning to introduce readers to our remarkable legacy of thought. Many educated Indians are woefully unaware of its contents, depth and range.

They are aware of some important names, and may have read a few texts, but on the whole, there is a regrettable ignorance with regard to the endless river of thought of which they are legatees. For such people, this book, I hope, will serve as an essential primer to understand the brilliance and continuity of our cerebral evolution, and inform them that the concept of nationhood is underpinned, since time immemorial, not only by a shared geography, but also the generous benediction of application of mind that, like some exquisite weave, binds us all together.

This infusion of knowledge is particularly important for us at this juncture, when we are poised to take our legitimate place at the high table of the world. For decades now, India has held an appeal for foreign observers. Some are overwhelmed by its surface diversity and cacophony, the pageantry of colours and cuisines and sartorial variations, the endless range of art and handicrafts, and, of course, the rich cultural heritage so visibly on display in music and dance. Others are bewildered by the number of deities and rituals, the infinite varieties of folklore, and the proverbial Babel of languages and dialects. There are still others who are attracted by the mystic appeal of Hinduism, and the many other religions that flourish here. But, in general, all these reactions appear to fit more into the label of 'exotica', which essentially means an 'interesting' or 'appealing' or even 'irresistible' multitude of people and traditions, spread out between the icy Himalayas and the balmy, sandy beaches of the coast.

The unfortunate part is that Indians themselves are quite happy with this kind of superficial appreciation. They are satisfied with the amusement—and occasional praise—of their 'quaintness' and seem to quite like their perceived eccentricity to be summed up in the decidedly condescending phrase: 'We are like that only.' This to my mind is an unacceptable threshold of self-esteem. We have to understand that underlying our vibrant diversity is the unity of what can only be described as the audacity of thought. It is this that enabled us to touch new heights in philosophical rumination, unmatched calculations in astronomy, foundational contributions in mathematics, including the invention of the 'zero', create one of the oldest systems of town planning, the first ever meditation on aesthetics, a unique tapestry of music, dance and rhythm not seen in any other part of the world, pioneering work on statecraft preceding Machiavelli by millennia, groundbreaking achievements in poetics, grammar, dramaturgy and literature, architecture, environment, and highly evolved notions of ethics, the goals of life and sources of anchorage for the ordinary person.

In other words, we have to understand that we are one of the most cerebral civilisations in the world, and cannot only be satisfied with surface appreciations that we are an ancient but diverse set of 'cute' people. The tragedy, of course, is that most of us are largely ignorant—apart from a cursory knowledge at best—about this past. This is the plight of most postcolonial societies. Long after political freedom has been won, the colonisation of the mind persists. This leads to either a lack of curiosity about our past, a false search for modernity without cultural rootedness, a sense of *heenta* or inferiority about our own heritage, and institutional amnesia, which includes the blanking out of, or skimming over, large parts of the essential knowledge corpus by our education system.

The opposite reaction occasioned by colonisation is a distortion of this heritage, either through exaggeration or misinterpretation. In this case, the pendulum swings to the other extreme, with people smarting from the deliberate colonial devaluation—even demeaning—of our past, seeking to over-glorify it, or worse, recreate it according to their agendas, such that one period of history is magnified disproportionately, others are looked down upon, and our manifest diversity is sought to be erased. Thus, there are claims made by so-called historians about aircrafts, advanced plastic surgery, artificial insemination and motor cars in ancient India, without any scientifically verifiable evidence, fuelled only by an overactive imagination and misplaced pride. Many of these conclusions are based on mythology—important for its wisdom and symbolism but not meant to be taken literally in every respect.

Religious evangelists also see everything through the prism of primacy or appropriation, thereby selectively rubbishing or diminishing the rich infusion of ideas that has come to us over millennia through assimilation. Both of these schools of thinking actually trivialise and caricature our profundity of thought, creative efflorescence and genuine achievements.

A word now about the format of the compendium. Firstly, a large part is about the foundational period of our civilisation, which can largely be called Indic. This is because this initial period of our history is by far the longest, stretching for close to or even more than 5,000 years. It was at this time that the philosophical framework of the Hindu faith evolved, taking the realm of ideas to a new high of refinement and loftiness. This is also the period when Buddhism and Jainism, both beginning as offshoots of Hinduism, made their dramatic intellectual foray as repositories of great depth of thought, introspection and wisdom. Apart from philosophy, it was in these initial millennia that kingdom states came up, political thought was coded, new milestones were set in science, unbelievable strides were made in the sectors of art, culture and literature, and great thought was invested in devising a framework to define the goals and values of life. Hence, the ideas of this period cannot be ignored in any meaningful compendium of thought. The dates for different works or authors in this section vary greatly in terms of exact determination, but the ones chosen are those which find the

greatest acceptability among scholars. However, to avoid any controversy, they should be taken as indicative.

However—and this is the second point—I have taken due care to give appropriate space to what happened after the Turkic invasion, and the syncretic and outstanding thought processes that resulted from this new interaction. Thirdly, and finally, the modern period of our history, and the great melting pot of ideas that marked our self-discovery in the final phase of British rule, and after Independence in 1947, have also been included.

In terms of the structure of the selected texts or ideas, I have chosen to either provide an important extract from a written text, or include an essay that describes a homogenous ideation, such as the remarkable Bhakti movement, some important thinkers and, of course, the great ideas of Sikhism and Sufism. What extract to choose has often posed a difficult problem, given the enormous choice available, but here I have exercised my editorial liberty, dictated by what appears to me to be brilliant, representing originality of thought and exposing an important aspect of our overall evolution of thought. Some texts, although important, are too abstruse for selection; in such cases an interpretation, or a flavour of the text, has been given. Other texts have been chosen for the information they provide and the substance and detail with which they deal with a subject, even if the quality of their prose could possibly be improved upon.

Poetry, which is synonymous with compressed thought, finds place, but here, in particular, the choice is so great that the larger purpose was merely to open a window to excite curiosity to enter the larger home replete with many, many more great voices. Brief contextual notes about the texts and individuals are duly provided. Some sections, including a few translations, are from my own books, especially *Adi Shankarcharya: Hinduism's Greatest Thinker* and *The Great Hindu Civilisation.* I would also like to emphasise that all the selected texts have been reproduced as originally published, with some minor editorial changes only when absolutely necessary.

By and large, the compendium tries to follow a chronological pattern, to illustrate the flow of ideas sequentially and root them in the changing historical context. However, there are exceptions, since on many occasions, the ideas of one period in one part of the country overlap with those of others. I have preferred—since it is in any case continuous—to have the 'river of thought' run without any break, indicative of a period or subject matter. Great care has also been taken in selecting the source material of the corpus. Wherever possible, I have tried to go back to early translations, many dating back to a hundred years or more, which retain a directness, freshness and spontaneity that best capture the brevity, intent and content of the original text.

Copyright access or permission has been duly obtained where possible, and due credit given to the source. I must also clarify that texts in the original language (except for the first text, the Nasadiya Sukta of the Rigveda, and some foundational texts of the Vedic period like the Brahma Sutras) have not been provided. Rather, their translation or meaning has been provided in English, while also providing the requisite reference material for any reader to easily access the text in its original language should they so desire. There was also a practical reason guiding this decision: the inclusion of all the original texts would have made the size of the book quite unmanageable.

My purpose is to create a collection—not perfect by any means—which would be useful as an essential primer in any library or home. The structure is such that the reader can dip into any section, to know more about a writer, a thinker, and the writings of that period. Ideally, this should whet the appetite to read and discover more about our thought heritage, and help bridge the gap between cursory or incomplete information and more definitive knowledge.

In this journey of labour and love, I must express my profuse thanks to Dr Mani Shankar Dwivedi, an outstanding Sanskrit scholar and researcher, who was always helpful and available to cross-check or find a particular text and its translation. My gratitude also to Karthika V.K., the exceptionally capable and patient editor and publisher of

Westland Books, and to her team, especially Amrita Talwar. A word of shukriya is also due to my secretary, Manish Tiwari, for all his organisational help. And, of course, to my wife Renuka, as always, a salute.

1

Nasadiya Sukta of Rigveda

The Vedas, and the Rigveda (circa 3500 BCE) in particular, are considered to be the foundation of Hinduism. The etymological meaning of Veda is 'sacred knowledge' or 'wisdom'. There are four Vedas: Rig, Yajur, Sama and Atharva. Together they constitute the samhitas that are the oldest textual basis of the Hindu religious system.

The Nasadiya Sukta starts with the 129th shloka of the 10th mandala of the Rigveda. These shlokas raise and answer the eternal question about the origin of life or Srishti. There are numerous translations and interpretations of these profound verses, which do not present a story of creation like those found in other religious texts. Instead, they encourage the listener to question whether one can ever know the details about the origin of the universe.

(10.129)

nasadasinno sadasittadanim nasidrajo no vyoma paro yat |
Kimavarivah kuha kasya sharmannambhah kimasidgahanam gabhiram || 1 ||

The non-existent was not, the existent was not; then the world was not, nor the firmament, nor that which is above (the firmament). How could there be any investing envelope, and where? Of what (could there be) felicity? How (could there be) the deep unfathomable water?

na mrutyurasidamrutam na tarhi na ratrya ahna asitpraketah |
anidavatam svadhaya tadekam tasmaddhanyannaparah kim chanasa ||2||

Death was not nor at that period immortality, there was no indication of day or night; THAT ONE unbreathed upon breathed of his own strength, other than THAT there was nothing else whatever.

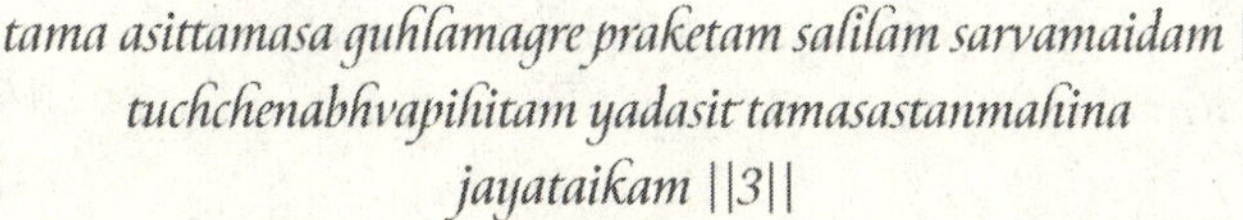

tama asittamasa guhlamagre praketam salilam sarvamaidam |
tuchchenabhvapihitam yadasit tamasastanmahina
jayataikam ||3||

There was darkness covered by darkness in the beginning, all this (world) was undistinguishable water; that empty united (world) which was covered by a mere nothing, was produced through the power of austerity.

kamastadagre samavartatadhi manaso retah prathamam yadasit |
sato bandhumasati niravindanna hrudi pratishya kavayo
manisha ||4||

In the beginning there was desire, which was the first seed of mind; sages having meditated in their hearts have discovered by their wisdom the connexion of the existent with the non-existent.

tirashchino vitato rashmireshamadhah svidasi duparisvidasi |
retodha asanmahiman asanna svadho avastat prayatih parastat ||5||

Their ray was stretched out, whether across, or below, or above; (some) were shedders of seed, (others) were mighty; food was inferior, the eater was superior.

Ko addha veda ka iha pravochatkuta ajata kuta iyam visrishtih |
arvagdeva asya visarjanaya atha ko veda yata ababhuva ||6||

Who really knows? Who in this world may declare it? Whence was this creation, whence was it engendered? The gods (were) subsequent to the (world's) creation; so who knows whence it arose?

iyam visrushtiryata ababhuva yadi va dadhe yadi va na |
yo asyadhyakshah parame vyomann so amga veda
yadi va na veda ||7||

He from whom this creation arose, he may uphold it, or he may not (no one else can); he who is its superintendent in the highest heaven, he assuredly knows, or if he knows not (no one else does).

—Translated by H.H. Wilson

2

Isha Upanishad

The Upanishads come at the very end of the corpus of the Vedas; they are also collectively called Vedanta, or the end of the Vedas, expounding the non-dual nature of the cosmos—Advaita. The word Upanishad literally means 'to sit down near' the feet of the master or teacher who shares with his pupils spiritual truths or wisdom. The authors of the Upanishads are not known, nor do we have their exact chronology. It appears certain that initially they were, like almost all ancient Hindu texts, orally transmitted from generation to generation, and only reduced to classical Sanskrit sometime around 600–400 BCE. The Upanishads do not constitute a single volume; in fact, their exact number is not known either, but by common consensus, there are about twelve principal Upanishads, which constitute perhaps the most profound philosophical texts of the Hindu faith.

Isha Upanishad (circa 3500–3000 BCE) is one of the shortest Upanishads, consisting of eighteen verses, embedded as the final chapter of the Yajurveda. 'Isha' means the Lord of the Universe. It is a key scripture of the Vedanta schools and an influential shruti for most schools of Hinduism.

All this is for habitation by the Lord, whatsoever is individual universe of movement in the universal motion. By that renounced thou shouldst enjoy; lust not after any man's possession.

Doing verily works in this world one should wish to live a hundred years. Thus it is in thee and not otherwise than this; action cleaves not to a man.

Sunless are those worlds and enveloped in blind gloom whereto all they in their passing hence resort who are slayers of their souls.

One unmoving that is swifter than Mind, That the Gods reach not, for It progresses ever in front. That, standing, passes beyond others as they run. In That the Master of Life establishes the Waters.

That moves and That moves not; That is far and the same is near; That is within all this and That also is outside all this.

But he who sees everywhere the Self in all existences and all existences in the Self, shrinks not thereafter from aught.

He in whom it is the Self-Being that has become all existences that are Becomings, for he has the perfect knowledge, how shall he be deluded, whence shall he have grief who sees everywhere oneness?

It is He that has gone abroad—That which is bright, bodiless, without scar of imperfection, without sinews, pure, unpierced by evil. The Seer, the Thinker, the One who becomes everywhere, the Self-existent has ordered objects perfectly according to their nature from years sempiternal.

Into a blind darkness they enter who follow after the Ignorance, they as if into a greater darkness who devote themselves to the Knowledge alone.

Other, verily, it is said, is that which comes by the Knowledge, other that which comes by the Ignorance; this is the lore we have received from the wise who revealed That to our understanding.

He who knows That as both in one, the Knowledge and the Ignorance, by the Ignorance crosses beyond death and by the Knowledge enjoys Immortality.

Into a blind darkness they enter who follow after the Non-Birth, they as if into a greater darkness who devote themselves to the Birth alone.

Other, verily, it is said, is that which comes by the Birth, other that which comes by the Non-Birth; this is the lore we have received from the wise who revealed That to our understanding.

He who knows That as both in one, the Birth and the dissolution of Birth, by the dissolution crosses beyond death and by the Birth enjoys Immortality.

The face of Truth is covered with a brilliant golden lid; that do thou remove, O Fosterer, for the law of the Truth, for sight.

O Fosterer, O sole Seer, O Ordainer, O illumining Sun, O power of the Father of creatures, marshal thy rays, draw

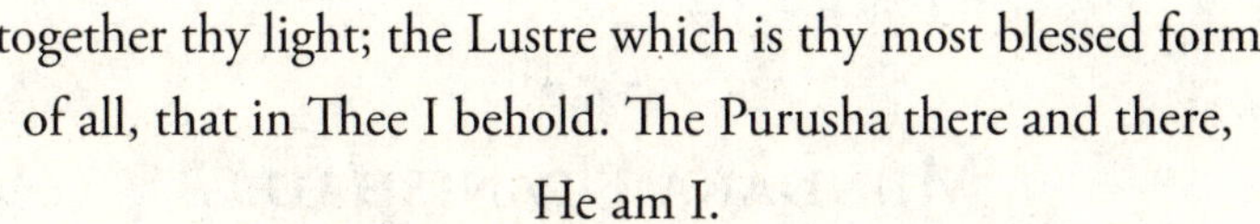

together thy light; the Lustre which is thy most blessed form of all, that in Thee I behold. The Purusha there and there, He am I.

The Breath of things is an immortal Life, but of this body ashes are the end. OM! O Will, remember, that which was done remember! O Will, remember, that which was done remember.

O god Agni, knowing all things that are manifested, lead us by the good path to the felicity; remove from us the devious attraction of sin. To thee completest speech of submission we would dispose.

—Translated by Sri Aurobindo

3
MUNDAKA UPANISHAD

Though written in the form of mantras, the object of the Mundaka Upanishad (circa 3500–3000 BCE) is to teach the knowledge of the Brahman, which cannot be attained by sacrifice or worship, but only by studying the Upanishads. Once the principal philosophy of this Upanishad is understood, all illusions fall away.

Om, O worshipful Ones, may our ears hear that which is auspicious, may we, well versed in the sacrifice, see with our eyes that which is auspicious. May we, singing your praise, enjoy our allotted span of life with strong limbs and healthy bodies.

May Indra, extolled in the scriptures, Pusah, the all-knowing, Tarksya, who protects us from harm and Brihaspati, who protects our spiritual lustre, grant us prosperity and further our welfare.

Om, Peace, Peace, Peace.

Om, Brahma, the creator of the universe, the protector of the world, arose before all the gods. He taught the knowledge of Brahman, which is the foundation of all knowledge, to his eldest son Atharvan. That knowledge Atharvan imparted in ancient times to Angir. He in turn taught it to Satyawaha, son of Bharadvaja, and the son of Bharadvaja passed it on to Angiras, the science thus descending from the greater to the lesser sages.

Saunaka, the renowned householder, once approached Angiras with reverence in the manner laid down by the scriptures, and asked: 'Venerable sir, what is that, knowing which, everything becomes known?' To him Angiras replied: 'The knowers of Brahman declare that there are two kinds of knowledge to be acquired, the higher as well as the lower.

Of these the lower consists of the Rig Veda, the Yajur Veda, the Sama Veda, the Atharva Veda, phonetics, ritual, grammar, etymology, metrics and astrology. And the higher is that by which the Imperishable is attained.

'That which is invisible, ungraspable, without origin or attributes, which has neither eyes nor ears, hands nor feet; which is eternal and many-splendored, all-pervading and exceedingly subtle, that Imperishable Being is what the wise perceive everywhere as the source of creation.

'As the spider sends forth and gathers in (its web), as herbs sprout upon the face of the earth, as hair grows upon the head and body of man, so, from the Immutable, springs forth the universe.

'By concentrated meditation Brahman expands; from Him matter is born, from matter life, mind, truth and immortality through works. From Brahman, the all-seeing, the all-knowing, whose energy consists of infinite wisdom, from Him is born Brahma, matter, name and form.

'This is the truth; the rituals which the seers beheld in the sacred hymns are elaborated in the three Vedas. Ye lovers of the truth, perform them constantly, for they are your paths to the world of good deeds. When the sacred fire is well kindled and the flames begin to move, offer your oblations with faith between the two portions of fire.

'For those whose fire sacrifice is not accompanied by the rites to be performed at the new moon and the full moon, at the four months of rain and at the first harvest, which is without guests and without offerings to all the gods, or which is performed contrary to scriptural injunctions; for such their hopes are destroyed in all the seven worlds.

'The Black, the Fierce, the Swift-as-mind, the Crimson, the Smoke-hued, the Scintillating, the Many-splendored—these are the seven swaying tongues of the fire. Whoever performs the rites and makes the offerings into these shining flames at the proper time, these in the form of the rays of the sun lead to where the lord of the gods resides.

'The radiant ones cry, "Come with us, come with us," as they carry him up on the rays of the sun. They speak pleasant words of sweetness and honour, saying, "This is the holy world of Brahma gained by your good works."

'Verily, frail are these rafts of the eighteen sacrificial forms which represent only the inferior work. The ignorant who acclaim them as the highest good fall repeatedly into the domain of old age and death. Though they consider themselves to be wise and learned, they are fools wandering aimlessly like the blind led by the blind.

'Revelling in multifarious ignorance, such people think they have achieved the goal of life. But being bound to passions and attachment they do not attain knowledge and sink down in misery when the effects of their good deeds are exhausted. Such bewildered minds regard sacrifices and good works as most important, and do not know any greater good.

Having reaped in heaven their rewards of good deeds they enter again this world or even a lower one.

'But those who live in the forest leading a life of austerity and faith, tranquil, wise and keeping the mendicant's rule, they, purged of all impurities, go by the solar gate to where the immutable, imperishable Being dwells.

'Having examined the worlds gained by deeds, the wise seeker should become indifferent to them, for the Eternal cannot be attained by works. To know that let him approach with humility a Guru who is learned in the scriptures and established in the Brahman. To such a seeker, whose mind is tranquil and senses controlled, and who has approached him in the proper manner, let the learned Guru impart the science of Brahman through which the true, Imperishable Being is realized.

'This is the truth. As from a blazing fire thousands of fiery sparks leap out, just so, my beloved, a multitude of beings issue forth from the Imperishable and, verily, fall back into it again.

'The divine Being is formless, eternal and pure, pervading within and without, anterior both to life and mind. He transcends even the highest immutable. From him are born life, mind and the senses; ether, air, fire, water and the all-supporting earth. Fire is his head, the sun and moon his eyes, space his ears, the Vedas his speech, the wind his breath, the universe his heart. From his feet the earth has originated; verily he is the inner self of all beings.

'From Him comes the fire fuelled by the sun; from the moon the rains which nourish herbs upon the earth. (Nourished by them) the male casts his seed into the female; thus are these many beings born of the divine Being. From Him are born the hymns of the Rig, Sama and Yajur Vedas; the sacrificial chants and the sacrifice; the ceremonies and the sacrificial gifts; the time of the sacrifice, the sacrificer and the worlds purified by the moon and illuminated by the sun.

'From Him are born the many gods and celestial beings; men, beasts and birds, the in-drawn breath and the out-breath; rice and barley; austerity and faith, truth, chastity and the law. From Him also are born the seven senses; the seven flames and their fuel, the seven oblations and the seven worlds in which move the life-breaths, seven and seven which dwell in the secret place of the heart.

'From Him are all these mountains and the oceans; from Him the multifarious rivers flow; from Him also are all the herbs and juices which, together with the elements, support the inner soul. Verily, that great Being is all this universe—sacrificial works, austerity and knowledge. O handsome youth, he who knows this immortal Being as seated in the secret caverns of the heart cuts asunder the knot of ignorance even during this life on earth.

'The Brahman is the mighty foundation, manifesting deep in the secret caverns of the heart. In it are established all that breathe, and move and see. Know this both as being and nonbeing, as the supremely desirable, greatest and highest of beings beyond all understanding. Luminous, subtler than the subtle, the imperishable Brahman is the abode of the worlds and all their peoples. It is life, it is speech, it is mind. It is reality and immortality. O beloved one, it is this which must be pierced; know it.

'Having taken a bow the great weapon of the secret Teaching, one should fix in it the arrow sharpened by constant meditation. Drawing it with a mind filled with That (Brahman), Penetrate, O good-looking youth, that Imperishable as the mark. The Pranava (Om) is the bow; the arrow is the self; Brahman is said to be the mark. With heedfulness is it to be penetrated, should become one with it as the arrow in the mark.

'He in whom are woven the sky, the earth and interspace, along with mind and all the life-breaths, know him as the one self and desist from other utterances. This is the bridge to immortality. Where all the nerves and arteries come together like the spokes of a chariot wheel at its hub, there, moving within the heart, he becomes manifold. Meditate on that self as Om; may your passage to the other shore beyond the darkness be pleasant and auspicious.

'The omniscient, the all-wise, whose glory is reflected here on earth, is the self-enthroned in the luminous city of Brahman, his ethereal heaven. Firmly established in mind, seated in the heart, he controls life and body. The wise by the higher knowledge see him clearly as the radiant blissful, immortal.

'When the Great Being is seen as both the higher and the lower, the knot of the heart is rent asunder, all doubts are dispelled and Karma is destroyed. In the highest golden sheath dwells the Brahman—stainless and indivisible. He is the light of all lights; it is he that the knowers of the self realize.

'There the sun does not shine, nor the moon and the stars; there these lightnings do not shine, how then this earthly fire? Verily everything shines only after his shining; his shining illuminates this entire cosmos. Verily the immortal Brahman is everywhere; in front and behind, to the north and the south, above and below, verily Brahman alone is this great universe.

'Two beautiful birds, closely bound in friendship, cling to a common tree. Of these one eats the delicious fruit with relish, while the other looks on without eating. Seated on the same tree one of them—the personal self—grieves on account of its helplessness. But when he sees the other—the worshipful lord in all his glory—his sorrow passes away from him.

'When the seer sees the golden-hued Lord, the Great Being who is the maker of the world and the source of Brahma the creator, then the wise one, shaking off good and evil, free from stain, attains unity with the supreme. Verily it is the divine spirit that shines forth in all beings. Knowing this, the wise one desists from unnecessary talk. Sporting in

the self, delighting in the self, yet involved in outer activity, such a one is the greatest among the knowers of Brahman.

'The Self within the body, pure and resplendent is attained through the cultivation of truth, austerity, right knowledge and chastity. When their impurities dwindle, the ascetics behold him. Truth alone triumphs, not untruth. By truth is laid out the divine path along which sages, their desires fulfilled, ascend to where Truth has its supreme abode.

'Vast, divine, beyond all thought processes shines the Brahman; subtler than the subtle, farther than the farthest. Yet it is nearer than the nearest, and the seer sees it within the secret heart. He cannot be grasped by the eye, by speech nor by the other sense organs. Nor can he be revealed by penance and austerities. Only when the mind becomes calm and purified by the grace of the higher knowledge does one, meditating, behold the great, indivisible Being.

'The subtle Atman within the body, pervaded by the fivefold life-force, is to be known by thought. The mind is constantly pervaded by the senses; when it is purified, the self shines forth. Whatever world the man of purified mind desires, whatever desires he wishes to fulfil, all these he attains. Therefore let whoever is desirous of prosperity worship the man of self-realization.

'The man of self-realization knows the supreme Brahman upon which the universe is based and shines radiantly. The wise, free from desire, worship the Brahman past beyond the

seed of rebirth. Whoever in his mind longs for the objects of desire is born again and again for their fulfilment; but one whose desire for the Brahman is fully satisfied, for such a perfected soul all his desires vanish even here in this life.

'Not by discourses, nor by intellectual analysis, nor through much learning can the Atman be attained. He is attained only by one whom he chooses; to such a one the Atman reveals its own form. This self cannot be attained by one without strength, nor by the careless, nor through improper austerities. But the wise who strive by all these means enter into the abode of Brahman.

'Having attained the Self the seers are fully satisfied with wisdom, perfect in their souls, non-attached and tranquil. Having realized the all-pervasive everywhere, these disciplined souls verily enter into the Brahman. Firmly established in the Vedantic wisdom through the yoga of renunciation, their consciousness purified, these seers at the end of time achieve immortality and liberation in the world of Brahman.

'Gone are the fifteen parts into their foundations; the senses into the corresponding deities; the deeds and the intellect into the supreme, immutable Being. As flowing rivers disappear into the ocean, losing their separate name and form, even so the seer, freed from name and form, becomes one with the effulgent Being, the highest of the high.

'Verily, he who knows the supreme Brahman himself becomes Brahman. In his lineage none is born who knows

not the Brahman. He crosses beyond sorrow; he crosses beyond sin. Liberated from the knots of the heart he becomes immortal.

'This very doctrine is declared in the Vedic verse. To them alone who perform the rites, who are well versed in the scriptures, who are firmly grounded in the Brahman, who tend the sacred fire with devotion, who have duly performed the rite of the head, should this knowledge of the Brahman be imparted. This is the truth imparted to his disciples in ancient times by the seer Angiras. Let no one who has not performed the rite study this.

'Salutations to the great seers
Salutations to the great seers.'

—Translated by Dr Karan Singh

4

Mahabharata: Yaksha Prashna and Shanti Parva

Besides the Bhagavad Gita, the Mahabharata (circa 3100–900 BCE) contains innumerable gems of wisdom. The Yaksha Prashna is found in the Aranya Parva and contains questions and answers on dharma and justice. Shanti Parva is the twelfth (and the longest) of the eighteen books that comprise the Mahabharata. It dwells on the duties and responsibilities of the king.

Yaksha Prashna

The Yaksha then said, 'What is it that maketh the Sun rise? Who keeps him company? Who causeth him to set? And in whom is he established?'

Yudhishthira answered: 'Brahma maketh the Sun rise; the gods keep him company; Dharma causeth him to set; and he is established in truth.'

The Yaksha asked, 'By what doth one become learned? By what doth he attain what is very great? How can one have a second? And, O king, how can one acquire intelligence?'

Yudhishthira answered, 'It is by the (study of the) Srutis that a person becometh learned; it is by ascetic austerities that one acquireth what is very great; it is by intelligence that a person acquireth a second; and it is by serving the old that one becometh wise.'

The Yaksha asked, 'What constituteth the divinity of the Brahmanas? What even is their practice that is like that of the pious? What also is the human attribute of the Brahmanas? And what practice of theirs is like that of the impious?'

Yudhishthira answered, 'The study of the Vedas constitutes their divinity; their asceticism constitutes behaviour that is like that of the pious; their liability to death is their human attribute; and slander is their impiety.'

The Yaksha asked, 'What institutes the divinity of the Kshatriyas? What even is their practice that is like that of the pious? What is their human attribute? And what practice of theirs is like that of the impious?'

Yudhishthira answered, 'Arrows and weapons are their divinity; celebration of sacrifices is that act which is like that of the pious; liability to fear is their human attribute; and refusal of protection is that act of theirs which is like that of the impious.'

The Yaksha asked, 'What is that which constitutes the Sama of the sacrifice? What the Yajus of the sacrifice? What is that which is the refuge of a sacrifice? And what is that which sacrifice cannot do without?'

Yudhishthira answered, 'Life is the Sama of the sacrifice; the mind is the Yajus of the sacrifice; the Rik is that which is the refuge of the sacrifice; and it is Rik alone which sacrifice cannot do without.'

The Yaksha asked, 'What is of the foremost value to those that cultivate? What is of the foremost value to those that sow? What is of the foremost value to those that wish for prosperity in this world? And what is of the foremost value to those that bring forth?'

Yudhishthira answered, 'That which is of the foremost value to those that cultivate is rain; that of the foremost value to those that sow is seed; that of the foremost value to those that bring forth is offspring.'

The Yaksha asked, 'What person, enjoying all the objects of the senses, endued with intelligence, regarded by the world and liked by all beings, though breathing, is not yet alive?'

Yudhishtira answererd, 'The person who doth not offer anything to these five, viz., gods, guests, servants, Pitris, and himself, though endued with breath, is not yet alive.'

The Yaksha asked, 'What is weightier than the earth itself? What is higher than the heavens? What is fleeter than the wind? And what is more numerous than grass?'

Yudhishthira answered, 'The mother is weightier than the earth; the father is higher than the heaven; the mind is fleeter than the wind; and our thoughts are more numerous than grass.'

The Yaksha asked, 'What is that which doth not close its eyes while asleep? What is that which doth not move after birth? What is that which is without heart? And what is that which swells with its own impetus?'

Yudhishthira answered, 'A fish doth not close its eyes while asleep; an egg doth not move after birth; a stone is without heart; and a river swelleth with its own impetus.'

The Yaksha asked, 'Who is the friend of the exile? Who is the friend of the householder? Who is the friend of him that ails? And who is the friend of one about to die?'

Yudhishthira answered, 'The friend of the exile in a distant land is his companion; the friend of the householder

is the wife; the friend of him that ails is the physician; and the friend of him about to die is charity.'

The Yaksha asked, 'What is that which sojourneth alone? What is that which is reborn after its birth? What is the remedy against cold? And what is the largest field?'

Yudhishthira answered, 'The sun sojourns alone; the moon takes birth anew; fire is the remedy against cold; and the Earth is the largest field.'

The Yaksha asked, 'What is the highest refuge of virtue? What of fame? What of heaven? And what, of happiness?'

Yudhishthira answered, 'Liberality is the highest refuge of virtue; gift, of fame; truth, of heaven; and good behaviour, of happiness.'

The Yaksha asked, 'What is the soul of man? Who is that friend bestowed on man by the gods? What is man's chief support? And what also is his chief refuge?'

Yudhishthira answered, 'The son is a man's soul; the wife is the friend bestowed on man by the gods; the clouds are his chief support; and gift is his chief refuge.'

The Yaksha asked, 'What is the best of all laudable things? What is the most valuable of all possessions? What is the best of all gains? And what is the best of all kinds of happiness?'

Yudhishthira answered, 'The best of all laudable things is skill; the best of all possessions is knowledge; the best of all gains is health; and contentment is the best of all kinds of happiness.'

The Yaksha asked, 'What is the highest duty in the world? What is that virtue which always beareth fruit? What is that which if controlled, leadeth not to regret? And who are they with whom an alliance cannot break?'

Yudhishthira answered, 'The highest of duties is to refrain from injury; the rites ordained in the Three (Vedas) always bear fruit; the mind, if controlled, leadeth to no regret; and an alliance with the good never breaketh.'

The Yaksha asked, 'What is that which, if renounced, maketh one agreeable? What is that which, if renounced, leadeth to no regret? What is that which, if renounced, maketh one wealthy? And what is that which if renounced, maketh one happy?'

Yudhishthira answered, 'Pride, if renounced, maketh one agreeable; wrath, if renounced leadeth to no regret; desire, if renounced, maketh one wealthy; and avarice, if renounced, maketh one happy.'

The Yaksha asked, 'For what may one be considered as dead? For what may a kingdom be considered as dead? For what may a Sraddha be considered as dead? And for what, a sacrifice?'

Yudhishthira answered, 'For want of wealth may a man be regarded as dead. A kingdom for want of a king may be regarded as dead. A Sraddha that is performed with the aid of a priest that hath no learning may be regarded as dead. And a sacrifice in which there are no gifts to Brahmanas is dead.'

The Yaksha asked, 'What constitutes the way? What, hath been spoken of as water? What, as food? And what, as poison? Tell us also what is the proper time of a Sraddha, and then drink and take away as much as thou likest!'

Yudhishthira answered, 'They that are good constitute the way. Space hath been spoken of as water. The cow is food. A request is poison. And a Brahmana is regarded as the proper time of a Sraddha. I do not know what thou mayst think of all this, O Yaksha.'

Shanti Parva

Yudhishthira said, 'How, O king, may a kingdom be consolidated, and how should it be protected? I desire to know this. Tell me all this, O bull of Bharata's race!'

Bhishma said, 'Listen to me with concentrated attention. I shall tell thee how a kingdom may be consolidated, and how also it may be protected.

A headman should be selected for each village. Over ten villages (or ten headmen) there should be one superintendent. Over two such superintendents there should be one officer (having the control, therefore, of twenty villages). Above the latter should be appointed persons under each of whom

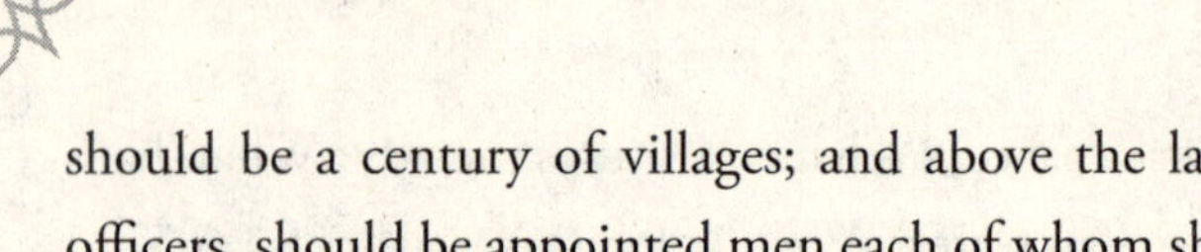

should be a century of villages; and above the last kind of officers, should be appointed men each of whom should have a thousand villages under his control.

The headman should ascertain the characteristics of every person in the village and all the faults also that need correction. He should report everything to the officer (who is above him and is) in charge of ten villages. The latter, again, should report the same to the officer (who is above him and is) in charge of twenty villages.

The latter, in his turn, should report the conduct of all the persons within his dominion to the officer (who is above him and is) in charge of a hundred villages. The village headman should have control over all the produce and the possessions of the village.

Every headman should contribute his share for maintaining the lord of ten villages, and the latter should do the same for supporting the lord of twenty villages.

The lord of a hundred villages should receive every honour from the king and should have for his support a large village, O chief of the Bharatas, populous and teeming with wealth.

Such a village, so assigned to a lord of hundred villages, should be, however, within the control of the lord of a thousand villages. That high officer, again, viz., the lord of a thousand villages, should have a minor town for his support.

He should enjoy the grain and gold and other possessions derivable from it. He should perform all the duties of its wars and other internal affairs pertaining to it.

Some virtuous minister, with wrathfulness should exercise supervision over the administration affairs and mutual relations of those officers. In every town, again, there should be an officer for attending to every matter relating to his jurisdiction.

Like some planet of dreadful form moving above all the asterisms below, the officer (with plenary powers) mentioned last should move and act above all the officers subordinate to him. Such an officer should ascertain the conduct of those under him through his spies. Such high officers should protect the people from all persons of murderous disposition, all men of wicked deeds, all who rob other people of their wealth, and all who are full of deceit, and all of whom are regarded to be possessed by the devil.

Taking note of the sales and the purchases, the state of the roads, the food and dress, and the stocks and profits of those that are engaged in trade, the king should levy taxes on them.

Ascertaining on all occasions the extent of the manufactures, the receipts and expenses of those that are engaged in them, and the state of the arts, the king should levy taxes upon the artisans in respect of the arts they follow.

The king, O Yudhishthira, may take high taxes, but he should never levy such taxes as would emasculate his people.

No tax should be levied without ascertaining the outturn and the amount of labour that has been necessary to produce it. Nobody would work or seek for outturns without sufficient cause.

The king should, after reflection, levy taxes in such a way that he and the person who labours to produce the article taxed may both share the value.

The king should not, by his thirst, destroy his own foundations as also those of others. He should always avoid those acts in consequence of which he may become an object of hatred to his people. Indeed, by acting in this way he may succeed in winning popularity.

The subjects hate that king who earns a notoriety for voraciousness of appetite (in the matter of taxes and imposts). Whence can a king who becomes an object of hatred have prosperity? Such a king can never acquire what is for his good.

A king who is possessed of sound intelligence should milk his kingdom after the analogy of (men acting in the matter of) calves. If the calf be permitted to suck, it grows strong, O Bharata, and bears heavy burthens. If, on the other hand, O Yudhishthira, the cow be milked too much, the calf becomes lean and fails to do much service to the owner.

Similarly, if the kingdom be drained much, the subjects fail to achieve any act that is great. That king who protects his kingdom himself and shows favour to his subjects (in the matter of taxes and imposts) and supports himself upon what is easily obtained, succeeds in earning many grand results.

Does not the king then obtain wealth sufficient for enabling him to cope with his wants? The entire kingdom, in that case, becomes to him his treasury, while that which is his treasury becomes his bed chamber.

If the inhabitants of the cities and the provinces be poor, the king should, whether they depend upon him immediately or mediately, show them compassion to the best of his power. Chastising all robbers that infest the outskirts, the king should protect the people of his villages and make them happy.

The subjects, in the case, becoming sharers of the king's weal and woe, feel exceedingly gratified with him. Thinking, in the first instance, of collecting wealth, the king should repair to the chief centres of his kingdom one after another and endeavour to inspire his people with fright.

He should say unto them, 'Here, calamity threatens us. A great danger has arisen in consequence of the acts of the foe. There is every reason, however, to hope that the danger will pass away, for the enemy, like a bamboo that has flowered, will very soon meet with destruction.

'Many foes of mine, having risen up and combined with a large number of robbers, desire to put our kingdom into difficulties, for meeting with destruction themselves.

'In view of this great calamity fraught with dreadful danger, I solicit your wealth for devising the means of your protection. When the danger passes away, I will give you what I now take. Our foes, however, will not give back what they (if unopposed) will take from you by force.

'On the other hand (if unopposed), they will even slay all your relatives beginning with your very spouses. You certainly desire wealth for the sake of your children and wives. I am glad at your prosperity, and I beseech you as I would my own children. I shall take from you what it may be within your power to give me.

'I do not wish to give pain to anyone. In seasons of calamity, you should, like strong bulls, bear such burthens. In seasons of distress, wealth should not be so dear to you.'

A king conversant with the considerations relating to Time should, with such agreeable, sweet, and complimentary words, send his agents and collect imposts from his people.

Pointing out to them the necessity of repairing his fortifications and of defraying the expenses of his establishment and other heads, inspiring them with the fear of foreign invasion, and impressing them with the necessity that exists for protecting them and enabling them to ensure the means of living in peace, the king should levy imposts upon the Vaisyas of his realm.

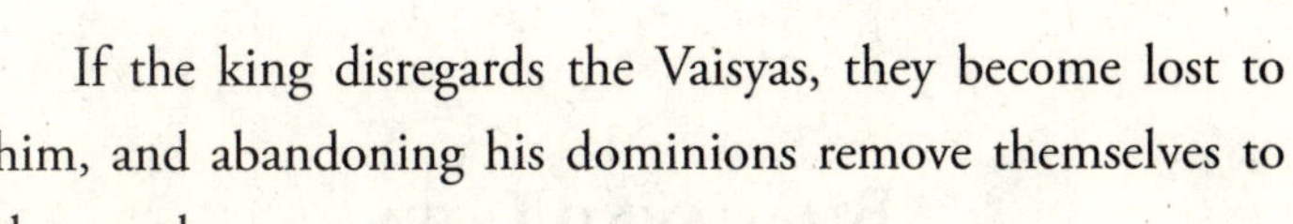

If the king disregards the Vaisyas, they become lost to him, and abandoning his dominions remove themselves to the woods.

The king should, therefore, behave with leniency towards them. The king, O son of Pritha, should always conciliate and protect the Vaisyas, adopt measures for inspiring them with a sense of security and for ensuring them in the enjoyment of what they possess, and always do what is agreeable to them. The king, O Bharata, should always act in such a way towards the Vaisyas that their productive powers may be enhanced.

The Vaisyas increase the strength of a kingdom, improve its agriculture, and develop its trade. A wise king, therefore, should always gratify them. Acting with heedfulness and leniency, he should levy mild imposts upon them.

It is always easy to behave with goodness towards the Vaisyas. There is nothing productive of greater good to a kingdom, O Yudhishthira, than the adoption of such behaviour towards the Vaisyas of the realm.

—Translated by K.M. Ganguli

5
Bhagavad Gita

The fourth chapter of the Bhagavad Gita (circa 500–100 BCE) is Gyana–Karma–Sanyasa–Yoga. In this chapter, Shri Krishna exalts Karma Yoga and imparts Transcendental Knowledge (the knowledge of the soul and the Ultimate Truth) to Arjuna.

Although there are many paths to God and many paths of worship or sacrifice, Krishna urges Arjuna to follow the path of Karma Yoga, or right action—all other paths are born of this primary path.

The fifth chapter describes the way of true devotion to the Supreme God. The paths of renunciation and the path of action are good but the path of Karma Yoga is more direct, it says.

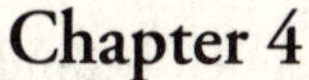

Chapter 4

The Blessed Lord said:

This imperishable yoga I declared to Vivasvan; Vivasvan taught it to Manu; Manu to Ikshvaku told it.

This, handed on down the line, the King–Sages knew. This yoga by great efflux of time decayed in the world, O Parantapa.

This same ancient yoga hath been today declared to thee by Me, for thou art My devotee and My friend; it is the supreme Secret.

Arjuna said:

Later was thy birth, earlier the birth of Vivasvan;
how then am I to understand that Thou declared it in the beginning?

The Blessed Lord said:

Many births have been left behind by Me and by thee, O Arjuna. I know them all, but thou knowest not thine, O Parantapa.

Though unborn, the imperishable Self, and also the Lord of all beings, brooding over nature, which is Mine own, yet I am born through My own power.

Whenever there is decay of righteousness, O Bharata, and there is exaltation of unrighteousness, then I Myself come forth.

For the protection of the good, for the destruction of evil-doers, for the sake of firmly establishing righteousness, I am born from age to age.

He who thus knoweth My divine birth and action, in its essence, having abandoned the body, cometh not to birth again, but cometh unto Me, O Arjuna.

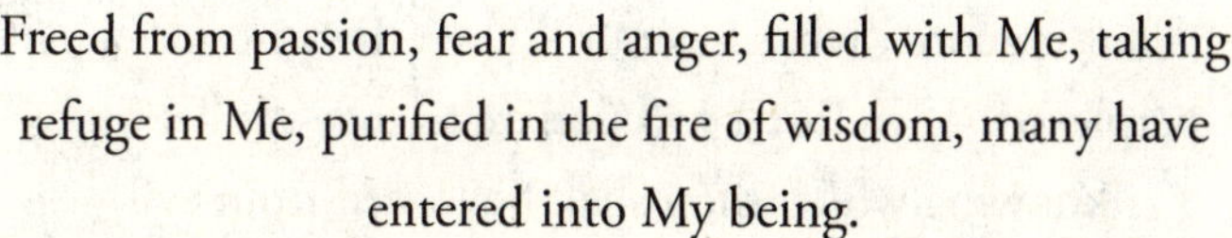

Freed from passion, fear and anger, filled with Me, taking refuge in Me, purified in the fire of wisdom, many have entered into My being.

However men approach Me, even so do I welcome them, for the path men take from every side is Mine, O Partha.

They who long after success in action on earth sacrifice to the Shining Ones; for in brief space verily, in this world of men, success is born of action.

The four castes were emanated by Me, by the different distribution of qualities and actions; know Me to be the author of them, through the actionless and inexhaustible.

Nor do actions affect Me, nor is the fruit of action desired by Me. He who thus knoweth Me is not bound by actions.

Having thus known, our forefathers, ever seeking liberation, performed action; therefore do thou also perform action, as did our forefathers in the olden time.

'What is action, what inaction?' Even the wise are herein perplexed. Therefore I will declare to thee the action by knowing which thou shalt be loosed from evil.

It is needful to discriminate action, to discriminate unlawful action, and to discriminate inaction; mysterious is the path of action.

He who seeth inaction in action, and action in inaction, he is wise among men, he is harmonious, even while performing all action.

Whose works are all free from the moulding of desire, whose actions are burned up by the fire of wisdom, him the wise have called a Sage.

Having abandoned attachment to the fruit of action, always content, nowhere seeking refuge, he is not doing anything, although doing actions.

Hoping for naught, his mind and self-controlled, having abandoned all greed, performing action by the body alone he doth not commit sin.

Content with whatsoever he obtained without effort, free from the pairs of opposites, without envy, balanced in success and failure, though acting he is not bound.

Of one with attachment dead, harmonious, with his thoughts established in wisdom, his works sacrifices, all action melts away.

The Eternal the oblation, the Eternal the clarified butter, are offered in the Eternal the fire by the Eternal; unto the Eternal verily shall he go who in his action meditateth wholly upon the Eternal.

Some Yogis offer up sacrifice to the Shining Ones; others sacrifice only by pouring sacrifice into the fire of the Eternal.

Some pour as sacrifice hearing and the other senses into the fires of restraint; some pour sound and the other objects of sense into the fires of the senses as sacrifice.

Others again into the wisdom-kindled fire of union attained by self-control, pour as sacrifice all the functions of the senses and the functions of life.

Yet others the sacrifice of wealth, the sacrifice of austerity, the sacrifice of yoga, the sacrifice of silent reading and wisdom, men concentrated and of effectual vows.

Yet others pour as sacrifice the outgoing breath in the incoming, and the incoming in the outgoing, restraining the flow of the outgoing and incoming breaths, solely absorbed in the control of breathing.

Others, regular in food, pour as sacrifice their life-breaths in life-breaths. All these are knowers of sacrifice, and by sacrifice have destroyed their sins.

The eaters of the life-giving remains of sacrifice go to the changeless Eternal. This world is not for the non-sacrificer, much less the other, O best of the Kurus.

Many and various sacrifices are thus spread out before the Eternal. Know thou that all these are born of action, and thus knowing thou shalt be free.

Better than the sacrifice of any objects is the sacrifice of wisdom, O Parantapa. All actions in their entirety, O Partha, culminate in wisdom.

Learn thou this by discipleship, by investigation, and by service. The wise, the seers of the Essence of things, will instruct thee in wisdom.

And having known this, thou shalt not again fall into this confusion, O Pandava; for by this thou wilt see all beings without exception in the Self, and thus in Me.

Even if thou art the most sinful of all sinners, yet shalt thou cross over all sin by the raft of wisdom.

As the burning fire reduces fuel to ashes, O Arjuna, so doth the fire of wisdom reduce all actions to ashes.

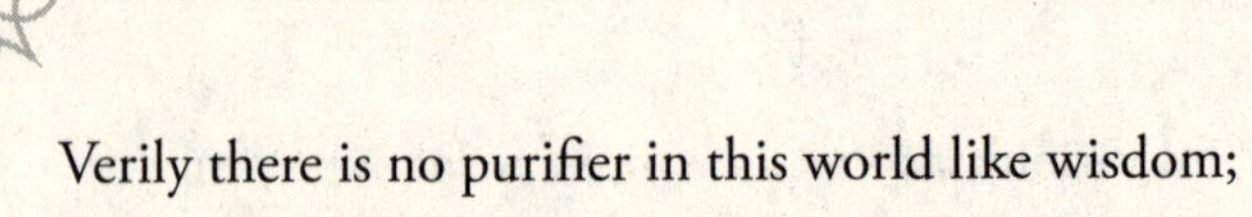

Verily there is no purifier in this world like wisdom; he that is perfected in yoga finds it in the Self in due season.

The man who is full of faith obtaineth wisdom, and he also who hath mastery over his senses; and having obtained wisdom he goeth swiftly to the Supreme Peace.

But the ignorant, faithless, doubting Self goeth to destruction; nor this world, nor that beyond, nor happiness, is there for the doubting Self.

He who hath renounced action by yoga, who hath cloven asunder doubt by wisdom, who is ruled by the Self, actions do not bind him, O Dhananjaya.

Therefore, with the sword of the wisdom of the Self cleaving asunder this ignorance-born doubt, dwelling in thy heart, be established in yoga. Stand up, O Bharata.

Chapter 5

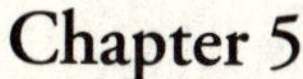

Arjuna said:

Renunciation of actions, thou praisest, O Krishna, and then also yoga. Of the two which one is the better? That tell me conclusively.

The Blessed Lord said:

Renunciation and yoga by action both lead to the highest bliss; of the two, yoga by action is verily better than renunciation of action.

He should be known as a perpetual ascetic, who neither hates nor desires; free from the pairs of opposites, O mighty-armed, he is easily set free from bondage.

Children, not sages, speak of the Sankhya and Yoga as different; he who is duly established in one obtains the fruits of both.

That place which is gained by the Sankhyas is reached by the Yogas also. He seeth who seeth that the Sankhya and the Yoga are one.

But without yoga, O mighty-armed, renunciation is hard to attain to; the yoga-harmonised Muni swiftly goes to the Eternal.

He who is harmonised by yoga, the Self-purified, Self-ruled, the senses subdued, whose Self is the Self of all beings, although acting he is not affected.

'I do not anything,' should think the harmonised one, who knoweth the Essence of things; seeing, hearing, touching, smelling, eating, moving, sleeping, breathing.

Speaking, giving, grasping, opening and closing the eyes, he holdeth: 'The senses move among the objects of the senses'.

He who acteth, placing all actions in the Eternal, abandoning attachment, is unaffected by sin as a lotus leaf by the waters.

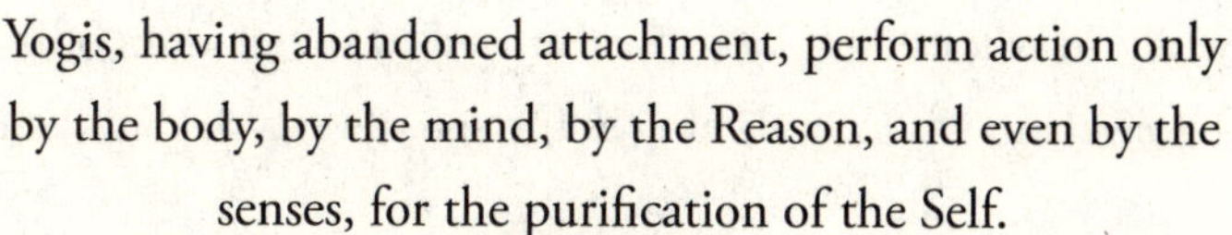

Yogis, having abandoned attachment, perform action only by the body, by the mind, by the Reason, and even by the senses, for the purification of the Self.

The harmonised man, having abandoned the fruit of action, attaineth to the Eternal Peace; the non-harmonised, impelled by desire, attached to fruit, are bound.

Mentally renouncing all actions, the sovereign dweller in the body resteth serenely in the nine-gated city, neither acting nor causing to act.

The Lord of the world produceth not the idea of agency, nor actions, nor the union together of action and its fruit; nature, however, manifests.

The Lord accepteth neither the evil-doing nor yet the well-doing of any. Wisdom is enveloped by unwisdom; therewith mortals are deluded.

Verily, in whom unwisdom is destroyed by the wisdom of the Self, in them wisdom, shining as the sun, reveals the Supreme.

Thinking on That, merged in That, established in That, solely devoted to That, they go whence there is no return, their sins dispelled by wisdom.

Sages look equally on a Brahmana adorned with learning and humility, a cow, an elephant, and even a dog, and an outcaste.

Even here on earth everything is overcome by those whose mind remains balanced; the Eternal is incorruptible and balanced; therefore they are established in the Eternal.

With Reason firm, unperplexed, the knower of the Eternal, established in the Eternal, neither rejoiceth on obtaining what is pleasant, nor sorroweth on obtaining what is unpleasant.

He whose Self is unattached to external contacts, and findeth joy in the Self, having self-harmonised with the Eternal by yoga, enjoys happiness exempt from decay.

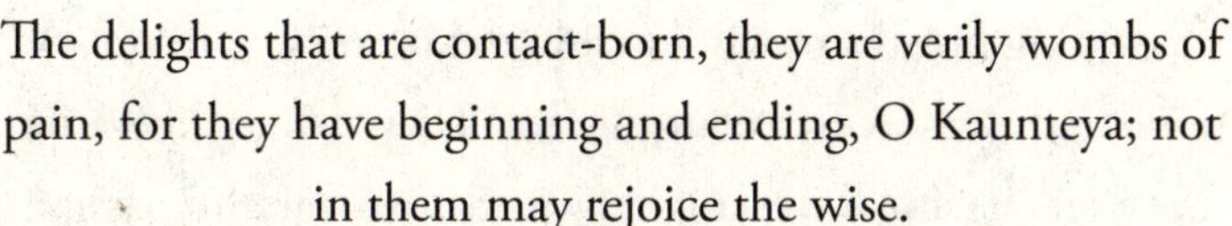

The delights that are contact-born, they are verily wombs of pain, for they have beginning and ending, O Kaunteya; not in them may rejoice the wise.

He who is able to endure here on earth, ere he be liberated from the body, the force born from desire and passion, he is harmonised, he is a happy man.

He who is happy within, who rejoiceth within, who is illuminated within, that Yogi, becoming the Eternal, goeth to the Peace of the Eternal.

Rishis, their sins destroyed, their duality removed, their selves controlled, intent upon the welfare of all beings, obtain the Peace of the Eternal.

The Peace of the Eternal lies near to those who know themselves, who are disjoined from desire and passion, subdued in nature, of subdued thoughts.

Having external contacts excluded, and with gaze fixed between the eyebrows; having made equal the outgoing and incoming breaths moving within the nostrils, with senses, mind and Reason ever controlled, solely pursuing liberation, the Sage, having for ever cast away desire, fear and passion, verily is liberated.

Having known Me, as the Enjoyer of sacrifice and of austerity, the mighty Ruler of all the worlds, and the Lover of all beings, he goeth to Peace.

—Translated by Annie Besant and Bhagavan Das

6

Bhumi Sukta of Atharvaveda

Atharvaveda (circa 1200–900 BCE) is the only Veda which is related to both worldly happiness and spiritual knowledge. Bhumi Sukta is a hymn comprising sixty-three mantras addressed to Mother Earth. It is an amazing illustration of the human endeavour to seek harmony and concord in the diversity of the Universe. The Earth is not for humans alone, but for others too, both animate and inanimate. Bhumi Sukta recognises the importance of Mother Earth for all entities and hence emphasises her protection. It is regarded as a beautiful depiction of environmental consciousness from over 3,000 years ago.

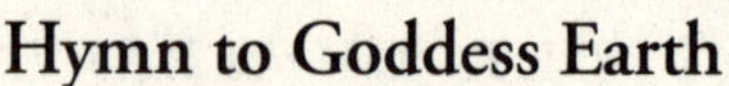

Hymn to Goddess Earth

Truth, greatness, universal order (rita), strength, consecration, creative fervour (tapas), spiritual exaltation (brahma), the sacrifice, support the earth. May this earth, the mistress of that which was and shall be, prepare for us a broad domain!

The earth that has heights, and slopes, and great plains, that supports the plants of manifold virtue, free from the pressure that comes from the midst of men, she shall spread out for us, and fit herself for us!

The earth upon which the sea, and the rivers and the waters, upon which food and the tribes of men have arisen, upon which this breathing, moving life exists, shall afford us precedence in drinking!

The earth whose are the four regions of space, upon which food and the tribes of men have arisen, which supports the

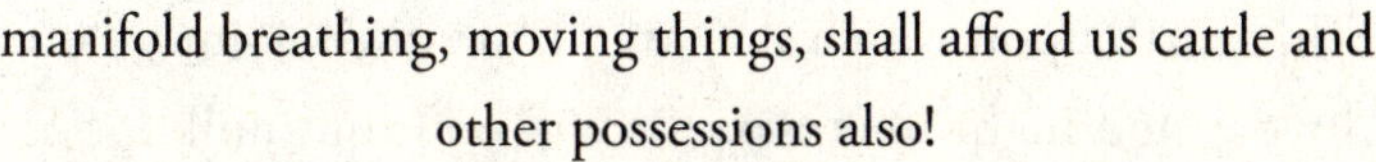

manifold breathing, moving things, shall afford us cattle and other possessions also!

The earth upon which of old the first men unfolded themselves, upon which the gods overcame the Asuras, shall procure for us (all) kinds of cattle, horses, and fowls, good fortune, and glory!

The earth that supports all, furnishes wealth, the foundation, the golden-breasted resting-place of all living creatures, she that supports Agni Vaisanara (the fire), and mates with Indra, the bull, shall furnish us with property!

The broad earth, which the sleepless gods ever attentively guard, shall milk for us precious honey, and, moreover, besprinkle us with glory!

That earth which formerly was water upon the ocean (of space), which the wise (seers) found out by their skilful devices; whose heart is in the highest heaven, immortal, surrounded by truth, shall bestow upon us brilliancy and strength, (and place us) in supreme sovereignty!

That earth upon which the attendant waters jointly flow by day and night unceasingly, shall pour out milk for us in rich streams, and, moreover, besprinkle us with glory!

The earth which the Asvins have measured, upon which Vishnu has stepped out, which Indra, the lord of might, has made friendly to himself; she, the mother, shall pour forth milk for me, the son!

Thy snowy mountain heights, and thy forests, O earth, shall be kind to us! The brown, the black, the red, the multi-coloured, the firm earth, that is protected by Indra, I have settled upon, not suppressed, not slain, not wounded.

Upon the firm, broad earth, the all-begetting mother of the plants, that is supported by (divine) law, upon her, propitious and kind, may we ever pass our lives!

Agni (fire) is in the earth, in the plants, the waters hold Agni, Agni is in the stones; Agni is within men, Agnis (fires) are within cattle, within horses.

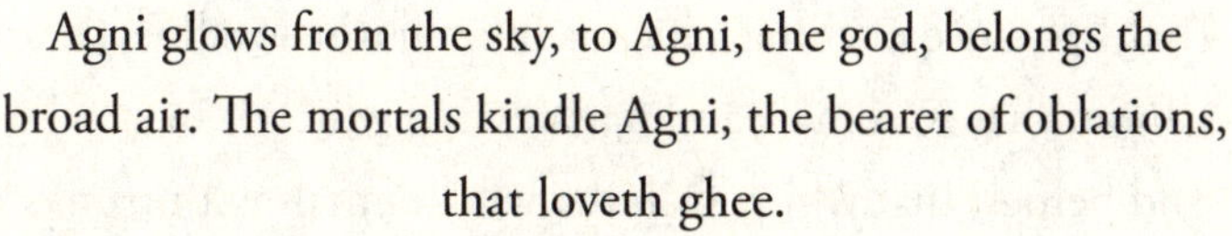

Agni glows from the sky, to Agni, the god, belongs the broad air. The mortals kindle Agni, the bearer of oblations, that loveth ghee.

The earth, clothed in Agni, with dark knees, shall make me brilliant and alert!

Upon the earth men give to the gods the sacrifice, the prepared oblation; upon the earth mortal men live pleasantly by food. May this earth give us breath and life, may she cause me to reach old age!

The fragrance, O earth, that has arisen upon thee, which the plants and the waters hold, which the Gandharvas and the Apsaras have partaken of, with that make me fragrant: not any one shall hate us!

That fragrance of thine which has entered into the lotus, that fragrance, O earth, which the immortals of yore gathered up at the marriage of Surya, with that make me fragrant: not any one shall hate us!

That fragrance of thine which is in men, the loveliness and charm that is in male and female, that which is in steeds and heroes, that which is in the wild animals with trunks (elephants), the lustre that is in the maiden, O earth, with that do thou blend us: not any one shall hate us!

Rock, stone, dust is this earth; this earth is supported, held together. To this golden-breasted earth I have rendered obeisance.

The earth, upon whom the forest-sprung trees ever stand firm, the all-nourishing, compact earth, do we invoke.

Rising or sitting, standing or walking, may we not stumble with our right or left foot upon the earth!

What, O earth, I dig out of thee, quickly shall that grow again: may I not, O pure one, pierce thy vital spot, (and) not thy heart!

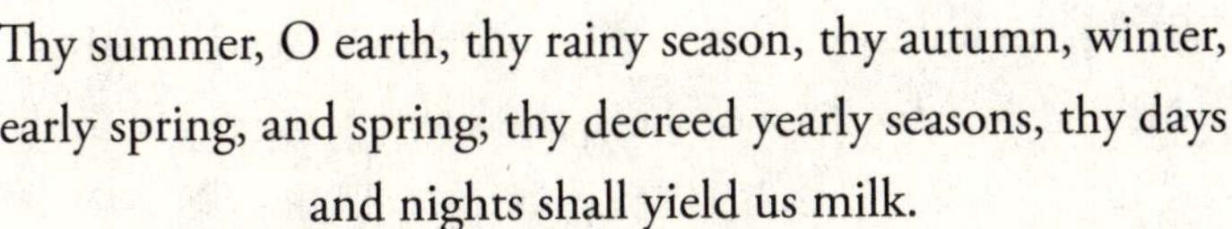

Thy summer, O earth, thy rainy season, thy autumn, winter, early spring, and spring; thy decreed yearly seasons, thy days and nights shall yield us milk.

The earth that holds people of manifold varied speech, of different customs, according to their habitations, as a reliable milch-cow that does not kick, shall she milk for me a thousand streams of wealth!

The serpent, the scorpion with thirsty fangs, that hibernating torpidly lies upon thee; the worm, and whatever living thing, O earth, moves in the rainy season, shall, when it creeps, not creep upon us: with what is auspicious (on thee) be gracious to us!

Thy many paths upon which people go, thy tracks for chariots and wagons to advance, upon which both good and evil men proceed, this road, free from enemies, and free from thieves, may we gain: with what is auspicious (on thee) be gracious to us!

The earth holds the fool and holds the wise, endures that good and bad dwell (upon her); she keeps company with the boar, gives herself up to the wild hog.

Thy forest animals, the wild animals homed in the woods, the man-eating lions, and tigers that roam; the ula, the wolf, mishap, injury (rikshika), and demons (rakshas), O earth, drive away from us!

The Gandharvas, the Apsaras, the Arayas and Kimidins; the Pisakas and all demons (rakshas), these, O earth, hold from us!

The earth upon whom the biped birds fly together, the flamingos, eagles, birds of prey, and fowls; upon whom Matarisvan, the wind, hastens, raising the dust, and tossing the trees—as the wind blows forth and back the flame bursts after.

The earth upon whom day and night jointly, black and bright, have been decreed, the broad earth covered and enveloped with rain, shall kindly place us into every pleasant abode!

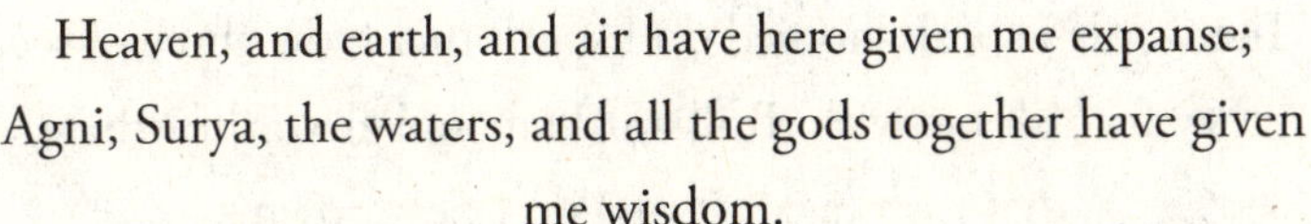

Heaven, and earth, and air have here given me expanse; Agni, Surya, the waters, and all the gods together have given me wisdom.

Mighty am I, 'Superior' (uttara) by name, upon the earth, conquering am I, all-conquering, completely conquering every region.

At that time, O goddess, when, spreading (prathamana) forth, named (prithivi 'broad') by the gods, thou didst extend to greatness, then prosperity did enter thee, (and) thou didst fashion the four regions.

In the villages and in the wilderness, in the assembly-halls that are upon the earth; in the gatherings, and in the meetings, may we hold forth agreeably to thee!

As dust a steed did she, as soon as she was born, scatter these people, that dwelt upon the earth, she the lovely one, the leader, the guardian of the world, that holds the trees and plants.

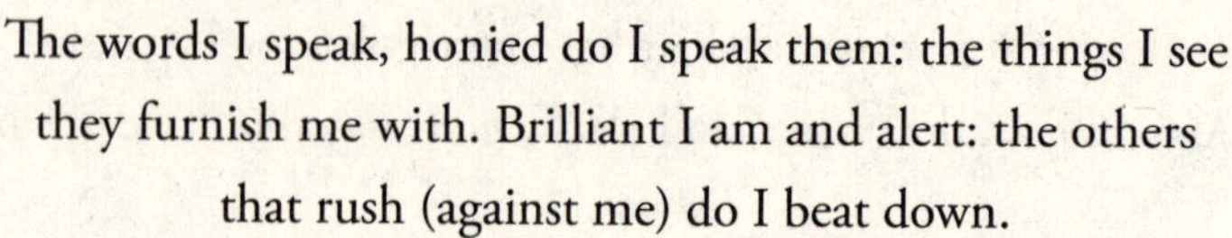

The words I speak, honied do I speak them: the things I see they furnish me with. Brilliant I am and alert: the others that rush (against me) do I beat down.

Gentle, fragrant, kindly, with the sweet drink (kilala) in her udder, rich in milk, the broad earth together with (her) milk shall give us courage!

She whom Visvakarman (the creator of all) did search out by means of oblations, when she had entered the surging (flood of the) atmosphere, she, the vessel destined to nourish, deposited in a secret place, became visible (to the gods) and the (heavenly) mothers.

Thou art the scatterer of men, the broadly expanding Aditi that yields milk according to wish. What is wanting in thee Prajapati, first-born of the divine order (rita), shall supply for thee.

Thy laps, O earth, free from ailment! Free from disease, shall be produced for us! May we attentively, through our long lives, be bearers of bali-offerings to thee!

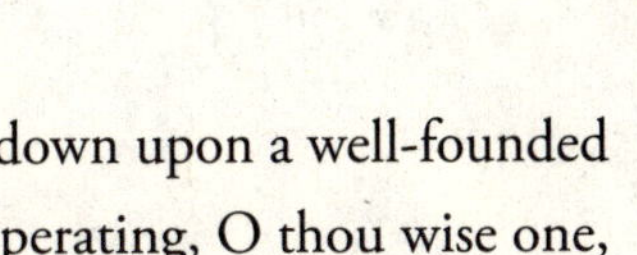

O mother earth, kindly set me down upon a well-founded place! With (father) heaven cooperating, O thou wise one, do thou place me into happiness and prosperity!

—Translated by Maurice Bloomfield

7
Puranas

'Purana' in Sanskrit means 'ancient' or 'old'. The Puranas (circa 1100–400 BCE) comprise some of the most ancient Indian literature about Hinduism. They are post-Vedic texts and are regarded as the fifth Veda.

The Puranas provide a detailed description of the universe, from creation to destruction and then to re-creation. They contain the spirit of the Vedas and were composed to popularise their philosophies and teachings. They were meant not for scholars but for ordinary people.

Introduction

The Puranas occupy a unique position in the sacred and secular literature of the Hindus, being regarded as next in importance only to the Vedas. In fact, they are said to be, like the Mahabharata, the fifth Veda, the Veda of the laity. They claim for themselves an equal antiquity and sanctity with the Vedas. They are closely akin to the smrtis both in form and substance. The Puranas are of inestimable value for the history of philosophy and religion, and are a veritable store-house for getting insight into all aspects and phases of Hinduism. Not a single Purana can be found to contain all these particulars; however, 'taken collectively, they may be described as a popular encyclopaedia of ancient and medieval Hinduism, religious, philosophical, historical, personal, social and political'.[1]

Purana: Meaning, Definition and Characteristics

The term Purana, according to its etymology as given in the Vayu Purana, means 'that which lives from ancient times'; the Matsya also describes the Puranas as 'containing records of past events'. Originally, therefore, the term signified 'ancient tale' or 'old narrative' in the Brahmana literature, as compared with Itihasa and Narasamsi, before it became associated with Purana as a class of literature. Puranas in the form of

legendary lore existed from times of antiquity, even prior to the revelation of the Vedas, and this was handed down to posterity. There was no Purana literature as such in those days of yore.

Though references in the Atharvaveda imply that the Purana had assumed some independent form of composition, it is not definite whether Puranas meant actual books at the time of the Atharvaveda. The Chandogya Upanisad shows that a definite work was intended by the term. It is in the Sutras, however, that we find reference to the existence of real Puranas.

Both Itihasa and Purana denoted history and both are mentioned together in Vedic literature, sometimes as separate words and sometimes as one compound word, but almost always associated with Gathas, Narasamsis, Vakovakyas, etc., which were all subjects of study in ancient times. In the later Vedic Age, Itihasa preponderated over Purana, but gradually the latter asserted itself. The characteristics of the Puranas have been mentioned in the classical definition of the term by Amarasimha (fifth century A.D.), which is also found in some Puranas, as Pańcalakshana, i.e., having five characteristics, which are, sarga (creation), pratisarga (dissolution and recreation), vamsa (divine genealogies), manvantara (ages of Manus) and vamsyanucarita (genealogies of kings). A variant reading has bhumyadeḥ samsthana (world geography) in place of vamsyänucarita.

None of the existing Puranas is in complete agreement with this definition; some contain much more than these, while others scarcely touch these and deal with other topics. It is further found that Pañcalakshana occupies but an insignificant part (about 1/40) of the extant Puranas. Thus it appears that religious instruction was not one of their primary aims, nor were they originally composed for sectarian purposes. These and other later additions such as däna (gifts), vratas (religious observances), tirthas (sacred places), sräddha (rites in honour of the manes), etc., which form the bulk of the contents of the extant Puranas and which are not covered by the definition, render the Pañcalaksana definition merely a theoretical thing, not an actual fact. In order to get over this difficulty the Puranas themselves stated that the Pañcalakṣaṇa definition was intended merely for the Upa-Purana (minor Purana) and the Maha-Purana (major Purana) has to satisfy the Dasalaksana (having ten characteristics) definition, which includes these additional topics: vrtti (means of livelihood), rakṣa (incarnations of gods), mukti (final emancipation), hetu (jiva, unmanifest), and apasraya (Brahman). These characteristics also leave out of account several of the features of the extant Purāṇas. Haraprasad Sastri has found in the Matsya, an advance over this definition, which may be said to be the nearest approach to the description of the Puranas. It says that besides the ten characteristics, the Puranas deal with the glorification of Brahma, Visnu, Surya and Rudra, as also with the dissolution and preservation of the world, and with dharma (righteous conduct), artha (economics and polity), kama (erotics) and mokşa (emancipation).

Even this comprehensive definition does not cover the entire ground traversed by the Puranas. The Purana tradition, like that of the Mahabharata, has all along been floating and dynamic, and the texts have been subjected to numerous revisions, additions, omissions and modifications. The only characteristic of a Purana is that it should be old. 'Anything old may be the subject of a Purana', observes Haraprasad Sastri, 'and it covers all the aspects of life'.[2]

Puranas: Their Number and Classification

There are eighteen Maha-Puranas and eighteen Upa-Puranas according to the traditional view. The list of the Maha-Purānas is given in almost all Purānas, mostly in the same order, and it is uniform, except for a couple of changes. The list runs: Brahma, Padma, Visņu, Vayu, Bhagavata, Naradiya, Märkandeya, Agni, Bhavisya, Brahmavaivarta, Varaha, Linga, Skanda, Vamana, Kurma, Matsya, Garuda and Brahmända. Some Puranas read Siva in place of Vayu, and Devi-Bhagavata instead of (Vaisnava) Bhagavata. Pusalker has shown that the Siva is not a Maha-Purana.[3] However, in order to accommodate these conflicting views, Pargiter takes

their number to be 19, by including both the Siva and Vayu,[4] and Farquhar further increases the number by including the Harivamsa in addition.[5] But there is absolutely no support for increasing the traditional number.

There is no uniformity in the enumeration of the Upa-Puranas, which, unfortunately, have been comparatively neglected so far. The Upa-Puranas are more sectarian in character, are comparatively late and of composite nature. There is very little of historical value in the Upa-Puranas. From a collation of the lists at different places, the following appear to be the eighteen Upa-Puranas: Sanatkumara, Narasimha, Nanda, Sivadharma, Durvasa, Naradiya, Kapila, Vamana, Usanas, Manava, Varuna, Kali, Maheśvara, Samba, Saura, Parasara, Marica and Bhargava. Hazra has collected the names of about a hundred Upa-Puranas,[6] of which hardly fifteen have appeared in print.

The Puranas can also be classified into ancient and later, according as they conform strictly to the Pañcalakṣaṇa definition or not. The less the number of additions which are foreign to the nature of the Puranas as defined by the Amarakosa, the older the Purana. Judging from this test, we may pronounce the Vayu, Brahmanda, Matsya and Vishnu as the ancient Puranas.

The Maha-Puranas have further been sub-divided according to their preferential treatment to Vishnu, Siva and other deities, and they are respectively styled Sättvika, Tamasa

and Rājasa, evidently from the Vaisnava standpoint. Thus, the Padma distribution is as under:[7]

(i) Sättvika—Vishnu, Naradiya, Bhagavata, Garuda, Padma and Varaha;
(ii) Tamasa—Matsya, Kürma, Linga, Siva, Agni and Skanda;
(iii) Rajasa—Brahmanda, Brahmavaivarta, Märkandeya, Brahma, Vämana and Bhavisya.

The Skanda enumerates ten Puranas as describing the greatness of Siva, four of Brahma and two each of Devi and Hari. The Matsya regards the Purana glorifying Agni as Rajasa, and those that glorify the Sarasvati and Pitrs (Manes) as Samkirna.

Basing his division on later Tamil works, Dikshitar classifies the Puranas into five groups as under:

(i) Brahma—Brahma and Padma;
(ii) Sürya—Brahmavaivarta;
(iii) Agni—Agni;
(iv) Siva—Siva, Skanda, Linga, Kurma, Vamana, Varaha, Bhavisya, Matsya, Märkandeya and Brahmanda; and
(v) Vişnu—Narada, Bhagavata, Garuda and Vishnu.

The most satisfactory grouping, however, has been attempted by Haraprasad Sastri, on a thorough and

critical examination of the contents of the Puranas. He divides them into six groups in accordance with their subject-matter.[8]

(i) The first group is the so-called encyclopaedias of literature, comprising the Garuda, Agni and Narada. These contain the abstracts of all the great works in Arts and Sciences in Sanskrit Literature. These deal, in addition to the usual Puranic material, with medicine, grammar, dramaturgy, music, astrology, etc.

(ii) The next group, which includes the Padma, Skanda and Bhavisya, mainly deals with tirthas and vratas. The original matter in these Purãnas has been lost out of recognition on account of various revisions of a drastic nature.

(iii) The Puranas, that underwent two general revisions which are apparent, form the third group, and comprise the Brahma, Bhagavata and Brahmavaivarta. In these Puranas, the original part is the kernel or the central portion, which has been added to twice—at both ends on each occasion.

(iv) The fourth group, called historical, comprises the Brahmanda and the lost Vayu. Haraprasad Sastri holds that excepting for a portion of the second part preserved in a manuscript, the genuine Vayu is lost;[9] the present Vayu may be merged in the Brahmanda.

(v) Sectarian works form the fifth group which consists of the Linga, Vamana and Märkandeya. The Linga deals with Linga Puja (worship of Linga as an emblem of Siva), while the Vamana is a handbook of Saiva sects according to Haraprasad Sastri. The Märkandeya deals with Devi.

(vi) Finally, old Purāṇas revised out of existence is the sixth group, including the Varäha, Kurma, and Matsya. One naturally expects these entire works to have been spoken by these various incarnations of Vişnu; but actually, Varäha speaks only about a half of the Varaha Purana; Matsya, only a third of the Matsya; and Kurma, only an eighth of the Kürma.

Puranas: Origin and Development

The Puranas contain different accounts of their origin. According to the Vishnu, after dividing the Veda and entrusting it to his four disciples, Vyasa compiled a Purana-Samhita with tales, anecdotes, songs and ancient lore, and taught it to his fifth disciple, Süta Lomaharsana (or Ro-), who divided that Purana into six versions and taught them to his disciples, three of whom each made a further collection. The six-fold Purana of Sûta is known as Romaharsanic collection, and the collections of his disciples are named after them, as Kasyapika, Sävarnika, and Samsapayanika. These four were regarded as the 'root-samhitas'. None of these is in existence at present. Súta had a son named Ugraśravas and he taught a samhita to him also. The Vishnu thus accounts for four root-samhitäs of the original Purana.

The Vayu says that the Puranas were compiled by Brahma before the Vedas were revealed to him, and the task of their preservation was given to the Sütas. The original Süta was born mystically out of the first sacrifice and was entrusted with preserving the tradition. This Süta is a holy and venerable Brahmana, quite distinct from the Süta of the Dharma-sastras, born of pratiloma wedlock between a Brahmana maiden and a Ksatriya male, as also from the residents of Magadha who were Sútas. Many a scholar has taken the Süta of the Puranas to be a non-Brahmana, which is evidently a mistake.

Haraprasad Sastri says that in the only genuine portion of the Vayu (referred to earlier) the number of the Puranas is given as ten, so that this represents, according to him, the next stage in the development of the Puranas, when their number was raised from four as given in the Vishnu, to ten. He states that the traditional number eighteen is the final stage.

B.C. Mazumdar holds that there was a separate Purana for each Vedic school as there were separate Brahmanas, Anukramanis, Upanisads, etc.; and regards the Agni, Vayu and Surya to be such original Puranas connected respectively with the Rg-, Yajus-, and Sama-vedas.

On account of the use of the word Purana in singular in the passages of the Atharvaveda, identity of language in the dynastic lists in the Puranas and the traditional account of there being a single Purana at the beginning, Jackson and others believe that there was only one Purana in the beginning. But the singular number has been used collectively to designate the group of Purana-Samhita. Again, different Puranas commence with different princes, and with different periods, and are the products of different places. Hence, there was no original single Purana, in the same way as there is no original single Veda or single Brahmana.

Tracing the genesis and development of the legendary lore from the earliest times to the period when the Purānas attained the status of eighteen Maha-Puranas, it appears that up to the period of the Atharvaveda, the Puranas signified only tales of old, and were allied with Itihasa, Gāthās, Narasamsis, etc. It is doubtful whether the term then conveyed any class of Purana literature. The Puranas in the Vedic Age were compiled by the Süta from the Vedic Vamsa, Akhyana, etc. The Bharata war was an important landmark in the development of the Puranas because their canon was fixed some four generations after the Bharata war and the genealogical accounts subsequent to this period were designated as 'future' in the Puranas. The next stage may be found in the Upanisadic period when chapters on cosmogony, which incorporate the Samkhya and Upanisadic ideas, were added in the Puranas along with those on the Ages of the Manus. The self-contradictory title Bhavisyat Purana employed by Apastamba indicates that in the period of the

Sütras the term Purana had become so specialised as to have lost its proper meaning and became merely a designation of a particular class of books. The Puranas of those days probably gave rise to the Pañcalakṣaṇa definition, and included sections on geography and bhakti (devotion). Matters on Hindu rites and customs, which are strictly the domain of the Smrtis and Dharmasastras, such as varnasramadharma, śräddha, dana, dikṣa, vratas, tirthas, etc., were incorporated into the Puranas, as shown by Hazra, not later than the middle of the fourth century AD. Liberties have all along been taken with the texts of the Puranas, and especially the ambition of the later compilers was to make the Puranas all-comprehensive and encyclopaedic like the Mahabharata and every successive generation tried to make the Purānas up-to-date by various devices.

Contents of the Puranas

According to the classical definition, as already stated, the Puranas as a whole deal with the evolution of the universe, recreation of the universe from the constituent elements, genealogies of gods and seers, groups of great ages included in an aeon (kalpa), and the history of royal families. The first three of these subjects may be said to contain early religion, mythology and philosophy as also cosmography and 'ages'. The last two topics deal with genealogies and supply us with traditional history. The Puranas also contain, besides, a good deal on supplementary topics of religious instruction, rituals, dana, vratas, bhakti, yoga, various incarnations of Vishnu and Siva, and also medicine, music, grammar, poetics, metrics, dramaturgy, astronomy and astrology, architecture, sculpture, iconography, polity, rajadharma, etc.

Philosophy, Cosmogony: The Puranas contain various accounts as to the creation of the world. Here we shall deal only with the accounts in the Vishnu Purana as they are sufficient to give an idea of the cosmogony of the Puranas. According to one account, when the self-existent Brahman, who exists in three successively proceeding forms Puruşa, Pradhana and Kála, enters Purusa and Pradhana, Mahat or Buddhi is produced from Pradhana. Buddhi produces Ahamkara and so are produced the five subtle elements (tanmatras), the gross elements (bhutas) and the eleven organs (jnänendriyas, karmendriyas, and manas). The highest deity, invested with the rajas (activity) guna, and known as Brahma, creates all beings; the same deity with the sattva (purity) guna, and known as Vishnu, preserves the universe, and in the awful form Rudra with the tamas (darkness) guna destroys it.

Another account narrates the nine creations, the first three, viz. the animal creation, the elemental creation and the organic creation, being known as the Prakrta Sárga (creation from Prakṛti), the next five as the Vaikṛta Sarga, and the last as the Kaumāra Sarga. In all these creations three gunas existed in different states of predominance.

In yet another account it is stated that Brahma assumed four different forms in succession, and from these were produced the demons (asuras), gods (devas), forefathers (pitrs) and the mankind (manusyas). Afterwards he produced all other living beings, creatures and vegetation. Then were produced the nine mind-born sons known as Rsis, and deities called Rudras, after whom were created the first Manu Svayambhuva and a woman Satarupā. These had two sons, Priyavrata and Uttänapäda, and a daughter. Daksa married the daughter and had 24 daughters, of whom 13 were married to Dharma and bore Love and other personified feelings, ten were married to other mind-born sons and Agni and the fore-fathers, and one, known as Sati, was married to Siva.

This creation lasts for a day of Brahma which is equal to 14 Manus or Manvantaras. At the close of each Manvantara, life of inferior creatures and lower worlds comes to an end, leaving the substance of the universe entire, and gods and sages unharmed. After the end of the fourteenth Manvantara or when Brahma's day closes, occurs the great dissolution called Naimittika Pratisarga in which all things come to an end by fire and water, from which only the Prakrta Creation escapes including the three qualities and Seven Rsis, etc. At the end of Brahma's night lasting for a Kalpa, he awakes and begins his creation again. All the Präkṛta Creation disappears only at the Präkṛta Pralaya, occurring at the end of the life of Brahma, when not only all the gods and all other forms are annihilated, but the elements are again merged into primary substance, besides which only spiritual being exists.

Kalpa, Manvantara, Yuga, etc.: The explanation of these theories involves a consideration of the question of Yugas (ages), Manvantaras (periods of Manus), etc. A human year is a day and night of the gods. 12,000 divine years or 4,320,000 human years constitute Caturyuga (four ages) or Mahayuga (great age) which is divided into four ages of progressive deterioration in the ratio of 4:3:2:1, respectively for Krta, Treta, Dvāpara and Kali. Each of these Yugas is preceded and followed by Sandhyās containing a tenth of the period of the Yuga. 1000 Caturyugas (i.e. 1000 x 4,320,000 human years) are equivalent to a day or night of Brahma, which is called a kalpa (aeon). Each kalpa comprises the periods of 14 Manus (fathers of mankind), each of whom presides over 71 Caturyugas with a surplus.

This chronological system of fitting in 71 four-age periods making a Manvantara in the cosmological scheme is purely hypothetical and a later elaboration. The idea of four ages seems to be an early one. Various theories have been put forth by scholars for explaining the Yugas and Manvantaras. Yuga appears to have meant any unit of time. Yuga has been variously taken to represent a quarter of a day, a month, a period less than a year, one year, four years, five years, ten years, one hundred years, one thousand years or ten thousand years on the strength of references in Sanskrit works. Daftary has published a monograph dealing with the astronomical method and its application to the chronology of ancient India. According to him, Yuga (also called Manvantara) was a period of four years (equivalent to a kalpa); the Maha-kalpa was a period of one thousand years, comprising Krta (four hundred), Treta (three hundred), Dvapara (two hundred) and Kali (one hundred); the first Krta began in 3102 B.C., and the Bharata war took place in 1197 B.C. Mankad has tried to show that all Yugas had at first an equal number of years, each having one thousand years at first and then twelve hundred years; the total of four Yugas being at first four thousand years and later four thousand eight hundred years; Manvantara was used for (a) a period from one Manu (generic dynastic title for a king) to another Manu, or (b) a period from a Manu (starter of a dynasty) to any king of his line; Caturyuga in the usual Purànic formula 'Caturyugaṇām hi samkhyātä sädhika hyekasaptatiḥ Manvantaram' was computed at forty years; the Manvantara Caturyuga method, employed for longer chronological computations, took a unit of forty years (termed as a Caturyuga) and in a given dynasty kept as many kings as the units of forty years were required. Manu's date has been taken to be 5976 B.C. and the date of Bharata war 3201 B.C.

No satisfactory explanation of the Manvantara Caturyuga theory has yet come forth. The division of time into four ages (Yugas), the Krta, Treta, Dvapara and Kali, according to Pargiter, had a historical basis, though later speculations have elaborated it into an amazing yet precise scheme of cosmogony, to which we have briefly referred. This theory of the four ages applies only to India and not to the whole world and thus the further elaboration of these ages in the 71 four-age periods making up a Manvantara is evidently a later development. As in later periods, great wars, conquests or political changes should be taken to have marked the end of one age and the coming in of another in the ancient period of traditional history. The Bharata war has been taken as having occurred at the close of the Dvapara age, and the Kali age began after the war. Earlier, Rama Dasarathi is said to have lived in the interval between the Tretă and Dvapara age. The Krta age appears to have ended with the destruction of the Haihayas and the Treta began with the reign of Sagara. Thus, in the scheme of genealogy before the Bharata war from Manu Vaivasvata to the participants in the great war which comprises 95 generations (according to Pargiter), the Krta covers forty generations (Nos. 1–40), the Tretä extends to twenty-five generations (Nos. 41–65) and the Dväpara to thirty generations (Nos. 66–95). These ages thus symbolize changes in the political conditions in India. Taking an average of 18 years for each generation, it may be stated that the Krta age covered (40 x 18) 720 years, Treta (25 x 18) 450 years, and Dvapara (30 x 18) 540 years, or that the historical period in India begins about 1800 years before the Bharata war. In other words, the great Flood, immediately after which the dynastic lists in traditional history begin, occurred about 1800 years before the Bharata war.

Cosmography: The account of the first Manu includes a description of the universe over which he ruled. Like chronology, most of the description is imaginary. The world is said to consist of seven concentric continents separated by encircling seas of different substances such as butter, milk, etc. Fabulous and mythological descriptions have been given of the nether regions comprising hells, and of the sun, moon, planets, stars and celestial worlds, etc. The innermost of the seven continents separated from the next by salt water is Jambudvipa which alone was subject to the law of Caturyugas. The most important region of Jambudvipa is Bharatavarşa or India, so called because the descendants of the Bharatas reside therein. Bharatavarsa is defined as the country that lies north of the ocean and south of the snowy mountains. It is said to contain seven main chains of mountains named Mahendra, Malaya, Sahya, Suktimat, Rksa, Vindhya and Päripätra. The Kirātas are stated to dwell on the east of Bharata; the Yadavas on the west, and the Brahmanas, Ksatriyas, Vaisyas and Sūdras in the centre. Detailed lists have been given of the rivers flowing from the Himalayas and seven mountain chains as also of several tribes inhabiting the various regions. The Mahabharata and other works also contain similar lists. The mention of Yavanas, Sakas and Pahlavas who came to India in the second and first centuries B.C. and of Hunas, who broke up the Gupta empire in the sixth century A.D., indicates that the geographical lists have been brought up-to-date, from time to time.

Dynastic Lists: The Puranas begin their genealogies with Manu, the saviour of humanity at the Flood. Vaivasvata Manu, the first king, had ten sons, among whom was divided the whole country. The eldest son had a dual personality as Ila or Ilā, and was the progenitor respectively of the Saudyumnas and the Alias. Ikṣvāku got the Madhyadeśa with its capital at Ayodhya, and his son Vikukşi continued the main Ikṣvāku branch of the Solar dynasty, and from another son Nemi sprang the Videhas. From Na-bhaga who ruled over the Yamuna descended the Rathitaras, known as 'Ksatriyan Brahmanas'. Dhrsta originated Dhrstakas who ruled over the Punjab. Saryati, founder of the Säryätas, ruled in Anarta, modern Gujarat, with its capital at Kusasthali (Dvārakā). Nabhanedişṭha ruled over modern Tirhut, and Visala in this line founded the Vaisala dynasty. From Karūsa came the Karūsas, the determined fighters, who occupied Badhelkhand and Shahbad. Not much is known about Narisyanta and Pramsu, and Prsadhra was probably excluded from his share.

From Pururavas Aila, born of Ila, who ruled over Pratisthäna (modern Pihan) started the Aila or Lunar dynasty. His son Ayu succeeded him at Pratisthāna, and another son Amavasu founded the Kanyakubja dynasty. Of his five sons, Nahuşa succeeded Ayu, Kṣatravṛddha established himself at Käsi, and Anenas gave rise to the Ksatradharmans. Nahuşa had five or six sons. Yati, the eldest, embraced asceticism, and Yayati, the great sacrificer, succeeded Nahusa. Yayati married Devayani and Sarmiṣṭhā, and had as sons Yadu and Turvasu (from Devayani), and Anu, Druhyu and Puru (from Sarmiştha), all founders of great dynasties. Puru continued the main line, and Pauravas, forerunners of the Kauravas and Pandavas, sprang from him. Yadu was the founder of the Yadavas, who included the Haihayas, Andhaka-Vrsnis, Satvatas, etc. From Anu descended the Anavas who branched off into Yaudheyas, Sauviras, Kaikayas, etc. Druhyu's descendants spread out into the Mleccha country beyond India, and Turvasu's line later merged in the Pauravas.

From Manu to the Bharata war have been given about 95 generations. After the Bharata war, the Puranas use the future tense for the subsequent dynasties, which are called dynasties of the Kali age, given only in seven Puranas. The account runs till about the period of the Guptas and Andhras.

Theology: The theology preached is heterogeneous. In preference to the Vedic deities of whom only Indra and Agni retain their premier positions, popular deities are praised in the Puranas. The three chief gods are Brahma, Vişņu and Siva. Varuna becomes the lord of the ocean, and his twin Mitra has disappeared. The Sun is highly extolled in some Puranas, but details of his worship are given in the Bhavisya. Yama, the god of the dead, punishes the sinners in his hells. Gandharvas and Apsaras are celestial musicians and nymphs. Under demons are classed the Asuras, Daityas, Danavas and Rākṣasas.

Of the trinity, Brahma is the creator, Vishnu the preserver, and Siva the destroyer. Sectarian Puranas preach the supremacy either of Vishnu or of Siva, but generally, the older Puranas glorify also the rival deity. The high watermark is found in the monotheistic teaching enunciating the unity of all three, and worship of any one of them according to the preference of the worshipper.

Incarnations: Ten incarnations of Visņu appear in most of the Puranas, of whom five (Matsya, Kürma, Varaha, Narasimha and Vamana) are mythological, four (Parasurama, Rāma, Kṛṣṇa and Buddha) are historical, and one (Kalki) is still future. Three of these, viz. Varaha, Narasimha and Vamana, of whom germs are found in Vedic literature, are said to be divya (divine) and the rest are mănuṣa (human). The Dasavatara (ten incarnations) theory suggests the idea of evolutionary process of human development. The fish emerges out of the early Palaeozoic seas, followed by the tortoise and boar in the Mesozoic period. Next came the man-lion and dwarf in the period of cavemen and bushmen. Parasurama represents the nomadic or hunter stage and Rama and Krsna, the fully civilised stage of city life.

In contrast to Vishnu, who appears on the celestial plane except when incarnated, Siva is a terrestrial god, forming part of the Hindu pantheon since prehistoric times. He is associated with Parvati, the Mother Goddess, and they have Skanda and Ganesa as sons. The Pasupata cult, praised in the Saiva Puranas, is reprobated in others. The Linga cult associated with Siva appears only in the later Puranas, as also the Sakta cult associated with the female counter-part of Linga worship.

There is also the worship of Pitrs (Manes) who are said to comprise seven groups, sometimes ranked with gods. They come into existence with gods in each manvantara. These pitrs are connected with Sraddha, about which elaborate particulars are given in the Puranas.

Heterodox systems: Among the heretical systems Jainism and Buddhism are condemned. Vişnu himself is represented as appearing as Mayamoha, who misguides the demons with the philosophies of darkness and ignorance, viz. those of the

Buddhists, Jainas and Carvākas. The term Nagna (naked) has been applied to Avaidika, i.e., a heretic, and includes these three. Käpälikas also figure as worst heretics.

Dharma, Artha, Käma and Mokṣa: These four aims of life form part of most of the Purānas. Under dharma is included religious teaching both Brahminical and popular. The doctrine of sin and punishment is distinctly laid down, with penance for the expiation of sins, and punishments in hells, of which description is given. The popular teaching consists of descriptions of tirthas and of pilgrimages to them, as also of vratas, dāna, etc.—the chief feature of all these being that they were available to all, including women and Šūdras to whom the Vedas were denied.

Artha (acquisition of wealth, or polity) may be found in the Rajadharma section appended to various Puranas dealing with the duties of kings and methods of administration, conduct of war and peace, etc.

Under Kama, we may include rules about marriage, duties of wife and women, which are illustrated by stories. Sitä and Savitri are cited as examples of perfect wifehood.

Mokṣa (final emancipation) was the aim placed before every human being. Transmigration was an article of faith with everyone. As means to the attainment of deliverance from the chain of successive rebirths were prescribed the paths of Yoga and Bhakti. Both Jñanayoga and Karmayoga have been taught. Bhakti is generally associated with Vishnu and Krsna.

Miscellaneous Matters: Medicine, veterinary science, architecture, scrutiny of gems, astrology, grammar, etc. are expounded in the Garuda and Agni. The latter further deals with archery, poetics, metrics, drama and music. The Matsya has a section on architecture.

—A.D. Pusalker, *Studies in the Epics and Puranas*

8

Kama Sutra of Vatsyayana

The Kama Sutra (circa 400–300 BCE) is a unique work of psychology, sociology, Hindu philosophy and sexology. It is an ancient Indian text which is considered to be the primary Sanskrit work on human sexuality. It is also one of the first systematic studies in world literature of human sexual behaviour.

On the Acquisition of Dharma, Artha and Kama

Man, the period of whose life is one hundred years, should practise Dharma, Artha, and Kama at different times and in such a manner that they may harmonize together and not clash in any way. He should acquire learning in his childhood, in his youth and middle age he should attend to Artha and Kama, and in his old age he should perform Dharma, and thus seek to gain Moksha, *i.e.*, release from further transmigration. Or, on account of the uncertainty of life, he may practise them at times when they are enjoined to be practised. But one thing is to be noted, he should lead the life of a religious student until he finishes his education.

Dharma is obedience to the command of the Shastra or Holy Writ of the Hindoos to do certain things, such as the performance of sacrifices, which are not generally done because they do not belong to this world, and produce no visible effect; and not to do other things, such as eating meat, which is often done because it belongs to this world, and has visible effects.

Dharma should be learnt from the Shruti (Holy Writ), and from those conversant with it.

Artha is the acquisition of arts, land, gold, cattle, wealth, equipages and friends. It is, further, the protection of what is acquired, and the increase of what is protected.

Artha should be learnt from the king's officers, and from merchants who may be versed in the ways of commerce.

Kama is the enjoyment of appropriate objects by the five senses of hearing, feeling, seeing, tasting, and smelling, assisted by the mind together with the soul. The ingredient in this is a peculiar contact between the organ of sense and its object, and the consciousness of pleasure which arises from that contact is called Kama.

Kama is to be learnt from the Kama Sutra (aphorisms on love) and from the practice of citizens.

When all the three, viz., Dharma, Artha, and Kama come together, the former is better than the one which follows it, *i.e.*, Dharma is better than Artha, and Artha is better than Kama. But Artha should be always first practised by the king, for the livelihood of men is to be obtained from it only. Again, Kama being the occupation of public women, they should prefer it to the other two, and these are exceptions to the general rule.

Objection 1

Some learned men say that as Dharma is connected with things not belonging to this world, it is appropriately treated in a book; and so also is Artha, because it is practised only by the application of proper means, and a knowledge of those means can only be obtained by study and from books. But Kama being a thing which is practised even by the brute creation, and which is to be found everywhere, does not want any work on the subject.

Answer

This is not so. Sexual intercourse being a thing dependent on man and woman requires the application of proper means by them, and those means are to be learnt from the Kama Shastra. The non-application of proper means, which we see in the brute creation, is caused by their being unrestrained, and by the females among them only being fit for sexual intercourse at certain seasons and no more, and by their intercourse not being preceded by thought of any kind.

Objection 2

The Lokayatikas say: Religious ordinances should not be observed, for they bear a future fruit, and at the same time it is also doubtful whether they will bear any fruit at all. What foolish person will give away that which is in his own hands into the hands of another? Moreover, it is better to have a pigeon today than a peacock to-morrow; and a copper coin which we have the certainty of obtaining, is better than a gold coin, the possession of which is doubtful.

Answer

It is not so. 1st. Holy Writ, which ordains the practice of Dharma, does not admit of a doubt.

2nd. Sacrifices such as those made for the destruction of enemies, or for the fall of rain, are seen to bear fruit.

3rd. The sun, moon, stars, planets and other heavenly bodies appear to work intentionally for the good of the world.

4th. The existence of this world is effected by the observance of the rules respecting the four classes of men and their four stages of life.

5th. We see that seed is thrown into the ground with the hope of future crops. Vatsyayana is therefore of opinion that the ordinances of religion must be obeyed.

Objection 3

Those who believe that destiny is the prime mover of all things say: We should not exert ourselves to acquire wealth, for sometimes it is not acquired although we strive to get it, while at other times it comes to us of itself without any exertion on our part. Everything is therefore in the power of destiny, who is the lord of gain and loss, of success and defeat, of pleasure and pain. Thus we see the Bali was raised to the throne of Indra by destiny, and was also put down by the same power, and it is destiny only that can re-instate him.

Answer

It is not right to say so. As the acquisition of every object presupposes at all events some exertion on the part of man, the application of proper means may be said to be the cause of gaining all our ends, and this application of proper means being thus necessary (even where a thing is destined to happen), it follows that a person who does nothing will enjoy no happiness.

Objection 4

Those who are inclined to think that Artha is the chief object to be obtained argue thus. Pleasures should not be sought for, because they are obstacles to the practice of Dharma and Artha, which are both superior to them, and are also disliked by meritorious persons. Pleasures also bring a man into distress, and into contact with low persons; they cause him to commit unrighteous deeds, and produce impurity in him; they make him regardless of the future, and encourage carelessness and levity. And lastly, they cause him to be disbelieved by all, received by none, and despised by everybody, including himself. It is notorious, moreover, that many men who have given themselves up to pleasure alone, have been ruined along with their families and relations. Thus, King Dandakya, of the Bhoja dynasty, carried off a Brahman's daughter with evil intent, and was eventually ruined and lost his kingdom. Indra, too, having violated the chastity of Ahalya, was made to suffer for it. In a like manner the mighty Kichaka, who tried to seduce Draupadi, and Ravana, who attempted to gain over Sita, were punished for their crimes. These and many others fell by reason of their pleasures.

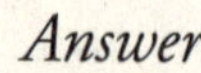

Answer

This objection cannot be sustained, for pleasures, being as necessary for the existence and well being of the body as food, are consequently equally required. They are, moreover, the results of Dharma and Artha. Pleasures are, therefore, to be followed with moderation and caution. No one refrains from cooking food because there are beggars to ask for it, or from sowing seed because there are deer to destroy the corn when it is grown up.

Thus a man practising Dharma, Artha and Kama enjoys happiness both in this world and in the world to come. The good perform those actions in which there is no fear as to what is to result from them in the next world, and in which there is no danger to their welfare. Any action which conduces to the practice of Dharma, Artha and Kama together, or of any two, or even one of them, should be performed, but an action which conduces to the practice of one of them at the expense of the remaining two should not be performed.

On the Arts and Sciences to Be Studied

Man should study the Kama Sutra and the arts and sciences subordinate thereto, in addition to the study of the arts and sciences contained in Dharma and Artha. Even young maids should study this Kama Sutra along with its arts and sciences before marriage, and after it they should continue to do so with the consent of their husbands.

Here some learned men object, and say that females, not being allowed to study any science, should not study the Kama Sutra.

But Vatsyayana is of opinion that this objection does not hold good, for women already know the practice of Kama Sutra, and that practice is derived from the Kama Shastra, or the science of Kama itself. Moreover, it is not only in this but in many other cases that though the practice of a science is known to all, only a few persons are acquainted with the rules and laws on which the science is based. Thus the Yadnikas or sacrificers, though ignorant of grammar, make use of appropriate words when addressing the different Deities, and do not know how these words are framed. Again, persons do the duties required of them on auspicious days, which are fixed by astrology, though they are not acquainted with the science of astrology. In a like manner riders of horses and elephants train these animals without knowing the science of training animals, but from practice only. And similarly the people of the most distant provinces obey the laws of the kingdom from practice, and because there is a king over them, and without further reason. And from experience we find that some women, such as daughters of princes and their ministers, and public women, are actually versed in the Kama Shastra.

A female, therefore, should learn the Kama Shastra, or at least a part of it, by studying its practice from some confidential friend. She should study alone in private the sixty-four practices that form a part of the Kama Shastra. Her teacher should be one of the following persons, viz., the daughter of a nurse brought up with her and already married, or a female friend who can be trusted in everything, or the sister of her mother (i.e., her aunt), or an old female servant, or a female beggar who may have formerly lived in the family, or her own sister, who can always be trusted.

The following are the arts to be studied, together with the Kama Sutra:

1. Singing.
2. Playing on musical instruments.
3. Dancing.
4. Union of dancing, singing, and playing instrumental music.
5. Writing and drawing.
6. Tattooing.
7. Arraying and adorning an idol with rice and flowers.
8. Spreading and arraying beds or couches of flowers, or flowers upon the ground.
9. Colouring the teeth, garments, hair, nails, and bodies, *i.e.*, staining, dyeing, colouring and painting the same.
10. Fixing stained glass into a floor.

11. The art of making beds, and spreading out carpets and cushions for reclining.
12. Playing on musical glasses filled with water.
13. Storing and accumulating water in aqueducts, cisterns and reservoirs.
14. Picture making, trimming and decorating.
15. Stringing of rosaries, necklaces, garlands and wreaths.
16. Binding of turbans and chaplets, and making crests and top-knots of flowers.
17. Scenic representations. Stage playing.
18. Art of making ear ornaments.
19. Art of preparing perfumes and odours.
20. Proper disposition of jewels and decorations, and adornment in dress.
21. Magic or sorcery.
22. Quickness of hand or manual skill.
23. Culinary art, i.e., cooking and cookery.
24. Making lemonades, sherbets, acidulated drinks, and spirituous extracts with proper flavour and colour.
25. Tailor's work and sewing.
26. Making parrots, flowers, tufts, tassels, bunches, bosses, knobs, &c., out of yarn or thread.
27. Solution of riddles, enigmas, covert speeches, verbal puzzles and enigmatical questions.
28. A game, which consisted in repeating verses, and as one person finished, another person had to commence at

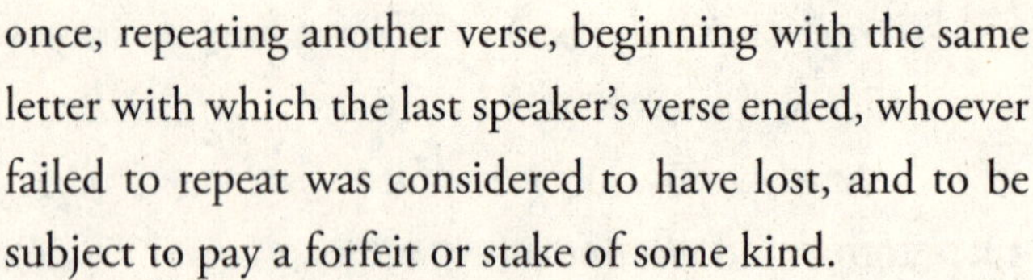

once, repeating another verse, beginning with the same letter with which the last speaker's verse ended, whoever failed to repeat was considered to have lost, and to be subject to pay a forfeit or stake of some kind.

29. The art of mimicry or imitation.
30. Reading, including chanting and intoning.
31. Study of sentences difficult to pronounce. It is played as a game chiefly by women and children, and consists of a difficult sentence being given, and when repeated quickly, the words are often transposed or badly pronounced.
32. Practice with sword, single stick, quarter staff, and bow and arrow.
33. Drawing inferences, reasoning or inferring.
34. Carpentry, or the work of a carpenter.
35. Architecture, or the art of building.
36. Knowledge about gold and silver coins, and jewels and gems.
37. Chemistry and mineralogy.
38. Colouring jewels, gems and beads.
39. Knowledge of mines and quarries.
40. Gardening; knowledge of treating the diseases of trees and plants, of nourishing them, and determining their ages.
41. Art of cock fighting, quail fighting and ram fighting.
42. Art of teaching parrots and starlings to speak.

43. Art of applying perfumed ointments to the body, and of dressing the hair with unguents and perfumes and braiding it.
44. The art of understanding writing in cypher, and the writing of words in a peculiar way.
45. The art of speaking by changing the forms of words. It is of various kinds. Some speak by changing the beginning and end of words, others by adding unnecessary letters between every syllable of a word, and so on.
46. Knowledge of language and of the vernacular dialects.
47. Art of making flower carriages.
48. Art of framing mystical diagrams, of addressing spells and charms, and binding armlets.
49. Mental exercises, such as completing stanzas or verses on receiving a part of them; or supplying one, two or three lines when the remaining lines are given indiscriminately from different verses, so as to make the whole an entire verse with regard to its meaning; or arranging the words of a verse written irregularly by separating the vowels from the consonants, or leaving them out altogether; or putting into verse or prose sentences represented by signs or symbols. There are many other such exercises.
50. Composing poems.
51. Knowledge of dictionaries and vocabularies.
52. Knowledge of ways of changing and disguising the appearance of persons.

53. Knowledge of the art of changing the appearance of things, such as making cotton to appear as silk, coarse and common things to appear as fine and good.
54. Various ways of gambling.
55. Art of obtaining possession of the property of others by means of mantras or incantations.
56. Skill in youthful sports.
57. Knowledge of the rules of society, and of how to pay respects and compliments to others.
58. Knowledge of the art of war, of arms, of armies, &c.
59. Knowledge of gymnastics.
60. Art of knowing the character of a man from his features.
61. Knowledge of scanning or constructing verses.
62. Arithmetical recreations.
63. Making artificial flowers.
64. Making figures and images in clay.

A public woman, endowed with a good disposition, beauty and other winning qualities, and also versed in the above arts, obtains the name of a Ganika, or public woman of high quality, and receives a seat of honour in an assemblage of men. She is, moreover, always respected by the king, and praised by learned men, and her favour being sought for by all, she becomes an object of universal regard. The daughter of a king too, as well as the daughter of a minister, being learned in the above arts, can make their husbands favourable to them, even though these may have thousands of other wives besides themselves. And in the same manner, if a wife becomes separated from her husband, and falls into distress, she can support herself easily, even in a foreign country, by means of her knowledge of these arts. Even the bare knowledge of them gives attractiveness to a woman, though the practice of them may be only possible or otherwise according to the circumstances of each case. A man who is versed in these arts, who is loquacious and acquainted with the arts of gallantry, gains very soon the hearts of women, even though he is only acquainted with them for a short time.

The Life of a Citizen

Having thus acquired learning, a man, with the wealth that he may have gained by gift, conquest, purchase, deposit, or inheritance from his ancestors, should become a householder, and pass the life of a citizen. He should take a house in a city, or large village, or in the vicinity of good men, or in a place which is the resort of many persons. This abode should be situated near some water, and divided into different compartments for different purposes. It should be surrounded by a garden, and also contain two rooms, an outer and an inner one. The inner room should be occupied by the females, while the outer room, balmy with rich perfumes, should contain a bed, soft, agreeable to the sight covered with a clean white cloth, low in the middle part, having garlands and bunches of flowers upon it, and a canopy above it, and two pillows, one at the top, another at the bottom. There should be also a sort of couch besides, and at the head of this a sort of stool, on which should be placed the fragrant ointments for the night, as well as flowers, pots containing collyrium and other fragrant substances, things used for perfuming the mouth, and the bark of the common citron tree. Near the couch, on the ground, there should be a pot for spitting, a box containing ornaments, and also a lute hanging from a peg made of the tooth of an elephant, a board for drawing, a pot containing perfume, some books, and some garlands of the yellow amaranth flowers. Not far from the couch, and on the ground, there should be a round seat, a toy cart, and a board for playing with dice; outside the outer room there should be cages of birds, and a separate place for spinning, carving, and such like diversions. In the garden there should be a whirling swing and a common swing, as also a bower of creepers covered with flowers, in which a raised parterre should be made for sitting.

Now the householder having got up in the morning and performed his necessary duties, should wash his teeth, apply a limited quantity of ointments and perfumes to his body, put some ornaments on his person and collyrium on his eyelids and below his eyes, colour his lips with alacktaka, and look at himself in the glass. Having then eaten betel leaves, with other things that give fragrance to the mouth, he should perform his usual business. He should bathe daily, anoint his body with oil every other day, apply a lathering substance to his body every three days, get his head (including face) shaved every four days, and the other parts of his body every five or ten days. All these things should be done without fail, and the sweat of the armpits should also be removed. Meals should be taken in the forenoon, in the afternoon, and again at night, according to Charayana. After breakfast, parrots and other birds should be taught to speak, and the fighting of cocks, quails, and rams should follow. A limited time should be devoted to diversions with Pithamardas, Vitas, and Vidushakas, and then should be taken the midday sleep. After this the householder, having put on his clothes and ornaments, should, during the afternoon, converse with his friends. In the evening there should be singing, and after that the householder, along with his friend, should await in his room, previously decorated and perfumed, the arrival of the woman that may be attached to him, or he may send a female messenger for her, or go for her himself. After her arrival at his house, he and his friend should welcome her, and entertain her with a loving and agreeable conversation. Thus end the duties of the day.

—Translation courtesy Kama Shastra Society

9

Arthashastra of Kautilya

Arthashastra (circa 300 BCE) is one of the most impactful texts ever composed on politics, philosophy, economics, military strategy, the functions of a state and society. It is a detailed manual on statecraft, governance and the science of living by Kautilya, one of ancient India's greatest minds. The principles of economic management, trade, taxation and wealth creation it sets out helped to sustain the Mauryan empire, which was one of the largest in the history of South Asia. The lessons and principles found in the Arthashastra continue to hold relevance in politics, governance and strategic thinking even today.

This Arthashastra is made as a compendium of almost all the Arthashastras, which, in view of acquisition and maintenance of the earth, have been composed by ancient teachers.

The King

The king who is well educated and disciplined in sciences, devoted to good government of his subjects, and bent on doing good to all people will enjoy the earth unopposed.

Restraint of the Organs Of Sense

The Shaking Off of the Aggregate of the Six Enemies

Restraint of the organs of sense, on which success in study and discipline depends, can be enforced by abandoning lust, anger, greed, vanity (maana), haughtiness (mada), and overjoy (harsha).

Absence of discrepancy (avipratipatti) in the preception of sound, touch, colour, flavour, and scent by means of the ears, the skin, the eyes, the tongue, and the nose, is what is meant by the restraint of the organs of sense. Strict observance of the precepts of sciences also means the same; for the sole aim of all the sciences is nothing but restraint of the organs of sense.

Whosoever is of reverse character, whoever has not his organs of sense under his control, will soon perish, though possessed of the whole earth bounded by the four quarters.

For example: Bhoja, known also by the name Daṇḍakya, making a lascivious attempt on a Brahman maiden, perished along with his kingdom and relations.

So also Karala, the Vaideha. Likewise Janamejaya under the influence of anger against Brahmans, as well as Talajangha against the family of Bhrigus.

Aila in his attempt under the influence of greed to make exactions from Brahmans, as well as Ajabindu, the Sauvira (in a similar attempt).

Ravana, unwilling under the influence of vanity to restore a stranger's wife, as well as Duryodhana, to part with a portion of his kingdom; Dambhodbhava as well as Arjuna of Haihaya dynasty being so haughty as to despise all people.

Vatapi, in his attempt under the influence of overjoy to attack Agastya, as well as the corporation of the Vrishnis in their attempt against Dvaipayana.

Thus these and other several kings, falling prey to the aggregate of the six enemies, and having failed to restrain their organs of sense, perished together with their kingdom and relations. Having driven out the aggregate of the six enemies, Ambarisha of Jamadagnya, famous for his restraint of the organs of sense, as well as Nabhaga, long enjoyed the earth.

The Life of a Saintly King

Hence by overthrowing the aggregate of the six enemies, he shall restrain the organs of sense; acquire wisdom by keeping company with the aged; see through his spies; establish safety and security by being ever-active; maintain his subjects in the observance of their respective duties by exercising authority; keep up his personal discipline by receiving lessons in the sciences; and endear himself to the people by bringing them in contact with wealth and doing good to them.

Thus with his organs of sense under his control, he shall keep away from hurting the woman and property of others; avoid not only lustfulness, even in dream, but also falsehood, haughtiness, and evil proclivities; and keep away from unrighteous and uneconomical transactions.

Not violating righteousness and economy, he shall enjoy his desires. He shall never be devoid of happiness. He may enjoy in an equal degree the three pursuits of life, charity, wealth, and desire, which are inter-dependent upon each other. Any one of these three, when enjoyed to an excess, hurts not only the other two, but also itself.

Kautilya holds that wealth, and wealth alone, is important, inasmuch as charity and desire depend upon wealth for their realisation.

Those teachers and ministers who keep him from falling a prey to dangers, and who, by striking the hours of the day as determined by measuring shadows, warn him of his careless proceedings even in secret, shall invariably be respected.

Sovereignty (rajatva) is possible only with assistance. A single wheel can never move. Hence, he shall employ ministers and hear their opinion.

The Source of Sovereign States

The Elements of Sovereignty

The king, the minister, the country, the fort, the treasury, the army and the friend, and the enemy are the elements of sovereignty.

Of these, the best qualities of the king are:

Born of a high family, godly, possessed of valour, seeing through the medium of aged persons, virtuous, truthful, not of a contradictory nature, grateful, having large aims, highly enthusiastic, not addicted to procrastination, powerful to control his neighbouring kings, of resolute mind, having an assembly of ministers of no mean quality, and possessed of a taste for discipline—these are the qualities of an inviting nature.

Inquiry, hearing, perception, retention in memory, reflection, deliberation, inference and steadfast adherence to conclusions are the qualities of intellect.

Valour, determination of purpose, quickness, and probity are the aspects of enthusiasm.

Possessed of a sharp intellect, strong memory, and keen mind, energetic, powerful, trained in all kinds of arts, free from vice, capable of paying in the same coin by way of awarding punishments or rewards, possessed of dignity; capable of taking remedial measures against dangers, possessed of foresight, ready to avail himself of opportunities when afforded in respect of place, time, and manly efforts, clever enough to discern the causes necessitating the cessation of treaty or war with an enemy, or to lie in wait keeping treaties, obligations and pledges, or to avail himself of his enemy's weak points, making jokes with no loss of dignity or secrecy, never browbeating and casting haughty and stern looks, free from passion, anger, greed, obstinacy, fickleness, haste and back-biting habits, talking to others with a smiling face, and observing customs as taught by aged persons—such is the nature of self-possession.

The qualifications of a minister have been described in the beginning, middle, and at the close of the work.

Possessed of capital cities both in the centre and the extremities of the kingdom, productive of subsistence not only to its own people, but also to outsiders on occasions of calamities, repulsive to enemies, powerful enough to put down neighbouring kings, free from miry, rocky, uneven, and desert tracts, as well as from conspirators, tigers, wild beasts, and large tracts of wilderness, beautiful to look at, containing fertile lands, mines, timber and elephant forests, and pasture grounds, artistic, containing hidden passages, full of cattle, not depending upon rain for water, possessed of land and waterways, rich in various kinds of commercial articles, capable of bearing the burden of a vast army and heavy taxation, inhabited by agriculturists of good and active character, full of intelligent masters and servants, and with a population noted for its loyalty and good character—these are the qualities of a good country.

The excellent qualities of forts have already been described.

Justly obtained either by inheritance or by self-acquisition, rich in gold and silver, filled with an abundance of big gems of various colours and of gold coins, and capable to withstand calamities of long duration, is the best treasury.

Coming down directly from father and grandfather (of the king), ever strong, obedient, happy in keeping their sons and wives well contented, not averse to making a long sojourn, ever and everywhere invincible, endowed with the power of endurance, trained in fighting various kinds of battles, skilful in handling various forms of weapons, ready to share in the weal or woe of the king, and consequently not falling foul with him, and purely composed of soldiers of Kshatriya caste, is the best army.

Coming down directly from father and grandfather, long-standing, open to conviction, never falling foul; and capable of making preparations for war quickly and on a large scale, is the best friend.

Not born of a royal family, greedy, possessed of a mean assembly of ministers, with disloyal subjects, ever doing unrighteous acts, of loose character, addicted to mean pleasures, devoid of enthusiasm, trusting to fate, indiscreet in action, powerless, helpless, impotent and ever injurious, is the worst enemy. Such an enemy is easily uprooted.

Excepting the enemy, these seven elements, possessed of their excellent characteristics are said to be the limb-like elements of sovereignty.

A wise king can make even the poor and miserable elements of his sovereignty happy and prosperous; but a wicked king will surely destroy the most prosperous and loyal elements of his kingdom.

Hence a king of unrighteous character and of vicious habits will, though he is an emperor, fall a prey either to the fury of his own subjects or to that of his enemies.

But a wise king, trained in politics, will, though he possesses a small territory, conquer the whole earth with the help of the best fitted elements of his sovereignty, and will never be defeated.

The Six-Fold Policy, and Determination of Deterioration, Stagnation and Progress

The Circle of States is the source of the six-fold policy. My teacher says that peace (sandhi), war (vigraha), observance of neutrality (asana), marching (yana), alliance (samsraya), and making peace with one and waging war with another are the six forms of state policy.

But Vatavyadhi holds that there are only two forms of policy, peace and war, inasmuch as the six forms result from these two primary forms of policy.

While Kautilya holds that, as their respective conditions differ, the forms of policy are six.

Of these, agreement with pledges is peace; offensive operation is war; indifference is neutrality; making preparations is marching; seeking the protection of another is alliance; and making peace with one and waging war with another is termed a double policy (dvaidhibhava). These are the six forms.

Whoever is inferior to another shall make peace with him; whoever is superior in power shall wage war; whoever thinks, 'No enemy can hurt me, nor am I strong enough to destroy my enemy,' shall observe neutrality; whoever is possessed of necessary means shall march against his enemy; whoever is devoid of necessary strength to defend himself shall seek the protection of another; whoever thinks that help is necessary to work out an end shall make peace with one and wage war with another. Such is the aspect of the six forms of policy.

Of those, a wise king shall observe that form of policy which, in his opinion, enables him to build forts, to construct buildings and commercial roads, to open new plantations and villages, to exploit mines and timber and elephant forests and at the same time to harass similar works of his enemy.

Whoever thinks himself to be growing in power more rapidly both in quality and quantity (than his enemy), and the reverse of his enemy, may neglect his enemy's progress for the time.

If any two kings, hostile to each other, find the time of achieving the results of their respective works to be equal, they shall make peace with each other.

No king shall keep that form of policy, which causes him the loss of profit from his own works, but which entails no such loss on the enemy; for it is deterioration.

Whoever thinks that in the course of time his loss will be less than his acquisition as contrasted with that of his enemy, may neglect his temporary deterioration.

If any two kings, hostile to each other, and deteriorating, expect to acquire equal amount of wealth in equal time, they shall make peace with each other.

That position in which neither progress nor retrogression is seen is stagnation.

Whoever thinks his stagnancy to be of a shorter duration and his prosperity in the long run to be greater than his enemy's, may neglect his temporary stagnation.

My teacher says that if any two kings, who are hostile to each other, and are in a stationary condition, expect to acquire equal amount of wealth and power in equal time, they shall make peace with each other.

'Of course,' says Kautilya, 'there is no other alternative.'

Or if a king thinks:

'That keeping the agreement of peace, I can undertake productive works of considerable importance and destroy at the same time those of my enemy; or apart from enjoying the results of my own works, I shall also enjoy those of my enemy in virtue of the agreement of peace; or I can destroy the works of my enemy by employing spies and other secret means; or by holding out such inducements as a happy dwelling, rewards, remission of taxes, little work and large profits and wages, I can empty my enemy's country of its population, with which he has been able to carry his own works; or being allied with a king of considerable power, my enemy will have his own work destroyed; or I can prolong my enemy's hostility with another king whose threats have driven my enemy to seek my protection; or being allied with me, my enemy can harass the country of another king who hates me; or oppressed by another king, the subjects of my enemy will immigrate into my country, and I can, therefore, achieve the results of my own works very easily; or being in a precarious condition due to the destruction of his works, my enemy will not be so powerful as to attack me; or by exploiting my own resources in alliance with any two (friendly) kings, I can augment my resources; or if a Circle of States is formed by my enemy as one of its members, I can divide them and combine with the others; or by threats or favour I can catch hold of my enemy, and when he desires to be a member of my own Circle of States, I can make him incur the displeasure of the other members and fall a victim to their own fury'—if a king thinks thus, then he may increase his resources by keeping peace.

Or if a king thinks:

'That as my country is full of born soldiers and of corporations of fighting men, and as it possesses such natural defensive positions as mountains, forests, rivers, and forts with only one entrance, it can easily repel the attack of my enemy; or having taken my stand in my impregnable fortress at the border of my country, I can harass the works of my enemy; or owing to internal troubles and loss of energy, my enemy will early suffer from the destruction of his works; or when my enemy is attacked by another king, I can induce his subjects to immigrate into my country', then he may augment his own resources by keeping open hostility with such an enemy.

Or if a king thinks:

'That neither is my enemy strong enough to destroy my works, nor am I his; or if he comes to fight with me like a dog with a boar, I can increase his afflictions without incurring any loss in my own works,' then he may observe neutrality and augment his own resources.

Or if a king thinks:

'That by marching my troops it is possible to destroy the works of my enemy; and as for myself, I have made proper

arrangements to safeguard my own works,' then he may increase his resources by marching.

Or if a king thinks:

'That I am strong enough neither to harass my enemy's works nor to defend my own against my enemy's attack,' then he shall seek protection from a king of superior power, and endeavour to pass from the stage of deterioration to that of stagnancy and from the latter to that of progress.

Or if a king thinks:

'That by making peace with one, I can work out my own resources, and by waging war with another, I can destroy the works of my enemy,' then he may adopt that double policy and improve his resources.

Thus, a king in the circle of sovereign states shall, by adopting the six-fold policy, endeavour to pass from the state of deterioration to that of stagnation, and from the latter to that of progress.

—Translated by R. Shamsastry

10

Teachings of the Buddha

Buddha (circa 563–483 BCE) was born during a period of great social and religious upheaval. Among Hindus, there was a general resistance to the stifling practices of the Brahmins. The Vedas, which were said to have been received directly from God, could not be questioned. But these scriptures were all in Sanskrit, a language the common people could not understand. They were dependent on the Brahmins for their interpretation.

Buddha's teachings challenged the prevailing Hindu–Vedic religion. They attracted a large number of people and over time Buddhism became the dominant religion in South and Southeast Asia.

Four Noble Truths and the Noble Eightfold Path

It is difficult to say what exactly are the teachings of the Buddha, who was mainly an ethical teacher and a mystic rather than a metaphysician, and who preached only orally. Yet, a fairly good account of his teachings can be gleaned. It may be said to be threefold—The Four Noble Truths, the Noble Eightfold Path and the Doctrine of Dependent Origination.

The Four Noble Truths (arya satya) are:

1. There is suffering (dukha): Life is full of misery and pain. Even the so-called pleasures are really fraught with pain. There is always fear lest we may lose the so-called pleasures and their loss involves pain. Indulgence also results in pain. That there is suffering in this world is a fact of common experience. Poverty, disease, old age, death, selfishness, meanness, greed, anger, hatred, quarrels, bickerings, conflicts, exploitation are rampant in this world. That life is full of suffering none can deny.

2. There is a cause of suffering (dukha-samudaya): Everything has a cause. Nothing comes out of nothing—*ex nihilo nihil fit.* The existence of every event depends upon its causes and conditions. Everything in this world is conditional, relative, limited. Suffering being a fact, it must have a cause. It must depend on some conditions. 'This being, that arises', 'the cause being present, the effect arises', is the causal law of Dependent Origination.
3. There is a cessation of suffering (dukh-nirodha): Because everything arises depending on some causes and conditions, therefore if these causes and conditions are removed the effect must also cease. The cause being removed, the effect ceases to exist. Everything being conditional and relative is necessarily momentary and what is momentary must perish. That which is born must die. Production implies destruction.
4. There is a way leading to this cessation of suffering (dukhanirodha-gamini pratipat): There is an ethical and spiritual path by following which misery may be removed and liberation attained. This is the Noble Eight-fold Path.

The Noble Eight-fold Path consists of eight steps which are: (1) Right faith (samyag drishti), (2) right resolve (sankalpa), (3) right speech (vak), (4) right action (karmanta), (5) right living (ajiva), (6) right effort (vyayama), (7) right thought

(smriti) and (8) right concentration (samadhi). This is open to the clergy and the laity alike.

In the old books we also find mention of a triple path consisting of Shila or right conduct, Samadhi or right concentration and Prajna or right knowledge. They roughly correspond to Darshana, Jnana and Charitra of Jainism. Shila and Samadhi lead to Prajna which is the direct cause of liberation.

Buddha's ethical 'middle path' is like the 'golden mean' of Aristotle. Self-indulgence and self-mortification are equally ruled out. In his very first Sermon at Saranatha he said: 'There are two extremes, O monks, from which he who leads a religious life must abstain. One is a life of pleasure, devoted to desire and enjoyment: that is base, ignoble, unspiritual, unworthy, unreal. The other is a life of mortification: it is gloomy, unworthy, unreal. The Perfect One, O monks, is removed from both these extremes and has discovered the way which lies between them, the middle way which enlightens the eyes, enlightens the mind, which leads to rest, to knowledge, to enlightenment, to Nirvana.'[10] This is the Noble Eight-fold Path contained in the Four Noble Truths.

Shunyavada

Shunyavada is one of the most important schools of Buddhism. Nagarjuna cannot be called its founder because it was present before him in the Mahayana Sutras, some of which are prior even to Ashvaghosha, and in Ashvaghosha. Nagarjuna is only the first systematic expounder of Shunyavada. However, it is to the glory of Nagarjuna that he seized these threads and wove them into unity; it is to the greatness of Nagarjuna that he developed these more or less scattered ideas almost to perfection in a thoroughly consistent manner.

Shunyavadins call themselves Madhyamikas or the followers of the Middle Path realized by Buddha during his Enlightenment, which Path, avoiding the errors of existence and non-existence, affirmation and negation, eternalism and nihilism, also at once transcends both the extremes. It is a great irony of fate that the followers of such a path are condemned by some as nihilists.

Unfortunately the word 'Shunya' has been gravely misunderstood. The literal meaning of the word, which is negation or void, has been the cause of much misunderstanding. The word is used by the Madhyamikas in a different philosophical sense. Ignoring the real philosophical meaning of the word 'Shunya' and taking it only in its literal sense, many thinkers, eastern and western, ancient, medieval and modern have unfortunately committed that horrible blunder which has led them to thoroughly misunderstand Shunyavada and to condemn it as a hopeless scepticism and a self-condemned nihilism. Shunya, according to the Madhyamika, we emphatically maintain, does not mean a 'nothing' or an 'empty void' or a 'negative abyss'. Shunya essentially means Indescribable (avachya or anabhilapya) as it is beyond the four categories of intellect (chatushkoti-vinirmukta). It is Reality which ultimately transcends existence, non-existence, both and neither. It is neither affirmation nor negation nor both nor neither. Empirically it means Relativity (pratitya-samutpada) which is phenomena (samsara); absolutely it means Reality (tattva) which is release from plurality (nirvana). The world is Indescribable because it is neither existent nor non-existent; the Absolute is Indescribable because it is transcendental and no category of intellect can adequately describe it. Everything is Shunya: appearances are *Svabhava-shunya* or devoid of ultimate reality and Reality is *Prapancha-shunya* or devoid of plurality. Thus Shunya is used in a double sense. It means the relative as well as the Absolute. It means Relativity as well as Reality. It means Samsara as well as Nirvana. That which is phenomenal, that which is dependent and conditional and therefore relative cannot he called ultimately real. Even as borrowed wealth cannot be called real capital. All appearances (dharmas) being relative (pratityasamutpanna), have no real origination (paramarthatonutpanna) and are therefore devoid of ultimate reality (svabhava-shunya or nissvabhava or anatman). But they are not absolutely unreal. They must belong to Reality. It is the Real itself which appears. And this Real is the Absolute, the Non-dual Harmonious Whole in which all plurality is merged (prapancha shunya or nishprapancha or advaya táttva). Shunya therefore does not mean 'void'; it means, on the other hand, 'devoid', so far as appearances are concerned 'of ultimate reality', and so far as Reality is concerned, 'of plurality'. It is clearly wrong to translate the word 'Shunya' as 'nothing or void'; and even to translate it as 'Relativity' as Prof Stcherbatsky has done, is but to represent only one aspect of it.

Ashvaghosha said that Tathata is neither Shunya nor Ashunya nor both nor neither because it transcends all categories of the intellect. 'All things in the world from beginning neither matter nor mind (empirical ego), nor consciousness (momentary and individual), nor non-being, nor being; they are after all, inexplicable.'[11] But this does not mean that there is no reality because it is the Real itself which appears. 'The divine nature of the Absolute Reality is not unreal.'[12]

The Shunyavadins take 'existence', 'is', 'affirmation', 'being' in the sense of absolute existence or ultimate reality; it means Eternalism. Those who maintain that the world exists are committing a great error because when we penetrate deep we find that this entire world with all its manifold phenomena is essentially relative and therefore ultimately unreal. And those who advocate non-existence or non-being are also committing a great error because they are denying even the phenomenal reality of the world. They are condemned by the Shunyavadins as nihilists (nastikas). Eternalism and Nihilism are both false. Intellect which is essentially discursive, analytic and relational involves itself in contradictions. All that can be grasped by it is essentially relative. It gives us four categories—existence, non-existence, both and neither and involves itself in sixty-two antinomies. It cannot give us Reality. Reality transcends all the categories and reconciles all the antinomies of intellect. It is to be directly realized through spiritual experience. It is the Non-dual Absolute in which all plurality is merged. We must rise above the subject-object duality of the intellect and the plurality of the phenomena.

—Chandradhar Sharma, *Indian Philosophy: A Critical Survey*

11

Nagarjuna

Nagarjuna is considered to be one of the most influential philosophers of the Buddhist tradition. He is said to have lived between 150 and 250 CE in southern India and authored several texts that expounded on the Madhyamaka school of philosophy, of which he was the founder.

Although little is reliably known of his life, several accounts exist by later Chinese and Tibetan scholars that testify to his influence and his defence of the Mahayana movement.

Pratyaya Pariksa

Examination of Relational Condition

The term, *pratyaya*, has been variously rendered as *yin-yuan* by Kumarajiva, as causality by Stcherbatsky, as *Bedingungen* by Walleser. All three renditions, it must be stated, do not do complete justice to the Sanskrit original but there is a feeling that all three translators have sensed the significance of the term and concluded with the best possible term under their command in conveying the idea. This is just an example of how difficult it is to translate an original idea into another language, a difficulty which is doubly so when the term is a philosophical concept.

We may perhaps venture to say at the outset that the term ought to be shorn of any notion of 'cause' or 'causality' as commonly interpreted. These notions would immediately set up a causal connection such that an effect or something is originated or produced out of something else. In other words, they would connote a one-to-one, cause-effect, occurrence of events which is definitely not the true intention of the Madhyamika. For this reason, it is proposed, not without shortcomings either, to coin the phrase, 'relational condition', in which the adjective, 'relational' refers to the ontological representation of an event or subject as related to the whole situation, whether significantly or not, in a certain moment; while the noun, 'condition', refers to the state of such an event or subject at that particular moment.

Thus, relational condition does reflect somewhat the modern idea of a four-dimensional view of events in nature but the comparison can never be completely carried out because the former has a pre-scientific origin while the latter has a strictly Western scientific base.

The chapter then discusses the important concept of *pratyaya* or relational condition. Nagarjuna immediately ties it in with the problem of origination or how experiential events come forth. He asserts emphatically that events or entities (a term synonymously used in reference to a unity of human experience) are never known or found to originate out of themselves, from others, from both themselves and others, and from the absence of causes (verse 1). Following fundamental Buddhist principles, he points out that four and only four types of relational condition are permissible, i.e., primary causal (*hetu*), appropriating or objectively extending (*alambana*), sequential or contiguous (*anantara*), and dominantly extending (*adhipateya*) (verse 3). But then, keeping in mind the concepts of being (*sat*) and non-being (*asat*), he methodically analyses the play of relational conditions in order to exhibit the inner contradiction or utter absurdity of premising anything in the entified form.

In such a way this chapter serves as an introduction to the rest of the chapters because the method or line of argument used recurs over and over again, almost *ad nauseam.* However, the reader must constantly keep in mind that the basic aim of Nagarjuna is to reveal the fact that experiential events are always in the nature of relational origination (*pratityasamutpada*). And, very early in a dedicatory verse, Nagarjuna sings praise to the Buddha's supreme teaching of relational origination. The verse contains the famous Eight-Noes or Negations which indirectly point at the blissful realm of existence. It expresses the whole philosophy of Madhyamika in a nutshell and thus could well be labelled the Madhyamika Creed.

I pay homage to the Fully Awakened One,
the supreme teacher who has taught
the doctrine of relational origination,
the blissful cessation of all phenomenal thought constructions.

(Therein, every event is 'marked' by):
non-origination, non-extinction,
non-destruction, non-permanence,
non-identity, non-differentiation
non-coming (into being), non-going (out of being).

Verse 1

At nowhere and at no time can entities ever exist by originating out of themselves, from others, from both (self-other), or from the lack of causes.

Verse 2

There are four and only four relational conditions; namely primary causal, appropriating or objectively extending, sequential or contiguous, and dominantly extending conditions. There is no fifth.

Note: Stcherbatsky asserts that the classification into four varieties belongs to the Sarvastivadins and that it is supplemented by a further classification into six different *hetus*, which probably are later than Nagarjuna, since they are not mentioned by him. (*The Conception of Buddhist Nirvana*; p. 164, fn. 6) On the other hand, S. Yamaguchi points out that the *Abhidharmamahavibhasasastra*, chuan 16 makes reference to the fact Nagarjuna is only trying to understand the method of the Sarvastivadins regarding their claim of the transmission of the true teachings of the Buddha. He further indicates that the four *pratyayas* also occur in the *Madhyamakavatara*. Thus there is no direct connection with the theory of six *hetus*.

Verse 3

In these relational conditions the self-nature of the entities cannot exist. From the non-existence of self-nature, other-nature too cannot exist.

Verse 4

The functional force does not inhere relational conditions, nor does it not inhere them. The relational conditions, vice versa, do not inhere the functional force, nor do they not inhere it.

Verse 5

Only as entities are uniquely related and originated can they be described in terms of relational conditions. For, how can non-relational conditions be asserted of entities which have not come into being?

Verse 6

Relational condition does not validly belong to either being or non-being. If it belongs to being, for what use is it? And if to non-being, for whose use is it?

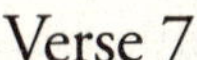

Verse 7

When a factor of experience does not evolve from being, non-being, nor from both being and non-being, how can there be an effectuating cause? Thus (such) a cause is not permissible.

Note: This verse treats the concept of the primary causal condition (*hetu-pratyaya*).

Verse 8

It is said that a true factor of experience does not have an appropriating or objectively extending relational condition. If it does not exist, then again, wherein is this type of relational condition?

Note: *Alambana* is normally translated as the object of cognition but here it hardly seems applicable to the concept of *dharma* (factor of experience).

Verse 9

It is not possible to have extinction where factors of experience have not yet arisen. In an extinguished state, for what use

is a relational condition? Thus the sequential or contiguous relational condition is not applicable.

Verse 10

As entities without self-nature have no real status of existence, the statement, 'from the existence of that this becomes' is not possible.

Note: This verse treats the concept of the dominantly extending relational conditional (*adhipati-pratyaya*). Stecherbatsky interprets the Sankrit phrase, *satidam asmin bhavatiti*, as the formula for the twelve-fold causal chain as found in the Nikayas. However, Ryotai Hatani points out as a note to this particular verse that the phrase is not to be restricted to the general formula on causation but should simply mean the significance of the existence of one entity from another. To be operative, the fourth cause (*adhipatipratyaya*) must assume the existence of an entity. However, Nagarjuna's fundamental standpoint is that of the non-self-nature (*nihsvabhava*) of an entity and therefore rules out any imputation of a causal or relational connection of entities in a one-to-one manner.

Verse 11

The effect (i.e., arisen entity) does not exist separated from relational condition nor together in relational condition. If

it does not exist in either situation, how could it arise out of relational conditions?

Verse 12

Now then, if non-entity arises from these relational conditions, why is it not possible that the effect (i.e., arisen entity) cannot arise from non-relational conditions?

Verse 13

The effect (i.e., arisen entity) has the relational condition but the relational conditions have no self-possessing (natures). How can an effect, arising from no self-possessing (natures), have the relational condition?

Verse 14

Consequently, the effect (i.e., arisen entity) is neither with relational nor without non-relational condition. Since the effect has no existing status, wherein are the relational and non-relational conditions?

—Kenneth K. Inada

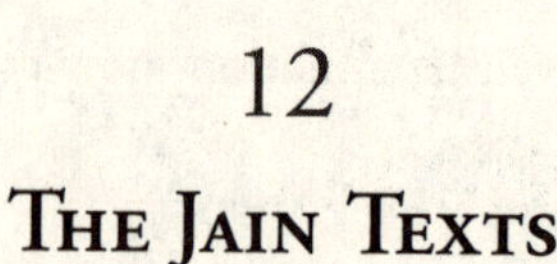

12

The Jain Texts

Jainism derives its name from the Sanskrit and Pali word 'jina', meaning 'victor'. A Jain is a follower of Jinas, who have conquered the illusion of birth and death and rediscovered Dharma. They are also known as Tirthankars. The last of the twenty-four Tirthankars, Mahavira Vardhamana (599–527 BCE), established the central tenets of Jainism: non-violence, truthfulness, non-stealing, chastity and non-attachment. Breaking barriers of caste, he organised his followers as monks (sadhus), nuns (sadhvis), laymen (shravaks) and laywomen (shravikas). This order is known as Chaturvidh Jain Sangh.

Syadvada

Syadvada which is also called Sapta-bhangi-naya is the theory of relativity of knowledge. Sapta-bhangi-naya means 'dialectic of the seven steps' or 'the theory of seven-fold judgment'. The word 'syat' literally means probable, perhaps, may be. And Syadvada is sometimes translated as the theory of probability or the doctrine of the may-be. But it is not in the literal sense of probability that the word 'syat' is used here. Probability suggests scepticism and Jainism is not scepticism. Sometimes the word 'syat' is translated as 'somehow'. But this too smacks of agnosticism and Jainism, again, is not agnosticism. The word 'syat' is used here in the sense of the relative and the correct translation of Syadvada is the theory of Relativity of knowledge. Reality has infinite aspects which are all relative and we can know only some of these aspects. All our judgments, therefore, are necessarily relative, conditional and limited. 'Syat' or 'Relatively speaking' or 'Viewed from a particular view-point which is necessarily related to other view-points' must precede all our judgments. Absolute affirmation and absolute negation both are wrong. All judgments are conditional. This is not a self-contradictory position because the very nature of reality is indeterminate and infinitely complex and because affirmation and negation both are not made from the same standpoint. The difficulty of predication is solved by maintaining that the subject and the predicate are identical from the point of view of substance and different from the point of view of modes. Hence categorical or absolute predication is ruled out as erroneous. All judgments are double-edged. Affirmation presupposes negation as much as negation presupposes affirmation. The infinitely complex reality (ananta-dharmakam vastu) admits of all opposite predicates from different standpoints. It is real as well as unreal (sadasadatmakam). It is universal as well as particular (vyavrtyanugamatmakam). It is permanent as well as momentary (nityanityasvarupam). It is one as well as many (anekamekatmakam). Viewed from the point of view of substance, it is real, universal, permanent and one; viewed from the point of view of modes, it is unreal, particular, momentary and many. The Jainas are fond of quoting the old story of the six blind men and the elephant. The blind men put their hands on the different parts of the elephant and each tried to describe the whole animal from the part touched by him. Thus the man who caught the ear said the elephant was like a country-made fan; the person touching the leg said the elephant was like a pillar; the holder of the trunk said it was like a python; the feeler of the tail said it was like a rope; the person who touched the side said the animal was like a wall; and the man who touched the forehead said the elephant was like the breast. And all the six quarrelled among themselves, each one asserting that his description alone was correct. But he who can see the whole elephant can easily know that each blind man feels only a part of the elephant which he mistakes to be the whole animal. Almost all philosophical, ideological and religious differences and disputes are mainly due to mistaking a partial truth for the whole truth. Our judgments represent different aspects of the many-sided reality and can claim only partial truth. This view makes Jainism catholic, broad-minded and tolerant. It teaches respect for others' points of view.

We can know an object in three ways through durniti, naya and pramana. Mistaking a partial truth for the whole and the absolute truth is called 'durniti' or 'bad judgment', e.g., the insistence that an object is absolutely real (sadeva). A mere statement of a relative truth without calling it either absolute or relative is called 'naya' or 'judgment', e.g., the statement that an object is real (sat). A statement of a partial truth knowing that it is only partial, relative and conditional and has possibility of being differently interpreted from different points of view is called 'pramana' or 'valid judgment' (syat sat). Every naya in order to become pramana must be qualified by syat. Syat is said to be the symbol of truth. It is relative and successive knowledge. It removes all contradictions among different points of view. To reject 'syat' is to embrace unwarranted absolutism which is directly contradicted by experience.

Everything exists from the point of view of its own substance, space, time and form and it does not exist from the point of view of others' substance, space, time and form. When we say 'This table exists', we cannot mean that this table exists absolutely and unconditionally. Our knowledge of the table is necessarily relative. The table has got innumerable characteristics out of which we can know only some. The table exists in itself as an absolutely real and infinitely complex reality; only our knowledge of it is relative. For us the table must exist in its own matter as made of wood, in its own form as having a particular shape, length, breadth and height, at a particular space and at a particular time. It does not exist in other matter, other form and at other space and time. So a table is both existent and non-existent viewed from different standpoints and there is no contradiction in it.

The Jaina logic distinguishes seven forms of judgment. Each judgment, being relative, is preceded by the word 'syat'. This is Syadvada or Sapta-bhangi-naya. The seven steps are as follows:

(1) Syadasti: Relatively, a thing is real.
(2) Syannasti: Relatively, a thing is unreal.
(3) Syadasti nasti: Relatively, a thing is both real and unreal.
(4) Syadavaktavyam: Relatively, a thing is indescribable.

(5) Syadasti cha avaktavyam: Relatively, a thing is real and is indescribable.
(6) Syannasti cha avaktavyam: Relatively, a thing is unreal and is indescribable.
(7) Syadasti cha nasti cha avaktavyam: Relatively, a thing is real, unreal and indescribable.

From the point of view of one's own substance, everything is, while from the point of view of other's substance, everything is not. As we have just remarked that we can know a thing in relation to its own matter, form, space and time as a positive reality, while in relation to other's matter, form, space and time it becomes a negative entity. When we affirm the two different stand-points *successively* we get the third judgment—a thing is both real and unreal (of course in two different senses). If we affirm or deny both existence and non-existence *simultaneously* to anything, if we assert or negate the two different aspects of being and non being together, the thing baffles all description. It becomes indescribable, i.e., either both real and unreal simultaneously or neither real nor unreal. This is the fourth judgment. The remaining three are the combinations of the fourth with the first, second and third respectively.

—Chandradhar Sharma, *Indian Philosophy: A Critical Survey*

The Four Hundred Quatrains

Moral Verses

(118) The path of virtue, like milk, is one;
The sects that teach it are manifold.

(122) Those who snare and keep encaged the partridge or the quail,
Which dwell in the wilds where beetles hum around the flowers,
Shall (in a later life) till black and hungry soil,
Their legs in fetters, as slaves to alien lords.

(134) Learning is a treasure that needs no safeguard;
Nowhere can fire destroy it or proud kings take it. Learning's the best legacy a man can leave his children. Other things are not true wealth.

(137) In the city of the gods, in the after-life,
We shall learn if there is any greater joy
Than that when wise men, with minds as keen as steel,
Meet together in smiling fellowship.

(156) You may bite the sugarcane, break its joints,
Crush out its juice, and still it is sweet.
Well-born men, though others abuse or hurt them

Never lose their self-respect in words of anger.
(170) The greatness of the great is humility.
The gain of the gainer is self-control.
Only those rich men are truly wealthy
Who relieve the need of their neighbours.
(195) People speak of high birth and low
Mere words, with no real meaning!
Not property or ancient glory makes a man noble,
But self-denial, wisdom and energy.
(202) This is the duty of a true man—
To shelter all, as a tree from the fierce sun,
And to labour that many may enjoy what he earns,
As the fruit of a fertile tree.
(219) Better hatred than the friendship of fools.
Better death than chronic illness.
Better to be killed than soul-destroying contempt.
Better abuse than praise undeserved.
(238) If I do not stretch out my hand and risk my life
For a friend in need,
May I reap the reward of one who seduces the wife of a friend,
While the wide world mocks me in scorn.
(365) Best is a life passed in penance,
Middling, that spent with those one loves,
Worst, the life of one never satisfied,
Clinging to rich men who care nothing for him.

(386) As a scroll read by one who well understands it,
As wealth to the man of generous spirit,
As a sharp sword in the warrior's hand,
Is the beauty of a faithful wife.

—Translated by G.U. Pope

13

Six Systems of Indian Philosophy

The Shad (six) Darshanas (showing the path) or the six systems of the Astika, considered to be the orthodox schools of Indian philosophy, are based on the Vedas. They seek to understand the nature of reality, the self and the ultimate purpose of life. They are called Sanatana Dharma and are collectively referred to as Hinduism today.

Systems that do not accept the authority of the Vedas are by definition Nastika systems or the unorthodox schools of Indian philosophy. They include the Charvaka, Buddhist, Jain, Ajivika and Ajnana philosophies.

The five schools of philosophy that preceded Shankara's systemic exposition of Vedantic metaphysics were the Nyaya, Vaisheshika, Sankhya, Yoga, and Purva Mimamsha. All these were essentially guided by two fundamental tenets, investigation or *mimamsha*, and reflection or *vichara*—about the ultimate nature of the world, and the consequential purposes of life. They overlapped in their concepts and reasoning in some respects, but their differences were equally marked, and in this sense, provide definitive proof of the eclectic milieu of those times, and the independence and robustness of thought they nurtured.

The *Nyaya Sutra* dates back to the third century BCE and is attributed to the sage Gautama. This school's principal preoccupation is with logic and dialectics, analysis and reasoning. To this end, the Nyaya relied primarily on four sources of knowledge: perception (*pratyaksha*), inference (*anumana*), analogy (*upamana*) and verbal testimony (*shabda*). Such tools were essential, the *Nyaya Sutra* stressed, to establish whether that which is posited exists or not. In other words, the importance of Nyaya lies in the fact that it set out the analytical framework for enquiry, and refused to accept anything only on face value or assertion.

The Vaisheshika school of the sage Kanada (third century BCE) relied closely on the tools of reasoning expounded upon by Nyaya, but went beyond to formulate what must arguably be the first philosophical doctrine based on the recognition of the atom.

All material objects, it asserts, are ultimately the product of four basic atoms found in earth, water, fire or air. Amazingly, for its times, the doctrine concludes that all finite objects can be broken down into parts and finally reduced to that one infinitesimal, indestructible and indivisible atom. A combination of atoms produces different products, which could, in their final form, be different from their constituent parts. The doctrine admits that in the evolutionary process, from the atom to a finite whole, the end result could be based on a dominant characteristic or *vishesha*, but essentially the worldview of the Vaisheshika is pluralistic.

While foundationally realistic in its approach, the Vaisheshika recognises that not all substances are material. The non-material aspects of cosmology include space, time, ether (*akasha*), mind and soul. At this point, somewhat reluctantly, Kanada accepts the possibility of a God or Ishwara who combined the four kinds of atoms and five non-material substances into an ordered universe. The essential tone of the philosophy, however, remains atheistic, since even while conceding the presence of god, it limits his role to the ordering of the universe, and not to the creation of the elements that constitute it.

The Sankhya school was essayed by Kapila in the seventh century BCE, and is one of the oldest systematised structures of thought in Hindu philosophy. In essence, the Sankhya posits a cosmic duality to the universe, consisting of Prakriti and Purusha. Prakriti, unlike the pluralistic atomistic view of the Vaisheshika, is a pervasive singularity, eternal and independent, from which the universe evolves. But this evolution happens only when Prakriti comes under the influence of Purusha, which stands for awareness or the sentient principle.

Until the influence of Purusha, Prakriti, representing the 'potentiality of nature'[13] lies latent, its three constituents, sattva, rajas and tamas, in equilibrium. Sattva stands for that which is pure; rajas signifies energy and activity; and tamas connotes inertia and stolidity.

This equilibrium is disturbed when Purusha interfaces with Prakriti, and evolution commences with all its manifest diversities. The emergence of the five cognitive organs—taste, touch, sight, sound and smell—and the five motor organs of movement are part of this evolution, as is the emergence of intellect (*buddhi*) and the ego (*ahamkara*). According to the Sankhya, this evolution is cyclical, with creation (*shrishti*) followed by dissolution (*pralaya*), and pralaya again followed by shrishti. For a human being, liberation consists in understanding the distinction between the material Prakriti and the sentient Purusha.

This understanding comes by lifting the veil of ignorance through the pursuit of jnana.

For sheer conceptualisation, there is an awe-inspiring grandeur to the cosmic architecture profiled by the Sankhya. What is especially interesting is that in the self-evolving cosmic drama that it structures, there is no place for god. As we shall see later, there are many aspects of this school that influenced Shankara, including, in particular, the emphasis on knowledge as the way to salvation, although he remained resolutely opposed to the duality of the system.

The Yoga school broadly accepts the worldview of the Sankhya, but fleshes out the physical discipline and meditational regimen required by an individual to realise the separation (*kaivalya*) of Purusha, pure consciousness, from the non-sentient Prakriti. The *Yoga Sutra* is attributed to Patanjali and is dated to sometime before 400 CE. Several scholars believe it to be of much greater antiquity, and it is very likely that even if composed later, the sutra codifies a tradition and practice from several centuries earlier.

The *Yoga Sutra* begins with this aphorism: *Yogah chitta vrittih nirodha*: Yoga is restraining the mind from discursive thought. This restraint, it believes, can be brought about by discipline, both physical and mental. In the sutra, discipline is outlined as an eightfold path, starting from *yama* (self-restraint), *niyama* (virtuous observances), *asana* (posture), *pranayama* (consciously controlling breath), *pratyahara* (withdrawal of the senses), *dharana* (concentrating the mind), *dhyana* (meditation), and *samadhi* (a trance-like state in which there is complete union with the subject of meditation).

Yoga literally translates to 'union', and the purpose of the entire regimen of the eightfold path is to prepare the disciple for this union with Purusha. Unlike the Vedantic system, which believes that enlightenment, based on jnana, can come to anybody at any time through direct anubhav or communion, Yoga provides to Sankhya a carefully structured complementary system of mental and physical exercises that it believes is a necessary pre-condition to moksha. On one essential point, however, Yoga differs from Sankhya, and that is in its acceptance of a personal god, who directs the cyclical evolutionary process from creation to dissolution.

The practice of dharma, through ritual action sanctified by the Vedas, is the principal focus of the Purva Mimamsha. Jaimini (circa 400 BCE) was its chief theoretician. This doctrine believes in karma or action, and not jnana as the path to salvation. Its preoccupation is with the practice and interpretation of Vedic rites and rituals, which are to be performed out of a sense of duty, and in the manner prescribed by the orthodox texts associated with the Vedas such as the *Brahmanas*.

The school believes that performing the obligatory rituals, and abstaining from those that are proscribed, will lead by itself to the elimination of evil and the attainment, through the purification of the soul, of moksha.

In the seventh century CE, Kumarila Bhatta wrote an extensive commentary on the original treatise of Jaimini. Shankara, who believed that jnana not karma is the path to salvation, met with Kumarila Bhatta, and had a definitive shastrartha or argumentation on this issue with Mandana Mishra.

—Pavan K. Varma, *Adi Shankaracharya: Hinduism's Greatest Thinker*

14

Adi Shankaracharya and His Doctrine of Advaita

Adi Shankaracharya was a revered Indian philosopher and theologian who lived in the eighth century. He put forth the doctrine of Advaita Vedanta. He propagated the ancient Hindu belief that the soul (Atman) was an inherent part of the Supreme Soul (Nirguna Brahman). Though he is best known for popularising Advaita Vedanta, his most important work was the unification of the six sub-sects, known as Shanmata. Shanmata literally means 'six religions' and is the worship of six supreme deities. Shankaracharya said that there was one Supreme Being (Brahman) and that the six supreme deities were a part of that one Brahman. He condemned the Mimamsa school of Hinduism which was based on ritual practices.

Shankaracharya's preachings and advocacy of Hinduism slowed down the spread of Buddhism across India and led to the revival of Hinduism.

Shankara's genius lay in building a complete and original philosophical edifice upon the foundational wisdom of the Upanishads. This philosophy validated what the Upanishads alluded to, but going far beyond, provided an entire system of intellectual enquiry and analysis. In this pursuit, he was the quintessential *paramarthachintakah*, one who wished to search for the ultimate truths behind the mysteries of the universe, and not just a *srishtichintakah*, one whose concerns are restricted to explicating the empirical world.

Thus, Shankara's was not an act of reiteration only. His originality lay less in his unflinching belief in the truths of the Upanishads, and more in the system of thought he devised to support his belief. 'With great ingenuity, remorseless logic, obvious sincerity, profound conviction and deep learning ... Shankara unfolded the teachings of (the Upanishads) and the *Vedanta Sutras* as he understood them.' In doing so, he developed 'independently a really remarkable "system" of idealistic philosophy and an unflinching monistic metaphysics, both of which are characteristically Shankara's own.'[14]

The most audacious part—and the lynchpin—of his philosophy was the conceptualisation of Brahman as the all-pervasive and only absolute force permeating the universe. For Shankara, Brahman is *urja* or infinite energy, pure consciousness, and unsullied awareness. It is intelligence personified—as can be inferred by the verifiable order in the universe, both at the micro and macro level. In fact, Shankara says that intelligence is Brahman's exclusive nature as saltiness is the unmistakable characteristic of a lump of salt.

The embodiment of perfect knowledge, Brahman is beyond knowledge, the knower or the known. It has no beginning, for it is eternal; it has no cause, for it is beyond the categories of time, space and causality; it has no end, for it always was and will always be. Its powers are unlimited; it is omnipotent and omniscient, a singular, indivisible fullness —*purna*—and universal force—*ekam eka sarvavyapi.*

A key aspect of Brahman is that it's completely transcendent. Does an intelligent force have to have a purpose? And, if so, does that purpose have to conform to conventional human comprehension? Can its purpose be judged by a goal that we believe is right, even if we accept that there is a notion of right in an absolute sense that has universal acceptance in our everyday, human life?

Everything in the cosmos is an emanation of Brahman, but it is beyond all activity and purpose as per our finite ways of thinking. Unchanging, it has no need to evolve or develop, grow or diminish. In its passivity, it's potentiality itself; in its aloofness, it's omnipotent; in its apparent purposelessness, it's infinite intelligence; and, in its indefinability, it's definitiveness itself. It is. Nothing without it is. And yet, in its undifferentiated fullness, its path is supremely overarching, beyond all compulsions of choice or will. Like the sun, it continues to shine even if there is no object to be illumined. Its uniformity (*ekarasa*) has no parts; its identity is divisionless (*akhanda*). In this sense, it is self-luminous, without the need of predication, conditionality or qualification. In Shankara's words, Brahman is 'eternally pure, intelligent and free, never changing, one only, not in contact with anything, and devoid of form.'[15]

Shankara endorses the Upanishadic injunction that Brahman is inexpressible. Any attempt to define it would circumscribe its infinitude. Neti, neti—not this, not this, is the best way to approach it, because, in this very negation is the assertion of its unlimited positivity. Shankara explains that it is 'not a thing in the empirical sense which we may indicate by words; nor is it an object like a cow which can be known by the ordinary means of knowledge. It cannot even be described by its generic properties or specific marks; we cannot say that it acts in this or that manner, since it is always known to be actionless. It cannot, therefore, be positively described.'[16]

But while Brahman is nirguna or attribute-less, it is not a void, or an indeterminate diffusion. This is where Shankara veers away definitively from the *shunyavada* of Buddhism which concludes that the ultimate truth is a void. Neti, neti, or not this, not this, implies not that Brahman is to be perceived negatively, but indicates a reluctance to dilute the infinity of

Brahman through definitions conceived by the human mind. In fact, Shankara is quite sharply critical of those who would want to interpret Brahman in negative terms. In his bhashya on the *Vedanta Sutras,* he says: 'Brahman, transcending space, attributes, motion, fruition and difference, which is Being in the highest sense, without a second, appears to the slow of mind no more than non-being.'

He reiterates this in his commentary on the *Mandukya Upanishad*: 'No, Brahman is not a void, never a non-entity. Brahman always underlies the changes and sustains them. All manifestations come out from that underlying sustaining ground. The ground that gives support to these changes and constantly sustains them cannot prove to be a mere void or non-entity. If the sustaining ground is held to be a non-entity—nothing—then, can mere 'nothing' give birth to the positive things of the world?'[17]

Quite to the contrary, therefore, Shankara's Brahman is positivity itself, pure being, characterised by existence (*sat*), consciousness (*chitta*) and bliss (*ananda*): *satchittananda*. To some this may appear contradictory. If, on the one hand, you say that Brahman is inexpressible and indefinable, how can you then ascribe to it such expressly defined features? Shankara gives a twofold answer. Firstly, these features are *inferred* from what Brahman is not. It is not non-existent, so it is sat, existence par excellence, unchanging through all the *kalas* (periods of time); it is not devoid of consciousness, so it is chitta, pure consciousness, the nature of absolute knowledge; and it is not of the nature of distress, so it is ananda, bliss supreme, the nature of absolute happiness. Secondly, the being of Brahman is experiential, not intellectual. The cognitive process, where the mind intervenes, can teach us intellectually about Brahman, but cannot provide the sublime experiential moment, where thought ceases and intuition takes over. We shall discuss this process in greater detail later, but suffice it to say at this stage that for Shankara, Brahman was absolute plenitude, a fullness that, once experienced, leaves an individual in no doubt about the certainty of its being.

Having posited the absolute immanence of Brahman as the only real in the universe, Shankara asserted that Brahman and Atman are the same. Human beings, who have the faculty of reflection and will, are more than the sum of their body and mind. There is in each of us an observer—*sakshin*—who stands apart from the incessant but transient preoccupations of the mind. This witnessing consciousness is above the sensory perceptions that govern our body. It may become dormant, or even ignored, in the perennial agitations of everyday life, but it exists in each of us as a focus of awareness (chitta shakti), only waiting to be discovered.

Matter and consciousness, says Shankara, are two separate realities. The first is the object, the second the subject. A subject and an object can never be the same. This subject in all of us is the Atman. The mind is in flux, our senses are volatile, and our body mutates, but the Atman is the changeless, all-knowing consciousness—*sarvapratyayadarshin*.

While the entire universe is an emanation of Brahman, Atman and Brahman are identical. Both are the substance of pure consciousness. One exists at the individual level, the other at the cosmic, but they are of each other, two sides of the same coin. When we peel away the empirically manifest—mind, body and senses—what is left is *nirvisheshachinmatram*—undifferentiated consciousness that is the characteristic of both Brahman and Atman. The objective and the subjective then become the same. *Atma cha brahm*—Atman is Brahman—says the Upanishads. We, at the level of consciousness are that, in conformity with the Upanishadic injunction—*Tat tvam asi*—That thou art. The same thought is mirrored in another mahavakya or 'great sentence' of the Upanishads: *Aham brahm asmi*—I am Brahman.

But, if there is one unchanging, eternal and all-pervasive consciousness and nothing else, both at the cosmic level and hidden away in our individual selves, what is this visible, pulsating plurality of the universe? If the real admits of no other to it, and permeates everything that exists, why do we have a derogation of that consciousness in our lives, and in the myriad aspects of the universe around us? Why do infinitude and finitude co-exist? Does the former dilute itself in creating the latter, or does the latter irrevocably change the former? If Brahman is indivisible, and beyond all mutation, how do we account for so many manifestations of that indivisibility? If the cause is beyond activity and completely self-sufficient, needing nothing beyond it, how do we see it giving rise to so many effects? If Brahman is all that exists, admitting of no duality, how do we explain the multiplicity of the universe? Is Brahman then but a notion, merely an intellectual construct, and the world the reality we cannot escape? Or, is the world an illusion, a cosmic sleight-of-hand, and Brahman and Atman the only reality?

Shankara's answer to this conundrum is to audaciously assert that this phenomenal world is real at one level, but Brahman is the only reality at the ontological level. In the midst of this bewildering plurality, Brahman continues to remain unchanging and eternal, immanent in everything, a witness to the empirical multiplicity but completely untouched or modified by it. Brahman, as the cause of all that is, ever was and ever will be, is present in the effect. But, in the dialectic between cause and effect, the latter is completely subsumed by the former, while the cause remains unaffected by the effect. The one remains the one, while the many proliferate as its reflection, as it were, without changing the essential nature of that one.

He explicates this by his theory of causation. The essential feature (*svabhava*) of the universal cause remains unchanged; the effect is only a transient condition (*avastha* or *vishesha*). Between cause and effect, there are two possible kinds of transactions. The first is called *parinamvada,* where the cause changes in order to produce the effect. The second is called *vivartavada,* where the effect is produced while the cause itself remains untransformed. Shankara explains the phenomenal world as vivartavada. The effect is neither latent in the cause, nor is its manifestation inevitable, and nor is it distinct from the cause. If inherently latent, it would have a substantive autonomy independent from the cause. If manifestation is inevitable, then it would in no way be dependent on the cause. And, if distinct, then it would create a duality that was completely unacceptable to the monism of Shankara.

For Shankara, Brahman is the cosmic cause from which the transient pluralities of name and form (*nama-rupa*) emerge, and into which they lapse. The names and forms can be endless, but the cause is one and unchanging. When a cause creates an effect without effort or volition, and without transforming itself, the causal process is called *nimitta karana.* The relationship between cause and effect has certain features, argues Shankara. Firstly, it is non-reciprocal: the substratum of the phenomenal world is Brahman, while Brahman itself is transcendent of the phenomenal world. Secondly, it is non-dependent: the empirical world visible to our sensory perceptions is dependent on Brahman, while Brahman is independent of them. Thirdly, cause and effect are non-different (*ananya*) and non-separate (*avyatirikta*).

Shankara's essential point is that the distinction between cause and effect is erroneous. Nothing can originate on its own; and so, if the effect has to have a cause, that can only be the cosmic ground or essence represented by Brahman. 'Cause alone is real and change is only phenomenal. The cause only appears to change into effect; what actually changes is the name and form. The clay and the pot have clay for their essence; but there is a change of name and form when the pot is made. Similarly, the space enclosed in the pot may appear to be an effect of infinite space, but it is manifestly one with the cause.'[18] A cloth and the threads woven to make it may appear to be different, but on deeper scrutiny, the cloth is only a different form of the threads. Devdatta (the equivalent of John Smith) remains Devdatta, says Shankara, even if his form changes when he sits or stands. 'A child in the womb is not reckoned as distinct in essence from the child that is born. We should not be misled by the manifestation of that which is latent. We cannot see the pattern of a cloth until it is unrolled. The plant is concealed within the seed....'[19]

The primal cause of all the diversity we see is, thus, Brahman. The phenomenal world is an emanation of it, and together the eternally whole and the infinitely divisible constitute a benevolent identity-indifference, *tadatmaya*. The difference of the effect from the cause is apparent, but the end, the product is not entirely illusory like a barren woman's son, or a square circle. The effects, consisting of the vast animate and inanimate forms inhabiting the universe, exist, but only relatively so. Shankara recognises three forms of reality: the extra-empirical (*paramarthik*); the empirical (*vyavaharik*); and the illusory (*pratibhasika*). From the viewpoint of higher knowledge, para vidya, the empirical has no authenticity or ultimate reality. However, from the plane of a lower level of knowledge (*apara vidya*), the empirical cannot be denied. Shankara, therefore, did not dismiss the ordinary world of name and form as entirely illusory, as some of his critics misinterpreted his philosophy to mean. He merely made the fundamental difference between the real and the unreal from an ontological point of view.

Brahman, as the unchanging, indivisible pure consciousness and energy pervading the cosmos, is eternal and, therefore, the only real; the world of our ordinary cognition, divided into false binaries of subject and object, is transient, and therefore, even if existent, cannot be real. It is subject to change, decline and decay. It exists but only ephemerally. It originates, subsists, and disintegrates. In a universe that has existed, as modern science now indicates, for close to fourteen billion years, entire galaxies have been born and died. Against the canvas of eternal time, their existence is as fragile as bubbles on water or a spark alight but briefly in the dark. Anything as transient cannot be real in an absolute sense. Beneath the near unlimited array of names and form, there has to be another reality, which is subject to neither origination nor eclipse. Nothing that is by definition volatile, or so vulnerable to mutation, or so inherently impermanent, can be the absolute. What is in incorrigible flux, coming into existence only to be extinguished, cannot be eternal. A foundation that is itself perennially unstable cannot uphold the ordered super structure of the universe. Shankara's purpose, thus, is not so much to deny the relative reality of the world in empirical terms as to assert its lack of substance in absolute terms. In his commentary on the *Taittiriya Upanishad*, Shankara succinctly sums it up: 'What is eternal cannot have a beginning and whatever has a beginning is not eternal.'

If the difference between the finite and the infinite is so stark, so unmistakable and crystal clear, why do we mistake one for the other? Shankara's answer is that it is due to *avidya* or nescience. Avidya creates an error of perception that blurs the distinction between the real and the unreal, the eternal and the transient. And to do so, it has, in each of us as human beings, the most responsive ground. To understand why, it is essential to follow Shankara's clinical analysis of what constitutes the individual human being, jiva, and how, by the very nature of our own limitations, *upadhis*, we become so readily the victims of the powers of avidya.

The finite world consists of five basic elements or mahabhutas: akasha or space, air, fire, water and earth. Akasha arises first, and from it, in ascending order, come air, fire, water and earth. Each of these elements has a primary quality associated with it. From akasha arises sound, from air, heat, from water, taste, and from earth, smell. All matter is a combination in varying form of these five elements and the qualities associated with them. Inert or inorganic matter is non-intelligent (*achetana*), serving a secondary purpose (*parartha*). Human beings are different. They have the power to think, reflect, reason and analyse. As compared to gross matter that is non-intelligent and lacks cognitive capacities, or other species that are guided primarily by instinct or biology, human beings have the power of discrimination and understanding, and the capacity to make choices. It is for this reason that the jiva or individual human being is the focus of Shankara's special observation.

In conformity with the findings of many other schools of Indic thought, the jiva is a complex compound. It too is constituted of the five basic elements that account for all animate and inanimate matter. In addition, it has five organs of perception, five of motion, five of breath and, most importantly, mind and intellect. Sight, sound, touch, taste and smell constitute its perceptional apparatus. Their corresponding organs are the eyes, ears, skin, tongue and nose. The five organs of motion are those that create speech, plus the hands, the legs, the anus and the genitals. Prana or the act of breathing is a vital function, and consists of five sub-classifications (*prana, apana, udana, samana* and *vyana*).

But the fundamental distinguishing human feature is mind and intellect, collectively called the *manas*, which interprets and structures what is received through the senses. The manas is located in an internal organ called the *antahkarana*, which has four identifiable segments. When merely an indeterminate cognitive faculty, it is called mind or manas; when that cognitive ability leads to understanding, it is called buddhi or intellect; when, as a consequence of such understanding, it creates self-consciousness, it is ego or ahamkara; and when, beyond the ego, it is in a state of higher concentration or awareness, it is chitta.

Each of the elements that constitute the jiva endow it with powers, many of which are unique; but, equally, they act as limitations to its ability to recognise the fundamental principle underlying the plurality of the universe. For instance, our sensory faculties, *indriyas*, are highly advanced, but they cognise objects only as per the categories of perception ordinarily comprehensible to the brain. We see objects when actually modern science reveals that shape and form are delusions of our mind, since all objects in their essence are nothing but a combination of empty space and waves of energy. The confusion with regard to the difference between the transcendental and the empirical is due, in part, to the limitations of our cognitive apparatus. As Dr S. Radhakrishnan says: 'As we perceive by our senses sound and colour, while the reality is mere vibrations, even so we see the variegated universe for the reality of Brahman.'[20]

However, the greatest barrier to our knowing our true self is the mind and the ego. Shankara treats the mind as *sukshma* or subtle matter. Observation shows that it is highly agile, perpetually unstable, constantly transient and congenitally volatile. Like a monkey forever jumping from one branch of a tree to another, it is never still. Like litmus paper, it takes on the colour of a ceaseless series of thoughts and impressions (*vrittis*). Its mode is reactive, completely in the grip of the external, whether objects or happenings. Rarely reflective and always mobile, it is forever a prisoner of memories, wants, and emotions, so prone to modification that thoughts often take birth and die in the same moment. It either lives in the past, or in an imagined future, but almost never at rest in the present. In short, the mind, and under its perennial shadow, the intellect, are powerful cognitive tools but, by their very nature, impulsive, fickle, capricious and unsteady, and thus, easy prey for the powers of avidya.

The ego is the second great obstacle. What is it that makes the ego so completely the central focus of our lives, making us almost oblivious to any other concern? The ego creates in each jiva a false sense of 'I-ness' that forms a near impenetrable barrier to the understanding of the unitary supremacy of Brahman–Atman. The cosmos, as science is revealing now, is in essence an undivided whole. Every part in it is inter-connected and inter-dependent within the unitary, pervasive energy of Brahman. And yet, the ego gives to each of us a sense of separateness. The universe then shrinks to a delusionary subjectivity, whose principal consequence is to foster the absurd notion that we, at our individual levels, are the prime movers of the world (*karta*), when actually we are only the agents of existence (*bhokta*). Existence then splits up into the artificial binary of a permanent subject and object. The limitless objective is reduced to the limited subject. With this I-ness comes the baggage of an entire range of emotions: want, desires, pride, ambition, joy, grief, envy, anger, pain, joy and hate. These emotions when added to our belief in a separate 'I' then become the limits of our make-believe world.

The manner in which we acquire this I-ness is worth observation. A newborn child has no sense of ego. But soon enough, he acquires a name or identity, a context of family and address, and the original innocence is lost. We become prisoners of our own simulated construct. This stubborn insularity obliterates all sense of reason or objectivity. Everything is seen from the prism of our notion of self. We forget that an inherent fragility beyond our capacities underlies our puny lives at the finite level. After all, a person, who is completely defined by his ego, can die tomorrow, given the fragility and uncertainty that governs our finite lives. Like a frog in the mouth of a serpent trying to catch an insect, we act as though we shall always be. The ego creates the illusion

of self-centred permanence that, in reality, is inherently ephemeral. Moreover, when juxtaposed to the infinite canvas of time and space, how can an individual believe that he or she is the karta, or the prime mover, when his own existence is more fleeting than the blinking of an eyelid?

The limitations of our sensory perceptions, the instability of our mind, and the false sense of ego that becomes a permanent adjunct to our lives, cumulatively create a jiva that revels in its own finitude oblivious to its real nature. The power of avidya becomes entrenched in direct proportion to the vulnerabilities of the jiva. It is for this reason that Shankara calls avidya natural (*naisargika*), eternal (*anant*) and beginning-less (*anadi*). Avidya is able to effortlessly make us devalue the real, while giving the unreal primacy. This error of perception (*dosha*), in which value is mistakenly attributed to something that is devoid of it, is called *adhyasha*, and it operates in a two-fold manner. Firstly, avidya has the ability to mask the truth of things (*avarana*), and secondly to misrepresent them (*vikshepa*). In this way, a veil of distortion hides the true nature of reality (*vastusvarupam*).

Avarana hides the pervasive reality of Brahman; vikshepa misrepresents it by making us believe that only the passing phenomenon of the world is real. As a result, the silent sakshin or observer within each of us becomes dormant, and the presence of the Atman is marginalised. It is important to remember that the finite jiva and the infinite Atman are not two separate entities. Atman–Brahman permeates all, but through the operation of avidya, the jiva becomes a reflection of the Atman in the shackles of finitude. Like the sword in a scabbard, the pure consciousness of the Atman is, to use Shankara's analogy, sheathed in ignorance. The self-limiting adjuncts or upadhis of our psychic apparatus hide the absolute from our reflective consciousness (*upadhi parichinna*). We are overwhelmed by the transient effects, and lose sight of the unchanging cause. We mistake chaitanya or pure consciousness for the transient plurality of the world. While Brahman is the original and permanent point (*bimba*), and the world only its reflection (*pratibimba*), we begin to see the reflection as the reality that defines our lives. As Shankara writes: 'The whole empirical reality, with its names and forms, which can be defined neither as being nor as non-being, rests upon avidya; while in the sense of highest reality, Being persists, without change or transformation.'[21]

Shankara's assertion that the world appearance (*jagat prapancha*) is neither being nor non-being makes a significant point. From the standpoint of Brahman, it is not, and can never be (*asat*); but from the distortion created by avidya, it is, and must always appear to be (*sat*). How do we explain this conundrum where both sat and asat have different validities? Shankara gives several analogies to do so. The most famous of these is that of the rope and the snake: the rope is the reality, but we mistake it to be a snake. Similarly, a piece of shell is mistaken to be silver; a crystal appears to be red in colour due to a red flower near it; a straight stick appears to be bent in water; a mirage in the desert appears to be real; and the sky, although colourless, appears to be blue. All of these are due to an error of perception creating false knowledge (*mithyasvarupah*).

The significant point, though, is that while the error lasts, the snake does exist in the mind of the perceiver, as does the silver, the red crystal, the bent stick, the mirage, and the blue sky. The distortion is manifest, but the perception until corrected is not non-existent. It is precisely in this way that the empirical world of our daily experience exists, and is assumed to be the only reality, but the moment it is tested against the higher reality represented by Brahman, the error in perception ends. Thus Shankara's intention is not to assert that avidya creates an entirely non-existent world. Such a world does exist, but only for so long as we do not remove the veil of avidya. His purpose is not so much to negate the world of sense–experience as to reinterpret it. 'What is actual has certainly no independent existence, yet it has existence: it is unreal only if we mistakenly attribute independence to it. The world is unreal but not illusory.'[22]

Given the omnipotence of Brahman, it must require a force of considerable power to mask its manifest reality. Avidya, at the individual level, is maya at the cosmic level, and both together, do, indeed, possess this kind of power.

Since Brahman is the only reality, and has no second, maya and avidya cannot but be a part of it. In fact, Shankara regards maya—that mysterious but cosmic veil of illusion—as the *bija* shakti—the seed power—of Brahman. It is Brahman that empowers this creative power, much like a spider weaves a web from its own body. The ground for the distortion created by maya remains Brahman. 'Even when a snake, a peice of silver, a mirage appears to arise, all these appearances are invariably found to be supported, in each case, by a sustaining ground on which they appear, viz., a rope, a shell, and the surface of a desert, unsupported by which these appearances cannot for a moment stand.'[23]

If Brahman and Atman, and maya and avidya, are essentially the same, and represent no duality, how do we explain the need for the empirical world, where the real and the unreal are seemingly coterminous? Shankara's candid answer is that it is inexplicable and indefinable: *anirvachaniya*. Ignorance exists. So does perfect knowledge. The eternal exists. But so does the transient. The one is never changing. Yet, it countenances ceaseless flux. That which is beyond all time and cause and beyond purpose co-exists with causal time and finitude. What then is the mysterious relationship between Brahman and maya, the progenitor of avidya?

—Pavan K. Varma, *Adi Shankaracharya: Hinduism's Greatest Thinker*

Brahma Sutra of Badarayana

Attributed to Rishi Badarayana, the Brahma Sutras (circa 200 BCE), the foundational texts of the Vedanta school of Hindu philosophy, are also known as the Vedanta Sutras, Sariraka Sutras and Uttara Mimamsa. Along with the Upanishads and the Bhagavad Gita, they form the core of Sanatana Dharma.

Badarayana uses the sutras to explore the nature of Brahman, the ultimate reality, and the relationship between Brahman and Atman (soul). He explains that Brahman is the only reality and that the individual soul is ultimately identical to Brahman. This realisation, known as moksha or liberation, is the ultimate goal of all human beings.

Four Sutras on the Enquiry into Brahman and Its Pre-requisites

athato brahmajijnasa || *1* ||

Now (after the attainment of the requisite spiritual qualities) therefore (as the results obtained by sacrifices etc., are ephemeral, whereas the result of the knowledge of Brahman is eternal), the inquiry (into the real nature) of Brahman (which is beset with doubts owing to the conflicting views of various schools of philosophical thought, should be taken up).

janmadyasya yatah || *2* ||

(Brahman is that omniscient, omnipotent cause) from which proceed the origin etc. (i.e. sustenance and dissolution) of this (world).

shastrayonitvat || 3 ||

The scriptures (alone) being the means of right knowledge (with regard to Brahman, the proposition laid in sutra 2 becomes corroborated).

tattu samanvayat ||4||

But that (Brahman is to be known only from the scriptures and not independently by any other means is established) because It is the main purport (of all Vedanta texts).

—Translated by Swami Vireswarananda

16

Thirukkural of Thiruvalluvar

Thirukkural (circa 300 BCE–500 CE) or the sacred Kural of Thiruvalluvar is an ancient book on practical philosophy. It is not a religious treatise but an ethical work dealing with the duties, conduct and character of various members of society like a householder, a hermit and various state officers. The couplets in the book are models of terseness and vividness, each one expressing in the briefest and most concise form the truth it seeks to convey. The sayings and thoughts in the Thirukkural offer profound insights on life, virtue and ethics.

16. Tolerance

151 Chief of virtues is to bear with revilers
Just as the earth bears its diggers.

152 To bear with others' evil is a good trait
Better it is to forget it.

153 To disregard hosting of guests is want of want
To endure fools is might of might.

154 Practise and preserve patience
To retain one's perfectness.

155 Who punish the offenders are despised
Who forbear are esteemed like gold.

156 Avenger's joy lasts only for one day
Forgiver's fame stays till Doomsday.

157 Though others do intolerable harm, pity them
And better it is to do no evil to them.

158 Conquer men who do evils by arrogance
Simply by your tolerance.

159 Who forbear evil words of the unrighteous
Are far purer than the ascetics.

160 Better are they who endure bitter insults
Than those who fast and do penance.

17. Not Envying

161 Value the unenvying nature of the heart
As the code of good conduct.

162 Of all the goodness nothing can equal
Being free from envy of one and all.

163 Who loves not virtue and wealth
Alone envies others' wealth.

164 Who know that envy causes misery
Will do no wrong out of envy.

165 To the envious, their envy itself is enough
Tho' enemies fail, it will bring grief.

166 Kin of those who envy charity to others
Perish without food and clothes.

167 Fortune herself will desert the envious
And direct her sister to the envious.

168 Envy, the matchless sinner, ruins wealth
And leads one to eternal evil path.

169 Wealth of the jealous and want of the just
Make enough food for thought.

170 No one has prospered through jealousy
Nor the unenvious have lost prosperity.

18. Not Coveting Others' Wealth

171 Coveting honest wealth by unfair means
Ruins family and begets crimes.

172 Who shrink from shame of injustice
Do no sinful deed of avarice.
173 Who seek eternal happiness
For petty joys, do no evil acts.
174 The spotless wise who've conquered five senses
Even in penury, won't covet others' riches.
175 Of what use is knowledge sharp and wide
If foolish deeds are done out of greed?
176 Who follows the path of virtue and grace
Perishes if he plots evils out of avarice.
177 Covet not wealth gained through greed
For its fruits rarely do good.
178 The way to keep one's wealth undwindled
Is not to covet wealth in another's hand.
179 Knowing their worth, Fortune stays with the wise
Who value virtue and covet not riches.
180 Thoughtless coveting leads to destruction
Greedless pride brings distinction.

19. Not Backbiting

181 Though one ignores virtue and does evils
It is good not to backbite others.
182 Worse is to smile before and slander behind
Than to decry virtue and do deeds not good.
183 Death is better than a life of backbiting
As death brings virtue's blessing.

184 You may utter heartless words to one's face
But backbite not ignoring after-effects.

185 Who extols virtue openly but not in the heart
Is by mean backbiting exposed.

186 One's worst faults will be sieved and revealed
If one gets others' faults exposed.

187 Who cannot foster friends thro' pleasing words
Lose friendship thro' slandering ones.

188 If they trumpet faults of even close friends
What will they not do to strangers?

189 Out of virtue the earth bears those
Who backbite with mean words.

190 If everyone sees his faults as he sees others'
Will any evil ever fall on living beings?

20. Not Speaking Vain Words

191 Who utters vain words displeasing all
Is despised by one and all.

192 Vain words spoken in public are worse
Than wrongs done to mates.

193 Long and vain speech trumpets
One's utter worthlessness.

194 One's vain and crude words before an assembly
Remove one's gains and goodness simply.

195 Whenever the good speak useless words
All esteem and eminence they lose.

196 Who speaks vain words call him not a man
Rather call him a chaff among men.

197 It's good for the perfect to utter not vain words
Even if they speak unjust words.

198 The wise who discern merit won't utter
Words that lack gains greater.

199 Men of clear wisdom and spotless vision
Even forgetfully utter not words in vain.

200 Always utter fruitful words
Never utter futile words.

21. Fear of Doing Evil

201 The wicked never fear the pride of evil
The good ever fear that evil.

202 Evil is feared more than fire
As evil begets evil ever.

203 Crown of wisdom is to shun evil
Even to foes who do evil.

204 Never plot evil against others even forgetfully
Or else virtue will ruin you surely
who plots others' ruin.

205 Plead not poverty for doing evil
For you'll become poorer still.

206 Who desire to avoid evil for themselves
Should eschew doing evil to others.

207 One may escape from deadly enmity but still
Enmity of the evil will chase and kill.

208 Destruction follows one who commits evil acts
Like the shadow following one's footsteps.

209 If you love yourself above all
Do no evil however small.

210 Who slips not from right path to do evils
Is guarded from all ills.

22. Duty to Society

211 Duty expects not anything in return
Just as rain expects none.

212 All riches that tireless efforts fetch
Are to help those deserving much.

213 Even in heaven and earth it's rare to find
A better deed than serving mankind.

214 He alone is alive who is in tune with the world
All others are deemed dead.

215 The wealth of the truly wise is like
The brimming village tank.

216 Abundant wealth of a benevolent person
Is like a fruit-laden tree in mid-town.

217 Wealth of a generous man is like a herbal tree
That becomes an unfailing remedy.

218 The dutiful even with dwindled affluence
Won't slacken in benevolence.

219 One who is generous feels very poor
When unable to do any favour.

220 The ruin that comes out of doing charity
Is worth buying by getting into slavery.

23. Charity

221 Giving to the poor alone is real charity
All else aim at recompense only.

222 Receiving is bad even tho' for the cause of good
Giving is good though heaven is denied.

223 Giving before one pleads penury
Marks the man of nobility.

224 Begging indeed is the most painful sight
Till one sees the beggar's face bright.

225 Great is the power of those who endure hunger
Greater is appeasing others' hunger.

226 Relieving the killing hunger of the needy
Is the safest treasury of the wealthy.

227 Fiery disease of hunger seldom touches
Those who share their meals.

228 The cruel who hoard and lose know not happiness
Of gladly helping the have-nots.

229 Eating all alone merely for hoarding
Is more painful than begging.

230 Nothing else is indeed so miserable as dying
But sweet it is when incapable of giving.

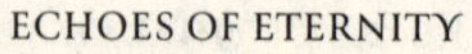

24. Fame

231 The only benefit in life is glory
That comes of charity.

232 Whatever spoken in the world in praise
Is the glory of alms-givers.

233 Nothing in the world remains undying
Except fame unique and towering.

234 Heaven will never acclaim even the gods
But men on earth with lasting laurels.

235 Fame in fall and life in doom
Are only to men of wisdom.

236 Enter a field and build up repute
If not, it's better to enter not.

237 Why do the fameless blame the despisers
Rather than blaming themselves?

238 To live without leaving a legacy of fame
Is to earn the whole world's blame.

239 The land that bears inglorious bodies
Will diminish in blameless yields.

240 Those who are blameless alone really live
The fameless are not considered alive.

25. Compassion

241 Wealth of wealth is the wealth of kindness
Worldly wealth even the mean possess.

242 By fair means seek and secure grace
All codes proclaim it as assistance.
243 Men of graceful heart would seldom pass
Into the world of darkness and distress.
244 Men of mercy who guard all beings
Are free from fear of evils.
245 Sorrows are not for those with merciful heart
This wind-blown world bears witness to it.
246 Who neglect virtue and life's purpose
Are graceless in their acts.
247 This world is not for the penniless
Nor is heaven for the graceless.
248 The poor may perhaps flourish some day
But the cruel prosper not any day.
249 Who performs charity without sympathy
Is like an unwise man seeking reality.
250 Imagine yourself facing the stronger
While oppressing the weaker.

—Translated by M. Rajaram

17

DHARMASHASTRAS

The Dharmashastras (circa 200 BCE-100 CE) are based on ancient Dharmasutra texts which, in turn, are based on the Vedas. The word 'Dharmashastra' never appears in the Vedic texts. There were several Dharmashastras, but only four have survived—Manusmriti, Yajnavalkyasmriti, Naradasmriti and Vishnusmriti. Manusmriti became famous during the colonial British era, though other Dharmashastras such as Yajnavalkyasmriti probably played a greater role in earlier times.

The various Dharmashastras contain very different ideas and customs, often conflicting with one another. Manusmriti prescribes the duties of each member of the four varna divisions (social classes) during the four ashrams. It was used to construct the Hindu law code by the British for India and other colonies in the region.

Dharma According to Manusmriti

Learn that Dharma, which has been ever followed by, and sanctioned by the heart of, the learned and the good, who are free from love and hate.

It is not right to be absorbed in desires—but there is in this world, no absolute absence of desire; for the study of the Vedas itself is prompted by desire, as also every act prescribed in the Veda.

Desire has its root in thought; sacrifices proceed from thought; vows and restraints—all these have been described as originating in thought.

No action is ever found in this world to be done by a man entirely without desires; whatever a man does is the outcome of desire.

Behaving in the right manner, in regard to these (desires), a man attains the position of immortals; and even in this world he obtains all the desires that he may have thought of.

The entire Veda is the root-source of dharma; also the conscientious recollection of righteous persons versed in the Veda, the practice of good (and learned) men, and their self-satisfaction.

Whatever dharma for whatever person has been described by Manu, all this is declared in the Veda; since the Veda embodies all knowledge.

Having fully perceived all this with the eye of knowledge, the learned man should enter upon his own Duties, resting upon the authority of the revealed Word.

For the man performing the duty laid down by the revealed word and the recollections obtains fame here, and after death, unsurpassed happiness.

The Veda should be known as the 'revealed word', and the Dharmashastra as the 'recollections'; in all matters, these two do not deserve to be criticised, as is out of these that Dharma shone forth.

If a twice-born person, relying upon the science of dialectics, should disregard these two sources, he should be cast out by good men—the detractor of the Veda being an infidel.

The Veda, the Smriti, the practice of cultured men, and what is agreeable to oneself—these directly constitute the fourfold means of knowing Dharma.

The knowledge of Dharma is ordained for those who are not addicted to the pursuit of wealth and pleasures; and for those seeking for the knowledge of Dharma, the revealed word is the highest authority.

Where there is conflict between two Vedic texts, both are held to be Dharma; both have been rightly pronounced by the wise to be Dharma.

—Translated by Ganganath Jha

18

Natyashastra of Bharat Muni

Bharata Muni's Natyashastra is a Sanskrit classic that was most likely composed between 200 BCE and 200 CE. It discusses the creation, techniques and significance of music, dance and theatre. Traditional artists and art forms still follow the rules prescribed in it.

Rasa Theory and Acharya Abhinavagupta

The spiritual quest of Hindu civilisation, and the deep thought that went into its structuring, could not but spill over into other areas of human endeavour. Art and culture was one such area. It is not my intention here to provide an account of the range of its creative canvas, be it in dance, music, theatre, literature, sculpture or architecture. There are countless books that deal with each of these subjects. The aim here is to focus on the approach to aesthetics, the cerebral rumination on what constitutes beauty and qualifies to be art. This is the unique aspect that deserves careful study in order to understand the distinguishing feature of the foundational period of our civilisation. In accordance with the contemplative philosophy that preceded the creation of artefacts, creativity was not a pursuit of excellence alone, but the definition of excellence itself was a consequence of a seminal reflection on what excellence should be.

Around 200 BCE, and possibly earlier, there lived an individual called Bharat Muni. As the word 'muni' connotes, he was a sage. Bharat wrote the *Natya Shastra*, consisting of thirty-six chapters and six thousand shlokas. At one level, the *Natya Shastra* was a compendium for the performing arts with a detailed manual of instructions. Its subjects included dramatic composition, structures of a play, construction of a stage, genres of acting, body movements, make-up, costumes, role and goals of an art director, musical scales, musical instruments and the integration of music with art performances. Such a comprehensive treatise was remarkable for its times even at the level of a manual. It is concrete evidence of the degree of sophistication of the performing arts so far back in our history. But the *Natya Shastra*'s real genius lay in what it outlined in chapters six and seven. This was the theory of rasa, spelling out the philosophy of aesthetics relating to art. This intellectual meditation on what the anubhav or artistic experience should be, both for the creator and the observer, and as an end in itself, was unknown to the world then, and still remains a remarkable contribution of India to the world of creativity.

We are talking here of a highly sophisticated and developed concept of the artistic experience at a time in human evolution when in many parts of the world people had not yet come down from trees. However, if you accept the Western understanding of the origin of aesthetics as a philosophy, you are likely to be told that it began with a series of articles on 'The Pleasures of the Imagination' by the journalist Joseph Addison in the magazine *The Spectator* in 1712. The word 'aesthetics' is derived from the Greek 'aesthetikos', but a quick search on internet will tell you that aesthetics as a branch of philosophy began only post-1712.

There is very little appreciation in Western and even Indian academia of the fact that this subject was fully elaborated upon in India some two thousand years earlier. That, of course, is the burden of ignorance colonised countries must bear, and live with even today in the cultural asymmetries of a globalising world. It is understandable too that while from the eighteenth century onwards there was a spirited discussion in the West on different facets of aesthetics, in India, where it all began, there was the frozen peace of intellectual inertness under colonial rule, the past forgotten, or excavated only as a museum relic.

But let's return to Bharat Muni and his theory of rasa. Rasa, Bharat says, is the essence, the very sap, the inner feeling, of the experience of art. The nature of this experience cannot but be related to the basic premises of Hinduism's spirituality which encompasses all creation and is inherent in all things. While Brahman itself is nirguna or attribute-less, for those who experience it, brahmanubhav, the overwhelming and unmistakable inferential, is a feeling of chit or total awareness, and ananda or absolute bliss. Ananda, or unalloyed joy, is the beej word of Hinduism. The essential nature of our Self or Atman is joy; Brahman, is joy; the world is joy. We are from joy, and we return to joy, which is our sole essence, prior to birth, during life, and on death. For reasons that we have discussed earlier, the joy which is the nature of our real Being, is pushed to the margins because the buddhi (mind), ever active and never still, and the ahamkara (ego), the futile sense of 'I'-ness, dominate our lives. The spiritual purpose of life then is to quieten the mind and vanquish the ego, so that the chit or the Atman, the silent and joyful observer within us, awakens and makes us aware of who we really are—purnta or unblemished joy and fulfilment. As Stella Kramrisch, one of the first Western observers to understand the linkage in Hindu art between the creative and the sublime, writes: 'Art originates in Mahat (The Great Consciousness) and evolves in buddhi. Subsequently, the ego apprehends and according to its limitations, modifies the work in progress, but it has no part in the creative process.'[24]

The purpose of art, then, must be to take us closer to anand. It must, in some way, jolt us away from our routine and mundane preoccupations, and transform our consciousness so that we are more predisposed to discover who we really are. The beautiful must be liberating. As a verse of the *Natya Shastra* says: 'Let Natya be the fifth Vedic scripture … leading to joy and spiritual freedom.' The Upanishadic dictum is—Raso vai saha: He is rasa. The 'He' is Brahman. Brahman is joy. Therefore the rasa, or the essence or relish or flavour of artistic experience has to be joyous, or such as to prepare us to experience the transcendent. 'The Hindu mind views the creative process as a means of suggesting or re-creating a vision, however fleeting, of a divine truth; and regards art as a means of experiencing a state of bliss akin to the absolute state of Ananda or jivanmukti.'[25] The aesthetic experience is then meaningful if it is, in some form, liberating from the contours that constrain our normal perceptions. The spiritual—and equally secular—notion of joy in Hindu spirituality frees us, even if momentarily, from our self-imposed shackles of routine existence. It is in this sense that we must understand what the *Vastu Sutra Upanishad* says: 'From the knowledge of art arises divine knowledge, and such knowledge leads to liberation.' The linkage of the creative to the spiritual transforms the artistic vision. Beauty then becomes 'less a property of things, art or otherwise, and more an experience and a state of being'.[26]

While the divine is juxtaposed with rasa, it should not be—and was never intended to be—seen exclusively in a religious sense. However, the spiritual notion of joy, which is dominant in Hindu philosophy, is relevant. The ananda of the experience of Brahman is used as a touchstone, a measure or definition, of the joy that art has the potential to create. The artist endeavours, through form, word, melody or dance to pursue this potential. Yet, dissonance is not ruled out. Obviously, art cannot be only about positive emotions of happiness. Sometimes, good art is also about discordance, about the less-than-happy things that abound in life. This is all, as we shall explain, factored in. But the theory of rasa still believes that the ultimate impact of art should be to elevate our consciousness. This can be done by what is inherently

joyous, and also by portraying the derogations from that joyousness. Both should lead to a sense of artistic fulfilment that, through the change in consciousness, makes us aware of what our true nature and that of the cosmos is—ananda.

Harsha Dehejia has a beautiful passage about the attraction of the Ananda–Brahman. 'In the ultimate analysis it is the ananda-brahman which holds the many and diverse manifestations of the Indian mind together, it is the ocean where all rivers meet, it is the still centre where all movement ends, it is the silent nada where all sounds end, this is the mind of the Buddha which understands all questions but does not need to provide an answer, this is the Krishna at the centre of the rasa-mandala who holds everything together and Vishnu on the adishesha, it is the formless vishranti that Shiva experiences when he is dancing the Ananda Tandava, it is the resting point beyond all forms. It is also the citta-vritti nirodha of Patanjali … This is the moment of perfect beauty beyond the beautiful.'[27] According to the theory of rasa, the artist is motivated by the search for the ananda within, although the artist expresses it without. 'The Indian artist sees the world with open eyes and the inner world with his eyes closed … God is the Nama (name), and a work of art is the body and the house in which the Formless, the Beyond Form, the Goal of Release and Source of all Forms, reveals itself … In Indian art the figures are, as it were, modelled by breath, which dilates the chest and is felt to carry the pulse of life through the body to the tips of the fingers. This inner awareness was given permanent shape in art.'[28]

In the invocation of rasa, Bharat identifies eight dominant bhavas or emotions. These are sringara (the sensual and the romantic), hasya (the comic), karuna (the pathetic and the sorrowful), raudra (the furious), vira (the heroic), bhayanak (the terrifying), vibhatsa (the disgustful or the odious) and adbhuta (the marvellous). Later commentators added a ninth, shantam (the quiescent). These bhavas act as vibhava (determinants), anubhava (consequents) and vyabhichari (transitory states of feelings) in the internalisation of rasa. As can be seen, the list of bhavas include those that are not simplistically about joy, such as the terrifying, the furious, the disgusting and the pathetic. But sorrow is only a temporary abeyance of joy, as disgust is of reverence, anger is of serenity and the ugly is of beauty. Taken together, in isolation or in any sequence of combination, the purpose of good art, Bharat believes, should be to alter, through these emotions, the consciousness of the viewer. It should trigger a disjunct from the mundane world, create a state of wonder and, ultimately, in that state of altered consciousness, bring the viewers closer to a confrontation with themselves, and what their real being is, which cannot but be the ability to see, even in the non-joyous, the possibility of ultimate joy.

Aesthetics then, for Bharat, is as much about the work of art as it is about the state of mind and the perception

of the viewer, the drishta. This involves the manner in which, at a secondary level of perception, he becomes an observer–participant in the act of seeing, drishti. While darshana is the surface act of seeing, dhrishti, derived from the noun 'drishya', is not just seeing or listening but internalising the seen and heard through perception, feeling and enlightened insight. The *Natya Shastra*'s concern is whether the drishta of beautiful art is in the frame of mind to undergo a transforming experience. For this, first and foremost, the observer has to have control over the mind. If the mind is preoccupied with an endless array of extraneous thoughts, or is in the grip of the ego, the ability to participate in the artistic experience is diminished, if not vitiated. It then becomes a superficial experience, where our indriyas, or sensory perceptions, are superficially active, and obstruct a non-subjective awareness. This devaluation of the communication between art and the viewer leads to the devaluation of the experience of rasa.

The complete aesthetic experience for the participant in art is possible only when the mind is stilled. The tranquil mind is conducive to the internalisation of the creative experience. Only a mind which realises the joy within can seek the true measure of the beauty without. This is the mental discipline which Hindu aesthetics demands of the viewer. When the creator of art is inspired by ananda, and the viewer's mind is both tranquil and in contemplative alertness, the appreciation of the beautiful takes place at another level of consciousness. 'In the antara hradaya akasha (internal space of the heart) is the realization of beauty in perfect form, where a perfect concord exists between viewer and viewed.'[29] In this conceptual sense, aesthetics links the spiritual with the creative. As the *Aitreya Brahmana* says: 'Now (He) glorifies the arts; the arts are refinement of the Self; with these the worshipper recreates the Self.'

Several seminal works were written elaborating the *Natya Shastra*'s theory of rasa. In the eighth century, Udbhata is credited with adding a ninth bhava to the eight mentioned by Bharat, namely, shantam, or tranquillity. Rudrata, a contemporary, added a tenth—affection. Lollata (early ninth century) and Dandin argued that bhavas could be many more; any heightened emotion could qualify to be a rasa. Nayaka (late tenth century) was of the view that rasa was experienced when the viewer overcomes unpleasant and worldly emotions.

However, the most influential commentator on rasa was Abhinavagupta (950–1020), a Shaivite philosopher from Kashmir, whose work, the *Abhinavbharti*, is a classic. Abhinavagupta referred to the *Natya Shastra* as *Natya Veda*. His focus was on perception—how is an art performance viewed? Does it represent tattva or a higher truth or plane of reality, or is it just aropa or a surface superimposition? Rasa, according to him, is a state of total transcendence, experienced

by one who has rasikatva, the cultivated ability to discern aesthetic constituents. It requires sahradayatva or an aesthetic susceptibility to focus on the art or artistic performance. This aesthetic predisposition is enabled by a heightened capacity of visualisation, which in its highest form is called pratibha. The spectator is then transported to a state of pure contemplation, where he or she goes beyond their subjective perceptions and attains a level of undifferentiated concentration which is akin to ananda. In that moment of ananda, 'the very language of name and form (nama and rupa) evoke that beyond form (pararupa and arupa)',[30] recalling the Upanishadic dictum—*Ekam rupam bahudya yeh karoti*: All forms are in the end the reproductions of one form. The vyakta, that which is expressed, is inspired by the avyakta, that which is unarticulated. Form becomes the expression of the formless, and the formless becomes the source of form. The need, Abhinavagupta emphasised, is to have rasiks or aesthetically oriented personalities, who are capable of experiencing such an emotion, and have the utsah (energy) and the exposure to pursue it.

The ancient and widely used expression 'Satyam Shivam Sundaram' is also related to a viewpoint on aesthetics. Satyam stands for the eternal truth. That truth is Brahman, the ultimate and unchanging reality, beyond attributes, but experienced as ananda or unalloyed bliss. Shiv is the saguna embodiment of Brahman. He is thus saubhagyakari

(auspicious), for he is the harbinger of the abundance of joy. That which is representative of the truth and is auspicious, is sundar or beautiful. A link is thus established between joy and beauty. One leads to the other, and connects the viewer of art with the art itself. The medium is Shiva. He presides over the panchakritya—creation, protection, destruction, removal of Maya and moksha. Art moves likewise from creation to liberation, destroying ignorance and the distortions of the ego, along the way.

The ananda, which Hindu aesthetics links to beauty, is not fragmented. On the contrary, it is overwhelmingly holistic, representing an indivisible wholeness that must infuse the entire canvas of artistic imagination. It follows that all artistic expression and experience has to be interlinked. Different branches of art may appear to be different, representing separate skills and training, but essentially the same notion of beauty permeates all forms of creativity. No one artistic endeavour can be viewed in isolation and, no one branch of art is complete without a knowledge of the others. The ancient treatise *Vishnudharmottara* (mid-fifth century) 'opens with a conversation between a king and a sage. The king desires to learn the whole meaning of art, but is told that he must know the theory of dancing. To this he agrees because the laws of dancing imply the principles that govern painting. But the sage further insists that the king shall begin by studying music and song, for without a knowledge of the arts, their

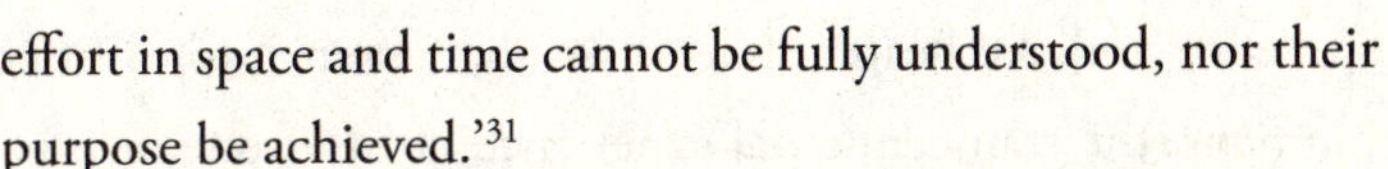

effort in space and time cannot be fully understood, nor their purpose be achieved.'[31]

The common spiritual inspiration for art shows in different mediums. The *Natya Shastra* enumerates 108 postures in Bharatnatyam dance. These can be seen in dance performances, as also in the magnificent Chola bronzes and in the stunning stone rendering of these entire set of stances in the Chidambaram temple. The Kathakali dance of Kerala comes alive in the wooden panels that depict its movements, or the wooden panels come alive in the dance performances they portray. The 108 types of movements of the *Natya Shastra* are brought alive in all cultural forms—Hindu, Buddhist and Jain. The beatitude on the faces of the ladies in the Ajanta frescoes mirrors the serenity of the magnificent Gandhara stone portrayals of the Buddha. Classical musical ragas sung in a temple at specific times of the day seem to have been composed to effortlessly enhance the worship of the deities. The poetry eulogising women finds expression in the seductively fulsome depictions of goddesses and apsaras carved in stone or sandstone. The same stillness, form and flux sets the tone of all art forms of ancient India, making it 'an organic whole where all dimensions of life are considered together in their essential relationship of interconnectedness and interdependence and overlapping'. This 'multi-layered concurrence', this 'unitary vision', is sourced in the theory of rasa, which is 'the ultimate experience of the creator, the spectator and the hearer alike … so that, even if for a brief moment, the transcendental experience of beatitude or bliss (ananda) can be evoked.'[32]

The Hindu theory of rasa, therefore, primarily establishes the ideal touchstone of beauty. This is the unchanging factor of all art. Having outlined the first principle, it sanctions a profusion of instructions, manuals and injunctions which are specific to any one particular form of art. Unity and multiplicity thus become the part of a singular discussion. This corresponds with the nirguna–saguna interface. Nirguna Brahman is the eternal and constant truth. Once the singularity of this ultimate truth is accepted, the saguna is free to encompass endless variations of that one truth. Kapila Vatsyayan has a remarkable analogy to illustrate this unified duality. She compares the Hindu vision with that of a double-reed flute: 'One reed is a perennial strain, a tonic, immutable trans-space and time; the other reed plays the tune of immediate time and space. The one is repetitive but stable; the other changing. The two together create the music that sounds different at different times.'[33] The unchanging reed is what is called sashvat and sanatan. The changing is parampara or specific tradition. The dialogue between the unconditioned and the conditioned, the unqualified and the qualified, and the unchanging and the contingent, is a continuum, in both the spiritual and the creative realm.

—Pavan K. Varma, *The Great Hindu Civilisation*

19

SHATAKAS OF BHARTRIHARI

The Shatakas of Bhartrihari (485–543 CE) include the Nitishataka, Shringarashataka and Vairagyashataka. The Nitishataka deals with ethics and morality, the Shringarashataka deals with love and the Vairagyashataka contains verses on austerity and renunciation.

Bhartrihari's works indicate great familiarity with the procedures of royal courts and, at first, appear to represent the aspirations of the common people. However, a closer reading reveals his disillusionment with worldly life as he fluctuates between the pursuit of worldly desires and those of the soul.

The Praise of Wisdom

When wise men dwell in poverty men whose words are adorned with polished sayings from the Sastras, and who impart sacred learning to their disciples then that prince in whose kingdom they dwell is chargeable with folly, and the wise men, though poor, are the rulers of the land. Should not those bad examiners be worthy of condemnation who (through) carelessness cause jewels to fall from their true value?

O kings! Cast off your pride before those who have the inward treasure of wisdom: they are not despoiled by robbers, but their treasure, always increasing, grows greater when it is shared with the needy: not even at the end of the world does it perish. Who indeed may compare with them?

Despise not wise men who have attained to knowledge of the truth. They are not held bound by riches, for they count wealth even as grass. The stalk of a waterlily will not bind an elephant who is infuriated by passion.

The Creator in his anger may hinder the swan from sporting in the lotus-bed, his dwelling; but he cannot take away his faculty of separating milk from water.

Bracelets are no ornament to a man, nor strings of pearls clear as the moon; nor yet bathing, nor perfumes, nor flowers, nor decorated hair. Perfect eloquence alone adorns a man.

Adornments may perish, but the ornament of eloquence abides for ever.

Wisdom, indeed, is the highest ornament that a man possesses. It is a valuable to be carefully guarded, for wisdom gains food, glory, and blessing. It is the lord of lords. Wisdom is as a friend to a man travelling in a distant land. Wisdom is honoured among kings even more than wealth. The man devoid of wisdom is but an animal.

If a man has patience, what need has he of armour? If he has anger in his heart, what further enemy need he fear? If he has knowledge, what need of fire to consume evil? If a friend, what need has he of divine medicines? If there are malicious people about him, why should he be afraid of serpents? If he has perfect wisdom, what need of riches? If he is modest, what need has he of ornament? If he give his mind to poetry, what need has he of power?

Be well disposed towards relatives; liberal to inferiors: always hate the evil; love the good; be obedient to princes; honour the wise. Be firm towards enemies; be respectful to venerable men; deal shrewdly with women. The man who frames his life after these precepts prospers in the world.

Intercourse with wise men takes away dullness of mind, elevates the intellect, inspires the speech with truthfulness. What will it not do for men?

May there be glory to wise men who are learned and accomplished poets! There is no fear that their renown shall wither or perish.

A virtuous son, an affectionate wife, a liberal master, a loving friend, a guileless kinsman, a mind not harassed by care, a handsome form, abiding riches, a mouth abounding in wisdom-these are the gifts which Hari, the giver of desires, the delight of the earth, bestows upon the man with whom he is pleased.

Abstinence from destroying life, keeping one's hands off another's wealth, speaking the truth, reasonable liberality according to one's power, not conversing with the wives of other men, checking the stream of covetousness, reverence towards spiritual fathers, compassion towards all creatures—this is the path of happiness, violating no ordinances, taught in all the Sastras.

The low-minded man does not make even the least effort in the pursuit of wisdom through fear of difficulties: if he has made any attempt, he stops when obstacles meet him. The noble-minded man may meet with repeated hindrances, but when he has once begun the pursuit of wisdom, he does not give it up.

Righteousness must be loved; evil must be avoided, even at the risk of death; wicked men must not be spoken to; a poor man, even though he be a friend, must not be asked for alms: even in adversity the foot must be constant, and the vow taught by good and great men must be conformed to, even if it be as difficult as to stand on the edge of a sword!

—Nitishataka, stanzas 15–28

The Praise of Riches

Our noble birth may go to the lower regions; our virtues may perish; our moral character may fall as if from a lofty mountain; our family may be consumed by fire; a thunderbolt may strike our might as it were an enemy: let us keep our money, for without this all the collected virtues are but a heap of grass.

These are all the same senses—exactly the same action—the same intellect undiminished: the same voice. But though a man may remain exactly what he was, yet, when deprived of the warmth which wealth gives him, he becomes someone altogether different. This is indeed wonderful!

If a man be wealthy, he is of good family, he is wise, he is learned in the Scriptures, he is virtuous, eloquent, beautiful. All the virtues attach themselves to gold.

A king is ruined through evil counsellors: an ascetic through society: a child by spoiling: a priest by not studying the Sacred Scriptures: a family by the evil behaviour of children: good manners by evil habits: modesty by wine: agriculture by want of care: affection by absence from home: friendship by want of love: possessions by mismanagement: money by waste and prodigality.

Giving, consuming, and loss, are the three ways by which wealth is diminished. The man who neither gives nor spends has yet the third way open to him.

A jewel is cut by the polishing stone; a conqueror in war is killed by weapons; the elephant is weakened by passion; the islands in a river become dry in the autumn; the moon wanes; young women become languid through pleasure, yet is their beauty nothing lessened: so noble men who have diminished their wealth by *giving* to the needy are still illustrious.

A man who is famishing longs for a handful of grain; but when he has revived, he looks on the whole earth as a mere handful of grass. So, objects seem great or small according to the condition of the men who possess them: it is the change in men's fortune which makes things seem greater or smaller.

If, O king! if you would enjoy this earth, which is as fruitful as a cow, nourish it as carefully as you would a calf. The earth brings forth fruits without end like the creeper of plenty if it is perpetually and carefully cultivated.

The behaviour of kings is as uncertain as the way of a courtesan. Now it is false, now true—now with harsh, now with agreeable words—now cruel, now merciful—at one time liberal, at another covetous—either always squandering money or heaping it together:

Authority, fame, the guarding of Brahmans, liberality, feasting, protection of friends: what profit is there to those who serve kings if they have not gained these six blessings?

Whatever fate has written on the forehead of each, that shall he obtain, whether it be poverty or riches. His abode may be the desert, but he shall gain no more if he lives even on Mount Meru. Let your mind be constant. Do not be miserable through envy of the rich. The pitcher takes up the same quantity of water whether it be from the well or the ocean.

'Who does not know that thou, O cloud, art the one support of the Chataka? Why, O most beneficent cloud l dost thou wait for our cry of misery?'

'Ah! Beloved Chtaka, hear and listen attentively to what I tell thee. The heavens have many clouds, but they are not all alike; some water the earth, others thunder and pour forth no rain.' Do not degrade yourself by asking alms of any one whom you may chance to meet.

Concerning Evil Men

Cruelty, causeless quarrels, the desire for another's wife or money, envy of the good, or of one's own relatives. These are the natural characteristics of wicked men.

An evil man should be avoided though he be adorned with learning. Is a snake less feared because it is ornamented with jewels?

The moderate man's virtue is called dullness; the man who lives by rigid vows is considered arrogant; the pure-minded is deceitful; the hero is called unmerciful; the sage is contemptuous; the polite man is branded as servile, the noble man as proud; the eloquent man is called a chatterer; freedom from passion is said to be feebleness. Thus, do evil-minded persons miscall the virtues of the good.

If a man be greedy, what further vice can he have? What sin can be worse than backbiting? What need has the truthful man of penances? What need has the pure minded man of a sacred bathing-place? What virtue is beyond generosity? If there be greatness of mind, what adornment is required? If a man be learned, what necessity is there of the society of others? If disgrace over take a man, why need he fear death?

The moon obscured by the daylight, a woman no longer young, a pond destitute of water-lilies, a handsome man who talks nonsense, a prince entirely devoted to money, a good man always in calamity, an evil man dwelling in a king's court—these are seven thorns in my mind.

A king full of wrath hath no friend. The sacred fire burns even the priest who offers the sacrifice if he touches it.

The man who preserves a respectful silence is considered dumb; the man who talks agreeably is considered forward; the man who stands close by is thought trouble some; he who stands far off, cold-hearted; the patient man is counted as faint-hearted; the impetuous man is called ill-bred. So difficult, indeed, are the laws by which behaviour is regulated, impossible to be learnt even by an ascetic.

Is it possible to take pleasure in the society of a low man, dissolute, whose evil is all evident, whose wicked acts are the result of former births, who hates virtue, and who lives by chance?

The friendships formed between good and evil men differ. The friendship of the good, at first faint like the morning light, continually increases; the friendship of the evil at the very beginning is great, like the light of mid day, and dies away like the light of evening. Deer, fish, and virtuous men, who only require grass, water, and peace in the world, are wantonly pursued by huntsmen, fishermen, and envious people.

—Nitishataka, stanzas 39–61

The Path of Enjoyment

In health there is the fear of disease; in pride of family the fear of a fall; in wealth the fear of the king; in honour the fear of abasement; in power the fear of enemies; in beauty the fear of old age; in the scriptures the fear of controversy; in virtue the fear of evil; in the body the fear of death. Everything on earth is beset by fear; the only freedom from fear is in the renunciation of desire.

What have we not attempted for the sake of those lives of ours which are as unstable as the drop of water on the lotus-leaf? Even we commit sin by boasting of our own virtues shamelessly before those rich men whose minds are senseless through the intoxicating power of wealth.

Homage be to time! The delights of the city, the great king with his crowds of courtiers, the counsellors which stand before him, the women with faces beautiful as the moon, the assembly of haughty princes, the bards, the reciters—these are all borne away by time, and become but a memory.

Setting Forth of Kala

Those from whom we were born have long since departed; they also with whom we grew up exist only in memory: we too, through the approach of death, become, as it were, trees growing on the sandy bank of a river.

In the house where there were many, now there is but one; where there was but one, there were many, and then again but one. So Kala and *Kali* toss day and night backward and forward as though they were dice, and play with men on the chessboard of this world as if they were chessmen.

Shall we dwell beside the divine river in a life of penance? or shall we desire the society of virtuous women? or shall we study the multitude of the scriptures, whose poetry is even as nectar? We know not what we shall do, seeing the life of man endures but the twinkling of an eye.

Surely the retreats amid the Himalayas, where the: Vidyadharas dwell among the rocks cooled by the spray of the Ganges, must have ceased to exist, since men enjoy that sustenance which they have gained from others to their own disgrace.

When may we sit at peace on the banks of the heavenly river, whose banks of sand are dazzling white in the moonlight? and when shall we, when the nights are perfectly still, wearied with the satiety of the world, utter cries of 'Siva! Siva! Siva!' while the tears flow from our eyes?

Mahadeva is the god we worship, and this river is the heavenly river; these caves are the dwelling, the abode of Bari. Kala, moreover, is our friend, and the rule of life which we observe has freedom from humiliation. What more need I say on this matter?

The Ganges falls from heaven on the head of Siva; from the head of Siva on to the mountain; from the top of the mountain to the earth, always falling lower and lower: even in so many ways is the fall of one whose judgment has departed from him.

Desire is like a river. Its waters are men's wishes, agitated by the waves of desire; love takes the place of crocodiles; the birds that fly about it are the doubts which haunt the mind. The tree of firmness growing on the bank is washed away by the flood; the whirlpools of error are very difficult to cross: the lofty banks are the cares of life. The ascetics who, pure in heart, have succeeded in crossing it successfully, are filled with joy.

As we look at the ever-changing three worlds, the desire hidden with us, violently attracted towards objects of sense, ceases to cross the path of our eyes or to enter into the way of our ears; for we have subdued the objects of sense which produce desire in us, and hold them bound by devotion, as an elephant attracted by his mate is kept from her by being tied to a post.

My days once seemed long when I used to suffer pain through asking favours from rich men, and they seemed too short for me to carry out all my aims, filled as they were with the desire for earthly objects. Now I sit on a stone in a mountain cave, and in the intervals of my meditation I am filled with laughter at the recollection of my former life.

Wisdom has not been gained free from spot; wealth has not been acquired; reverence towards our elders has not been practised by us; we have not even dreamt of love. If this has been our existence, then have we lived a life even like the life of a crow, which hungers for the food of others.

When all our wealth is gone, then with hearts full of tenderness, recollecting how the path of action in the world leads to evil, we in a sacred grove, with the rays of the autumn moon shining on us, will pass our nights occupied alone in meditation, at the feet of Siva.

I am satisfied with bark clothing; thou takest pleasure in thy magnificence: there is no difference between the contentment of both of us. The man whose desires are unlimited is poor indeed; who that is satisfied with what he has can be either rich or poor?

Relaxation from toil at one's own will, food gained without degradation, friendship with noble-minded men, a mind not agitated by contact with external things this is the result of the highest vow of tranquillity. I know not, though I have carefully thought thereupon, by what strict penance this perfect state may be gained.

The hand serves for a cup; food is gained by begging; the sky with its pure expanse serves for a garment; the earth is a couch. Those whose freedom from attraction to objects of sense has been brought to such perfection as this are fortunate, contented in their own minds, and they uproot action, casting away all the many forms of pain which attend upon it.

Masters are difficult to please; kings change from one thing to another in their minds with the swiftness of horses; our desires are great, and our minds aim at high things. Old age consumes our bodies; death puts an end to our lives. 0 my friends l there is no glory in this world for a wise man but that which he gains by penance.

Pleasure is like the lightning that flashes in the canopy of cloud; life is like the fleeting clouds that are torn asunder by the storm; the ardent desires of the young are transitory. Owise men! You who know the uncertainty of human affairs, gain wisdom by meditation on the Supreme Spirit; for perfection is easily gained by means of constant contemplation.

A man who is wise and understanding, being pained by hunger, will go from door to door throughout the huts of a sacred village, and will beg alms where he sees the door-post blackened by the smoke of the sacrifices offered by the learned priests who dwell within; and he will bear before him his pot covered with a white cloth: he will not live in misery from day to day among families as wretched as himself.

'Are you a Chandala? are you a Brahman? are you a Shudra, or an ascetic, or a lord of devotion whose mind is skilled in meditating on the truth?' Ascetics, when men ask them such questions as these with loud voices, feel neither pleasure nor anger, but pursue their course in quietness.

O my friend l fortunate are those who have cast off the many bonds of this world, and from within whose minds desire £or earthly objects, like the poison of a serpent, has departed. They spend the night, bright with the clear shining of the autumn moon, in the border of the forest, thinking on nothing but the greatness of their good fortune.

Cease to wander wearily in the thicket of sense. Seek that better way which, in a moment, brings freedom from trouble. Unite thyself to the Supreme Spirit, and abandon thy own state as unsteady as the waves. Take no more pleasure in things perishable. Be calm, O my heart!

O my friend l live on fruits and nuts, lie on the bare ground; let us rise up and go into the forest clothed in new soft bark garments. In that retreat we shall not hear the voices of those rich men whose minds are blind through ignorance, and whose voices are troubled through the confusion of their minds.

O my mind! It the delusion which envelops thee be cleared away, pay devotion to the god of the mooncrest, who takes

delusion away from man. Fix your thought on the stream of the heavenly river. For what certainty is there [in earthly things], in waves and bubbles, or in flashes of lightning, or in women, or in the tongues of flame, or in serpents, or in the rushing of a stream.

If there are songs before thee, if there are elegant poets from the southern regions on one side of thee, if behind damsels bearing the fans with tinkling anklets, taste, my friend, the pleasures of sense which thou mayest gain from these things. If thou hast them not, then plunge, O my mind! into devout contemplation, freeing thee from all thought.

Wise men! Have nothing to do with women who are only pleasing from their beauty, in whose society is a transitory delight. Rather follow after women who are compassionate, amiable, and intelligent: the beautiful forms of women adorned with tinkling jewels will not avail thee in Naraka.

Abstinence from destroying life, keeping one's hands off another's wealth, speaking the truth, seasonable liberality according to one's power, not conversing with the wives of other men, checking the stream of covetousness, reverence towards spiritual fathers, compassion towards all creatures—this is the path of happiness, violating no ordinances, taught in all the Sastras.

O mother Lakshmi! Grant me yet further that I may not be filled with desire. May I not be filled with the longing after

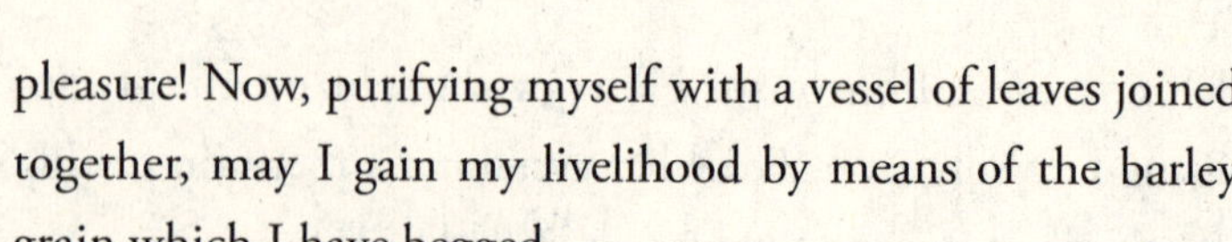

pleasure! Now, purifying myself with a vessel of leaves joined together, may I gain my livelihood by means of the barley grain which I have begged.

You were to me even as myself; I was as yourself to you. Such were our feelings to one another. How has it come about that we have been changed, and that we no more £eel the same sympathy one for another?

O woman! Why dost thou shoot forth at me those beautiful glances from thy half-opened eyes? Cease! Cease! Thy toil is in vain! I am as it were changed! My youth has departed from me; my dwelling is in a forest; my infatuation ha left me. I look on the favours of this world only as so much grass.

This woman, with eyes that have stolen the beauty of the lotus, unceasingly casts her glances towards me. What does she wish? My infatuation has departed; the arrows of cruel love, producing immoderate heat and fever, have left me.

Is not a palace delightful to dwell in? Are not songs charming to hear? Is not the society of friends, whom we love as our own lives, alluring? Yet wise men retire away from all these things into the forest, considering them like the light of a lamp which burns unsteadily through the wind of the wings of a wandering moth.

Are there no more roots growing in the caves; have the mountain torrents1 ceased to flow; do the trees no longer bear fruit; has the bark with which you may gain your clothing withered on the trees, that you cast off your self-respect and fall down before haughty men, who have gained a little wealth with difficulty, and who regard you with supercilious contempt?

Surely the retreats of the Himalayas, the abode of the Vidyadharas, where the rocks are cooled by the spray of the Ganges, surely these places must have ceased to exist, since men enjoy food which they gain from others to their own disgrace.

When Meru the magnificent mountain falls from its place, destroyed at the end of the age; when the ocean, the abode of multitudes of great monsters, is dried up; when the earth resting on her mountains comes to an end, how can there be any abiding-place for the body, which is as unstable as the ear of a young elephant?

When shall I, O Shiva! whose drinking-cup is my hand, who have no garment but the sky, who live solitary, peaceful, free from desire, able to uproot action-when shall I attain to union with the Supreme Soul?

Thou mayest have gained glory and the accomplishment of all thy desires: what further? Thy foot may have been placed on the neck of thine enemies: what further? Thou mayest have bestowed thy riches on thy friends: what further? Thou mayest live thousands of years: what further?

One may have been clothed in rags: what then? One may have worn a magnificent silk garment: what then? One may have had only one wife: what then? Or a retinue of horses and elephants and attendants: what then? One may have enjoyed good fare: what then? Or eaten poor food at the end of the day: what then? What matters either state if you know not the glory of the Supreme One who destroys all evils?

Thou hast paid worship to Siva; thou hast lived in fear of death and birth in a future state; thou hast detached thyself from love for thy own family; thou hast not been blinded by love; thou hast dwelt in a forest ·apart from men; thou hast been freed from the evil contact of the world. [If thou hast passed thy life thus], then thou hast vairagya-freedom from attachment to outward things.

Meditate on the Supreme Being, who is eternal, who grows not old, above all things, expanding by his own will. What profit is there in the delusions of the world? If a man be truly seeking unity with the Supreme Being, all earthly pleasures and powers seem worthy only of the notice of low-minded men.

O mind! thou canst enter Patala, thou canst skim over the heaven and cross the breadth of this world in a moment of thought. How is it that thou dost not even by accident meditate on the Supreme Being, who is spotless, dwelling within himself? So thou mightiest gain tranquillity.

We, as men devoid of intelligence, think within ourselves that day and night repeat themselves indefinitely; and so we run each to our tasks unswervingly, and we take up each separate work where we laid it down. Alas! how is it that we

are not ashamed of our folly? We endure the torments of this world while we are wholly occupied in enjoying 'the same objects of sense over and over again.

The earth is his delightful couch, the arms of the creepers are his pillow, the heaven is his canopy, the winds his fan, the moon is his twinkling lamp. The sage, rejoicing because he has been freed from desire, lives in peace and happiness, as though he were the lord of the universe.

The man who has gained great power finds even the sovereignty of the universe tasteless. Do not seek pleasure in the enjoyment which comes from 'flattery, dress, or feasting; for the only delight which is supreme is everlasting, and continually grows. Seize upon it, for, compared to the sweetness of that, all the three worlds are devoid of pleasure.

What profit is there in the Vedas, or in the Smriti, or in the reading of Puranas and the tedious Sastras, or in the bewildering multitude of ceremonial acts which lead to an abode in the tabernacles of heaven? All else is as the mere haggling of merchants, in comparison with the final fire which will consume the creations of this wearisome burden of sorrow called existence, that fire which will make us enter into the sphere of joy and unite us with the Supreme Soul.

Life is as uncertain as the waves of the sea; the glory of youth remains but a short time; wealth passes away like a thought; all the pleasure in the world endures but a lightning-flash through the heavens; the embraces of your beloved whom you clasp to your breast will not be for long. Direct your thoughts to the Supreme Being; for you must cross the sea of life with all its fears and alarms.

How should a wise man be anxious after a small portion of this world? Is the mighty ocean ever stirred up by the gambols of a little fish?

When the darkness of love had filled me with ignorance, women seemed the only objects for which to live. Now, since I have anointed my eyes with the ointment of discrimination, the sight of all things has become clear to me, and I behold the three worlds as the Creator.

Delightful are the rays of the moon; delightful the grassy places of the forest; delightful the society of beloved friends; delightful the tales of the poets; delightful the face of one's beloved sparkling with the tear-drops of rage. But who cares any more for these delights when his mind reflects on their uncertainty?

An ascetic lives on alms, remote from men, self-con trolled, walking in the path of indifference, giving or not giving, it matters not which. He is clothed in a torn cloak made from rags cast into the street; he has no pride, no self-consciousness; he is free from desire; his sole pleasure is rest and quietness.

O earth, my mother! O wind, my father! O fire, my friend! O water, my consort! O sky, my brother! I salute you with my hands joined. I am full of glory through the merit which I have gained through my union with you. O may I enter into the Supreme Being!

As long as the tabernacle of the body is well and strong; as long as old age is far off; as long as the senses are unimpaired; as long as there is no diminution of life; so long will the wise man make great efforts to gain eternal glory for himself. What is the use of digging a well when the house is on fire?

We have not studied knowledge while upon the earth-knowledge which tames the hosts of disputants and is suitable for a well-trained man: our fame has not been exalted to the skies by the sword-point which splits the hard forehead of the elephant; we have not tasted the juice of the lower lip of the soft mouth of the beloved one at the time of moon-rising. Alas! Youth has passed fruitlessly, like a lamp in an empty house.

In good men knowledge is the destruction of pride; in others it is the cause of haughtiness: a solitary dwelling frees ascetics from attraction to objects of sense; it is the cause of extreme attraction towards desire in those who are wounded by it.

The desires in our own minds have faded: youth has passed into old age: even the very virtues in our own bodies have become barren since they are no longer recognised as virtues. What can we do? All-powerful time is hastening on, and death is coming on us to end our lives. what can we do but resort to the feet of Siva? There is no other means of salvation for us.

When the mouth is dry, a man drinks water which is sweet to him; when pained with hunger, he eats rice and other vegetables. But he is mistaken if he imagines that the removal of the pain caused by hunger and thirst is a pleasure.

I will bathe in the waters of Ganges: I will honour thee, O lord! with pure fruits and flowers. I will meditate upon thee; I will sit on a couch of stone in a mountain cave; I will feed on fruits with peaceful mind; I will reverence the voice of my spiritual father. When shall I, lying at thy feet, O enemy of love! by thy favour be freed from the pain of desire, seeking alone the path of meditation?

Thou whose bed is a slab of rock; thou whose dwelling is a cave, whose clothes are the bark of trees, whose companions are the antelopes, whose food is the tender fruits, whose drink is water from the cascades, whose wife is the sciences: such as these are indeed the supreme lords; they pay homage to no man.

While there is the Ganges near us, whose rays kiss the head of Siva, and furnishes us abundant livelihood, with bark garments made from the banyan trees that grow on its banks, what sage would even look at the face of women as they sit filled with extreme misery, and with pain produced by the fever of calamity, unless he felt compassion for his distressed family?

If wise men forsake Benares, alas l to what other place should they resort? For in the gardens of Benares are manifold pleasures, and penances practised of exceeding difficulty; a small ragged piece of cloth is looked upon as a splendid

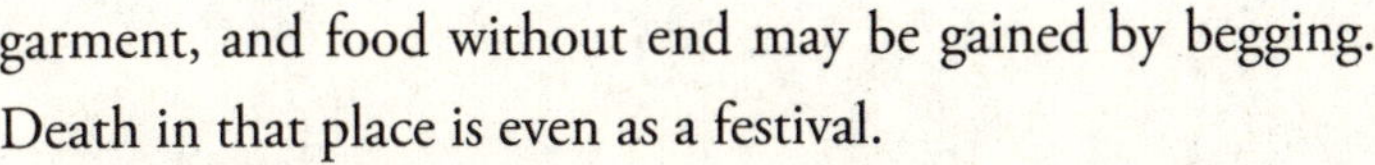

garment, and food without end may be gained by begging. Death in that place is even as a festival.

'Our lord sleeps; now is the time for his rest: you may not enter, for if he wakes up and see you, he will be angry.' So, say the guardians at the palace gate.

Pass them by and enter the temple of that lord who is t ruler of the universe-that shrine which gives boundless bliss, full of love, where the speech of rough doorkeepers is not heard.

Dear friend, unyielding destiny, like an almighty potter, places the mind of man upon the wheel of care, like a lump of clay and makes him revolve, that wheel which is ever moving through all the manifold evils of life, visiting men as though with the rod of affliction.

There is no difference for me between Siva, the lord of the world, the slayer of Janu, and Vishnu, the soul of the universe; therefore, I worship the deity who bears the moon-crest.

I am satisfied with the divine voice which sheds forth words over my mind sweeter than honey, richer than butter. Alms content me; bark clothing satisfies me; I care nothing for wealth gained in a state of slavery to objects of sense.

—Vairagyashataka, stanzas 35–100, translated
by Rev. B. Hale Wortham

20

Sri Nimbarkacharya and His Doctrine of Dvaitadvaita

Sri Nimbarkacharya (circa 600–700 CE), also known as Nimbarka, Nimba Daitya and Niyamananda, was a leading proponent of Dvaitadvaita (Dvaita–Advaita) or dualistic–non-dualistic philosophy. He popularised the worship of Radha and Krishna.

Sri Nimbarkacharya laid the foundations of Nimbarka Sampradaya. He believed that the Jiva and the world were both separate from, and identical with, the Brahman. According to him, all animate and inanimate objects are a part of God and all souls are a part of the Supreme Soul.

In South India, Sri Ramanujacharya brought into practice the 'Sri Sampradaya' (the religious tradition in which Sri Mahalakshmi plays the pivotal role of the mediatrix in the redemption of the jivas) and was responsible for spreading and expanding the Vishistadvaita Darshana. Sometime after Acharya Ramanujacharya, Sri Nimbarkacharya, who had generated a flowing current of devotion sweeping everybody around Mathura, began to worship, adore and serve Sri Radha Krishna. He was the originator of 'Premalakshan Bhakti' (devotion with intense love as its main feature) and the Acharya (Preceptor) of the Doctrine of Dvaitadvaita. He was an Acharya of the Vaishnava tradition. He was born at Arunashrama near Vaiduryapattana on the banks of Godavari River in the Telugu region of India. Sri Nimbarka was born in the 11th century, soon after Sri Ramanujacharya but before the advent of Sri Madhvacharya. He is considered to be an incarnation of Surya Deva (the Sun God). His father's name was Arunamuni and his mother's name was Jayanti Devi. Although Nimbarkacharya's birth took place in South India, he spread devotion to Vishnu around Mathura. Even today, this tradition is largely prevalent in North India, in and around Mathura and parts of Bengal. It has not been possible to ascertain the exact year of Nimbarkacharya's birth despite all the research so far. But there is sufficient evidence to indicate that his birth took place after Acharya

Ramanunjacharya. Acharya Nimbarka's disciple, Harivyasdev has written in one of his texts that the Acharya's birth took place on the auspicious third day of the half of the lunar month of Vaishak. But the year of birth has not been mentioned therein. Scholars say that the Acharya lived on the earth in the year Samvat 1164. The Acharya has written a treatise on the Vedanta Sutras called the *Vedantaparijatasaurabh*. He has also written a sacred text called the *dashashloki* or *Sidhanta Ratna*.

The Doctrine of Dvaitadvaita Brahma

The Universe, the Jiva and Brahman are the objects of enjoyment/experience, the enjoyer/the one who experiences and the controller respectively. They are actually different from each other. The inherent form or nature of the Universe as well as the Jivas as also their present states and future transformations are all dependent on the will of Brahman and are pervaded by the Brahman. In this way, the Universe and the Jivas exhibit identity with the Brahman. It is by the desire and resolve of Ishvara, who is beyond thought, who is eternal, and who is a past master in generating events that have not happened before, that the Universe is created. Therefore the Universe is the consequence of Brahman. Sri Ramanujacharya's Doctrine states that the Brahman is the one efficient cum material cause. This tenet is explained by Nimbarkacharya as follows: Sentient and insentient substances in their subtle states and in possession of their inherent powers are created in the most fundamental form by the Brahman using his own powers, and therefore Brahman is the material cause. Further, because Ishvara gives Jivas knowledge about the fruits of their karmas which they must necessarily enjoy or experience, having become otherwise unfit for true knowledge, being bound helplessly by their past deeds and suffering contraction of remembrance (of auspicious things) and, further, because Ishvara also introduces to the Jivas the means for such enjoyments/experiences, He becomes the efficient cause as well.

Jiva

The Jiva (individual soul) is of the intrinsic nature of knowledge, self-luminous, of the nature of consciousness/intelligence and atomic in size. It is also the knower, the doer, and the enjoyer or the one who experiences. It is entirely dependent upon Sri Hari. In each body, the Jiva is quite different from the other which means that the Jivas are innumerable.

These essential characteristics of the Jivas are obscured by Maya since times without a beginning. As a result, each Jiva is unable to recognise its true nature. Nevertheless, by God's grace devotees can realise their true inherent nature. Jivas are of three types. These are '*baddh*' (bound), '*mukta*' (liberated) and '*baddha-mukta*' (bound-free). All jivas are the Paramatma's '*sphulinga*' (a flame or spark of a fire). Just as a

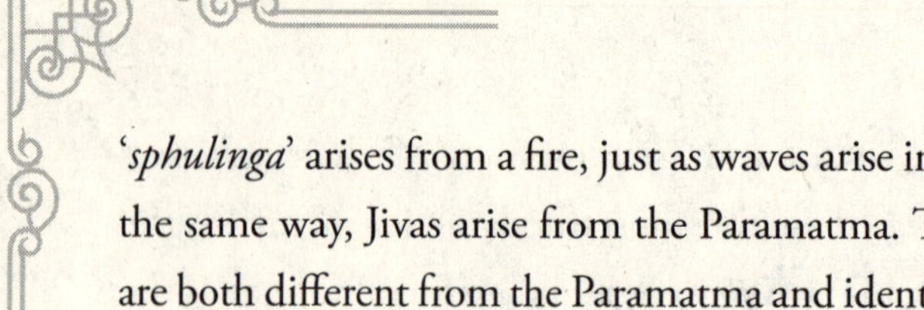

'*sphulinga*' arises from a fire, just as waves arise in the ocean, in the same way, Jivas arise from the Paramatma. Therefore Jivas are both different from the Paramatma and identical too. Since the Jivatma is embodied, it is different from the Paramatma but because the Jivatma within the body has arisen from the Paramatma, like the spark of a fire or waves of the ocean, the Jivatma also has an essential identity with the Paramatma.

The Universe

In the opinion of Nibarkacharya, the Universe is not an illusion but is real and true. It is the consequential effect of Brahman. Without the Brahman and by itself, the Universe has no independent existential reality. From this point of view we may say that the Universe is, in a way, not real. The 'Pradhan Tattva' (truths about primordial matter) are three in number, as follows:

1. '*Aprakrut*' (non-material, spiritual stuff which is the eternal superhuman creation of Ishvara)
2. '*Prakruti*' (inert, insentient matter) endowed with the 'sattva', 'rajas' and 'tamas' gunas.
3. '*Kala*' (Time).

Just as the countless Jivas are eternal, these three truths are also without a beginning or an end.

Discussion on Moksha

Ignorance is without beginning and eternal. Karmas impelled by ignorance obscure the pure nature of the Jivatma. It is only by the merciful grace of Ishvara that it becomes possible for the Jivatma to dispel ignorance. Ishvara's merciful grace manifests itself from constant loving devotion.

Prapatti (self surrender to God) or delivering/entrusting the Atma or the Self to Ishvara is the only way to moksha (final liberation from transmigration and worldly existence). Even in the state of moksha, the Jivatma remains distinct from Ishvara. Nevertheless, because the Jivatma is, at the same time, a projection or an emanation of Brahman, it is identical with the Brahman. This is the essence of the '*Bhedabhed*' (difference in non-difference) Doctrine. In the state of moksha, the Jivatmas are identical in form with the Brahman but they do not get dissolved into Brahman nor do they get fully absorbed in Brahman and further, the processes of creation of the Universe as well as its dissolution remain the domains of action of the Brahman and not the Jivatmas.

Hence, viewed from this perspective, Brahman and the Jivas are different realities but because the Jivas have been created out of Brahman, they are also non-different from the Brahman.

—Swami Satya Prasad Dasji, *Indian Philosophy*

21

Sri Ramanujacharya and His Doctrine of Vishishtadvaita

Ramanujacharya (1017–1137) was a Vaishnavite saint from Tamil Nadu. He advocated the philosophy of Vishishtadvaita (qualified non-dualism), emphasising the eternal relationship between the individual soul (Jiva) and the Supreme Being (Vishnu). His Vishishtadvaita competed with the Dvaita (theistic dualism) philosophy of Madhvacharya and the Advaita Vedanta (non-dualism) philosophy of Adi Shankaracharya.

He disagreed with Advaita Vedanta and said that while Brahman was the ultimate reality, at the same time, the universe was real and was a manifestation of the Brahman. His teachings encouraged temple worship and inspired the Bhakti movement across India.

Ramanuja was born in Sriperumbudur, South India in the year 1017 CE—and whose millennium was celebrated in 2017—some two hundred years after the death of Shankara. Even as a child, he acquired a mastery of the Vedanta doctrine, and adopting the life of a sanyasi, settled down in Srirangam. He wrote several highly regarded treatises on Vedanta, and seminal commentaries on the *Brahma Sutra* and the *Bhagavad Gita.* Although, he did not seek to consciously differ from Shankara, he is ultimately associated with the doctrine of Vishista Advaita, or qualified non-dualism, which was different from Shankara's unyielding non-dualism, and moulded Advaita towards a personalised theism.

Ramanuja did not contest Shankara's assertion that Brahman is supreme, all-knowing, omnipotent and omnipresent, characterised by the experience of sat (being), chitta (consciousness), and ananda (bliss). However, he did not support Shankara's assertion that Brahman is attribute-less. He argued that pure consciousness is an untenable construct. A thing without any attributes is as good as being non-existent, and if it has attributes, it cannot be pure consciousness. It is not possible 'for the mind to apprehend an undifferentiated object. What is known is necessarily known as characterised in some way.'[34] Shankara's inference that Brahman is '*nirguna*' is, Ramanuja asserts, a misreading of the Upanishads. What the Upanishads actually intend to indicate is that 'some qualities are denied while there are still others characterizing it.'[35]

If Brahman, although supreme, is not without attributes, then it must be determinate, a whole, no doubt, but with verifiable elements. These, according to Ramanuja, are the individual souls, their bodies, inanimate matter and, overseeing them all, Ishwara or God. The absolute, therefore, is not unqualified and indeterminate, but has internal differences (*svagatabheda*), which are real and have separate autonomy (*chidachidvishishtha*). They may be dependent on Brahman, but are not subsumed into 'nothingness' by it.

It follows then that the empirical world is not an illusion. To say that it is purely phenomenal, a product of the illusionary powers of maya, is wrong. Nor can it be dismissed as a product of avidya or nescience. To explain the empirical as 'inexpressible' or anirvachaniya, as Shankara does, is illogical. There is nothing logically inconsistent in accepting that the infinite can give rise to the finite, or that there can be diversity within unity, and a coherence between a whole and its parts.

As a follow up to this argument, Ramanuja articulated his own theory of causation, *satkaryavada*. This was different to Shankara's theory—vivartavada, which we have discussed earlier. Basically, vivartavada does not accept that the effect is different from the cause. The effect could represent the one, unchanging cause in a different form—like a pot does clay—but that does not make it, in essence, different from the cause. This theory was different to that of parinamavada, espoused by other schools of Hindu philosophy, that the cause actually undergoes a change when giving rise to the effect.

Ramanuja postulates a third variant. The cause, he argues, can be the eternal basis, *adhara*, but the effect, even while dependent on it, *adheya*, can have its own independently verifiable attributes, *visheshana*. Brahman is, indeed, the essential substance or *dravya* underlying all reality, and the inner self, *sarvantaratmatvam,* of all things, but individual human beings, jiva, and all other empirical phenomena, are its visheshana—adjectives or attributes—which are *distinct* from it. In other words, if Brahman is the supreme personality, Ishwara or God is its perfect manifestation, and the soul, as embodied in human beings, are imperfect entities. It is the role of Ishwara to guide the imperfect to the perfect, and the perfect to the supreme.

At one stroke then, Ramanuja, while not disputing the supremacy of Brahman, gave to human beings an autonomy, in which they could, through their efforts and the grace of Ishwara, strive towards salvation. In such a saguna world of attributes, Ramanuja's chosen path for salvation was not jnana or knowledge as Shankara emphasised, nor karma or action as the mimamshaks advocated and Shankara decried, but bhakti or devotion.

In fact, on the foundations of his philosophical divergence with Shankara, Ramanuja built an elaborate and appealing edifice of the art of complete surrender, *prapatti,* to the grace, prasada, of Ishwara. What is more, he invested considerable thought to the elaboration of what constituted bhakti. At one level, it was, as is commonly understood, the exhilaration of devotion. At another, it required the conscious acquisition of certain virtues, such as *vimoka,* the constant longing for god, *abhaysa*, the continuous thinking about god, *dana* or charity, *daya* or compassion, *arjavam* or integrity, *satyam* or truthfulness, and *ahimsa* or non-violence. Simple devotion, at the level of prayers or visiting temples, is a lower form of bhakti. But bhakti, reinforced by such virtues and emotionally exalted by prapatti, the complete surrender to god, is, argues Ramanuja, the surest path to salvation, and has the sanction of the Upanishads, the *Bhagavad Gita,* and the *Brahma Sutra.*

Ramanuja's greatest contribution thus was not the denial of Brahman, but the inclusion within its pervasive supremacy, of the validity of devotion to a personal god, and in so doing provide, for ordinary mortals, an alternative form of spirituality to the remote intellectual aloofness of the nirguna Brahman of Shankara. In the structure of Advaitic thought, he provided the philosophical key to open the gates of bhakti.

As Dr S. Radhakrishnan writes:

The sense of personal communion with God involves a real fellowship with an 'other' divine personality. The nirguna Brahman, which stares at us with frozen eyes regardless of our selfless devotion and silent suffering, is not the god of religious insight. Shankara's method, according to Ramanuja, leads him to a void, which he tries to conceal by a futile play of concepts. His nirguna Brahman is a blank.[36]

With Brahman as the background, Ramanuja's focus became Ishwara, a personalised god, accessible to his devotees. For him, he was Vishnu, who symbolised to perfection the supreme spirit, and subsumed within himself the other two members of the Hindu divinity—Brahma and Shiva. In contrast to Shankara's partiality to Shiva—although this was never exclusive and he wrote devotional stotras to Vishnu as well—Ramanuja unleashed a wave of Vaishnava devotion that has left a very marked impact on the evolution of Hinduism.

In the Vaishnava tradition, the world is dependent on the grace of Vishnu, in his role of supporter (*prakari*), controller (*niyanta*), and the sole refuge (*seshi*). The relation of man to such an Ishwara is not one of inhibition. God became a friend, a parent, a child, a confidante, and even a beloved. Through his grace, in any relationship of devotion chosen by a devotee, he is the guarantor of moksha, guiding the dependent soul beyond its mortal barriers. Once these barriers are broken, the liberated soul can reach heaven. Ramanuja goes beyond the normal restraints of philosophy to actually essay such a heaven, where a congregation of liberated souls enjoy the pleasures of crystal-clear streams, fruit laden trees, music and delicious food, and a wonderful climate all through the year.

Ramanuja's Vaishnava theism gave philosophical backing to earlier traditions of Vishnu worship as evidenced in the *Vishnu Purana*, the *Harivamsha* and the *Bhagwata Purana*, as also the later poet–saints called the Alwars in South India. However, once Ramanuja laid the philosophical framework for a Vishnu-focused theism, his thought process was taken much further by later thinkers like Madhava, Nimbarkar, Vallabha and Chaitanya.

—Pavan K. Varma, *Adi Shankaracharya: Hinduism's Greatest Thinker*

22

Sri Madhvacharya and His Doctrine of Dvaita Philosophy

Sri Madhvacharya (1238–1317) is also known as Purna Prajna and Ananda Tirtha. He was a revered philosopher, theologian and spiritual leader who made significant contributions to the fields of Vedanta and Dvaita (dualism) philosophy. He believed that divinity was separate from human consciousness or the soul. Unlike other philosophers of his time, he considered Maya to be a realistic creation of Brahman, not an illusion.

He disagreed with Adi Shankaracharya's philosophy of Advaita Vedanta and Ramanujacharya's philosophy of Vishishtadvaita Vedanta, though he also believed that the path of liberation was through the grace of God. Madhvacharya's Vaishnavism is called Sad-Vaishnavism to distinguish it from the Sri-Vaishnavism of Ramanujacharya.

Sri Madhvacharya was born after Sri Ramanujacharya. After the Advaita Doctrine of Sri Shankaracharya, the Vishistadvaita Doctrine of Sri Ramanujacharya was propounded. Under the powerful influence of this Darshana, Vedic knowledge and devotion to Sri Vishnu began to spread like a flood. In order to strengthen these paths of knowledge and devotion, two Acharya were born in the 12th century. One was Nimbarkacharya and the other Madhvacharya. Both were Acharyas of the Vaishnava faith. Nimbarkacharya propounded the 'Dvaitadvaita Darshana and by advocating a new form of the path of 'Premalakshana' (Loving Devotional Service), he made it easier for devotees to practise devotion to God. This tradition was propagated mostly in the North of India.

In this millennium, in the year 1238, in the southern part of Udipi in southern Karnataka, in Pajak area of Bele Village, Sri Madhvachya was born in a Tulu Brahmin family. His father's name was Madhyageha. His father was a scholar of the Vedas and the Upanishads. His mother's name was Vedavati. Sri Madhvacharya's childhood name was Vasudev. Even as a youth, he was initiated into the order of Sanyasis by Achyutaprekasha.

He was then named Purnapragnya. After becoming a Sanyasi, Purnapragnya studied the Vedas and other Scriptures under Achyutapreksha. During the course of these studies, questions posed by Purnapragnya regarding logic and reasoning would often perplex his Guru. In attempting to answer such questions, Achyutapreksha, who was a follower of the Advaita Doctrine, found that his knowledge was scattered and inadequate. However, he was immensely pleased with Purnapragnya's great scholarship and brilliance, and bestowed upon him the title of 'Vedanta Samrat' (Emperor of Vedanta). Around this time, Purnapragnya became famous by the name of Anandatirtha. Sometime later, Anandatirtha accompanied his Guru on a pilgrimage. They visited various holy places. Enroute, they had debates and discussions regarding the Shastras with many scholars and learned men. Because of their own learning and intellectual brilliance, they were able to defeat many scholars, and in due course reached Trivandrum. At that place, there was a debate with Vidyashankar of Sringeri Matha. Thence, after visiting the Holy Region of Srirangam, they returned to Udupi. Here, Anandatirtha wrote a Bhashya (Commentary) on the Bhagawad Geetha and founded the Dvaita Philosophy of Religion. Subsequently, he wrote a Bhashya on the Vedanta Sutras.

Taking this Bhashya along with himself, he set out on a pilgrimage to Kashi. At Kashi, he held discussions with many scholars on various aspects of the Scriptures. Thereafter, he proceeded to Haridwar and stayed there, engaging himself in fasting, vow of silence, and intense meditation. Sometime later, he set out on a pilgrimage to Badarikashrama (Badrinath). There he pondered deeply over the Scriptures and in the process, he crystallised the tenets of the Dvaita Doctrine. From

Badarikashrama he returned back to Haridwar. Although he had initially composed the Commentary on the Brahma Sutras at Udipi, at Haridwar he was able to refine it further on the basis of his discussions at Kashi and his own deep reflections at Badarikashrama, and gave the Commentary a firm and definitive shape. At the same place, Anandatirtha accepted a disciple of the faith, and after initiating that disciple into the order of the Sanyasis, named him Padmanabhatirtha. Later, the same disciple was to become the successor.

The Acharya built a temple to Sri Krishna at Udupi. This temple is considered to be the main centre of pilgrimage for followers of the Madhva Traditional Order. This Acharya lived on Earth for 79 years, 6 months and 20 days. But under what circumstances did his demise actually take place? Where did it take place? No evidence regarding these questions has been found so far but it is known that after nominating Padmanabhatirtha as his successor, and after handing over the care of the Sri Krishna temple at Udupi to eight of his disciples, the Acharya left Udupi one day without informing anyone. Some scholars are of the opinion that, according to old history, the Acharya may have proceeded to Badarikashrama and may have expired there.

The Doctrine of Sri Madhvacharya

Just as the doctrine of Sri Ramanujacharya is famous by the name of Sri Vaishnava tradition, the doctrine of Sri

Madhvacharya is well known as the 'Sadsampradaya' (The True Tradition). Whereas, the Sri Ramanuja tradition is based on a trio of different truths, the Sri Madhvacharya tradition is based on five different truths.

Brahman

The Paramatma is endowed with infinite auspicious attributes. Compared to Sri Lakshmi and the Jiva, the attributes possessed by the Paramatma such as knowledge, power, bliss etc. are infinitely larger. He is the 'Karta' (doer or instrumental agent) of the eight-fold activity of creation, maintenance, destruction, control, knowledge, repetition, bondage and liberation. He is entirely different from inert, insentient matter, the Jivas, and Prakruti (considered as Mahalakshmi here). All the limbs/ aspects of Bhagawan are pervaded with knowledge and bliss. Whereas the bodies of human beings are full of bones, flesh etc., the body of the Paramatma is filled with auspicious attributes like knowledge etc. to an infinite degree. Bhagawan is by himself completely independent. There is but one Ishvara. Vasudev, Sankarshan, Padhyumna, and many other forms are adopted by Him alone.

Sri Lakshmi

Sri is different from the Paramatma. but is dependent upon the Paramatma. She is the 'charanasewak' (loving, devoted, and intimate servant) of Ishvara. She is eternally liberated.

She is free of the corporeal body, which means that she possesses a divine, transcendental image or form. She is all pervading in space and time like the Paramatma.

Jiva

The Jiva is associated with worldly or material life. In its worldly existence, it is subject to defects like ignorance etc. Jivas are infinite in number. Jivas can be classified into three categories, namely '*Muktiyogya*' (those fit to attain mukti or liberation), '*Nityasamsari*' (those who are ever transmigratory) and '*Tamoyogya*' (those who have base or vile qualities and deserve to be consigned to hells and other dark worlds of existence).

'*Muktiyogya Jivas*' are of five types, namely, Gods, Rishis, Manes, Emperors like Raghu and others, and the '*Uttam Manushya*' (Best of Humans).

'*Uttam Manushyas*' are of two types, namely, '*Chaturguna Upasaka*' (those who worship/adore four qualities of the Paramatma) and '*Ekaguna Upasaka*' (those who worship/adore one quality of the Paramatma).

'*Nitya Samsari*' (Ever Transmigratory) Jivas are always trapped in worldly life, and experience pleasure and pain throughout. They are innumerable and keep moving between heaven, earth and hell all the time.

'*Tamoyogya*' (Those with Base/Vile Qualities).

Jivas are of four types, namely, '*Daitya*' (demons who are sons of Diti), '*Rakshasas*' (demons, goblins in general),

'*Pishachas*' (evil/malevolent spirits) and '*Adhamas*' (low, mean, despicable humans).

'*Muktiyogya*' Jivas take pride in *Brahman.*

'*Nitya Samsaris*' take pride in rebirth. '*Tamoyogya Jivas*' are proud of the Age of Kali.

Prakruti

This tradition holds that Prakruti is the material cause of the Universe. It is also verily the material cause of Time and the Gunas. This Prakruti is of inert, insentient nature, and it is eternal and '*avyapta*' (non-pervasive). Its presiding deity is Goddess '*Rama*'. Prakruti is the '*lingasharir roop*' (of the form of the subtle frame or body) of all Jivas and is at the same time different from the body. The creation and expansion of the three gunas as well as elements such as 'Mahat' and others are due to this Prakruti alone.

Of the three gunas mentioned above, the '*shuddha sattvaguna*' (the pure quality of sattva) is of use for the '*lilasharir*' (the body meant for sport or pastime) of the liberated Jivas. Creation proceeds from the '*Rajoguna*' (the quality of Rajas, whose main characteristics are activity and passion). The Presiding Deity of Sattvaguna is Goddess Lakshmi, that of the Rajoguna is the Deity of the Earth and Sri Durga is the Deity of Tamasguna. Out of these three Gunas, '*Mahat*' (The Great Principle or Buddhi or Intellect) emerges and it is the body of Brahma. From '*Mahat*' arises '*Ahankar'* (The Ego

Principle). Ahankar has three forms, namely, '*Vaikarik*' (The Principle of Evolution and Expansion), '*Tejas*' (The Principle of Light/Energy) and '*Tamas*' (The Principle of Indolence and Delusion). Of these, the Deity of the Principle of Evolution and Expansion is Sri Garuda. The Deity of '*Tejas*' is Sri Sesh and that of '*Tamas*' is Sri Rudra.

The Concept of Moksha or Final Liberation

'*Upasana*' (Worship and Adoration) is the main expedient for securing '*moksha*'. There are two aspects of '*upasana*', one is the form of adherence to and practice of the injunctions contained in the Scriptures and the other is of the form of meditation. Continuous study of the Scriptures results in knowledge as it actually is. Meditation is the setting aside of all thoughts related to material aspects of life and focusing one's thoughts entirely upon Bhagawan. This alone is called '*Nidhiabhyas*'. Reflection upon the Scriptures, listening and recollection, gradually dispels ignorance, doubts, and illusory or false knowledge. The conviction expressed by the phrase '*that is exactly so*' is also called '*Nidhiabhyas*'. In this manner, through '*Nidhiabhyas*' we get the higher or divine knowledge. And from such knowledge, we develop intense devotion.

—Swami Satya Prasad Dasji, *Indian Philosophy*

23

Sri Vallabhacharya and His Doctrine of Shuddhadvaita

Sri Vallabhacharya or Vallabha (1478–1530) was a devotional philosopher who founded the Pushti sect and preached Shuddha Advaita (pure non-dualism) or Monism within the Vaishnava traditions. His school of philosophy is known as Rudrasampradaya or Pushtimarg. He was a Bhakti preacher and considered Sri Krishna, Vishnu's eighth incarnation, to be the highest Brahman.

In Vallabha's interpretation of the Vedanta, Brahman and the universe were one and the same. Brahman manifested as matter and as souls. Bhakti, with true love for God, was the only means of salvation. Vallabha accepted the authority of the Upanishads, Bhagavad Gita and the Brahma Sutra, as well as the Bhagavata Purana.

The founder of the 'Pushti Marg' (the Path of Grace) Sri Vallabhacharya was born at Champaranya near Kashi (Varanasi) in Samvat 1565 on Vaishak Krishna Ekadasi (in the lunar month of Vaishak on the auspicious eleventh day of the dark half) to a Telugu Brahmin couple who hailed from Kankarvad village in South India. His father's name was Sri Laxmanbhattaji and his mother's name was Yellamagaru. He was also known by the name of Sri Mahaprabhuji or Sri Acharyacharan. He is said to be an incarnation of 'Vaisvanara' (Agni or God of Fire). He was a master of all the Vedic Scriptures. He was initiated into the 'ashtadshakshargopalamantra' by Sri Bilvamangalacharya of the Sri Rudra Sampradaya. He was initiated as a 'tridandi sanyasi' by Swami Narayanendratirth. He was married to Mahalakshmi the daughter of Sri Devabhattaji and in due course two sons were born—Sri Gopinath and Vittalnath. Sri Mahaprabhu made three all-India pilgrimage tours wearing only a dhoti and a shawl. Because of his scholarship, simplicity, an attitude in which service was considered the highest and such other qualities, he was duly honoured by Rajas and Maharajas in their kingdoms whichever he visited. Once, in an assembly of scholars in the Vijayanagara kingdom of Krishnadevaraya, there were debates and discussions on the meanings of the shastras between pundits of different faiths which went on for 28 days and in the end, Sri Mahaprabhu emerged victorious. Subsequently, he set out to propagate and spread devotion to Sri Vishnu Bhagawan.

To fit and deserving aspirants for knowledge, he gave the 'nama-nivedan mantra' and initiated many into the faith. Amongst them 84 initiated devotees are important. Each of those places where Sri Mahaprabhuji conducted the systematic recitation of the Srimad Bhagavatam is considered as Sri Mahaprabhuji's 'baithak' (a sacred sect, a place where people gather to listen/converse). Of these, the maximum number of such 'baithaks' are in Rajasthan and Gujarat. As such there are 84 main 'baithaks'. The most important 'baithak' of the Vallabhacharya tradition is Nathdwar in Rajasthan. In 1576, with the help of Purnmal Khattri, it was built in a very grand and beautiful style. There, even today, the service of the Lord is carried out according to the age-old customs of this tradition. Among the numerous texts written by Sri Vallabhacharya are *Prasthanatrayi Vyasutra Bhasya (Anu Bhasya), Geetha Bhasya, Upanishad Bhasya, Jaimini Sutra Bhasya, Bhagwad Tikka Subhodhini, Pushti Pravaha Maryada, Siddhanta Rahasya*, etc.

Before terminating his existence on this Earth, in three and a half shlokas (verses) he advised his sons and those serving him to serve the Lord. In this tradition, 'Bal Krishna' (Lord Krishna in childhood form) is mainly worshipped. Devotees awaken in themselves 'vatsalyabhava' (the sentiments of tenderness and affection which parents feel for their off-spring) by worshipping and serving the childhood form of Lord Sri Krishna. The Grace of the Lord and devotion to Him are considered most essential in this tradition.

The Doctrine

Essentials of the doctrine of Sri Vallabhacharya are contained in the following verse:

Sadrupam Krishnarupam jagadidamakhilam
brihisuchyaprakalpo jeevonuhu
Vrajapaticharane savvasaraiva bhaktihi |
Sakaram brahmatadyad vrajabhuvi ramate
schitdanandarupa-mithyakaraprakaro
Vilasatu satatam Vallabhacharya margaha ||

The whole Universe is real; it is Sri Krishna's own form. Existence and bliss are hidden in it. The atomic Jivas are also part of Him. The Lord of Vraja (Sri Krishna Paramatma) is both the means and the fruit (end) to be attained. Sri Krishna who is existence—consciousness—bliss personified, who is an unimaginable mass of bliss and who indulged in divine sports and dalliances in 'Vraja Bhumi' (the Holy Land of Brindavan, Mathura and surrounding areas), is verily the Parabrahman himself. In this manner, let the Shuddhadvaita Doctrine grow and flourish in the hearts of the devotees.

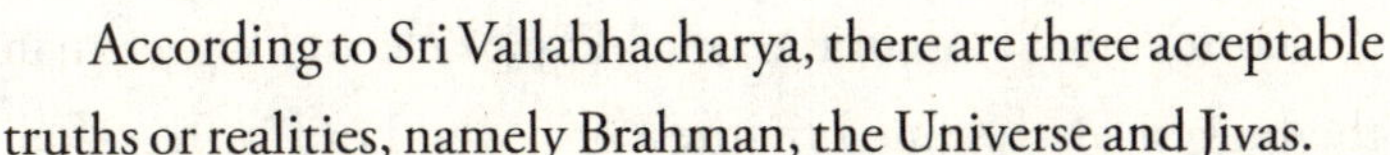

According to Sri Vallabhacharya, there are three acceptable truths or realities, namely Brahman, the Universe and Jivas.

Brahman

Lord Sri Krishna exists at all times everywhere. He is all-knowing and all-pervading. The perishable Universe is the primordial material manifestation of the Lord. All contrary or hostile Dharmas are also part of the Lord. This means that all Dharmas have divine elements in them. Despite being completely independent, the Lord is dependent upon his devotees. Even though the Lord is birthless, He takes birth in the Universe countless times. Although He is '*Atmaram*' (a yogi who is completely content with the knowledge of the self or the realisation of the Self), he yearns for His devotees. Three forms of Brahman have been described. These are '*Adhidaivik*' (of divine origin), '*Adhyatmik*' (relating to the self, spiritual) and '*Antaryami*' (the inner controller). Accepting Purushottam Sri Krishna alone as the Parabrahman, contemplation of innumerable beautiful forms and delightful sports have been regarded as the hymns for the manifestation of bliss in one's life. The Universe is the ground for the Brahman's sports and dalliances. The entire Universe is the Brahman's own creation caused by His sporting activities.

Samo mashkena, samo nagena | Anorniyan mahato mahiyan ||

Forms smaller than the smallest particle and bigger than the biggest are assumed by the Lord. The Lord is free of all material aspects. The Paramatma is the doer of everything, the enjoyer of everything, and all Scriptures, Doctrines and Sciences are vested in Him.

Jiva

Whenever the desire arose in the Lord to indulge in some sport or dalliance, concealing his supremely blissful nature, He manifested himself as His Ray or Emanation, in the form of a Jiva. In the embodied state in worldly life, along with its blissful nature, the Jiva's other virtues such as its glory etc. all disappear. With the disappearance of '*aishvarya*' (glory, grandeur), '*veerya*' (strength, power), '*yash*' (fame, renown) and '*sri*' (fortune, prosperity), other qualities such as '*paradhinata*' (dependence, servility), '*deenata*' (poverty, apathy, meekness) and all such inferior, mean or vile qualities arise in the Jiva. With the disappearance of knowledge and detachment, attachment to worldly things increased. In other words, the Jiva turns away from '*aishwarya*', '*veerya*', '*yash*' and '*sri*' and becomes attached to 'paradeenatha', 'deenata' and 'sarvahinatva'.

In the Srimad Bhagavad Gita (ch 15/7), Bhagawan himself said that in the World, the ancient and eternal Jivatma is a part of Him (a ray or emanation). It has been said in the Shruti as stated above that this Jiva is atomic in size and can be realised through consciousness.

Esho anuratma chetasa veditvyaha

Valagrashtabhagasya shatadhakalpitasya cha |
Jeevaanuhu sah cha vigneyaha so anantyaya kalpate ||

An indication of the size of the Jiva can be had from the fact that it is a hundred times smaller than the front tip of a strand of hair. Nevertheless, it exists as if it pervades the entire body. This is like the lamp which is stationary at one place but its light spreads all around. Just like the flame of a fire, the Jiva has separated from the Paramatma as His emanation. From a fire, thousands of flames emanate and sparks are thrown out, and yet the strength of the fire does not diminish thereby. In the same manner, innumerable Jivas emanate and separate out from the Paramatma. But the Lord continues to be all powerful. Consciousness subsists in the Jeeva just like the fragrance present in a flower and soothing coolness in sandalwood. The Universe, the Jivas, and the Lord are eternal truths. Jivas are considered to be of three types, namely, '*Pushti Jiva*', '*Maryada Jiva*' and '*Pravaha Jiva*'.

'*Pushti Jivas*' exist depending completely upon Bhagawan's grace and become eligible to participate in the Lord's eternal sports and pastimes.

'*Maryada Jivas*' are those who follow the sacred precepts and rules of the Vedas and eventually attain various higher worlds.

'*Pravaha Jivas*' are those who remain engrossed in the world and worldly life and always hanker for enjoyment of worldly happiness.

In determining the nature of the relationship of Brahman with the Jivas and Universe, Sri Vallabhacharya's contention was that the Jiva is a real part of Brahman and the World is also a real part of Brahman. Because there is no difference between the part and the whole, the Jivas, the Universe, and the Brahman are not different from each other. The only difference is that in the Jiva that portion, which is a part of the Brahman's bliss, remains covered and hidden whereas in the case of inert matter both the portions representing Brahman's bliss as well as consciousness remains hidden.

The Material World or the Universe

The World is real because the Lord has himself assumed that form.

Sat eva saumyedamagra asit

O saumya! This world is real—it is the form of Krishna.

Sa atmanam svayamakurute

The Lord himself has assumed the form of this World.

Sa hai tavanasa

Because a desire arose in Him to engage in sports and dalliance, the Lord assumed the form of the Universe.

Sarva khalvidam brahma

This Universe that we behold is a form of the Brahman.

Aham krutsnasya jagataha prabhavaha

I am the originator of the entire Universe (Gita 7/6).

In Sri Vallabhacharya's doctrine, there is a clear distinction between the material world and worldly life. The material world is not an illusion, it is real and true. The material world is a form of Ishvara. However, worldly life is an illusion, of the form of a delusion. Worldly life is defined in terms of the 'Ahambhava'; the Jivatma forgets its basic nature which is akin to Brahman. Ishvara is both the material as well as efficient cause of the world. Ishvara creates the world by His will or resolve but does not undergo any change in His essential form. He is alone as the Creation and He is alone also the Creator.

—Swami Satya Prasad Dasji, *Indian Philosophy*

24

Sri Chaitanya Mahaprabhu and His Doctrine of Achintyabhedabheda

Chaitanya Mahaprabhu (1486–1534) was a spiritual teacher from Bengal. His devotees believe he was Lord Krishna himself. He founded Gaudiya Vaishnavism and promoted the worship of Lord Vishnu as the Supreme Being. Gaudiya Vaishnavism teaches the acceptance of Bhakti Yoga as the method of realising the ultimate truth.

Chaitanya Mahaprabhu popularised the Maha Mantra or Hare Krishna Mantra. He also composed a prayer of eight verses in Sanskrit, called 'Siksastakam'. This is the only written record of his teachings.

Gaurang or Chaitanya Mahaprabhu became a great Vaishnava Acharya of Northern India. This Acharya of Sri Krishna Bhakti in the Vaishnava tradition was born in the village of Navadveep in Bengal in the year Vikram Samvat 1542 (1486 AD) on the full moon day of the month of Phalgun in the evening in Simha Lagna when there was an eclipse of the moon. His father's name was Jagannath Mishra and his mother's name was Shachidevi. Chaitanya Mahaprabhu's boyhood names were Chaitanya Deva and Nimayi. The Swami was very fair complexioned and therefore he came to be called Gaurang.

Navadveep is a famous place in Bengal. At that time, the Muslim invasion of India was underway. Navadveep happened to be the capital of Bengal. There was a centre of learning (university or college) in that place. Students from all parts of India would come there to pursue their studies. Sri Gaurang was extraordinarily intelligent. He studied under Sri Vasudev Sarvabhauma Bhattacharya. Within a short time he completed his studies of Nyaya Shastra. Thereafter, he was married to a girl called Vishnupriya. After marriage, he began to attend to the householder's duties because his father had expired when Gaurang was still a student and his elder brother Vishwaropa had, much earlier, taken sanyasa (joined the order of sanyasis). Consequently, Sri Gaurang began to look after his mother.

Even as a householder, Sri Chaitanya Mahaprabhu would be engrossed in the worship and adoration of Sri Krishna. Then, at the age of 24, he abandoned the householder's life and became a sanyasi (one who belongs to the order of those who have formally renounced everything in life). His Guru's name was Sri Keshavabharathi. After becoming a sanyasi, when Sri Gaurang (Sri Chaitanya) Mahaprabhu reached Puri and beheld Sri Jagannathji (the Presiding Deity of Jagannath Puri temple), he was so overwhelmed with loving devotion that he became intoxicated with love for the Lord and began dancing and singing devotional songs and presently, while doing so, fell down unconscious within the temple. Soon after becoming a sanyasi, for about 6 years, he went on pilgrimages to different parts of India. He propagated devotion to Sri Krishna. He would often be completely absorbed in singing the hymns of Sri Hari and worshipping the Lord. Till the very end of his life, like an intoxicated person, he would constantly chant the names of Sri Krishna Paramatma. Two Acharyas named Nityanand and Advaita would always be by the side of Chaitanya Swami. The Swami established the Order of Succession of Acharyas of his tradition and appointed both these Acharyas as Heads of the Order. In accordance with Swamiji's commands, both these Acharyas began to teach the Precepts of their Swami's doctrine. The chief disciples of Sri Chaitanya Mahaprabhu were Roop, Sanatan, Jeev, Raghunath Bhatt, Raghunath Das and Gopal Bhatt.

The Doctrine

In this tradition, the deity of worship is Sri Krishna. Sri Krishna is Bhagawan himself. It is Sri Krishna Paramatma alone who manifests himself in the form of Brahma, Vishnu and Mahadeva, and creates, sustains and destroys the Universe. From Age to Age, He incarnates upon this Earth to establish Dharma, to destroy Adharma, and to protect the people. Sri Krishna (Vishnu Bhagawan) is the Supreme Truth. He is the infinite ocean of love and compassion. He is without a second. He is existence–consciousness–bliss personified. Since He is beyond Maya (The Lord's own power of illusion), He is '*Nirguna*' (without attributes). He is all-knowing and all-powerful. And because he is the repository or storehouse of auspicious qualities which are endless in magnitude, He is also '*Saguna*' (with attributes). Through His '*Parashakti*' (omnipotent higher powers), He invokes his '*Aparashakti*' (lower powers) and the '*Adhyashakti*' (the first potential power of creation) and through these He creates the Universe. From this perspective, the Paramatma is both the material as well as the efficient cause of the Universe.

The two truths, namely, the Universe and the Jivas, are entirely supported by Ishvara and completely dependent upon Him. However, they are both different as well as identical with Ishvara. The nature of this difference as well as non-difference at the same time is considered in this doctrine

to be beyond thought or inconceivable, and therefore, this Darshana is named '*Achintyabhedabheda*'.

Ishvara's Secret and Inconceivable Powers

This is similar to the analogy of the light present in the Sun and the heat present in a fire. In the same manner, Sri Krishna Paramatma possesses His powers. These powers have no independent existence. They are dependent upon Ishvara. The nature of the relationship between Ishvara and his powers can best be described by the term '*Bhedabhed*' (Co-Existent Difference and Non-Difference).

The 'Shaktis' (Powers or Potencies or Energies) of Ishvara are of three types, namely, '*Chittashakti*' (Innate Potency or Power), '*Jivashakti*' (the Jiva Potency), and '*Mayashakti* (the Power of Illusion). These powers can be described respectively as '*Antarang*' (Inward Acting), '*Tatastha*' (Peripheral or Marginal), and '*Bahiranga*' (Extraneous or External). The '*Chittashakti*' is used to create '*Vaikunta*' (Celestial Abode of Sri Hari). In Vaikunta, there is only '*Shuddha Sattva*' (Non-Material, Incorruptible Spiritual Stuff). '*Maya*' cannot make any ingress there.

Jivas are brought into existence by means of the '*Tatasthashakti*' (the Jiva Potency). Ishvara sets into motion the creation of the Universe from the '*Mahat Tattva*'. Further proliferation and expansion is done by Brahmaji. Men who have realised the ultimate knowledge behold Sri Krishna in the form of the Parabrahman. Sri Krishna Yogis come to know Sri Krishna in the form of the Paramatma while Devotees come to know Him in the form of Bhagawan. Countless forms are assumed by Bhagawan which are classified into three categories, namely, '*Svayamroopa*' (His Transcendental Form), '*Tadokatmaroopa*' (the Forms Emanating from That), '*Aveshtaroopa*'. '*Matsya*' (Fish), '*Kurma*' (Tortoise), and '*Narasimha*' (Man–Lion) are examples of his incarnations for sport. Rishi Sanatkumar, Narad Muni, Emperor Pruthu, Brahma, Sri Sesh (the Primordial Serpent) and others are examples of '*Aveshta*' incarnations. Prosperity, glory, power and might are vested in them alone. Rishi Sanatkumar has the power of knowledge, Narada Muni has the power of devotion, Brahma has the power of creation, and Sri Ananth (Lord Sesh) has the power of upholding.

Devotion Is the Means for Liberation

In this tradition, loving devotion is accorded the highest importance. Devotion to God is considered to be the only means of attaining final liberation. Mahaprabhu Chaitanya would teach devotees that every person has equal rights to practice devotion to Bhagawan. People of every caste or creed can purify themselves through devotion. Following this tenet, Chaitanyaswami initiated people from the lower castes into the faith and made them his disciples. Sri Chaitanya Mahaprabhu's tenet was that loving devotion occupies the highest place. There are five types of 'bhavas' (sentiments) which give characteristic flavour to Loving Devotion. These are '*Shanta*' (of the nature of serenity or peacefulness), '*Dasya*' (of the nature of loving servitude), '*Sakhya*' (of the nature of close companionship or friendship), '*Vatsalya*' (of the nature of tender love and care which parents feel for their offspring), and '*Madhurya*' (of the nature of sweet and blissful union). The sentiment with which Rishis like Sanat, Sanandan and others practised devotion is of the nature of '*shanta bhava*'. The sentiment with which most ordinary folks express their devotion is called '*dasya bhava*'. The feeling of devotion in the Pandavas is called '*sakha bhava*'. The sentiment with which Nandji and Yashoda expressed their devotion is termed '*vatsalya bhava*'. The fifth one, namely '*madhurya bhava*' has been hailed by Chaitanyaprabhu as the best of all. Radha and other Gopis served the Lord with the '*madhurya bhava*'. Chaitanya Prabhu too practiced devotion to the Lord with his mind and body immersed in the '*madhurya bhava*'.

In this tradition, the chanting of the names of the Lord is considered the most important devotional activity. In the Kali Yuga, the recollection or remembrance of the Lord's names is deemed as an excellent expedient for all aspirants.

Harernama harernama harernamaeva kevalam
Kalau nathyeva nasyeva nastyaeva gatiranyatha

In this way, the remembrance or recollection of the names of the Lord has been regarded as the best means available. In addition to the remembrance of the Lord's names, fasting, dancing and such other means numbering 64 in all have been considered acceptable. The service of the Guru has also been accorded considerable importance in this tradition. The trio of Ishvara, the Guru, and Mantra have been accepted as one.

Thus in this traditional order, the Guru is given due importance. It is enjoined that the words of the Guru should be deemed as the words of the Lord himself and accorded due importance. The Goswamis in the traditional order of succession alone are considered to be eligible to be installed as Gurus. Brahmacharis (celibate aspirants) are eligible to join the order but only married men can become Acharyas who head the organisation.

Sri Chaitanyamahaprabhu has preached a 32-syllable 'tarakbrahmaharinam mahamantra' (a great mantra consisting of the Brahman Sri Hari's names which constitute a means of deliverance from the bondage of samsara) with the intention of uplifting Jivatmas in this Kali Yuga. This mantra is as follows:

Hare Krishna Hare Krishna
Krishna Krishna Hare Hare
Hare Rama Hare Rama
Rama Rama Hare Hare

In this Tradition, it is the practice to apply a high 'tilak' (traditional marking) of 'gopichandan' (the sacred soil of Dwarka or Brindavan) on the forehead. On both the hands, the chest opposite the heart and other areas of the body are stamped with the words 'Radha Krishna' and they also carry the 'japamala' (rosary, beads for chanting).

Literature pertaining to this tradition is available in Sanskrit and Bengali. Roop and Sanatan Goswami have written many texts. Some of these are, 'Vidgadhamadhav', 'Ujjwalneelamani', 'Danakelikaumudi', 'Bahustavavali', 'Ashtadasha Leelakand', 'Padmavali', 'Govindabirudavali', 'Laghubhagavata', 'Bhaktirasamrutasindhu', 'Vrajavilasavarnan', 'Geethavali', 'Vaishnavatoshit', 'Haribhaktitivilas', 'Bhagavatamrut', and 'Siddhantasar'. Even today these texts are accorded the status of ancient holy texts.

Moksha

In this Vaishnava faith, Mukti is considered to be of two types. One is 'Aishvaryalabh or Svargabhog' (the acquisition of wealth, prosperity and power or the enjoyment of heavenly pleasures) and the other is residence in Vaikunta. Devotees who reach Vaikunta by means of worship and adoration of the Lord will never get trapped again in the cycle of birth and deaths and transmigration. Four types of Mukti have been accepted. However, 'Sayujyamukti' is given maximum importance.

—Swami Satya Prasad Dasji, *Indian Philosophy*

25

Sri Ramcharitmanas

Sri Ramcharitmanas (circa 800 BCE) is one of the most revered scriptures in Hinduism. It was composed in the sixteenth century by the poet-saint Goswami Tulsidas. It narrates the story of Sri Rama, an incarnation of Lord Vishnu.

The events in Sri Ramcharitmanas take place during the Treta Yuga. Through the divine lilas of Sri Rama, the scripture explores human values and the concept of dharma. It offers spiritual guidance and moral teachings to all Hindus, and contains the precepts of Sanatana Dharma. Sri Rama is the embodiment of truth and morality. He is the ideal son, the ideal husband, the ideal sibling, the ideal householder, the ideal warrior and, above all, the ideal leader and king.

Nirgun–Sagun Brahma and Stutis

In the Ramcharitmanas, Tulsidas says that according to the sages (men of wisdom), the Vedas and the Puranas, the Nirguna Brahman (attributeless and formless Absolute) and Saguna Brahman (Absolute with attributes and form) are the same. He also says that Shri Ram is the all-pervading Brahma.

There are two aspects of God—the one unqualified and
the other qualified. Both these aspects are unspeakable,
unfathomable, without beginning and without parallel.
To my mind, greater than both is the Name, that has
established Its rule over both by Its might.

There is no difference between qualified Divinity and
the unqualified Brahma: so declare the sages and men
of wisdom, the Vedas and the Puranas. That which is
attributeless and formless, imperceptible and unborn,
becomes qualified under the influence of the devotee's love.

How can the Absolute become qualified? In the same way as water and the hail-stone are non-different in substance. Infatuation is out of the question for Him whose very Name is like the sun to the darkness of error.

Shri Ram, who is Truth, Consciousness and Bliss combined, is like the sun; the night of ignorance cannot subsist in Him even to the smallest degree. He is the Lord whose very being is light; there is no dawn of understanding in His case (for the dawn presupposes night and night there is none in the sunlight of Shri Ram).

Joy and grief, knowledge and ignorance, egoism and pride—these are the characteristics of a Jiva (finite being). Shri Ram is the all-pervading Brahma; He is supreme bliss personified, the highest Lord and the most ancient Being. The whole world knows it.

He walks without feet, hears without ears and performs actions of various kinds even without hands. He enjoys all tastes without a mouth (palate) and is a most clever speaker even though devoid of speech.

He touches without a body (the tactile sense), sees without eyes and catches all odours even without a nose (the olfactory sense). His ways are thus supernatural in every respect and His glory is beyond description.

In deep waters the fish are as happy as ever, just as those who have taken refuge in Shri Hari (i.e., myself) never fall into trouble of any kind. With full-blown lotuses the lake appears as charming as when the absolute Brahma appears with form.

Of His own free will the Lord descends on earth for the sake of gods, Earth, cows and the Brahmanas. Spurning all the varieties of final beatitude the worshippers of His qualified form (come down and) remain with Him even on earth.

The doing of Shri Ram when appearing in an embodied form, Bhavani, cannot be logically interpreted by the power of reason or speech. Realizing this, those who know the truth about Him and are full of dispassion adore Shri Ram, discarding all theological speculation.

Shri Ram's Adoration by Lord Shiva

Hail to You, Ram, Spouse of Rama (Sita), Reliever of the afflictions of worldly existence! Protect this servant, who is obsessed with the fear of transmigration. O King of Ayodhya, Ruler of the gods, Lord of Lakshmi, all-pervading Master! Having fled to You for refuge, I implore You: pray, extend Your protection to Me.

By disposing of Ravana who possessed as many as ten heads and twenty arms, You rid the earth of many a severe scourge. The hosts of demons were a veritable swarm of moths that were reduced to ashes by the fierce glow of Your fire-like arrows.

An exceedingly beautiful jewel of the terrestrial globe, You have armed Yourself with an excellent bow, arrows and quiver. You are a radiant sun as it were to disperse the thick darkness prevailing in the night of pride, gross ignorance and attachment.

The hunter in the form of lust has laid low the human deer by piercing his heart with the shafts of evil desire: O Lord! Pray, kill the hunter and thus save the life of these poor helpless creatures, lost as they are in the wilderness of sensuality, O Hari!

People are stricken with a host of diseases and bereavements, which are surely the result of neglecting Your feet. Those men who cherish no love for Your lotus-feet continue to drift in the fathomless ocean of mundane existence.

They are ever most wretched, impure and unhappy, who have no devotion to Your lotus-feet. On the other hand, they who derive their sustenance from Your stories hold the saints and the eternal Lord (Yourself) as constantly dear to them.

They are free from passion, greed, pride and arrogance; prosperity and adversity are alike to them. That is why sages give up forever all faith in Yoga (mental discipline) and gladly become Your servants.

With a pure heart and under a solemn pledge they constantly and lovingly adore Your lotus-feet. Regarding honour and ignominy alike, all such saints move about happily on earth.

O Hero of Raghu's line, invincible and exceedingly staunch in battle, indwelling as a bee the lotus-heart of sages, I take refuge in You. I repeat Your Name and bow to You, O Hari; You are a sovereign remedy for the disease of birth and death and an enemy of pride.

I constantly greet You, Lakshmi's Spouse, supreme abode of goodness, amiability and compassion. O Delight of the Raghus, put an end to all pairs of contrary experiences (such as joy and sorrow, pleasure and pain, attraction and repulsion, etc.); O Ruler of the earth, just cast a glance on this humble servant.

Rudrashtaka or a Hymn of Eight Verses Addressed to Lord Shiva by Shri Ram

Reflecting on my awful fate, the Brahmana prostrated himself before Lord Shiv and, with joined palms and his voice choked with emotion, he prayed as follows:

I adore You, the guardian of the south-east quarter and Ruler of the whole universe, eternal bliss personified, the omnipresent and all-pervading Brahma manifest in the form of the Vedas. I worship Lord Siva, shining in His own glory, devoid of material attributes, undifferentiated, desireless, all-pervading consciousness, having nothing to wrap about Himself except ether (or enveloping ether itself).

I bow to the supreme Lord, who is devoid of form, transcendent and extra-cosmic, beyond speech, understanding and sense perception, terrible yet gracious, the seed of the mystic syllable OM, the Ruler of Kailasha, the Devourer even of the great Time-Spirit and the abode of virtues.

I adore the all-merciful Shankara, the universal Lord, who is loved by all and yet unfathomable, who is possessed of a form white as the snow-clad Himalaya, and radiant with the beauty of a myriad Cupids, whose head sparkles with the lovely stream of the Ganga, whose brow is adorned by the crescent moon and neck coiled by serpents, who has tremulous pendants hanging from His ear-lobes, is possessed of beautiful eyebrows and large eyes, who has a cheerful countenance and a blue speck on His throat, and who has a lion-skin wrapped round His waist and a garland of skulls round His neck.

I take my refuge in Bhavani's Spouse, the supreme Lord, terrible, exalted, intrepid, indivisible, unborn and invested with the glory of a myriad suns, who roots out the threefold agony and holds a trident in His hand and who is accessible only through love.

Beyond number, ever blessed, bringing about universal destruction at the end of each round of creation, a source of perpetual delight to the virtuous, Slayer of the demon Tripura, Consciousness and Bliss personified, dispeller of delusion, be propitious, my Lord, be propitious, O Destroyer of Cupid.

So long as they worship not the lotus-feet of Uma's Lord, there is no happiness nor peace nor cessation of suffering for men either in this world or in the next. Therefore, be propitious, my Lord, dwelling as You do in the heart of all living beings.

I know not Yoga (concentration), nor Japa (the muttering of prayers) nor ritual. I simply bow to you at all times and at every moment, O Sambhu! Pray, protect me, my lord, miserable and afflicted by sufferings attendant on old age and birth (and death) as I am, O Lord Shambhu!

This hymn of eight verses was uttered by the Brahmana in order to propitiate Lord Hara. Shri Shambhu is pleased with those men who devoutly repeat it.

—Pavan K. Varma, *The Greatest Ode to Lord Ram: Tulsidas's Ramcharitmanas*

26

THE BHAKTI MOVEMENT

The Bhakti movement was a spiritual and social reform movement from around the eighth to the twelfth century. It promoted personal devotion to God instead of ritualistic practices. It helped to break caste barriers, promoted equality and made spirituality accessible to all.

The Bhakti movement led to the revival and expansion of Hinduism. Shiva and Vishnu became the primary gods, and a large number of tribal gods and goddesses were assimilated into the mainstream Hindu religion by making them subsidiary to Shiva and Vishnu.

The Bhakti movement started in South India and spread to the entire country. It included the lower castes and broke the Vedic monopoly of the Brahmans. It aimed to reform society by removing the barriers of caste, creed and gender that stood between the devotee and God, and the need of a priest for praying to God.

Jnaneshvara, Namadeva, Tukaram, Chandidasa, Vidyapati, Surdas, Bihari, Jayadeva, Chaitanya Mahaprabhu, Ramananda, Tulsidas, Kabir, Basavanna, Allama Prabhu, Tikkana, Yerrapragada, Potana, Vemana, Aantaal, Mirabai, Lal Ded

How did Hinduism survive the onslaught of the proselytising Turkic invaders? This is an important question, since the Islamic rule that followed used the powers of the state to propagate the superiority of Islam and believed in converting as many infidels as possible to its faith. There are examples, like that of Indonesia, where an overwhelmingly Hindu and Buddhist population almost entirely converted to Islam in the space of three centuries, after Islamic sultanates were established there at the beginning of the thirteenth century. What was it that happened in India that gave it relative immunity from the proselytising prowess of Islamic rulers who ruled almost the entire country for over six centuries?

The simple answer to this is that Hinduism reinvented itself through the Bhakti movement, enabling a democratic decentralisation of the Hindu faith, so widespread in nature, and so full of ardour and conviction, that it has few parallels in history. Many Hindu temples—which played a pivotal role in the preservation and dissemination of religion—were razed; there did occur a fundamental discontinuity in the cerebral conversations that allowed Hindu civilisation to evolve and rejuvenate itself; centres of learning and repositories of scriptures and commentaries were, indeed, destroyed; the practice of Hinduism in structures hitherto taken for granted received a serious setback; Hindus were discriminated against through instrumentalities like the jiziya and pilgrim taxes. But Hinduism escaped the confining cage intended to contain it by simply slipping through the crevices. It rediscovered itself, not through the institutional support that it had earlier enjoyed through the patronage of kings, or on the basis of the injunctions of the Brahminical class, but by embracing the masses of its followers directly. In this process, faith and its perpetuation became part of an inner world of devotion, surrender and personal belief; the formal apparatus of religion became largely superfluous; the priestly class was relatively marginalised; and formal rituals were seen as mostly unnecessary. The net outcome was the reinvention of Hinduism through a powerful reform movement which looked inward rather than outward, and drew its sustenance from the people at large rather than the dictates of a rarefied elite at the top. A rainbow-coloured butterfly of this nature—combining devotional fervour, individual autonomy and social irreverence could hardly be killed by the conqueror's sword.

Hinduism had always been a way of life—it did not have only one book, nor one god, nor one church, nor one set of prescriptive rituals. Such a religion was structured to evade destruction because of the variable nature of its belief systems and practices, and the absence of any one central pillar which, if demolished, could endanger the entire edifice. At the same time, Hinduism had also developed very strong foundations of thought and practice in the millennia prior to the Islamic invasion. An important aspect of this strength was the ability to evolve and adapt. We have seen in detail how the nirguna aspect of divinity transitioned to the philosophical sanction for saguna practice. The foundations of devotional theism were laid by Ramanuja in the eleventh century. In creating space for the devotion to a personal god, Ramanuja, and the philosophers who followed him, were responding to a felt need. The *Bhagwata Purana*, dated to the eighth century, narrated the delightful exploits of Krishna as a child, and his irresistible attractions as a lover. The Krishna of the Bhagwad Gita, written centuries earlier—who had asked for personal surrender from his devotees—now descended from the pedestal of exalted divinity to a god ready for appropriation at a personal level. Jayadeva's *Gita Govinda* (twelfth century), which immortalised the love lore of Radha and Krishna, took this process further. Around the same time as the *Bhagwata Purana*—and even earlier—the sects of the Nayanars and Alvars in the south were propagating a new form of bhakti for Shiva and Vishnu respectively, which dispensed with ritual and formal rites of worship. These developments prior to the Islamic invasion had prepared Hindus for the democratisation and decentralisation of their religion. The

Bhagwata was translated from the original Sanskrit to almost all the regional languages. There were forty translations in Bengali alone.

The linguistic appropriation by vernacular languages of a religious tradition that was earlier largely propagated through Sanskrit, played a very significant role in ensuring the pan-Indian spread of the Bhakti movement. One of the earliest manifestations of this renaissance was seen in Maharashtra. Jnaneshvara (1271–1296) wrote the *Bhavarthapadika*, also called the *Jnaneshvari*, which was a long commentary on the Bhagwad Gita. Written in Marathi, it soon acquired huge popularity, especially since it was written to a rhyme and metre that could be sung and chanted; its appeal was enhanced by examples and analogies that related to the ordinary life of its lay readers. Jnaneshvara, also known as Jnanadeva, was a member of the Varkari sect which commenced regular, popular pilgrimages to the Vithoba Temple in Pandharpur dedicated to Vishnu. The pilgrims, drawn from all sections of society, participated in spontaneous kirtans during their journey, giving to their faith a new and increasingly popular mass base.

Namadeva (1270–1350), who was born around the same time as Jnaneshvar but lived for five decades more, was also a great devotee of Vithoba. Namadeva's hymns, expressed in commonly understood language, are characterised by a deep and intense devotion that was internalised by Hindus at large.

I die unless Thou succor bring,
O haste and come, my God and King!
To help me is a trifling thing,
Yet Thou must haste, my God and King!
O come (how Nama's clamours ring)
O haste and come, my God and King![37]

Breaking new ground, Namadeva showed scant regard for the hierarchies of caste. His inner circle included a barber, a gardener, a potter, a woman (Janabai, the maid), and Chokha, an 'untouchable'. His simple but powerful message was that where there was devotion, social hierarchies or ritualistic purity did not matter.

The Muslims razed the temple at Pandharpur, but could not destroy the Bhakti movement. The movement received a new impetus from Eknath (1533–1599), who republished the *Jnaneshvari* and wrote learned commentaries on Valmiki's Ramayana, and the *Bhagwata Purana*. 'But Eknath did more. He invented, as it were, a new form of deep religious life that needed no institutions or monasteries, no resignation from the world. He was a family man, devoted, austere, whose life was regulated around his hearth and his manuscripts, and yet he was a mystic. He showed how, whatever obstacles the Muslims put in the way, the Hindu could aspire to the deepest experience of his religion within the ordinary framework of life. Every day he practiced

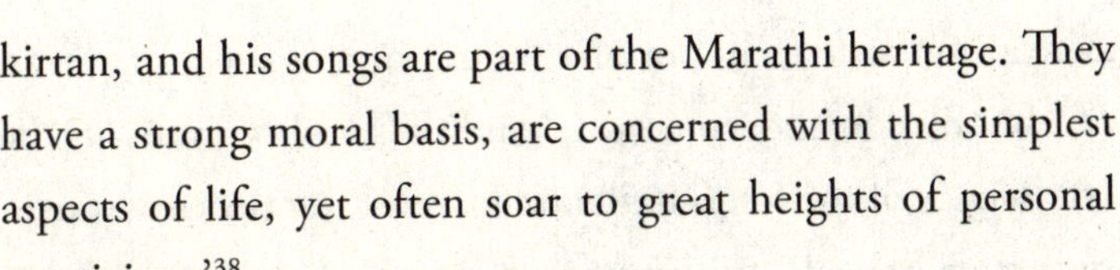

kirtan, and his songs are part of the Marathi heritage. They have a strong moral basis, are concerned with the simplest aspects of life, yet often soar to great heights of personal mysticism.'[38]

If Namadeva was a Brahmin, Tukaram (1598–1650), arguably the greatest of the Bhakti poets of Maharashtra, came from a humble rural family of grain traders. His hymns expressed an irresistible longing for the ecstasy of the highest spiritual experience, in the face of which the ritualism and ceremony of organised religion mattered little. In writing of his personal yearning for union with the Absolute, he transported his audience to a new level of personal interface with religion.

As on the bank the poor fish lies
And gasps and writhes in pain,
Or as a man with anxious eyes
Seeks hidden gold in vain—
So is my heart distressed and cries
To come to thee again
Thou knowest, Lord, the agony
Of the lost infant's wail,
Yearning his mother's face to see.
(How oft I tell this tale!)
O, at Thy feet the mystery
Of the dark world unveil![39]

Bengal too was an important centre for the rise and spread of the Bhakti movement. Chandidasa, who lived at the confluence of the fourteenth and fifteenth centuries, wrote in his native Bengali and is regarded by many as the founder of modern Bengali literature. His poetry had an intensity borne out of personal experience. He was the village priest but was deeply in love with a washerwoman named Ramini. It was a liaison deeply frowned upon by the village community, but in keeping with the irreverence towards caste shown by many leading figures of the Bhakti movement, Chandidasa was not willing to disown it. On the contrary, he derived sustenance and inspiration from the story of the love between Radha and Krishna.

Indeed, Krishna and Radha were the focus of other writers, too, of the Bhakti school. Vidyapati (1352–1448), a younger contemporary of Chandidasa, lived in Mithila, Bihar, and wrote in the language he knew best—Maithili. Surdas (1483–1563) wrote in Braj, the language of the region around Mathura. Braj was also the choice of expression for Bihari (1595–1664), court-poet of Jayasimha, the ruler of the kingdom of Amber in Rajasthan. Govindadasa, in the sixteenth century, wrote in Brajaboli, a local dialect having elements of both Bengali and Maithili.

All these poets acquired immense popularity. Their compositions had a sensuous simplicity, deriving strength from being based on the local idiom and turn of phrase.

To the masses they provided a scripture that could be comprehended without effort and was thoroughly enjoyable for its lyrical informality. There was a directness of appeal in their writings that invoked an immediacy of response. Their lines sat easily on the tongue of the worshipper. Not surprisingly, the development of kirtans—the fast tempo, community singing of devotional songs—had a direct correlation with the popularity of these works. By this time, Jayadeva's *Gita Govinda* and Bilvamangala's *Krishnalilamrita* (eleventh century) had also been translated into other regional languages. The cumulative result was that the worship of Krishna, and especially his love lore with Radha, shifted from the sanctum sanctorum of the temple to the dust and din of daily life. Krishna's sensual love-play made a transition from the refined if passionate milieu of Sanskrit poetics to the earthy and seductive medium of the lingua franca of the masses. Radha and Krishna, humanised by Jayadeva, were now depicted in as many situations as it was possible for human lovers to find themselves in. It was a case of the divine imitating the human, and the human being enriched by the divine. The Lord and his consort were removed from the rarefied atmosphere of lotus-leaved arbours and ethereal jungle thickets, and placed with poetic adroitness in more familiar settings. Their rasa leela continued with unabated ardour, but in new situations that were inspired by—and related to—the humdrum routine of ordinary people. Thus,

Chandidasa's Krishna saw Radha as she emerged from the river in the village, twisting her sari to dry like any village belle would do:

Who was that girl?
Friend, who was that girl
Inflaming the river
With her fair skin?
The gold necklace
On the peak of her breasts
Shone as the moon on the mountain snow,
The darkness in tears,
The shadows of the moon,
A flood of black hair rolled up on her hips.
She rose from the river
Like a slice of the moon,
Glistening in twilight dark.
As I stood watching
And losing myself,
She walked away wringing and twisting my soul
Together with her sari—dripping, blue.
My heart still shivers in a fever of love.[40]

Bihari's eyes saw Krishna and Radha exchange secret messages as Radha sat in a gathering of elders:

When he saw Radha
Sitting among the elders
You know what the wily Krishna did?
He brushed his forehead with a lily
Implying
'Say yes, dear beloved,
See, I'm even falling at your feet!'
Clever Radha
Consenting,
Flashed her mirrored ring
At the sun
And hid away her hand
In the mounds of her breasts
As though to say:
'When the sun sets under the hills Lover,
I will come to you.'[41]

In the popular psyche, Krishna and Radha became the universal symbol for the lover and the beloved. Krishna was the ideal nayak, hero, and Radha the ideal nayika, heroine. As a genre, the poetry about them came to be known as riti-kala or sringara-kala. The furtively ecstatic world of Radha, the woman in love, is of particular interest to these poets. Her transition from adolescence to womanhood, her inner turmoil, her uncertainties, the simplicity and intensity of her feelings, the shadow play between desire and her innate shyness—these themes fascinated them. Surdas described Radha's first meeting with Krishna—the burning sensual denouement under the as yet opaque surface of innocence:

'Who are you, my fair one?' the Dark One asks,
'And where is your family, your house?
You've never been seen in Braj lanes.'
'Never you mind—I stay in my yard
And play behind my gate, never venture out
Where, I've heard, Nanda's boy is bound
To steal our butter and curd.'
'Now what of yours could I possibly steal?
Come on, let's both of us play.'
The gourmet of love, Sur's Lord, with his words
Disarms poor Radha, simple girl.[42]

What we are seeing here is the appropriation of divinity to a personal level of devotion that is quite beyond formal structures of religion.

Surdas was the foremost disciple of Vallabhacharya, or Vallabha (1471–1531), a Telugu philosopher who propounded the Shuddha Advaita doctrine, and founded the Krishna sect of Vaishnavism in the Braj region of northern India. Vishambhar Mitra, universally known as Chaitanya (1486–1534), was the Bengali mystic who took Vaishnava bhakti to new heights. For his followers, he was Shri Krishna

Chaitanya Mahaprabhu, the very incarnation of Krishna. Chaitanya argued that divinity was characterised by several shaktis, the three principal ones being jiva shakti, maya shakti and svarupa shakti. Individual souls were the emanation of the Lord's jiva shakti; the manifest world was a creation of the Lord's maya shakti; the expression of the Lord's own bliss was svarupa shakti. The relation between these shaktis was one of achintyabhedabheda or inconceivable oneness and difference, wherein each was different but all were one with Krishna. For Chaitanya, Krishna was not only the avatar of Vishnu, but also the highest manifestation of the divine, its supreme rasa. In this aspect, when he unites with Radha, the highest Shakti, the result is an irresistible experience of madhurya or sweetness, which is what the devotee must aspire to. It is said that for the evolution of his philosophy, Chaitanya sent six Goswamins, or theologians, to Vrindavan, to actually experience this madhurya. His form of worship required not temples or abstruse scriptures, but ecstatic singing and dancing, and the chanting of the Hare Krishna Maha mantra, the essence of the Gaudiya Vaishnava sect he founded. While his focus was not expressly on social reform, his practice of bhakti rejected the distinctions of caste and promoted a devotional egalitarianism that greatly increased its attraction.

The many-splendoured personality of Krishna, the butter-stealing adorable child and the passionate lover, lent itself easily to the rise of the Bhakti cult around him. But maryada purushottam Rama was also included in a very significant way. Ramananda (1400–1470), was probably born in south India, where he was a follower of the Vaishnava order set up by the philosopher Ramanuja. Later he migrated to Varanasi and established his own sect, the Ramanandis. Notwithstanding the popularity of Valmiki's Ramayana and other works based on the epic, there is no proof of a cult exclusively devoted to Rama prior to this. Ramananda looked upon Rama as the supreme God; Sita, his shakti, and Hanuman, his faithful devotee, were part of this devotional triad. 'Ramananda was strongly opposed to the restrictions and injustices of caste. He threw his sect open to all, and his twelve personal disciples are said to have included women, an "outcaste", and even a Muslim. This frank egalitarian basis and the exclusive use of the vernacular set the sect apart from many others.'[43] Unfortunately, like much other valuable Hindu heritage lost following the Muslim invasion, only one hymn of Ramananda is extant.

The person who let loose a tidal wave of bhakti for Rama was Goswami Tulsidas (1532–1623). His magnum opus, the *Ramcharitmanas*, which literally translates into 'the splendid lake of Rama's exploits', is arguably the greatest ode to Lord Rama. Like other writers of the Bhakti movement, Tulsidas, although well-versed in Sanskrit, chose to write in Awadhi, the language of the masses in northern India. Following the basic narrative of Valmiki, Tulsidas's *Ramcharitmanas* was an epic in itself—12,800 lines divided into 1,073 stanzas and seven kandas or sections. It also ranks among the greatest works of literature in the world, using a scintillating rhyme and metre that could be memorised and chanted with ease by the common devotee. Its soaring popularity has led to it being compared to the Bible for most Hindus, especially in north India. Mahatma Gandhi regarded it 'as the greatest book in all devotional literature'.

Tulsidas was, indeed, partial to the Brahman class, to which he himself belonged. However, his main contribution was to provide a philosophical argument which, overarching the dichotomy between nirguna and saguna, rendered the redeeming powers of bhakti to Rama as the sole and only fulfilling spiritual pursuit—*Aguna saguna dui Brahma sarupa, akath, agaath, anaadi anoop*: Nirguna and saguana are two aspects of the same Brahman—unspeakable, unfathomable, eternal and unparalleled. But unalloyed bhakti to Rama is greater than both, because even the mere recital of His name is a guarantor of salvation. There is no need, therefore, to waste time on the philosophical quibble over nirguna or saguna—*Binu pada chalai sunai binu kana, kara binu karam karai bidhi nana, anana rahita sakal rasa bhogi, binu bani bakata bada jogi*: The devotee immersed in pure devotion can walk without feet, hear without ears, perform tasks without hands, enjoy all taste without a sense of taste and speak eloquently without a tongue. Tulsidas does not negate the nirguna Brahman. But his argument is—*Aguna, aroopa, alakh aj joi, bhagata prema bas saguna so joi*: Even Brahman—attribute-less, formless, imperceptible and unborn—takes the form of Rama due to the bhakt's devotion.

Tulsidas is in his element explaining the power of bhakti which, for him, is the greatest and easiest path to redemption for an ordinary mortal. It is a complete and independent path to salvation; it is above the dialectics of jnana and vijnana, above knowledge and reasoning. Indeed, knowledge is subordinate to bhakti. The path of bhakti is easily accessible, where the grace of the Lord is effortlessly obtained. Bhakti creates detachment to worldly things and fills the devotee with divine love. In a beautiful chaupai or quartet, Tulsidas says that when a devotee's body vibrates with joy in singing the praises of Rama, when the speech quivers with ecstasy, and the eyes brim over with tears in surrendering to Rama, and he or she is completely free from pride, desire and ego, then Rama is entirely accessible to the devotee. In the face of this joy, nothing else matters. Rama, in the words of Tulsidas, says exactly this to Shabri, who belonged to the lowest scale of the social ladder but had spent her entire life in selfless devotion to him—*Jati paati kula dharma badhai, dhana bala parijana guna chaturai, bhagati heena nara sohai kaisa, binu jala barid dekhia jaisa*: Caste, kinship, lineage, dharma, reputation, wealth, family, accomplishments and ability mean nothing for a person lacking in bhakti, who is of no more worth than a cloud without water. Interestingly, while certainly qualifying to belong to the Vaishnava school of bhakti, Tulsidas effortlessly bridges the divide with the Shaivas—in his *Ramcharitmanas*, Rama pays fulsome tribute to Shiva, and Shiva is all praise for Rama.

In Punjab, the great Guru Nanak (1469–1539), who founded the Sikh faith, was greatly influenced by the Bhakti movement. Sikhism, under Nanak, and the nine Gurus who followed him, the last being Guru Gobind Singh (1666–1708), created a remarkably sublime and powerful monotheistic faith of nirguna bhakti. In clear Vedantic tones, its mul mantar or fundamental prayer—Ik Onkar: There is only one Supreme Being—made a powerful call of universal spiritual appeal. Like Brahman, the Sikh Absolute is nirankar (formless), akal (timeless), karta purakh (the Creator), agam agochar (incomprehensible and invisible) and is Waheguru (wonderous Teacher). The religion emphasised the non-duality of divinity—*Ek noor te sab jag upja*: From one luminous light the entire universe arose. In this one statement, it pole-vaulted above conventional religious orthodoxies.

Of great importance in the Sikh faith is mehar, kirpa, karam or the Grace of God. Guru Nanak taught that to obtain this, the most important form of worship is bhakti. Guru Arjan, in the *Sukhmani Sahib*, recommended that true religion is one of loving devotion to God. Selfless devotion and service can lead to Sach Khand or the Realm of Truth, which is the final union with the spirit of God, akin to the Advaita notion of brahmanubhav. Thus, Sikhism considers simran (the meditative remembrance of God) and japna (chanting or kirtan of God's name) to be an essential part of religious practice. The singing of the Guru's hymns as contained in the Guru Granth Sahib—the only divine symbol of worship recognised by Sikhism—was practised through the shabad kirtans. The passages of the Guru Granth Sahib were poetically composed in rhyme, and lent themselves easily to exceptionally soulful musical compositions based on thirty-one ragas of classical music. Religious practice also strongly emphasised the importance of seva or service of humankind, and this included vand chakko or giving to the needy for the benefit of the community. Even today, the Sikhs are in the forefront of community service. Their Gurudwaras are now, as then, open to all, regardless of religion, background, caste or race. The langar or free vegetarian meals served there are also accessible to all, without recognising any distinctions of caste, creed or status.

Unlike other Bhakti movements of that period, the Sikh faith was forced to assume a military profile in order to resist and fight Muslim oppression. Two of the Sikh Gurus, Guru Arjan and Guru Tegh Bahadur, were brutally executed by Mughal emperors Jahangir and Aurangzeb respectively, and both for the same reason—refusal to convert to Islam. The tenor of Sikhism, however, was emphatically eclectic.

Sikh scriptures refer to Hindu deities like Shiva, Brahma, Parvati, Lakshmi, Rama and Krishna, as also to Allah—not for purposes of worship but only to indicate alternate names of that One God. The Guru Granth Sahib, which was compiled by Guru Gobind Singh in 1678, contains the hymns of not only the Sikh Gurus but also includes the traditions and teachings of thirteen Hindu Bhakti movement sants, including Ramananda and Namadeva. It also includes a Muslim Sufi, Sheikh Farid and Kabir, who states in the Guru Granth Sahib: 'I am not Hindu nor Muslim.'

Kabir (1440–1518) was the most outspoken iconoclast of the Bhakti movement. He was born in Varanasi, and either born a Muslim or brought up by a Muslim weaver family. However, early in life, he became a disciple of Ramananda, imbibing not only his devotionalism but also his strong leaning towards Advaita philosophy. In earthy and colloquial language—Awadhi, Braj Bhasha, even Bhojpuri—easily understood by the masses, and expressed through pithy and earthy dohas called 'bani', he advocated the search for inner truth through humility, renunciation, detachment, meditation, solitude, kindness, love and bhakti. For him, God could be called Rama or Hari, or Allah or Khuda, but the spirit of Vedantic monism is clearly identifiable in his compositions, and his collection of lyrics is often called *Nirguni Bhajans*:

If God be within the mosque, then to whom does this world belong?
If Ram be within the image which you find upon your pilgrimage
Then who is there to know what happens without?
Hari is in the East, Allah is in the West,
Look within your heart, for there you will find both Karim and Ram
All the men and women of the world are His living forms
Kabir is the child of Allah and of Ram:
He is my Guru, He is my Pir.[44]

Kabir was eloquent in his contempt for religious ritual, holy scriptures and hypocritical preachers:

There is nothing but water at the holy bathing places;
and I know that they are useless since I have bathed in them.
The images are all lifeless, they cannot speak;
I know, for I have cried aloud to them.
The Puranas and the Koran are mere words;
lifting up the curtain, I have seen.[45]

Belonging to a family of low-caste weavers, he had little time for the restrictions of caste or status:

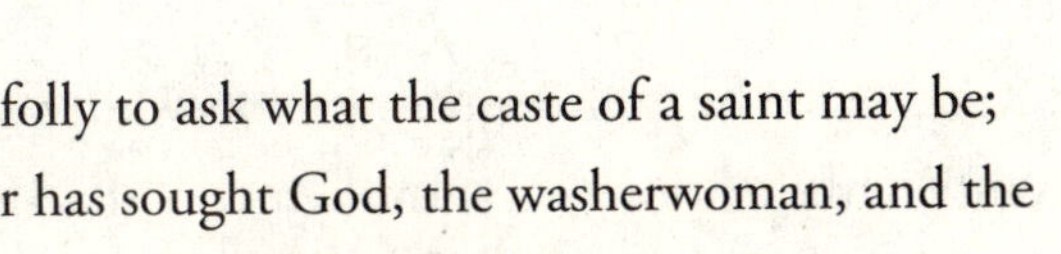

It is but folly to ask what the caste of a saint may be;
The barber has sought God, the washerwoman, and the carpenter—
Even Raidas was a seeker after God.
The Rishi Svapacha was a tanner by caste.
Hindus and Muslims alike have achieved that End,
where remains no mark of distinction.[46]

It is said that when Kabir died, both Hindus and Muslims claimed his body. His teachings were preserved and propagated by a community of his followers called the Kabirpanthis. Kabir is emblematic of the organic unity of the Bhakti movement—he was the disciple of Ramananda and, in turn, Guru Nanak was greatly influenced by Kabir.

Something quite remarkable was afoot in south India too. The Nayanars and Alvars, whom we have mentioned earlier, can be called the founders of the Bhakti movement, and it is instructive to remember that many of the icons of the Bhakti movement in the north, like Vallabha or Ramananda, came from the south. The Nayanars were devotees of Shiva, and were led by a group of sixty-three Tamil saints during the sixth to eighth centuries CE. During the reign of the great king Raja Raja Chola I (947–1014), the hymns of the Nayanars were compiled in a series of volumes called *Tirumurai*, also referred to as the *Tamil Veda*. The Alvars, literally meaning 'those immersed in meditation', were followers of Vishnu and of Krishna, led by twelve supreme saints who lived around the seventh to the tenth century. The hymns of the Alvars were also collated in a volume, the *Nalayira Prabandhan*, a collection of 4,000 songs. Both the Nayanars and Alvars, while travelling from place to place, practised an intense mystical devotion bordering on ecstasy, which emphasised prapatti or complete surrender to the Lord. Their followers came from all classes, including the lowest castes; they shunned rituals and believed in direct, personal communion with the Absolute, in which there was no place for the intermediary role of the priestly class.

The powerful Virashaiva devotional movement in Karnataka had its roots in the Tamil Nayanar tradition. The Virashaivas were 'heroic worshippers of Shiva' and are also called the Lingayats. They rejected temple worship, rituals and Brahminical supremacy, replacing it with direct personalised worship of Shiva without gender, caste or class discrimination. Their only form of worship was the Ishtalinga, a necklace with a pendant that contains the image of the Shivalinga. Basavanna (1105–1167), who was the most towering figure of the Lingayat Virashaiva sect, is also called 'Bhakti Bhandari', literally 'the treasurer of devotion'. Basavanna's vachanas or hymns, intensely lyrical and devotional, movingly evoked the yearning for personal communion with Shiva, and railed against archaic social customs, taboos and superstitions, image worship, rituals like yajna and the sacrifice of animals, and the caste system. His Lord was Kudalasangamadeva, which stands for Shiva in the town of Kappadisangama in Karnataka, where three rivers meet—the Lord of the Meeting Rivers:

The rich
will make temples for Shiva.
What shall I,
a poor man,
do?
My legs are pillars
the body the shrine,
the head a cupola
of gold.
Listen, O lord of the meeting rivers,
things standing shall fall,
but the moving ever shall stay.[47]

Stressing the importance of bhakti, he ridicules the paraphernalia of organised religion and temple worship:

How can I feel right
about a god who eats up lacquer and melts,
who wilts when he sees fire?
How can I feel right?
about gods you sell in your need,
and gods you bury for fear of thieves?
The lord of the meeting rivers,

self-born, one with himself,
he alone is the true god.[48]

Allama Prabhu was a contemporary of Basavanna, and along with him (and Akka Mahadevi) is considered the patron saint of the Lingayat movement. The Kannanda poet Camarasa has written a powerful account of his life; given Allama's highly mystical vachanas, the book is appropriately titled *The Achievement of Nothingness*. The unitary consciousness of surrender and grace between a devotee and Shiva, unmediated by the externalities of religion, was the theme of Allama's writings also:

With your alchemies,
you achieve metals,
but no essence.
With all your manifold yogas,
you achieve
a body, but no spirit.
With your speeches and arguments
you build chains of words
but cannot define the spirit.
If you say
you and I are one,
you were me
but I was not you.[49]

Along with bhakti, Basava and Allama Prabhu were powerful social reformers too. As in the Sikh tradition, they emphasised the importance of seva or service of humanity. 'Work is worship', Basava taught, and compassion the greatest virtue. 'Where is religion without loving-kindness?' is one of his most popular sayings in Kannada. His rejection of orthodoxy and ordained social hierarchies is borne out by his constructing—with the fullest help of Allama Prabhu—the Anubhav Mantapa or 'the hall of spiritual experience' in the city of Kalyan, where he was chief minister in the court of King Bijjala II. Men and women from all social and economic backgrounds could come to the Mantapa to openly discuss spiritual questions, or any other matter of public importance. An institution like this, predating the Din-i-Ilahi of Akbar by centuries, could only be possible in the wake of the widespread social and religious reform ignited by the Bhakti movement. Even today, the Lingayats are a powerful sect in Karnataka, spearheading Shaivite bhakti, and often, given their numerical strength, determining who wins political power in the state.

Although Shiva was the dominant theme, Vaishnava literature also found a place in the Kannada Bhakti tradition. Madhava, the philosopher of qualified monism who followed in the footsteps of Ramanuja, was born in 1199 in a village near Udupi in Karnataka. A scholar, he wrote learned commentaries on the *Brahma Sutra*, the Gita and the Upanishads, and a gloss on the *Bhagwata Purana*. Unlike

Ramanuja's Vishist Advaita, which was a qualified monism, Madhava was openly dualistic in his approach. For him, God, souls and the world were eternally three different entities. The Upanishadic statement *Tat tvam asi* did not mean that the soul and Brahman are identical but only that the soul has qualities *similar* to Brahman. Madhava concedes that Brahma is the embodiment of supreme perfection, but asserts that Vishnu, as its embodiment, is unfettered in his powers as the creator, maintainer and destroyer of the world. Lakshmi, Vishnu's consort, is co-eternal with him and represents his creative energy. A devotee's only way to salvation is through uninhibited bhakti, for only devotion can move the Lord to extend his grace. Madhava takes Ramanuja's emphasis on bhakti to another level of fervour. The devotees are encouraged to brand their body with Vishnu's symbols, and carry out all the rites, pilgrimages and sacrifices, making worship, in thought and practice, the only means to moksha. The Vijayanagara kings provided a further fillip to Vaishnava bhakti. They had the Mahabharata, the Ramayana and the *Bhagwata Purana* translated into Kannada, and spurred by their popularity, dasas or mendicant singers sang hymns in praise of Vishnu, Krishna and Rama. The visit of Chaitanya to the south in 1510 further strengthened this trend.

In Andhra Pradesh, there was the influence of Nimbarka, a Telugu Brahmin who lived a little earlier than Madhava, and postulated a theory of dvaitadvaita, or dualistic non-dualism.

This theory specifically refutes the predicateless character of Brahman, and breaks further from Adi Shankaracharya by arguing that Brahman, actually, undergoes parinama or actual change, while creating the dependent yet autonomous entities of Jiva and Prakriti. What is created is both different from Brahman, and yet not entirely different since its existence is dependent on Brahman. The material cause of creation is the power of Shakti inherent within Brahman. This interdependent world of similar yet different entities is governed by Ishvara, the supreme God, which Nimbarka, as part of the Vaishnava school, identifies with Krishna. As stressed by Ramanuja, and reiterated later by Madhava, Nimbarka also believes that bhakti and prapatti, total devotion and surrender infused with love, are the means for Brahmasakshatkara or the realisation of God.

On these philosophical foundations, the writer Nannaya (eleventh century) partially finished a popular translation of the Mahabharata into Telugu; the seminal work was completed by Tikkana (1220–1300) and Yerrapragada (1280–1350). Telugu versions of the Ramayana and the Puranas soon followed. Potana (1400–1475), who lived an indigent life in the countryside, did a widely read translation of the *Bhagwata Purana*. Vemana, who belonged to a low caste, spread Shiva bhakti through his highly popular gnomic verses, which became famous for their ferocious attack on ritualistic orthodoxies and conventional religious practices:

What are you the better for smearing your body with ashes?
Your thoughts should be set on God alone;
For the rest, an ass can wallow in dirt as well as you.
The books that are called the Vedas are like courtesans,
Deluding men, and wholly unfathomable;
But the hidden knowledge of God is like an honourable wife.
He that fasts shall become (in his next birth) a village pig;
He that embraces poverty shall become a beggar;
And he that bows to a stone shall become like a lifeless image.[50]

An important aspect of the Bhakti movement was the rise of trail-blazing women devotees, who refused to be straitjacketed in the conventional stereotype of submission, subordination and inferiority to men. Aantaal, regarded as one of the twelve Alvar saint-poets, lived in the ninth century in Tamil Nadu. She was found abandoned under a tulsi plant by Periyalvar Timmoli, the great Alvar saint-poet, and he adopted her. She had no family of her own and never married. Mirabai was born in 1498, daughter of a nobleman of the house of Mewar. It is said that as a child she was given an image of Krishna and grew so fond of it that her mother jokingly remarked that Krishna would one day be her bridegroom. Her childhood and youth were one of considerable grief and frustration. Her mother died when she was still very young. Her father was mostly away at war. In 1516, she was married to Prince Bhoja Raj, heir to the throne of Marwar. The marriage was childless and her husband died very soon after they were married. Mira spoke of herself as a celibate.

The significant common factor in Aantaal and Mira is that they looked upon Krishna as their husband. Both believed that in their previous lives they were gopis in Vrindavan. Mira considered herself to be an incarnation of the gopi Lalita, mentioned in the *Bhagwata Purana*. Aantaal decided to marry the Lord himself in the form of Ranganatha of Thiruvarangam (the reclining form of Vishnu).

Aantaal has left behind two important works. In the *Tirupaavai*, a poem of thirty stanzas, she evokes Krishna by comparing him with the rainfall that produces fertility. Her second and longer work of 143 verses is much more explicitly sensuous. In a dream, she sees herself married to Vishnu, but Krishna remains elusive. Her burning desire for physical contact with him is the dominant theme here:

He entered inside me and crushed me to pieces; he let
my life escape and enjoys seeing me dance (in agony).
My bones are melting, my eyes find no sleep
for many days. I am whirling, and drown
in the sea of suffering without the boat,
the Lord of Venkata.
I have lost the beauty of my breasts and my

red lips, since Hrishikesha violated me.
In the sole desire to be united with him my breasts
grew large and jumped in joy. Now
they make my life melt away and cause
such agony.[51]

It is interesting that such impassioned and sensuous devotional writing has some parallels in the West as well. In the sixteenth century, Teresa of Avila fantasised about how a beautiful angel 'thrust a long dart of gold tipped with fire through my heart several times so that it reached my very entrails'. The pain, she wrote, was so real that she 'was forced to moan aloud, yet it was so surpassingly sweet that I would not wish to be delivered from it.'[52]

To return to Aantaal, the unredeemed intensity of her fantasies has an explosive and violent finale:

Whether I weep or whether I worship him, he
won't show his form to me.
He does not come to embrace me, to hold me close,
to enter me and wrap himself around me …
Press down, flatten out, tie up tightly my breasts
to remove the stain of dedicating them to His
Beautiful strong arms …
He did not enquire after me, did not bother that
I was melting, crushed.
I shall tear off with their very roots these

breasts of mine,
For they gained nothing from looking at Him
who robs and plunders and is full of deceit.
I shall throw them towards His chest to extinguish
their burning.[53]

It was the ethos of the Bhakti movement that, notwithstanding such unabashed and transparently sensuous language to express her devotion for Krishna, Aantaal is counted among the most prominent and revered Alvar saints. She was considered an incarnation of Lakshmi. The great Vijayanagara king Krishnadevaraya composed an epic poem in Telugu, *Amuktamalyada*, dedicated to her and the viraha or suffering she experienced in being separated from Krishna or from Vishnu. Even today, many south Indian Vaishnava temples have a separate shrine for her.

Mirabai's songs, collectively known as her *Padavali*, are perhaps less sensual but no less intense. They profile a highly intimate and personal world in which nothing seems to exist except Krishna, the object of her desire. Like Aantaal, Mira too is wed to the Lord in a dream:

Sister, the Lord of the Poor
Came to wed me in a dream.
Fifty-six crores of deities formed the bridal procession.
And the bridegroom was the Lord of Braj.

In my dream I saw the wedding-arch constructed
And the Lord took my hand.
In my dream
I underwent a wedding ceremony
And entered the married state.
Giridhara has revealed himself to Mira:
Her fortunes stem
From good deeds in past births.[54]

Mira is consumed by her desire to give her all to Krishna:

Giridhara is my true lover:
On beholding His beauty, I long for him much.
As night falls I set out to see him
And at break of dawn I return.
Day and night I sport in His company
I please Him in any way I can.
Whatever he clothes me in, that I wear.
Whatever he offers, that I eat.
My love for him is ancient and long-standing.
Without Him I could not live.
Wherever he places me, there I remain.
If he sold me into slavery,
I would acquiesce.
Mira's Lord is the courtly Giridhara
She offers herself in sacrifice again and again.[55]

Like Aantaal, Mira was a rebel. Her fanatical obsession with Krishna led her to become increasingly oblivious to the norms of conventional behaviour imposed on women in her conservative times. She began to receive sadhus, holy men, in the women's quarters, and travel to temples in the city all by herself. Her husband's family was not amused and, it is said, an attempt was made to poison her. Her involvement with Krishna was, however, unwavering:

I donned anklets and danced
The people said 'Mira is mad.'
My mother-in-law declared
That I had ruined the family's reputation.
The king sent me a cup of poison
Which I drank with a smile.
I have offered body and mind
To the feet of Hari
And will drink the nectar of His holy sight.
Mira's Lord is the courtly Giridhara:
My Lord, to thee will I go for refuge.[56]

In addition to Aantaal and Mira, there was, in Kashmir, Lal Ded (1320–1392), also known as Lalleshwari, whose Shaivite bhakti mysticism, expressed in Sanskrit poems called Vakhs, had a deep impact on the psyche of Kashmiris. Among the Nayanar saints was Karaikkal Ammaiyar. She left her husband,

and after a pilgrimage to the Himalayas, settled in a cremation ground in the town of Alankatu, where she wrote hymns (included in the *Tirumurai*) describing how, oblivious to her feminine attributes, she just rejoiced in Shiva's divine dance among the dead:

She has shrivelled breasts
and bulging veins,
in place of white teeth
empty cavities gape.
With ruddy hair on her belly
a pair of fangs, knobbly ankles and long shins
the demon woman wails at the desolate cremation ground
where our Lord,
whose hanging matted hair
blows in all eight directions
dances among the flames
and refreshes his limbs
His home is Alankatu.[57]

As remarkable was Mahadevi, known also as Akka or elder sister, who lived at the time of Basavanna. For her, Shiva was her beloved and husband, and she had no time for any worldly suitors, nor for her husband, Kaushika, the local chieftain. When Kaushika tried to force himself on her, she left her home and became a wandering mendicant, discarding even her garments, covered only by her tresses. In this state, she reached the Anubhav Mantapa in Kalyan, where followed a remarkable dialogue between her and Basavanna. When she was asked who her husband was, she simply said 'Chennamallikarjuna', meaning the 'Lord white as jasmine'—the name of Shiva in the temple where as a child she fell in love with him. When asked why she was in the nude, her deeply evocative reply was:

Till the fruit is ripe inside
the skin will not fall off.
I'd a feeling it would hurt you
if I displayed the body's seals of love.
O brother don't tease me
needlessly. I'm given entire
into the hands of my Lord
white as Jasmine.[58]

The remarkable fact is that this wild-looking, completely unconventional woman was admitted into the Lingayat order. The vachanas she wrote constitute some of the most powerful poetry not only in the Virashaiva sect but in the entire corpus of the Bhakti movement:

Like a silkworm weaving
her house with love
from her marrow,

and dying
in her body's threads
winding tight, round
and round
I burn
desiring what the heart desires.
Cut through, O lord,
my heart's greed,
and show me
your way out,
O lord white as jasmine.[59]

What is most striking is the social iconoclasm of these women poets, their rebellion against conventional expectations and their sheer joy in revealing their devotion to the Lord irrespective of the consequences. Here, Mahadevi Akka expresses this irreverence with aplomb:

I have Maya for mother-in-law;
the world for father-in-law;
three brothers-in-law like tigers;
and the husband's thoughts
are full of laughing women;
no god, this man.
And I cannot cross the sister-in-law
But I will

give this wench the slip
and go cuckold my husband with Hara, my lord.[60]

The women icons of the Bhakti movement posed a challenge to gender orthodoxies and traditional notions of male superiority sanctioned by texts like the *Manusmriti*. The intense passion of these uninhibited female devotees led to a point of view that bhakti could be pursued best only if the devotees imagined themselves to be women. Many of the early hymns in Tamil and Telugu are by male poets writing in a woman's voice. Chaitanya was considered by many of his followers to be an incarnation of Radha, and his mystic–ecstatic form of worship openly encouraged male devotees to imagine themselves in the role of the gopis. We have it on record that several eminent saints experienced the loss of their manhood in moments of the deepest communion with Krishna. The Gujarati saint Narsi Mehta, born a century before Mira, wrote: 'I took the hand of that lover of the gopis in loving converse … I forgot all else. Even my manhood left me. I began to sing and dance like a woman. My body seemed to change and I became one of the gopis … At such moments I experienced moments of incomparable sweetness and joy.'[61] In the south, the eminent Vaishnava exponent, Vedanta Desika, used to wear the clothes of a woman while worshipping Krishna. An annual festival is still held in Chennai in memory of the saint in which his image, dressed as a woman, is taken out in a procession.

The Radha–Vallabhis emerged as a distinct group within the cult of Krishna bhakti in the sixteenth century CE. The founder of this movement was Hita Harivansh (1503–1553). The most important of his works was the *Radha Sudha Nidhi* in which he lauded Radha; she was a veritable ocean of nectar, whereas Krishna was but a drop. The most extreme sect in the glorification of Radha was that of the Sakhi-bhavaks, which assumed the form of a separate grouping by the end of the eighteenth century, and derived its greatest strength from Bengal and the Mathura district. Its followers believed that they could worship Krishna *only* by imagining themselves to be gopis. Swami Ramakrishna Paramahamsa (1836–1886), the towering Bengali saint also strongly believed that he could best achieve a vision of Krishna only if he approached him as a woman. 'As an adult, Ramakrishna undertook a systematic discipline of devotion as a woman of Krishna … For about six months (he) wore women's clothes and ornaments (sari, gauze scarf, bodice, artificial hair) and mimicked the movements, speech, smile, glance, and gestures of women.'[62]

The Bhakti movement was Hinduism's response to the violent and proselytising Islamic invasion. In this sense, it was as much about renewal as it was about self-preservation. If Hinduism had not shown the suppleness and energy to reinvent itself, and had remained brittle and fossilised as in earlier structures without the mass support enabled by the Bhakti movement, it may have suffered the same fate that befell it (and Buddhism) in Indonesia with the advent of Islam. Hinduism had existed for millennia before Islamic rule, but it was more a top-down model, although vibrant local adaptations even then enriched the overall tradition, and influenced those at the pinnacle. However, with the Bhakti movement, kirtans, hymns in the regional languages, and simplified and personal forms of worship and ardent devotion, erupted from the bottom half of the social pyramid, and significantly expanded Hinduism's outreach to the masses where they were not only participants but initiators of religious and spiritual practice. 'The bhakti poet-saints were in dialogue with their own civilization, the Brahminical part of it and its pretensions. Actually, they were in a passionate dialogue of the human soul with itself, yearning for union with God.'[63] In this process, it became a reform movement as well, as many orthodoxies, especially relating to caste and gender discrimination, were upended. As A.K. Ramanujan writes: 'In the lives of the bhakti saints 'the last shall be first': men wish to renounce their masculinity and to become as women; upper caste males wish to renounce pride, privilege and wealth, seek dishonour and self-abasement, and learn from the untouchable devotee.'[64] Certainly, in great part, the Bhakti movement was an attack on rigid caste hierarchies, the supremacy of the Brahminical order and the ritualistic paraphernalia of conventional religious orthodoxies. This does not mean that the subordination of women or the oppression of the lower castes was eliminated. But it did constitute a consistent and prolonged interrogation of these inequalities, and thus took Hinduism towards a much needed re-examination of some of its earlier sacrosanct dictums in religious practice and social interactions.

—Pavan K. Varma, *The Great Hindu Civilisation*

27

Narsinh Mehta

Narsinh Mehta was a fifteenth-century Gujarati poet-saint whose verses in devotion to Lord Krishna are considered to be among the earliest poems in the Gujarati language. Five hundred years later, bhajans composed by him continue to be sung. One of these, Vaishnav Jan To Tene Kahiye Je was a favourite of Mahatma Gandhi's and gained popularity across India as a consequence.

Vaishnav Jan To Tene Kahiye Je

A good human being is one
Who feels the pain of others
One who helps those in misery
And does not let pride enter his mind

A good human being tolerates and praises the entire world
And does not say bad things about anyone
Keeps his words, actions and thoughts pure
(To such a person) Your mother is blessed!

A good human being sees everything equally, rejects greed and avarice
Considers someone else's wife/daughter as his mother
The tongue may get tired, but will never utter lies
And will never even touch someone else's property.

A good human being who does not succumb to worldly attachments
Who has become staunchly detached from worldly pleasures

Who has been addicted to the elixir coming from the name of Ram

For whom all the religious sites are in the mind

Who has no greed and deceit
Who has renounced all types of desires and anger
The poet Narsi would like to see such a person
Whose virtue brings salvation to the entire family.

28

The Japji and the Rehras

The Sikh religion emphasises prayer as a means of worship. The Japji and the Rehras are the morning and evening prayers of the Sikhs. They are the sacred routes to understand the true Guru.

The Japji was composed by Guru Nanak (1469–1539), the founder of the Sikh faith. It consists of hymns in praise of 'The One God who is Truth' and appears at the beginning of the Guru Granth Sahib, the holy book of the Sikhs. The Rehras are a prayer of thanks, recited at the end of the day in gratitude and also for inspiration. They contain hymns by five Sikh Gurus—Guru Nanak, Guru Amar Das, Guru Ram Das, Guru Arjan and Guru Gobind Singh.

1

Not by thought alone can He be known,
Though one thinks a hundred thousand times;
Not in solemn silence
Nor in deep meditation.
Though fasting yields
an abundance of virtue
It cannot appease the hunger for truth.
No, by none of these,
Nor by a hundred thousand other devices,
Can God be reached.
How then shall the truth be known?
How the veil of false illusion torn?
O Nanak, thus runneth the writ divine,
The righteous path—let it be thine.

2

By Him are all forms created,
By Him infused with life and blessed,
By Him are some to excellence elated,
Others born lowly and depressed.
By His writ some have pleasure,
others pain;

By His grace some are saved,
Others doomed to die, re-live, and die again.
His will encompasseth all, there be none beside.
O Nanak, He who knows, hath no ego and no pride.

3

Who has the power to praise His might?
Who has the measure of His bounty?
Of His portents who has the sight?
Who can value His virtue, His deeds, His charity?
Who has the knowledge of His wisdom,
Of His deep, impenetrable thought?
How worship Him who creates life, then destroys,
And having destroyed doth re-create?
How worship Him who appeareth far
Yet is ever present and proximate?
There is no end to His description,
Though the speakers and their speeches be legion.
He the Giver ever giveth,
We who receive grow weary,
On His bounty humanity liveth
Form primal age to posterity.

4

God is the Master, God is truth,
His name spelleth love divine,
His creatures ever cry: 'O give, O give',
He the bounteous doth never decline.
What then in offering shall we bring
That we may see his court above?
What then shall we say in speech
That hearing may evoke His love?
In the ambrosial hours of fragrant dawn
On truth and greatness ponder in meditation,
Though action determine how thou be born,
Through grace alone comes salvation.
O Nanak, this need we know alone,
That God and truth are two in one.

5

He cannot be proved, for He is uncreated;
He is without matter, self-existent.
They that serve shall honoured be,
O Nanak, the Lord is most excellent.
Praise the Lord, hear them that do Him praise,
In your hearts His name be graven,
Sorrows from your soul erase

And make your hearts a joyous haven.
The Guru's word has the sage's wisdom,
The Guru's word is full of learning,
For though it be the Guru's word
God Himself speaks therein.
Thus run the words of the Guru:
'God is the destroyer, preserver and creator,
God is the Goddess too.
Words to describe are hard to find,
I would venture if I knew.'
This alone my teacher taught,
There is but one Lord of all creation,
Forget Him not.

28

As a beggar goes a-begging,
Bowl in one hand, staff in the other,
Rings in his ears, in ashes smothered,
So go thou forth in life.
With earrings made of contentment,
With modesty thy begging bowl,
Meditation the fabric of thy garment,
Knowledge of death thy cowl,
Let thy mind be chaste, virginal clean,
Faith the staff on which to lean.
Thou shalt then thy fancy humiliate,

With mind subdued, the world subjugate.
Hail! And to Thee be salutation.
Thou art primal, Thou art pure,
Without beginning, without termination,
In single form, forever endure.

38

If thou must make a gold coin true
Let thy mint these rules pursue.
In the forge of continence
Let the goldsmith be a man of patience,
His tools be made of knowledge,
His anvil made of reason;
With the fear of God the bellows blow,
With prayer and austerity make the fire glow,
Pour the liquid in the mould of love,
Print the name of the Lord thereon,
And cool it in the holy waters.
For thus in the mint of truth the word is coined,
Thus those who are graced are to work enjoined.
O Nanak, by his blessing have joy everlasting.

—Translated by Khushwant Singh

So Purakh Niranjan, Hari Purakh Niranjan

Guru Ram Das

He is immaculate and beyond comprehension.
There are many ways of worshipping Him.

Our Lord is without blemish, our Lord is untainted by illusion
He is beyond comprehension, endless and beyond reach;
All worship You, the real author of all creation;
All creatures are created by You, You are their provider and giver;
O men of God, ponder over Him! He is the remover of all sorrows;
He Himself the Lord, and the servant,
Says Nanak, of what worth is a mere human?

You dwell in every body, flowing uninterrupted,
You are the only one in every one;

Some You endow with riches, others You reduce to beggary,
It is all a part of Your inscrutable design;

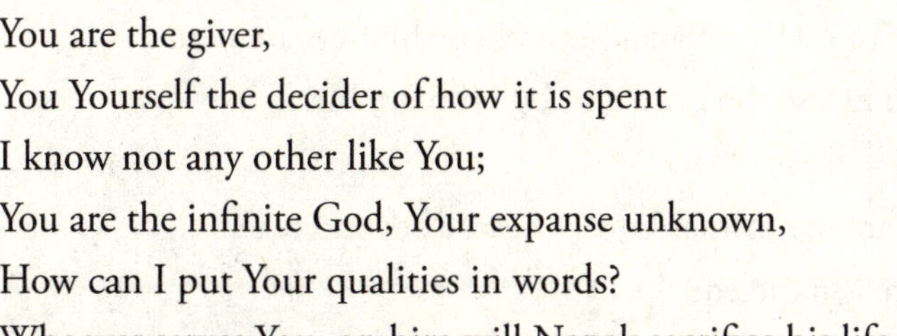

You are the giver,
You Yourself the decider of how it is spent
I know not any other like You;
You are the infinite God, Your expanse unknown,
How can I put Your qualities in words?
Whoever serves You, on him will Nanak sacrifice his life.

Those who meditate on You, those who worship You,
Will live in peace for all their lives;
Those who meditate on You, will gain salvation
And be freed from the noose of Yama;

Those who worship the Lord who is without fear
They will themselves be freed of fear;
Those who serve the Lord
Will merge in the person of the Lord;
Twice blessed are they who contemplate God
Nanak will give his life for them.

The treasury of Your worship is beyond count
Your worshippers worship You in infinite ways;
Worship You who are infinite and without end;
Many are the ways to worship You
Many forms of penance and endless the forms of prayer;

Many a sacred text is read,
Many a way to serve You, including the six karmas;

Says Your slave Nanak, those worshippers are best
Who please the Lord and by Him are blest.

You are the primal Lord, Creator beyond reach
There is none equal to You;
From age to age You are the only one
Forever the only one who gives stability;
What pleases You comes to pass
What You do comes to be;
You created all that exists
You will take it all back as You will;
Your slave Nanak sings Your praises
Who knows all that is worth knowing.

—Translated by Khushwant Singh with Reema Anand

29

Amir Khusrau Dehlavi

(1253–1325)

Dye Me in Your Hue

Dye me in your hue, my love,
You are my man, oh beloved of Almighty;
Dye me in your hue.
My scarf, and the beloved's turban,
Both need to be dyed in the hue of spring;
Whatever be the price for dyeing, ask for it,
You can have my blossoming youth in mortgage;
Dye me in your hue.
I have come and fallen at your door step,
For you to safeguard my pride, my dignity,
You are my man, Oh beloved of Almighty,
Dye me in your hue.

Abu'l Hasan Yamin ud-Din Khusrau, better known as Amir Khusrau, was a prolific Indo-Persian poet, singer, musician and scholar. He popularised several poetic forms, including the ghazal and the qawwali that carried both Indian and Persian traditions. He was a mystic and a spiritual disciple of the Sufi saint Nizamuddin Auliya.

Just a Glance

You've taken away my looks, my identity, by just a glance.
You've taken away my looks, my identity, by just a glance.
By making me drink the wine of love-potion,
You've intoxicated me by just a glance;
My fair, delicate wrists with green bangles on them,
Have been held tightly by you with just a glance.
I give my life to you, Oh my cloth-dyer,
You've dyed me in yourself, by just a glance.
I give my whole life to you Oh, Nijam,
You've made me your bride, by just a glance.
You've taken away my looks, my identity, by just a glance.

—Translation courtesy PoemHunter.com

30

BABA BULLEH SHAH

(1680–1757)

Bulla, Who Knows Who I Am?

Bulla! I know not who I am
Nor am I a believer of the mosque,
Nor am I in rituals of the infidel
Nor am I the pure inside the impure.
Nor am I inherent in the vedas,
Nor am I present in intoxicants.
Nor am I lost nor the corrupt.
Nor am I union, nor grief,
Nor am I intrinsic in the pure/impure
Nor am I of water, nor of land.
Nor am I fire nor air.
Bulla! I know not who I am

Syed Abdullah Shah Qadri, popularly known as Bulleh Shah, was a Punjabi Islamic philosopher and Sufi poet. The simplicity with which he addressed complex issues of life and humanity contributed to his popularity. He decried bigotry and rituals. For him, love was the essence of God.

Nor am I Arabic, nor from Lahore,
Nor am I the Indian city of Nagour.
Nor hindu or a turk from Peshawar.
Nor did I create differences of faith,
Nor did I create Adam and Eve
Nor did I name my self.
Beginning or end, I just know the self,
Do not acknowledge duality.
There's none wise than I.
Who is this Bulleshah
Bulla! I know not who I am.
Nor am I moses, nor Pharoah
Nor am I fire nor wind.
I do not stay in Nadaun city. (City of innocents)
Bulleshah, who is this man standing?
Bulla! I know not who I am
Bulla! I know not who I am.

One Point Contains All

One point contains all;
Learn about the One, forget the rest.
Forget hell and the terrible grave;
Leave the ways of sin and purify
Your heart.

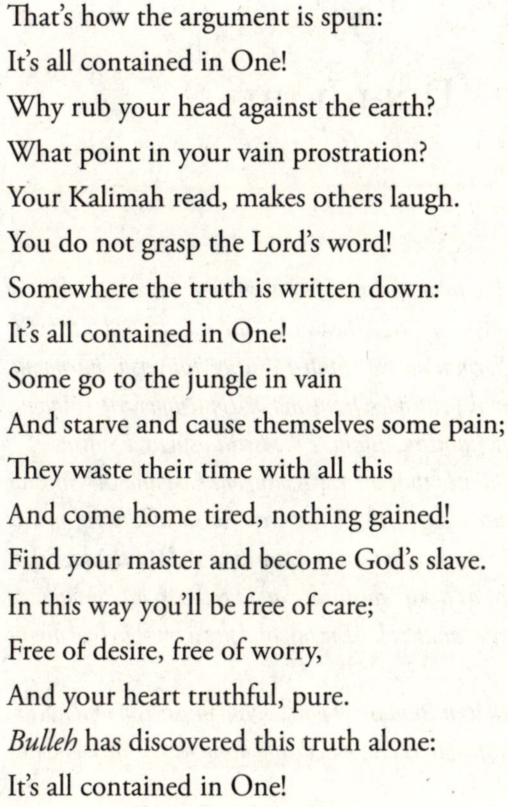

That's how the argument is spun:
It's all contained in One!
Why rub your head against the earth?
What point in your vain prostration?
Your Kalimah read, makes others laugh.
You do not grasp the Lord's word!
Somewhere the truth is written down:
It's all contained in One!
Some go to the jungle in vain
And starve and cause themselves some pain;
They waste their time with all this
And come home tired, nothing gained!
Find your master and become God's slave.
In this way you'll be free of care;
Free of desire, free of worry,
And your heart truthful, pure.
Bulleh has discovered this truth alone:
It's all contained in One!

—Translation courtesy PoemHunter.com

31
Din-i-Ilahi

Tauhid-i-ilahi (divine monotheism) was a religion introduced by the Mughal emperor Akbar in 1582. The word 'Din' was applied later. The basic purpose of its formation was Sulh-i-Kul or universal harmony. This religion borrowed principles from major contemporary religions, including Hinduism, Jainism, Islam, Zoroastrianism and Sufism.

Din-i-Ilahi proclaimed that there was only one God and the emperor was God's representative on earth. There were no sacred books, priests or places of worship. The religion was primarily a code of conduct that promoted virtues such as piety, abstinence and kindness, and prohibited sins such as lust, slander and pride. The sun and fire were objects of divine worship.

This religion, with its mishmash of philosophy, mysticism and nature worship, garnered few followers and practically disappeared after Akbar's death.

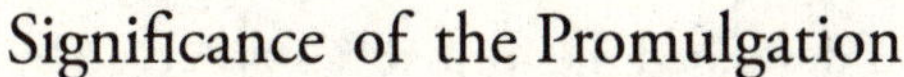

Significance of the Promulgation

The Sufi creed of the Din-i-Ilahi was promulgated in the beginning of the year 1582. According to Bartoli, there was a formal council before the promulgation of the Din-i-Ilahi, and an old Shaikh (Mubarak) was sent to proclaim in all quarters that in, a short time, the law to be professed throughout the Mughal Empire would be sent from the court and that they should make themselves ready to take it for the best and accept it with reverence, whatever it might be. We do not know anything more about the embassy of Mubarak; moreover, the tone and language do not fit in with the happy saying of Akbar, 'Why should I claim to guide men before I myself am guided?'

Principles of the Din-i-Ilahi

Smith says that the principles of the system were not properly defined and there was a good deal of uncertainty as to its meaning till 1587. Really, it was 'undefined', as it was no new religion: it was the summing up of the old. In the absence of any written treatise on the subject there was much scope for imagination. Von Noer is of opinion that the system was like that of the Freemasons or Illuminati. So, it was not necessary to declare it in public. Badauni also says that the Mujtahid of

the new religion was the only repository of the fundamentals of the faith. Badauni's narrative relates only to the exterior rituals of the creed and described the formalities observed by Akbar. Badauni gave his reader hardly any new information about the principles of the creed. Like an ordinary Mulla he identified the fundamentals with the collaterals, and formalities were mistaken for principles. Abul Fazl in Ain No. 77 on the subject of 'His Majesty as the spiritual guide of the people', began in a Sufic strain but left the subject with a pious wish, 'should my occupations allow sufficient leisure and should another term of life be granted me, it is my intention to lay before the world a separate volume on the subject'. His 'occupations' gave him no leisure, nor 'another term of life was granted' to him and we have lost a separate volume on the subject. The Portuguese missionaries who visited the court during this period had their peculiar mode of describing things, they generally mixed up gossip with fact which more often than not deprived truth of its essence if there was any. The only author who narrated the fundamentals of the Din-i-Ilahi was Mohsin Fani, who has described a part of it in his famous Dabistan-i-Mazahib. The Dabistan did not directly discuss the Din-i-Ilahi but has indirectly expressed inner principles of the system through the mouth of the Philosopher in course of a dialogue. The authority of Mohsin Fani was Mirza Shah Muhammad, son of Baigh Khan, who knew it directly from Azam Khan—a member of the Din-i-Ilahi. Mohsin Fani was a sympathetic observer unlike Badauni or Portuguese priests; and there is a touch of romance in his way of speaking a thing. The Philosopher of the Dabistan, who represented the Emperor at the end of a general debate where the champions of other faiths were present, propounded the Din-i-Ilahi in ten virtues:

1. Liberality and beneficence.
2. Forgiveness of the evil doer and repulsion of anger with mildness.
3. Abstinence from worldly desires.
4. Care of freedom from the bonds of the worldly existence and violence as well as accumulating precious stores for the future real and perpetual world.
5. Wisdom and devotion in the frequent meditation on the consequences of actions.
6. Strength of dexterous prudence in the desire of marvellous actions.
7. Soft voice, gentle words, pleasing speeches for everybody.
8. Good treatment with brethren, so that their will may have the precedence to our own.
9. A perfect alienation from creatures and a perfect attachment to the Supreme Being.
10. Dedication of soul in the love of God and union with God the preserver of all.

The whole philosophy of Akbar was: 'The pure *Shast* and the pure sight never err.' Great stress was thus laid on purity of individual life and purity of outlook on affairs of life. Practices followed by Akbar and his 'Happy Sayings', as quoted by Abul Fazl, bear out the truth that lay behind Akbar's philosophy.

In discussing the Sufi system of Akbar, we cannot lose sight of its rituals and priests, ceremonies and practices, initiations and symbols of brotherhood of the Sufi creed, for they are the concomitant parts of the system. Indeed, in every religion whether primary or subsidiary, formalities are given as much prominence as the ideal to be worshipped. The development of a religion has in its background the religious experience of the propounder. The difference amongst great religious systems is based not on any difference in the ultimate ideal, for the object of worship is almost everywhere the same, but what they differ in, is in the form of worship. The war is on the *path* but not on the *destination*. Really speaking, the formalities and rituals are no ends in themselves, but are only means to some end. But unfortunately the history of religion has shown that the forms apparently are regarded as ends, and ends lose themselves in the labyrinths of forms; and more new creeds have developed not by way of difference of fundamentals but by way of formalities, rituals and ceremonies.

Priests

In the Din-i-Ilahi, there was no priesthood and that is why Blochmann opines, 'Akbar solely relying on his influence and example, had established no priesthood and had appointed no proper persons to propagate his faith.' Von Noer says, 'There was no priesthood in the Din-i-Ilahi, it being confined to the select few.' But to us it appears that the Din was never regarded by Akbar as a new religion and therefore, there was no need of a separate priesthood and separate church so natural and so common to the promulgation of a new faith. Moreover, in Islam there is no priesthood and it has been condemned in unequivocal terms by the orthodox. From the Islamic point of view, Akbar is justified in not having any priesthood in the system. Tajuddin was the expounder of the exterior rites of the creed. The Mujtahids were Abul Fazl and his brother Faizi. Azam Khan is said to have learnt the rules of the new order from Abul Fazl, who, according to Badauni, was the repository of the rules of *discipleship*. In fact, separate priests were not necessary, nor a mosque, for it was a Sufi order of Islam within Islam, depending on the individual experience of the follower and was only open to men who had attained a certain stage of development based on capacity. Akbar before allowing anyone to enter into the order made a 'clearing search' and 'every strictness and reluctance was shown by His Majesty in admitting novices'.

Of course, it could not be a fact that all those who entered into the order were, without exception, actuated by a deep religious conviction; in some, royal favour was the prime object, 'though His Majesty did everything to get this out of their heads'. Nor did Akbar himself play the part of a Pope, as Smith would have his readers believe, for Akbar himself used to say, 'Why should I claim to guide men before I myself am guided?' Like his great Indian predecessor Asok, 1800 years back, he issued a general order to all state officials to look after the spiritual development of all subjects.

'The Governor ought not to oppose the creed and religion of the creatures of God; in as much as a wise man chooses not his loss in the affair of this perishable world, how should he knowingly tend to perdition in the religious world which is permanent and eternal? lf God be with his faith, then thou thyself carriest our controversy and opposition against God; and if God fails him and he knowingly takes the wrong way, then he proves to himself a rule of erroneous profession, which demand pity and assistance, not enmity or contradiction; he, who acts, and thinks well, bears friendship to every sect.' In the same Farman his officers were 'required to show veneration for those who were distinguished by devotion to incomparable God, and pray in the morning and evening and at midnight'.

Toleration was the basis of these instructions. Du Jarric informed us that Akbar often used to say, 'God ought to be worshipped with every kind of veneration.' Unconsciously his doctrine of non-intervention in religion was the best missionary for the propagation of the Din as Akbar conceived it. Again, he says, 'If the people wished it, they might adopt his creed and His Majesty declared that religion ought to be established by choice and not by violence.' Indeed, the Quran says that if God wished the whole world might have been Islamised but when God has not willed it, what right has man to compel people to come to Islam by force; Badauni says that some people asked Akbar why he did not make use of the sword, the most convincing proof, such as Shah Ismail at Persia had done. Akbar replied, 'Confidence in him as a leader was a matter of time and good counsel, and he did not require the sword.' To Salim, Akbar said, 'Are not five-sixths of all mankind either unbelievers or Hindus? If I were actuated by motives similar to those which thou ownest, what would remain to me but to destroy them all?' (Shea and Troyer, p. cxlvii.)

—Makhanlal Roychoudhury, *The Din-i-Ilahi or The Religion of Akbar*

32

Mir Taqi Mir

(1723–1810)

All plans have gone amiss, all recipes have failed,
This ailing heart, you see, has undone me at last.
Groaning, grieving I spent my youth, as age arrived I closed my eyes,
Having passed a sleepless night, I dozed off at dawn.
Unjustly we helpless mortals are charged with having sovereign wills,
He doth what He wills, we are to blame in vain.
All revellers and drinkers hold Thee in respect,
Crooked and clever, sharp and sly, all kneel to Thee.
Even in my frenzied state seldom did I misbehave,
For miles after him I went, but knelt at every stage.
Why talk of Mecca or Kaaba, who cares for pilgrimage?
Dwellers of the street of love, greet these places from afar.
In the light and shade of life, this is our only role,

Mir Taqi Mir's ghazals speak of romantic love, with its ecstasy as well as its agony, presenting philosophical insights through seemingly straightforward verses.

Wailing we move from night to morn, from morn,
somehow, to eve.
I had grasped her silver arms, but then I let them go,
A fool I was to trust her word, to harbour wishful thoughts.

The head that feels proud today because it wears a crown,
In the din of lamentation tomorrow will be drowned.
Whoever finished safe the voyage of his life?
Every traveller on this road has been waylaid.
Even the prison could not subdue my manic state,
Stoning alone may now suppress my wild unrest.
So glistens the tear on the eyelid perched,
A fragment of my diamond heart, it may seem to you.
Breathe gently, tread softly, friend!
Highly fragile is the glassware of this world.
Come sharp and attend to the heart-consumed Mir,
Who knows when this morning lamp suddenly expires.

33

Bahadur Shah Zafar

(1775–1862)

I am not the apple of any eye, nor the joy of any heart,
A handful of useless dust, no purpose I discharge.
I've lost my strength and shape, I'm severed from my friend,
I'm the spring of the garden, laid waste by fall.
I'm a friend to no one, nor a foe to aught,
I'm the star-crossed fate, I'm the ruined resort.
Why should someone sing my dirge, or come to lay a wreath?
I'm the tomb of helplessness, better left in dark.
I'm not a lilting song, which others may hear or heed,
I'm the wail by severance caused, a cry of anguished heart.

Bahadur Shah Zafar was the last Mughal ruler of India. He had a gift for poetry, music and calligraphy. His acute awareness of his lack of power is reflected in many of his poems.

34

Mohammed Ibrahim Zauq

(1790–1854)

Commissioned by life we come, commanded by death we go,
Sans our will we come, sans will we go.
Even if given Khizar's life, we will but complain:
'A while ago here we came, in another while we go.'
What a poor player am I in the game of life!
Every move on my part makes a dismal show.
Good, if the world doesn't engage our heart and soul,
But what to do? Uninvolved, we cannot run this show.
Declaim not your virtues, too strong is Fate,
Your wit and my wisdom must before her bow.
Has the world been faithful to anyone on earth?
Move along the tide of time as it ebbs and flows.
Carried on the wings of love, here we quit this grove,
What care we whether or not the morning breeze now blows.

Mohammed Ibrahim Zauq was appointed a poet laureate in the Mughal court in Delhi at the age of nineteen. He was a deeply religious man and his ghazals deal with religious and ethical themes.

35

Asadullah Khan Ghalib

(1797–1869)

To have met my friend was not my fate,
A longer life'd have entailed a longer wait.
Did I trust your word, indeed? What a wrong belief!
I sure had died of joy, had I believed it true.
My heart alone could tell about your half-drawn arrow,
Could it leave a sting behind, had it pierced the marrow?
What use this friendship which cannot but advise,
O for a friend! to physic my sorrow, to heal my heart.
Mortifying is sorrow, no doubt, but how can one escape?
If not to pangs of love, we are to pangs of living a prey.
Calamitous is the night of severance, terrible beyond words,
I'd die with pleasure, had I to die but once.
Why didn't I drown in a river ere this disgrace?
There couldn't have been a funeral, there wouldn't be a grave.

Mirza Asadullah Khan, known as Ghalib, was a poet laureate in the court of the last Mughal emperor, Bahadur Shah Zafar. He is considered to be the last classical Persian poet of India and remains greatly popular for his Urdu poetry, especially his ghazals.

It takes an age for a sigh to bear fruit,
Who lives long enough to vanquish your locks?
A hundred crocodiles lie coiled in the web of every wave,
See what happens to the droplet ere it becomes a pearl.
Love demands patience, desire will not wait,
What hues should my heart reflect, till it bleeds to death?
True, you'd respond without least delay,
But ere you come to know, I'd be no more.
The reflection of the sun heralds the dew-drop's doom,
I too await your kindly glance.
Short is our span, as the twinkling of an eye,
The glamour of the court is but the glimmer of the spark.
Who but death can cure, Asad, the sorrows of this life,
A taper anyway shall burn, right till the dawn.

All my hopes stand belied,
No prospect is in sight!
Death will come when it will come,
Why comes not sleep at night?
I once could laugh at the state of my heart,
But nothing can make me laugh today.
To pray and penance is good, I know,
But my mind is not disposed this way.
There must be something that holds my tongue,
Not that I know not how to speak.
If you can't see my scalded heart,

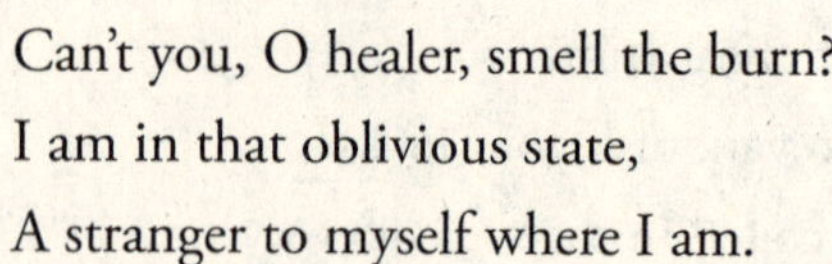

Can't you, O healer, smell the burn?
I am in that oblivious state,
A stranger to myself where I am.

To me this world is a children's fair,
A play goes on 'fore me all day and night.
The throne of Suleman is a plaything to me,
The miracles of Christ are oft-told tales.
The world exists only in name,
Illusory—all material things.
The desert hides itself in dust as I approach,
The river flows prostrate rubbing its brow on earth.
True, I am self-conscious, self-adorning; why not,
When I behold a beauty as perfect as mirror?
Set before me a draught of wine, should you like to see,
The blossoming of my tongue, the beauty of my speech.
Faith holds me back, heresy goads me on,
Kaaba stands behind me, pantheon ahead.
Men rejoice at union, but do they ever die?
Lo, I pay with life for the desire of the parting night.

—Translated by K.C. Kanda

36

Suryakant Tripathi 'Nirala'

She Breaks Stones

Beside a road in Allahabad
I saw her
        Breaking stones.

No tree to give her shade,
A dark skin,
Firm, tightly-cupped breasts,
Eyes fixed on the ground,
Thoughts of the night before
Going through her mind,
She brought down the heavy hammer
Again and again, as though it was
A weapon in her hand.
Across the road—
A row of trees, high walls,
The mansions of the rich.

Suryakant Tripathi 'Nirala' (1899–1961) was a poet, writer, storyteller, novelist and composer. He is considered one of the four pillars of the Chhayavaad neo-romantic movement of Hindi literature.

The sun climbed the sky.
The height of summer.
Blinding heat, and the loo blowing hard,
Scorching everything in its path.
The earth under the feet
Like burning cotton wool,
The air filled with dust and sparks.
It was almost noon,
And she was still breaking stones.

As I watched,
She looked at me once,
Then at the houses opposite,
Then at her ragged clothes.
Seeing there was no one around,
She met my eyes again
With eyes that spoke of pain<br.
But not defeat.

Suddenly, there came the notes of a sitar,
Such as I had not heard before.
The next moment her young body
Quivered and as sweat
Trickled down her face, she lifted

The hammer, resuming work,
As though to say,
	I'm breaking stones.

—[1935] Translated by Arvind Krishna Mehrotra

37

Maithili Sharan Gupt

Panchavati: An Introduction

The full moon's mesmerising rays
Appear to skim the lake and sand,
As moonlight, fresh, diffuses over
Surfaces of sky and land.
The earth transmits a joyous pulse
From melodies of green grass blades.
On cue, the trees begin to sway—
A gentle westerly pervades.
The shaded woods of Panchavati
Enclose a modest leaf abode,
And keeping watch from a high rock
Is a young prince who's calm, composed.
This warrior, why's he still awake
When all creation's deep in sleep?
He's used to pomp and luxury;
Now he's constrained by vows to keep.

Maithili Sharan Gupt (1886–1964) was a pioneer of Khari Boli poetry. He was honoured with the title of 'National Poet' by Mahatma Gandhi.

What's this brave youth's avowed purpose
That sleep's been sacrificed like this?
The jungle's where he must now live
While abnegating princely bliss.
That which he dutifully guards,
What wealth resides in that abode?
In whose defense, his body, mind
And soul are thoroughly bestowed.
To cleanse our tainted mortal world,
She who accompanies her Lord,
And now resides in this leaf hut,
Is Lakshmi, whom three worlds adore.
She represents a brave clan's pride:
It's apt she's guarded by the brave.
It's lonely, night has just set in,
And nightly beasts can act depraved.
Even though there's no one nearby,
It's hard to silence a man's mind.
He starts conversing with himself,
As thoughts, replies, are intertwined.
Every so often, he looks up,
And joyfully surveys the scene.
All to himself, the fearless warrior
Advances thoughts that are pristine.
How fresh, how dazzling the moonlight!
O, how devoid of noise tonight!

How beautiful the night's sweet odour,
Does anything here lack delight?
Things haven't stopped, they're on the move,
Accompanying nature's dance,
But they continue so sequestered,
As though they're in a peaceful trance!
The beautiful earth scatters pearls
Whilst everyone is fast asleep.
When dawn takes hold, the morning sun
Recovers them in one fell sweep.
Later the sun opts for a break,
Bestowing on the lovely evening
A gentle, almost zero darkness,
Which gives to dusk a fresh new meaning,
Whence glittering like liquid dew,
The moon's rays take a happy turn,
And soulful nature shows her joy
By shedding tears of sweet concern.
For errors made unknowingly,
Indeed she punishes us harshly,
But then she nurtures both the young
And old just as impartially.
It feels like 'twas just yesterday,
Yet thirteen years have gone so fast!
Seeing us come deep in the jungle
Had made our father full aghast.

The time will come soon when our term
In this deep jungle will be over,
But what would be more satisfying
Than wealth I've gained from this exposure?
My noble brother will then take
On weighty tasks of governance.
Busy he'll be with royal duties,
And won't give us a fleeting glance.
Keeping in mind the good he'll do,
I certainly won't feel denied.
Don't we aristocrats all know
How to take such things in stride?

—Translated by Paddy Raghunathan

38

Ramdhari Singh 'Dinkar'

Identity

A crippled clamour of emptiness,
seeking to fill the silence in my heart.
I wander, searching for light in darkness,
I am, I hear, a treasury of light.

Night seeks her dawn, burning candles of stars,
I too, await my dawn.
A hundred times, I lived and died,
Have I found yet, the bridge across the Unknown?

In the dew-drop on flower petal,
I am a world of multi-hued dreams.
What care I, sooner or later, I will wilt
For I am a flower, a modest offering,

A burning, a pain, a heartache
Oh woe! I am someone's lost love.

Ramdhari Singh 'Dinkar' (1908–1974) was a Hindi poet, essayist and academic. He was known for his nationalist poetry and received the Sahitya Akademi Award, the Padma Bhushan and the Jnanpith Award.

Fallen to earth, from the flower-garden,
beloved son of the evergreen tree

Shouldering my burden of sorrow,
my life is a little sweeter now.
With anguish, precious wealth of poets,
I string together my tears in verse.

Why pride in my own light,
I am but the dust from the pyre, the ash.
Where I am, the earth will tell you,
She who has consumed me a hundred times.

Yet the world looks not with hatred upon me,
For I am a man, a wonder of creation.
Oh Devotee, lift me from the dust where I lie!
I am a garland for your beloved God.

Oh mighty ocean, what shall I make of your roar?
I am a voice, loud, of this age and its mores
A hard fearsome voice of lightning,
I am the twang of catastrophe's bow,

The suppressed fire of a ravenous hunger,
I am the wordless wail of the suffering.

Oh vigilant world, take care, beware!
I am the tumultuous ocean of catastrophe.

A captive storm, forbidden motion,
I am a waterfall dammed.
Who am I, what is my desire,
I am helpless, a pen constrained.

39

Amrita Pritam

To Waris Shah

Speak from the depths of the grave,
to Waris Shah I say
and add a new page to your saga of love today.

Once wept a daughter of Punjab,
your pen unleashed a million cries,
a million daughters weep today.
to you Waris Shah they turn their eyes.

Awake, decry your Punjab,
O sufferer with those suffering!
Corpses entomb the fields today,
the Chenab is flowing with blood.
Mingled with poison by some,
are the waters of five rivers,
and this torrent of pollution,
unceasingly covers our earth.

Amrita Pritam (1919–2005) was the recipient of several awards, including the Sahitya Akademi Award, the Padma Shri and the Padma Vibhushan. Her novel Pinjar *(1950) was made into an award-winning film in 2003.*

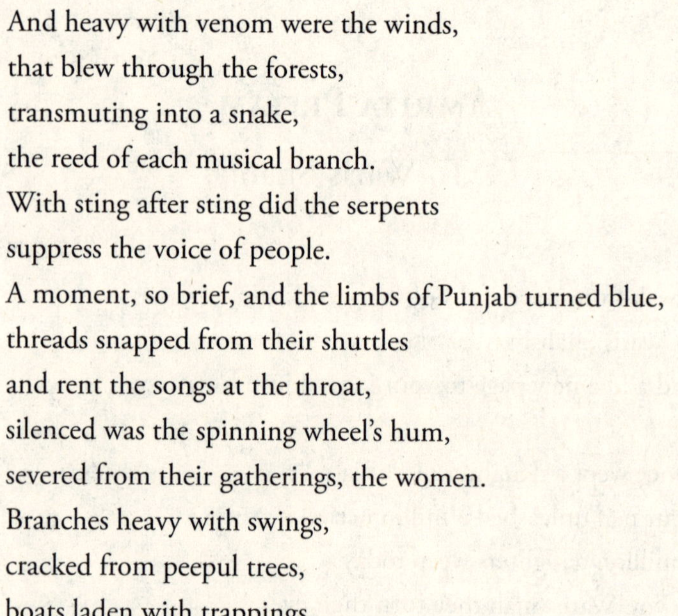

And heavy with venom were the winds,
that blew through the forests,
transmuting into a snake,
the reed of each musical branch.
With sting after sting did the serpents
suppress the voice of people.
A moment, so brief, and the limbs of Punjab turned blue,
threads snapped from their shuttles
and rent the songs at the throat,
silenced was the spinning wheel's hum,
severed from their gatherings, the women.
Branches heavy with swings,
cracked from peepul trees,
boats laden with trappings,
loosened from anchors to sink.

Despoilers of beauty and love,
each man now turned a Kedu
where can we seek for another like
Waris Shah today?

Only you can speak from the grave,
to Waris Shah I say
add another page
to your epic of love today.

—Translated by Amrita Pritam

40

Sahir Ludhianvi

Taj Mahal

The Taj, mayhap, to you may seem, a mark of love supreme
You may hold this beauteous vale in great esteem;
Yet, my love, meet me hence at some other place!

How odd for the poor folk to frequent royal resorts;
'Tis strange that the amorous souls should tread the regal paths
Trodden once by mighty kings and their proud consorts.
Behind the facade of love my dear, you had better seen,
The marks of imperial might that herein lie screened
You who take delight in tombs of kings deceased,
Should have seen the hutments dark where you and I did wean.
Countless men in this world must have loved and gone,
Who would say their loves weren't truthful or strong?

Abdul Hayee (1921–1980), popularly known as Sahir Ludhianvi, is regarded as one of the greatest poets and film lyricists in Urdu and Hindi. His work gave a new direction to the poetry of the Indian Progressive Writers' Movement. He received the Padma Sri and two Filmfare Awards.

But in the name of their loves, no memorial is raised
For they too, like you and me, belonged to the common throng.

These structures and sepulchres, these ramparts and forts,
These relics of the mighty dead are, in fact, no more
Than the cancerous tumours on the face of earth,
Fattened on our ancestor's very blood and bones.
They too must have loved, my love, whose hands had made,
This marble monument, nicely chiselled and shaped
But their dear ones lived and died, unhonoured, unknown,
None burnt even a taper on their lowly graves.

This bank of Jamuna, this edifice, these groves and lawns,
These carved walls and doors, arches and alcoves,
An emperor on the strength of wealth, Has played with us a cruel joke.
Meet me hence, my love, at some other place.

—Translated by K.C. Kanda

41

Gopaldas Neeraj

Let Us Have a Different Religion

Let us have a different religion
That allows a human to be human
Let its fragrance transcend borders
Reach our neighbours and beyond
The Ganga is aflame, so are the Jhelum and others
Enraged with hatred between brothers
No place remains where there can be peace
Is there such a place? Someone tell me please!
Why love is lost, to understand this
Let us call dusk at dawn to answer it!
Trust this new doctrine makes us humane
When I am hurt, you feel the pain.
If I am hungry, you are unable to nibble
If I weep, tears from your eyes dribble
We live as if two souls
In which one heart beats
Presently all music is bored

Gopaldas Saxena 'Neeraj' (1925–2018) used both Hindi and Urdu in his work. He was the recipient of numerous literary awards, including the Sahitya Shiromani, the Padma Shri and the Padma Bhushan.

Songs are silent, poems gored
This is when you call on Neeraj
He will have you all
with his rhythm floored.

—Translated by R.K. Karnani

42

Dushyant Kumar

Ghazal

The pain has risen mountain-high, it must now melt and flow
From this Himalaya a new Ganga should burst and flow

The walls are tottering now, swaying like curtains
But we wanted to shake up the foundation

In each road, each lane, each city, each village
Even a corpse should walk swinging its arms

It's not my purpose just to cause an uproar
I strive that these circumstances must change

If not in my breast then surely in yours
A fire must burn, somewhere a fire must burn.

—Translated by Harish Trivedi

Dushyant Kumar (1931–1975) was one of the foremost poets of the twentieth century. He wrote poetry, plays and novels, but was best known for his Hindi ghazal writing.

43

Namdeo Dhasal

Tree of Violence

Comes the Day, Passes the Day
We walked the way
We shouldn't have walked

As we went further, even the darkness became familiar
A lonesome wind reeling through the city's autobiography

An ethos of treachery
A search for the root of agony

Yesterday, only darkness rustled like a million leaves here
Today, the whole inner world is electrified
After so long it's started to rain
On the untouchable earth

We lived the day as it came to us
We shut out the day as it went away!

—Translated by Dilip Chitre

Namdeo Dhasal (1949–2014) was a Marathi poet, writer and Dalit activist. He was one of the founders of the Dalit Panthers, an organisation that worked towards ending caste discrimination.

44

Gulzar

Old Woman

Old woman, with you I have shared
Everything about life
Food, drink, clothes, all that make a home
Sleep, and all our wakeful nights
From the birth of our children, to their settling down,
And finally, moving on,
Every stage of my life
I have shared with you
With you I have shared the grief of parting
Quarrel, reconciliation, solitude, too
All my tricks I shared with you, truths and lies as well
My pain you have borne
And all your pain has passed through my pores
We have lived together
But how is it possible for us to die together?
One of us one day

Sampooran Singh Kalra 'Gulzar' (b. 1934) is a lyricist, poet, novelist, songwriter, screenwriter and film director. He has received the Sahitya Akademi Award, the Dadasaheb Phalke Award and the Padma Bhushan, as well as a Grammy.

Will have to leave the other
At the funeral pyre
And return alone.

—Translated by Pavan K. Varma

45

Raja Rammohun Roy

Raja Rammohun Roy (1772–1833) was a socio-religious reformer who contributed to the abolition of the practice of sati. He also advocated the elimination of the purdah system and child marriage. In 1828, he formed the Brahmo Samaj, which was against idol worship and caste discrimination. The title 'Raja' was bestowed upon him by the Mughal emperor Bhahadur Shah Zafar, though it was not recognised by the British.

The Crusade Against Suttee

Burning Widows Alive: Pros and Cons

The reason you have now assigned for burning widows alive is indeed your true motive, as we are well aware; but the faults which you have imputed to women are not planted in their constitution by nature; it would be, therefore, grossly criminal to condemn that sex to death merely as a precaution. By ascribing to them all sorts of improper conduct, you have indeed successfully persuaded the Hindu community to look down upon them as contemptible and mischievous creatures, whence they have been subjected to constant miseries. I have, therefore, to offer a few remarks on this head.

Women are in general inferior to men in bodily strength and energy; consequently, the male part of the community, taking advantage of their corporeal weakness, have denied to them those excellent merits that they are entitled to by nature, and afterwards they are apt to say that women are naturally incapable of acquiring those merits. But if we give the subject consideration, we may easily ascertain whether or not your accusation against them is consistent with justice. As to their inferiority in point of understanding, when did you ever afford them a fair opportunity of exhibiting their natural capacity? How then can you accuse them of want of understanding? If, after instruction in knowledge and wisdom, a person cannot comprehend or retain what has been taught him, we may consider him as deficient; but as you keep women generally void of education and acquirements, you cannot, therefore, in justice pronounce on their inferiority. On the contrary, Lilavati, Bhanumati, the wife of the prince of Karnat, and that of Kalidasa, are celebrated for their thorough knowledge of all the *Sastras*: moreover in the *Brihadaranyaka Upanishad* of the *Yajur Veda* it is clearly stated that Yajnavalkya imparted divine knowledge of the most difficult nature to his wife Maitreyi, who was able to follow and completely attain it!

Secondly. You charge them with want of resolution, at which I feel exceedingly surprised: for we constantly perceive, in a country where the name of death makes the male shudder, that the female, from her firmness of mind, offers to burn with the corpse of her deceased husband; and yet you accuse those women of deficiency in point of resolution.

Thirdly. With regard to their trustworthiness, let us look minutely into the conduct of both sexes, and we may be enabled to ascertain which of them is the most frequently guilty of betraying friends. If we enumerate such women in each village or town as have been deceived by men, and such men as have been betrayed by women, I presume that the number of the deceived women would be found ten times greater than that of the betrayed men. Men are, in general, able to read and write, and manage public affairs, by which means they easily promulgate such faults as women occasionally commit, but never consider as criminal the misconduct of men towards women. One fault they have, it must be acknowledged; which is, by considering others equally void of duplicity as themselves, to give their confidence too readily, from which they suffer much misery, even so far that some of them are misled to suffer themselves to be burnt to death.

In the fourth place, with respect to their subjection to the passions, this may be judged of by the custom of marriage as to the respective sexes; for one man may marry two or three, sometimes even ten wives and upwards; while a woman who marries but one husband desires at his death to follow him, forsaking all worldly enjoyments, or to remain leading the austere life of an ascetic.

Fifthly. The accusation of the want of virtuous knowledge is an injustice. Observe what pain, what slighting, what contempt, and what afflictions their virtue enables them to support! How many Kulin Brahmans are there who marry ten or fifteen wives for the sake of money, that never see the greater number of them after the day of marriage, and visit others only three or four times in the course of their life. Still amongst those women, most, even without seeing or receiving any support from their husbands, living dependent on their fathers or brothers, and suffering much distress, continue to preserve their virtue; and when Brahmans, or those of other tribes, bring their wives to live with them, what misery do the women not suffer? At marriage the wife is recognized as half of her husband, but in after-conduct they are treated worse than inferior animals. For the woman is employed to do the work of a slave in the house, such as, in her turn, to clean the place very early in the morning, whether cold or wet, to scour the dishes, to wash the floor, to cook night and day, to prepare and serve food for her husband, father, mother-in-law, sisters-in-law, brothers-in-law, and friends and connections! (For amongst Hindus more than in other tribes, relations reside together, and on this account quarrels are more common amongst brothers respecting their worldly affairs.) If in the preparation or serving up of the victuals they commit the smallest fault, what insult do they not receive from their husband, their mother-in-law, and the younger brothers of their husband? After all the male part of the family have satisfied themselves, the women content themselves with what may be left, whether sufficient in quantity or not. Where Brahmans or Kayasthas are not wealthy, their women are obliged to attend to their cows, and to prepare the cow-dung for firing. In the afternoon they fetch water from the river or tank, and at night perform the office of menial servants in making the beds. In case of any fault or omission in the performance of those labours they receive injurious treatment. Should the husband acquire wealth, he indulges in criminal amours to her perfect knowledge and almost under her eyes, and does not see her perhaps once a month. As long as the husband is poor, she suffers every kind of trouble, and when he becomes rich, she is altogether heart-broken. All this pain and affliction their virtue alone enables them to support. Where a husband takes two or three wives to live with him, they are subjected to mental miseries and constant quarrels. Even this distressed situation they virtually endure. Sometimes it happens that the husband, from a preference for one of his wives, behaves cruelly to another. Amongst the lower classes, and those even of the better class who have not associated with good company, the wife, on the slightest fault, or even on bare suspicion of her misconduct, is chastised as a thief. Respect to virtue and their reputation generally makes them forgive even this treatment. If unable to bear such cruel usage, a wife leaves her husband's house to live separately from him, then the influence of the husband with the magisterial authority is generally sufficient to place her again in his hands; when, in revenge for her quitting him, he seizes every pretext to torment her in various ways, and sometimes even puts her privately to death. These are facts occurring every day, and not to be denied. What I lament is, that, seeing the women thus dependent and exposed to every misery, you feel for them no compassion, that might exempt them from being tied down and burnt to death…

...We should not omit the present opportunity of offering up thanks to Heaven, whose protecting arm has rescued our weaker sex from cruel murder, under the cloak of religion, and our character, as a people, from the contempt and pity with which it has been regarded, on account of this custom, by all civilized nations on the surface of the globe.

—From *Selected Works of Raja Rammohun Roy*

46

Ishwar Chandra Vidyasagar

Ishwar Chandra Bandyopadhyay (1820–1891), who became famous as Pandit Ishwar Chandra Vidyasagar, was a scholar, teacher, author and philanthropist. As the principal of Sanskrit College, Calcutta, he allowed non-Brahmins, including those from lower castes, to study there. He introduced English and Bengali as mediums of instruction, in addition to Sanskrit.

He brought about a revolution in the Bengali education system by changing the way the Bengali language was written and taught. His own book Borna Porichoy *(an introduction to the Bengali alphabet) is still the first book given to a Bengali child, almost 170 years after it was first published.*

Marriage of Hindu Widows

Many Hindus are now thoroughly convinced of the pernicious consequences arising from the practice of prohibiting the marriage of widows. Many are already prepared to give their widowed daughters, sisters and other relations in marriage, and those who dare not go so far acknowledge it to be most desirable that this should be done.

Whether the marriage of widows is consonant to our Sastras is a question which, a short while ago, was discussed by some of the principal Pundits of our country. But, unfortunately, our modern Pundits, carried away in the heat of controversy by a passion for victory, become so eager to maintain their respective dogmas that they entirely lose sight of the subject they are investigating; and hence there is no hope of arriving at the truth of any question by convening an assembly of Pundits and setting them to debate on it. At the discussion above alluded to, each party considered itself victorious and its antagonist foiled. It is easy, therefore, to conceive how the question was decided. In fact, nothing was settled as to the point at issue. One great object, however, has been gained, and that is that most people, since that period, have been extremely anxious to ascertain the truth of this matter. Perceiving this eagerness I have been led to enquire into the subject; and, in order to lay before the public at large the result of my enquiries, I publish this treatise in the vernacular language of the country: so that after an impartial examination the Hindu public may judge whether the marriage of widows ought to be practised or not.

In entering upon this enquiry we should, first of all, consider that since the marriage of widows is a custom which has not prevailed among Hindus for many ages, in seeking to give our widows in marriage we propose an innovation and are bound to show that the custom is a proper one; for if it be otherwise, no man, having any regard for religion, would consent to its introduction. It is, therefore, highly necessary to establish first the propriety of this custom. But how is this to be done? By reasoning alone? No. For it will not be admitted by our countrymen that mere reasoning is applicable to such subjects. The custom must have the sanction of the Sastras; for in matters like this, the Sastras are the paramount authority among Hindus, and such acts only as are conformable to them are deemed proper. It must, therefore, first be settled, whether the marriage of widows is a custom consonant or opposed to the Sastras.

At the very outset of the enquiry as to whether the marriage of widows is consonant or opposed to our Sastras, we find it necessary to decide what are those Sastras, the sanction or prohibition of which will determine the propriety or impropriety of the practice. Certainly, Vyakarana (Grammar), Kavya (Poetry), Ahankara (Rhetoric), Darsana (Philosophy) and the like are not Sastras of this kind. It is only the works known as Dharma Sastras, that is to say, the works comprising the whole body of ceremonial and religious observances, moral duties, and municipal law, that are everywhere regarded as the Sastras to be referred to in deciding such questions.

Now, it should be enquired, what Dharmas have been enjoined in the Parasara Sanhita for widows. We find in the 4th chapter of this work the following passage:

'On receiving no tidings of a husband, on his demise, on his turning an ascetic, on his being found impotent or on his degradation—under any one of these five calamities, it is canonical for women to take another husband. That woman, who on the decease of her husband observes the Brahmacharya (leads the life of austerities and privations), attains heaven after death. She, who burns herself with her deceased husband, resides in heaven for as many Kalas or thousands of years as there are hairs on the human body or thirty-five millions.'

Thus, it appears that Parasara prescribes three rules for the conduct of a widow: marriage, the observance of the Brahmacharya and burning with the deceased husband. Among these, the custom of concremation has been abolished by order of the ruling authorities; only two ways, therefore, have now been left for the widows; they have the option of marrying or of observing the Brahmacharya. But in the Kali Yuga, it has become extremely difficult for widows to pass their lives in the observance of the Brahmacharya and it is for this reason that the Philanthropic Parasara has, in the first instance, prescribed marriage. Be that as it may, what I wish to be clearly understood is this—that as Parasara plainly prescribes marriage as one of the duties of women in the Kali Yuga under any one of the five above enumerated calamities, the marriage of widows in the Kali Yuga is consonant to the Sastras.

It being settled by the arguments above cited, that the marriage of widows in the Kali Yuga is consonant to the Sastras, we should now enquire whether in any Sastras, other than the Parasara Samhita, there is a prohibition of this marriage in the Kali Yuga. For it is argued by many that the marriage of widows was in vogue in the former Yugas, but has been forbidden in the Kali Yuga. It should be remembered, however, that in the Parasara Samhita, the Dharmas, appropriated to the Kali Yuga only, have been assigned and among those Dharmas the marriage of widows has been prescribed in the clearest manner. It can, therefore, never be maintained that widows have been forbidden to marry in the Kali Yuga. Under what authority this prohibitory dogma is upheld, is a secret known only to the prohibitionists.

Some people consider the texts of the Vrihannaradiya and Aditya Puranas, quoted by the Smartta Bhattacharya Raghunandana in his article on marriage, as prohibitory of the marriage of widows in the Kali Yuga. Those texts are, therefore, cited here with an explanation of their meaning and purport.

Vrihannaradiya Purana:

'Sea voyage; turning an ascetic; the marriage of twice-born men with damsels not of the same class; procreation on a brother's wife or widow; the slaughter of cattle in the entertainment of a guest; the repast on flesh-meat at funeral obsequies; the entrance into the order of a Vanaprastha (hermit); the giving away of a damsel, a second time, to a bridegroom, after she has been given to another; Brahmacharya continued for a long time; the sacrifice of a man, horse, or bull; walking on a pilgrimage till the Pilgrim dies, are the Dharmas the observance of which has been forbidden by the Munis (sages) in the Kali Yuga.'

Nowhere in these texts can any passage be found forbidding the marriage of widows.

An adequate idea of the intolerable hardships of early widowhood can be formed by those only whose daughters, sisters, daughters-in-law and other female relatives have been deprived of their husbands during their infancy. How many hundreds of widows, unable to observe the austerities of a Brahmacharya life, betake themselves to prostitution and foeticide and thus bring disgrace upon the families of their fathers, mothers and husbands. If the marriage of widows be allowed, it will remove the insupportable torments of life-long widowhood, diminish the crimes of prostitution and foeticide and secure all families from disgrace and infamy. As long as this salutary practice will be deferred, so long will the crimes of prostitution, adultery, incest and foeticide flow on in an ever increasing current; so long will family stains be multiplied; so long will a widow's agony blaze on in fiercer flames.

In conclusion, I humbly beseech the public to attend to these circumstances, and after having duly weighed all that have been said respecting the consonancy of the marriage of widows to the Sastras, to decide whether the marriage of widows should or should not prevail.

—From *Marriage of Hindu Widows*

47

Dadabhai Naoroji

Dadabhai Naoroji (1825–1917) was an Indian Independence activist, political leader, businessman, scholar and writer who served three terms as the president of the Indian National Congress. He became the first Indian to be appointed a professor at Elphinstone. In 1902, he was elected as a member of the Liberal Party in the House of Commons and thus became the first Indian member of the British Parliament. He became widely known for his unfavourable opinion of the economic consequences of British rule in India.

Poverty and Un-British Rule in India

In order to give briefly some indication of the scope and object of this book, I make some introductory remarks.

The title of the book is 'Poverty and un-British Rule in India,' i.e., the present system of government is destructive and despotic to the Indians and un-British and suicidal to Britain. On the other hand, a truly British course can and will certainly be vastly beneficent both to Britain and India.

Common sense will suggest this to any thoughtful mind. These evils have ever since gone on increasing, and more and more counterbalancing the increased produce of the country, making now the evil of the 'bleeding' and impoverishing drain by the foreign dominion nearly or above £30,000,000 a year in a variety of subtle ways and shapes; while about the beginning of the last century the drain was declared to be £3,000,000 a year—and with private remittances, was supposed to be near £5,000,000—or one-sixth of what it is at present. If the profits of exports and freight and insurance, which are not accounted for in the official statistics, be considered, the present drain will be nearer forty than thirty millions; speaking roughly on the old basis of the value of gold at two shillings per rupee.

Mr Montgomery Martin, after examining the records in the India House of a survey made in 1807–1814 of the condition of some provinces of Bengal and Behar, said in 1835 in his 'Eastern India': 'It is impossible to avoid remarking two facts as peculiarly striking—first the richness of the country surveyed, and second, the poverty of its inhabitants … The annual drain of £3,000,000 on British India has amounted in thirty years, at 12 per cent (the usual Indian rate) compound interest to the enormous sum of £723,900,000 sterling … So constant and accumulating a drain, even in England, would soon impoverish her. How severe then must be its effects on India when the wage of a labourer is from twopence to threepence a day.' He also calculates the result of the drain of £5,000,000 a year. What then must be or can be the effect of the unceasing drain which has now grown to the enormous amount of some £30,000,000 a year, if not famines and plagues, destruction and impoverishment!

Mill's *History of India* (vol. VI, p. 671) says: 'It is an exhausting drain upon the resources of the country, the issue of which is replaced by no reflex; it is an extraction of the life blood from the veins of national industry which no subsequent introduction of nourishment is furnished to restore.'

Sir George Wingate has said (1859): 'Taxes spent in the country from which they are raised are totally different in their effect from taxes raised in one country and spent in another.

In the former case the taxes collected from the population … are again returned to the industrious classes … But the case is wholly different when the taxes are not spent in the country from which they are raised … They constitute … an absolute loss and extinction of the whole amount withdrawn from the taxed country … might as well be thrown into the sea … Such is the nature of the tribute we have so long exacted from India … From this explanation some faint conception may be formed of the cruel, crushing effect of the tribute upon India … The Indian tribute, whether weighed in the scales of justice or viewed in the light of our own interest, will be found to be at variance with humanity, with common sense, and with the received maxims of economic science' ('A Few Words on Our Financial Relation with India.' London: Richardson Bros. 1859).

Lord Salisbury, as Secretary of State for India, in a Minute (26/4/1875) said [C. 3086-1-(1884, p. 144)]:

'The injury is exaggerated in the case of India, where so much of the revenue is exported without a direct equivalent. As India must be bled the lancet should be directed to the parts where the blood is congested or at least sufficient, not to those (the agricultural people) "which are already feeble from the want of it".'

This was said twenty-six years ago, and those who were considered as having sufficient blood are also being brought lower and lower. The 'want of blood' among the agricultural

population is getting so complete that famines and plagues like the present are fast bleeding the masses to death.

Lord Lawrence, Lord Cromer, Sir Auckland Colvin, Sir David Barbour, and others have declared the extreme poverty of India.

But the drain is not all. All the wars by which the British Indian Empire is built up have not only been fought mainly with Indian blood, but every farthing of expenditure (with insignificant exceptions) incurred in all wars and proceedings within and beyond the frontiers of India by which the Empire has been built up and maintained up to the present day has been exacted from the Indian people. Britain has spent nothing.

There is the great injustice that every expenditure incurred even for British interest is charged to India. Under the recommendation of the late 'Royal Commission—Indian Expenditure and Apportionment' the British Government has done a very small justice in refunding about £250,000 a year. Even for such trifle of justice we are thankful, and hope that this may lead to further justice. But it is necessary for us to have the help of the recognition and voice of the British public to ensure this.

The utter exhaustion and destruction from all these causes is terrific, and cannot but produce the present famines, plagues, etc. What would Britain's condition be under a similar fate? Let her ask herself that question. The Anglo-Indians always shirk that question, never face it. Their selfishness makes them blind and deaf to it.

Despotism

I need only say that the people of India have not the slightest voice in the expenditure of the revenue, and therefore in the good government of the country. The powers of the Government being absolutely arbitrary and despotic, and the Government being alien and bleeding, the effect is very exhausting and destructive indeed.

Sir William Hunter has truly said:

'I cannot believe that a people numbering one-sixth of the whole inhabitants of the globe, and whose aspirations have been nourished from their earliest youth on the strong food of English liberty, can be permanently denied a voice in the government of their country. I do not believe that races … into whom we have instilled the maxim of "no taxation without representation" as a fundamental right of a people, can be permanently excluded from a share in the management of their finances.'

Un-British and Suicidal to Britain

A committee of five members of the Council of the Secretary of State for India have declared the British Government to be exposed to the charge of keeping promise to the ear and breaking it to the hope (Report, 20th January, 1860).

Lord Lytton, as Viceroy of India, in a Minute referred to in the despatch of the Government of India of 2nd May,

1878, said: 'No sooner was the Act (1833) passed than the Government began to devise means for practically evading the fulfilment of it … We have had to choose between prohibiting them and cheating them, and we have chosen the least straightforward course ... are all so many deliberate and transparent subterfuges for stultifying the Act and reducing it to a dead letter … I do not hesitate to say that both the Government of England and of India appear to me up to the present moment unable to answer satisfactorily the charge of having taken every means in their power of breaking to the heart the words of promise they had uttered to the ear.' (First Report of the Indian National Congress.)

The Duke of Argyll has said: 'We have not fulfilled our duty or the promises and engagements which we have made.' (Hansard, 11/3/1869)

Lord Salisbury, in reply to Lord Northbrook's pleading for the fulfilment of British solemn pledges, said it was all 'political hypocrisy'. (Hansard, 9/4/1883)

Suicidal to Britain

Sir John Malcolm says: 'We are not warranted by the history of India, nor indeed by that of any other nation in the world, in reckoning upon the possibility of preserving an Empire of such a magnitude by a system which excludes, as ours does, the Natives from every station of high rank and honourable ambition … If we do not use the knowledge which we impart it will be employed against us … If these plans are not associated with the creation of duties that will employ the minds which we enlighten, we shall only prepare elements that will hasten the destruction of our Empire. The moral evil to us does not thus stand alone. It carries with it its Nemesis, the seeds of the destruction of the Empire itself.'

Mr John Bright: 'I say a Government like that has some fatal defect which at some not distant time must bring disaster and humiliation to the Government and to the people on whose behalf it rules.' (Speech in the Manchester Town Hall, 11/12/1877.)

The Duke of Devonshire pointed out that 'it is not wise to educate the people of India, to introduce among them your civilisation and your progress and your literature and at the same time to tell them they shall never have any chance of taking any part or share in the administration of the affairs of their country except by their getting rid the first instance of their European rulers.' (Hansard, 23/8/1883)

Lord Randolph Churchill, as Secretary of State for India, has said in a letter to the Treasury:

'The position of India in relation to taxation and the sources of public revenue is very peculiar, not merely from the habits of the people and their strong aversion to change, which is more specially exhibited to new forms of taxation, but likewise from *the character of the Government* which is *in the hands of foreigners who hold all the principal administrative*

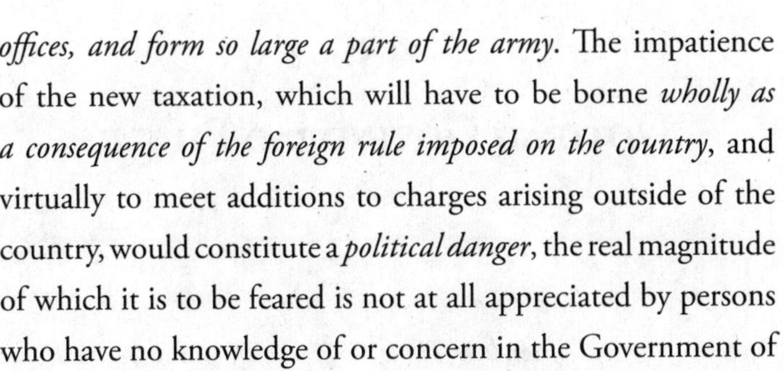

offices, and form so large a part of the army. The impatience of the new taxation, which will have to be borne *wholly as a consequence of the foreign rule imposed on the country*, and virtually to meet additions to charges arising outside of the country, would constitute a *political danger*, the real magnitude of which it is to be feared is not at all appreciated by persons who have no knowledge of or concern in the Government of India, but which those responsible for that Government have long regarded as of *the most serious order*.'

Lord George Hamilton candidly admits: 'Our Government never will be popular in India.' Again, 'our Government never can be popular in India'. (*Times*, 16/6/1899)

How can it be otherwise? If the present un-British and suicidal system of government continues, commonsense tells us that such a system 'can never' and 'will never' be popular. And if so, such a deplorable system cannot but perish; as Lord Salisbury truly says, 'Injustice will bring the highest on earth to ruin.' Macaulay has said, 'The heaviest of all yokes is the yoke of the stranger.' And if the British rule remains, as it is at present, a heavy yoke of the stranger and the despot, instead of being a true British rule and a friendly partner, it is doomed to perish. Evil is not, and never will be, eternal.\

—From *Poverty and Un-British Rule in India*

48
Jyotirao Govindrao Phule

Jyotirao 'Jyotiba' Govindrao Phule (1827–1890) was a socio-cultural reformer, activist, teacher, thinker and writer. He challenged the prevailing caste system and the social restrictions imposed on the lower classes. He coined the term 'Dalits' for all people considered lower caste and untouchables. In his mission to educate women and girls, he was supported by his wife Savitribai Phule, whom he had taught to read and write.

Jyotirao denounced the Vedas and blamed the Brahmins for designing the exploitative and inhuman laws that kept Shudras and Atishudras in slave-like conditions. He started the Satya Shodhak Samaj with the aim of freeing society from caste discrimination.

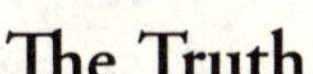

The Truth

Ganapatrao Daryaji Thorat: Who are the votaries or followers of the Truth?

Jyotirao Govindrao Phule: (1) Our Creator has created all human beings. All men and women are by birth independent, and are entitled to enjoy all due *human rights.* Those who accept this view are the votaries or followers of *the Truth.*

(2) Our Creator has created the Sun (Solar system) and the stars and planets of the galaxy in the vast void. He or she who does not venerate or worship any of these, or a freak star or any stone or metal icon as the true Creator—should be designated as the votaries or followers of *the Truth.*

(3) Our Creator has created all things in this world. Those who do not allow all human beings to enjoy all these things so created, but dedicate or offer them all to the Creator, a useless exercise, and who do not recite His name—an empty ritual—should be designated as the votaries or followers of *the Truth.*

(4) Those who allow all human beings to enjoy all the (good) things created by our Creator and who also allow

them to thank and glorify the Creator—should be designated as the votaries or followers of *the Truth*.

(5) Those who do not trouble any human beings created by our Creator (in His goodness) unnecessarily, should be designated as the votaries or followers of *the Truth*.

(6) Our Creator has graciously bestowed *all human rights* on all men and women, without any distinction. No particular man or a group (gang) of men has any right to oppress any human being. Those who do not so oppress their fellow beings should be designated as the votaries or followers of *the Truth*.

(7) Our Creator has bestowed full religious and political autonomy (freedom) on all human beings. So nobody is justified in troubling other persons. Those who respect other persons' rights scrupulously and do not trouble others in any way should be designated as the votaries or followers of *the Truth*.

(8) Our Creator has created all human beings. Each woman will choose one man as her husband, and each man will choose one woman as his wife. Barring such legitimate instances (cases, examples), if all men and women behave towards all other human beings as brothers and sisters, they should be designated as the votaries or followers of *the Truth*.

(9) Our Creator has given all human beings full freedom to express, to write down and to publish (propagate) their personal opinions and views regarding the human rights (which He has so kindly bestowed upon them all). Those who

take scrupulous care not to harm other human beings while exercising the above-mentioned freedom in their personal lives should be designated as the votaries or followers of *the Truth*.

(10) Those who accept this (divine) dispensation of our Creator, and who do not look down upon and do not oppress other human beings in respect of their (different) religious or political opinions or views, should be designated as the votaries or followers of *the Truth*.

(11) Those who accept the view that our Creator has endowed all human beings with the requisite capacity to hold (and enjoy) any position of authority in matters of religion, or village administration or revenue administration, in consonance with their innate ability and capability, should be designated as the votaries or followers of *the Truth*.

(12) In accordance with the dictates of our Creator, all human beings have rights regarding matters of religion, or village administration or revenue administration, such as their freedom (to enjoy these rights), their property, their defence and their protection from being oppressed. Those who do not hamper these rights should be designated as the votaries or followers of *the Truth*.

(13) Such men and women as take proper care of their parents in their old age and honour duly other senior (aged) worthies or those who honour such people duly (as mentioned in the previous clause) should be designated as the votaries or followers of *the Truth*.

(14) Those men or women who do not consume narcotics such as opium or heroin or who do not imbibe wine (as per the direction of the doctors) and who do not commit any acts of injustice (to others) or who do not give any quarter to those who indulge in such habits, should be designated as the votaries or followers of *the Truth*.

(15) There may be men or women who may have occasion to destroy vermin like lice, bed-bugs etc, or scorpions, reptiles like snakes, and ferocious animals like wolves, tigers and lions, as also greedy men who may murder other human beings, or suicides. Excepting persons in this category, those men or women who do not kill their fellow-beings or do not give aid and comfort to such murderers should be designated as the votaries or followers of *the Truth*.

(16) Those men or women who do not tell lies either for their own selfish ends or to harm the interests of others and who do not assist liars should be designated as the votaries or followers of *the Truth*.

(17) Men or women who do not indulge in immoral acts or who do not treat with respect persons indulging in such acts should be designated as the votaries or followers of *the Truth*.

(18) Men or women who do not commit theft of any kind, or who do not help such thieves should be designated as the votaries or followers of *the Truth*.

(19) Men or women who do not set fire to others' dwellings or belongings, or who do not befriend persons doing such

acts should be designated as the votaries or followers of *the Truth*.

(20) Men or women who, for personal gains, do not rebel against the princes (of Indian States) ruling over their subjects in a just manner, or against any other justly constituted administration, or against the officers or administrators (representatives) chosen voluntarily by the subjects, causing untold misery to lakhs of families, or who do not help persons so rebelling, should be designated as the votaries or followers of *the Truth*.

(21) There are (selfish and crooked) persons who brag loudly that the religious Scriptures have been composed for the common weal of all the people in this world, but who keep them tightly under their own vicious grasp and refuse even to show them to other fellow-citizens. Men or women who do not trust such treacherous braggarts should be designated as the votaries or followers of *the Truth*.

(22) Men or women who do not regard either themselves or their blood-relations or their own kith and kin or their own friends and companions only as pre-eminent, sacrosanct or specially privileged *hereditarily*, and who do not regard other human beings as of mean lineage or as unholy—such persons should be designated as the votaries or followers of *the Truth*.

(23) Men or women who, on the dubious authority of their spurious and wicked Scriptures, do not stigmatise other

human beings as hereditary slaves (helots, thralls) or who do not pay respect to those who stigmatise others—should be designated as the votaries or followers of *the Truth*.

(24) Men or women who, in order to perpetuate their own domination, do not discriminate against other people's children while imparting instruction to them in the schools, or who condemn persons so discriminating should be designated as the votaries or followers of *the Truth*.

(25) Men or women who, while dispensing justice in Courts of law, award due punishment to the guilty in accordance with the canons of justice *impartially* and fairly, and who condemn those who act unjustly and partially in such cases, should be designated as the votaries or followers of *the Truth*.

(26) Men or women who honour farmers or other artisans who earn their livelihood honestly, the hard way, and who pay respect to those who diligently help the farmers and allied classes, should be designated as the votaries or followers of *the Truth*.

(27) Men or women who do not look down upon persons earning an honest livelihood by working as unskilled labourers under a cobbler (a Chamar), but who, moreover, praise persons aiding such artisans, should be designated as the votaries or followers of *the Truth*.

(28) Men or women who, without engaging in any useful activity, putting on spurious religiosity, do not exploit

the ignorant masses by threatening them with dire doom consequent upon the baleful influence of the inauspicious planets, and who also do not write spurious, wicked books the better to feather their own nests unjustly, should be designated as the votaries or followers of *the Truth*.

(29) Men or women who do not deceive superstitious fools by posing to be (all-knowing) astrologers or as witch-doctors (or faith-healers) or who do not aid or abet such impostors should be designated as the votaries or followers of *the Truth*.

(30) Men or women who do not pretend to be mercenary devotees to propitiate imaginary gods and who do not earn an unrighteous livelihood by engaging in ceaseless recitations only to fleece and exploit the ignorant folk or who do not honour persons aiding and abetting such exploiters—should be designated as the votaries or followers of *the Truth*.

(31) Men or women who do not create dissensions among the ignorant folk in order to make an unrighteous living (livelihood) or who do not associate themselves even remotely with persons indulging in such irreligious practices should be designated as the votaries or followers of *the Truth*.

(32) Men or women who do not discriminate against human beings created by our Creator or who do not make any (artificial) distinctions in their dealings with them regarding their food habits or the mode of their apparel, but conduct

themselves with pure hearts to them, should be designated as the votaries or followers of *the Truth*.

(33) Men or women who do not discriminate against human beings, but who are ever ready to help, to the best of their ability, lepers, physically handicapped persons or orphans, or honour those helping such persons should be designated as the votaries or followers of *the Truth*.

Ganapatrao: The above-mentioned (thirty-three) rules or commandments conclusively prove that our compassionate Creator has not compiled in book-form the rules of ideal conduct guiding human beings in their dealings with one another. Do you agree with this hypothesis?

Jyotirao: Your point is well taken. Our Creator has created the majestic Solar system as also other planets and stars in the vast inter-stellar spaces—particularly the earth inhabited by human beings. Rather than feeling contented and happy about the way those human beings conduct themselves towards one another ideally—in consonance with the ethical rules and commandments laid down by Him, suppose He had been pleased to write a holy book or Scripture so that all the human beings inhabiting this earth should follow the straight and narrow path of *Truth*. In that (unlikely) event, He would surely have defined, impartially, the fundamental human rights of all men and women, without discriminating among them and He would have taken care to write that religious book or Scripture in a universal language which would have been understood by diverse people speaking diverse languages (all over the world).

Ganapatrao: Who, then, must have written the different religious books and Scriptures which wax so eloquent about the human rights of *men* only?

Jyotirao: All these different religious books and Scriptures have been composed by *compassionate, philanthropic Saints*, in which they have tried to propound the rights of *men* only, as per the authors' perceptions.

Ganapatrao: This thought has just occurred to me. *Firstly*, in the '*Aryan religion*', the Aryans have supplanted our universal Creator, and they presume to style themselves as the 'earth-gods' of the ignorant folk. *Secondly*, Jesus is called the Son of the Creator (of the Universe). And *thirdly*, in Islam, Muhammad is called the *Paigambar* (Carrier of the message, the Messenger) of our Creator. I shall be grateful to you if you will kindly enlighten me on all these (abstruse) points.

Jyotirao: *Firstly*, the Aryans presumed to be Vedantic experts on the authority of their wholly illogical, philosophical arrogance (deceitfulness), rendered our Creator redundant, and subsequently supplanted Him. They further grew all-powerful and have become the 'earth-gods' of the ignorant, defeated folk (in India). *Secondly*, Jesus, in the evangelism preached by him about the Creator, regarded Him as the (kind) Father of us all, and instructed them, with a great hope, for the redemption of his ignorant brethren. That is why all the Christians revere him as the *Son of God* and also as their Saviour. *Thirdly*, Muhammad has recorded in the *Holy Quran* many details about the Creator's powers (authorities, officers). The kernel of his preaching, as presented there, highlights the fact that our Creator has sent Muhammad into the world to lead all mankind to the path of righteousness. He used to preach this philosophy to all people openly and forcefully. That is why all the Muslims belonging to the *Shiya* and *Sunni* Sects regard him as the *Paigambar* or the Messenger (Carrier of the Message) of our Creator.

Ganapatrao: Dear Tatyasaheb, you say that all these Scriptures (religious books) were written by holy men. I would like to know if any holy woman has written any Scriptures.

Jyotirao: If a holy woman had written any Scripture, then men would not have been able to ignore the due rights of women and they would also not have waxed so eloquent about their own rights. If women were learned enough, then men would never have been able to be so partial and deceitful.

Ganapatrao: If these great and holy men have propounded some facts of Truth in their religious books (Scriptures) regarding the rights of men, then why are their followers so deeply divided among themselves?

Jyotirao: The reason for these deep divisions among them, according to me, is as follows: They do not think in an impartial and dispassionate (rational) manner about their own religion or about other (people's) religion, but hold (believe) obdurately and obstinately that their own religion has the monopoly of Truth. I am convinced that if all of us think impartially and dispassionately about our (different) religions, we would never be so foolish or rash to dub other people's religion as untrue (spurious).

Ganapatrao: Secondly, even though they think impartially and dispassionately about all the religions, then how is it they are so antagonistic to one another? There is no valid reason for it.

Jyotirao: That is because they do not take a balanced (impartial) view about the holy founders of the different religions as also about the logical deductions regarding the extent of truth reflected in the conduct of the ignorant followers of those religions.

Ganapatrao: If we accept your explanation, then it appears that people in ancient times were not as tolerant and accommodating as people in modern times.

Jyotirao: Undoubtedly so. If the people in ancient times were as tolerant and accommodating as the modern ones, it stands to reason that they would never have condemned the Shudras and Ati-Shudras to the meanest level in society. They would also never have condemned the children of those whom they had vanquished on the battlefield to the status of *serfs, helots, slaves*, and forced them to serve them eternally in that capacity. It is a cruel fact that some people did exercise this wholly iniquitous right over the Shudras and hence their 'learned and saintly' authors dared not record this evil practice in any of their so-called Sacred Books. This fact proves that they (the Aryans) were of an *obdurate, uncompromising* and *vindictive nature*.

Ganapatrao: I grant that not even an uncultured, uncivilised barbarian would have dared record such a barbarous practice in his religious books or Scripture. I shall be grateful to you if you would kindly enlighten me upon the nature of the *Ideal Sacred Book*.

Jyotirao: Men and women should not discriminate against one another (should treat others justly) irrespective of the consideration of their villages, or Presidencies, or Countries or Continents or irrespective of the religious beliefs which they profess, but they should regard themselves as *members of one world-wide family*, should behave amicably and in unison, observing strictly the truthful doctrine (path). Only thus can they please their Creator and become his dear children. Only such (virtuous) persons should be designated as the votaries or followers of *the Truth*. If all human beings had followed this noble principle and had been the votaries of *the Truth*, then the deified Parashuram, (and his) minions—the police, the judges and the guards in various prison-houses—would have been rendered redundant (they would have been dispensed with).

Ganapatrao: I request you, Tatyasaheb, to give your final ruling (opinion) about the (ideal) religion to be followed by all the human beings in this wide world.

Jyotirao: Dear Ganapatrao, all the Sacred Books (Scriptures) compiled by different holy persons do contain some element of Truth, as per their own perceptions and in consonance with the spirit of their times. In that (ideal) family, the lady (of the house) may, if she likes, embrace Buddhism after studying the Buddhist religious scripture; her husband may embrace Christianity, if he likes (if he so chooses) after studying the Old and the New Testaments (of the Bible); their daughter may embrace Islam if she so chooses after studying the Quran; and their son may embrace the Universal Religion of Truth, if he so chooses, after studying the 'Universal Religion of Truth' (by Mahatma Phule, 1891). And all these members of the family (the parents, the son and the daughter) should lead peaceful lives, should never envy or hate the other persons' religion, and all of them should behave towards one another in a spirit of love and understanding, always bearing in their minds that they are the Creator's children, and hence are the members of (belonging to) the Creator's own family. By following this righteous path, they will, indeed, be the blessed citizens of our Creator's Kingdom.

Ganapatrao: That is enough (for me). If each one of those Sacred Books invariably contains some element of *the Truth*, then I am quite convinced that all the religions which are in vogue in this universe are the children of the *Universal Truth*.

Jyotirao Phule: Now all of you should reflect deeply for yourselves whether the followers (votaries) of all the religions should bow down reverently before the *Universal Truth*, or the manner in which the *Universal Truth* should honour the followers (votaries) of all the religions (in the world). Let it be! As all men and women have every right to conduct themselves towards others without hurting or harming them (in any way), (so, I exhort you all) to treat all men and women as your own brothers and sisters, without discriminating among them in any way so that you will be truly blessed in the eyes of our Creator (the Governor, the Ruler of us all)!

—Translated by P.G. Patil

49

Ramakrishna Paramahamsa

Gadadhar Chattopadhyay (1836–1886), who came to be known as Sri Ramakrishna Paramahamsa, was a mystic and a yogi. He translated complex concepts of spiritual philosophies into logical and easily intelligible parables, stories and anecdotes. After practising different versions of Hinduism, Islam and Christianity, he came to the conclusion that all religions are different paths that lead to the same goal—the realisation of God.

His chief disciple Swami Vivekananda founded the Ramakrishna Mission to propagate his thoughts and teachings.

Master and Disciple

Second Visit

M.'s second visit to Sri Ramakrishna took place on the southeast verandah at eight o'clock in the morning. The Master was about to be shaved, the barber having just arrived. As the cold season still lingered he had put on a moleskin shawl bordered with red. Seeing M., the Master said: 'So you have come. That's good. Sit down here.' He was smiling. He stammered a little when he spoke.

Sri Ramakrishna (to M.): 'Where do you live?'

M: 'In Calcutta, sir.'

Sri Ramakrishna: 'Where are you staying here?'

M: 'I am at Baranagore at my older sister's—Ishan Kaviraj's house.'

Sri Ramakrishna: 'Oh, at Ishan's? Well, how is Keshab now? He was very ill.'

M: 'Indeed, I have heard so too, but I believe he is well now.'

Master's Love for Keshab

Sri Ramakrishna: 'I made a vow to worship the Mother with green coconut and sugar on Keshab's recovery. Sometimes, in the early hours of the morning, I would wake up and cry before Her: "Mother, please make Keshab well again. If Keshab doesn't live, whom shall I talk with when I go to Calcutta?" And so it was that I resolved to offer Her the green coconut and sugar.

'Tell me, do you know of a certain Mr Cook who has come to Calcutta? Is it true that he is giving lectures? Once Keshab took me on a steamer, and this Mr Cook, too was in the party.'

M: 'Yes, sir, I have heard something like that; but I have never been to his lectures. I don't know much about him.'

Sri Ramakrishna on M.'s Marriage

Sri Ramakrishna: 'Pratap's brother came here. He stayed a few days. He had nothing to do and said he wanted to live here. I came to know that he had left his wife and children with his father-in-law. He has a whole brood of them! So I took him to task. Just fancy! He is the father of so many children! Will people from the neighbourhood feed them and bring them up? He isn't even ashamed that someone else is feeding his wife and children, and that they have been left at his father-in-law's house. I scolded him very hard and asked him to look for a job. Then he was willing to leave here.

'Are you married?'

M: 'Yes, sir.'

Sri Ramakrishna (with a shudder): 'Oh, Ramlal! Alas, he is married!'

Like one guilty of a terrible offence, M. sat motionless, his eyes fixed on the ground. He thought, 'Is it such a wicked thing to get married?'

The Master continued, 'Have you any children?'

M. this time could hear the beating of his own heart. He whispered in a trembling voice, 'Yes, sir, I have children.'

Very sadly Sri Ramakrishna said, 'Ah me! He even has children!'

Thus rebuked M. sat speechless. His pride had received a blow. After a few minutes Sri Ramakrishna looked at him kindly and said affectionately: 'You see, you have certain good signs. I know them by looking at a person's forehead, his eyes, and so on. Tell me, now, what kind of person is your wife? Has she spiritual attributes, or is she under the power of avidya?'

M: 'She is all right. But I am afraid she is ignorant.'

Master (with evident displeasure): 'And you are a man of knowledge!'

M. had yet to learn the distinction between knowledge and ignorance. Up to this time his conception had been that one got knowledge from books and schools. Later on he gave up this false conception. He was taught that to know God is knowledge, and not to know Him, ignorance. When Sri Ramakrishna exclaimed, 'And you are a man of knowledge!', M.'s ego was again badly shocked.

God with and Without Form

Master: 'Well, do you believe in God with form or without form?'

M., rather surprised, said to himself: 'How can one believe in God without form when one believes in God with form? And if one believes in God without form, how can one believe that God has a form? Can these two contradictory ideas be true at the same time? Can a white liquid like milk be black?'

M: 'Sir, I like to think of God as formless.'

Master: 'Very good. It is enough to have faith in either aspect. You believe in God without form; that is quite all right. But never for a moment think that this alone is true and all else false. Remember that God with form is just as true as God without form. But hold fast to your own conviction.'

The assertion that both are equally true amazed M.; he had never learnt this from his books. Thus his ego received a third blow; but since it was not yet completely crushed, he came forward to argue with the Master a little more.

God and the Clay Image

M: 'Sir, suppose one believes in God with form. Certainly He is not the clay image!'

Master (interrupting): 'But why clay? It is an image of Spirit.'

M. could not quite understand the significance of this 'image of Spirit'. 'But, sir,' he said to the Master, 'one should explain to those who worship the clay image that it is not God, and that, while worshipping it, they should have God in view and not the clay image. One should not worship clay.'

God the Only Real Teacher

Master (sharply): 'That's the one hobby of you Calcutta people—giving lectures and bringing others to the light! Nobody ever stops to consider how to get the light himself. Who are you to teach others?

'He who is the Lord of the Universe will teach everyone. He alone teaches us, who has created this universe; who has made the sun and moon, men and beasts, and all other beings; who has provided means for their sustenance; who has given children, parents and endowed them with love to bring them up. The Lord has done so many things—will He not show people the way to worship Him? If they need teaching, then He will be the Teacher. He is our Inner Guide.

'Suppose there is an error in worshipping the clay image; doesn't God know that through it He alone is being invoked? He will be pleased with that very worship. Why should you

get a headache over it? You had better try for knowledge and devotion yourself.'

This time M. felt that his ego was completely crushed. He now said to himself: 'Yes, he has spoken the truth. What need is there for me to teach others? Have I known God? Do I really love Him? "I haven't room enough for myself in my bed, and I am inviting my friend to share it with me!" I know nothing about God, yet I am trying to teach others. What a shame! How foolish I am! This is not mathematics or history or literature, that one can teach it to others. No, this is the deep mystery of God. What he says appeals to me.'

This was M.'s first argument with the Master, and happily his last.

Master: 'You were talking of worshipping the clay image. Even if the image is made of clay, there is need for that sort of worship. God Himself has provided different forms of worship. He who is the Lord of the Universe has arranged all these forms to suit different men in different stages of knowledge.

'The mother cooks different dishes to suit the stomachs of her different children. Suppose she has five children. If there is a fish to cook, she prepares various dishes from it—pilau, pickled fish, fried fish, and so on—to suit their different tastes and powers of digestion.

'Do you understand me?'

Need of Holy Company and Meditation in Solitude

M. (humbly): 'Yes, sir. How, sir, may we fix our minds on God?'

Master: 'Repeat God's name and sing His glories, and keep holy company; and now and then visit God's devotees and holy men. The mind cannot dwell on God if it is immersed day and night in worldliness, in worldly duties and responsibilities; it is most necessary to go into solitude now and then and think of God. To fix the mind on God is very difficult, in the beginning, unless one practises meditation in solitude. When a tree is young it should be fenced all around; otherwise it may be destroyed by cattle.

'To meditate, you should withdraw within yourself or retire to a secluded corner or to the forest. And you should always discriminate between the real and the unreal. God alone is real, the Eternal Substance; all else is unreal, that is, impermanent. By discriminating thus, one should shake off impermanent objects from the mind.'

God and Worldly Duties

M. (humbly): 'How ought we to live in the world?'

Master: 'Do all your duties, but keep your mind on God. Live with all—with wife and children, father and mother—and serve them. Treat them as if they were very dear to you, but know in your heart of hearts that they do not belong to you.

'A maidservant in the house of a rich man performs all the household duties, but her thoughts are fixed on her own home in her native village. She brings up her Master's children as if they were her own. She even speaks of them as "my Rama" or "my Hari". But in her own mind she knows very well that they do not belong to her at all.

'The tortoise moves about in the water. But can you guess where her thoughts are? There on the bank, where her eggs are lying. Do all your duties in the world, but keep your mind on God.

'If you enter the world without first cultivating love for God, you will be entangled more and more. You will be overwhelmed with its danger, its grief, its sorrows. And the more you think of worldly things, the more you will be attached to them.

'First rub your hands with oil and then break open the jack-fruit; otherwise they will be smeared with its sticky milk. First secure the oil of divine love, and then set your hands to the duties of the world.

'But one must go into solitude to attain this divine love. To get butter from milk you must let it set into curd in a secluded spot; if it is too much disturbed, milk won't turn into curd. Next, you must put aside all other duties, sit in a quiet spot, and churn the curd. Only then do you get butter.

'Further, by meditating on God in solitude the mind acquires knowledge, dispassion, and devotion. But the very same mind goes downward if it dwells in the world. In the world there is only one thought: "woman and gold".

'The world is water and the mind milk. If you pour milk into water they become one; you cannot find the pure milk any more. But turn the milk into curd and churn it into butter. Then, when that butter is placed in water, it will float. So, practise spiritual discipline in solitude and obtain the butter of knowledge and love. Even if you keep that butter in the water of the world the two will not mix. The butter will float.'

Practice of Discrimination

'Together with this, you must practice discrimination. "Woman and gold" is impermanent. God is the only Eternal Substance. What does a man get with money? Food, clothes, and a dwelling-place—nothing more. You cannot realize God with its help. Therefore money can never be the goal of life. That is the process of discrimination. Do you understand?'

M: 'Yes, sir. I recently read a Sanskrit play called *Prabodha Chandrodaya*. It deals with discrimination.'

Master: 'Yes, discrimination about objects. Consider—what is there in money or in a beautiful body? Discriminate

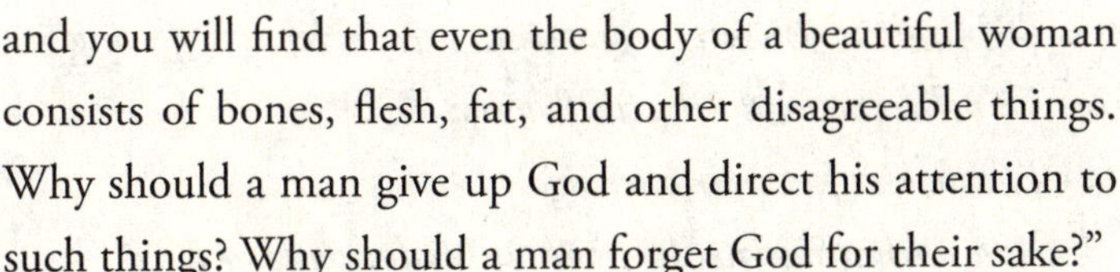

and you will find that even the body of a beautiful woman consists of bones, flesh, fat, and other disagreeable things. Why should a man give up God and direct his attention to such things? Why should a man forget God for their sake?"

How to See God

M: 'Is it possible to see God?'

Master: 'Yes, certainly. Living in solitude now and then, repeating God's name and singing His glories, and discriminating between the real and the unreal—these are the means to employ to see Him.'

Longing and Yearning

M: 'Under what conditions does one see God?'

Master: 'Cry to the Lord with an intensely yearning heart and you will certainly see Him. People shed a whole jug of tears for wife and children. They swim in tears for money. But who weeps for God? Cry to Him with a real cry.'

'The Master sang:

Cry to your Mother Syama, with a real cry, O mind!
And how can She hold Herself from you?
How can Syama stay away?
How can your Mother Kali hold Herself away?

O mind, if you are in earnest, bring Her an offering
Of bel-leaves and hibiscus flowers;
Lay at Her feet your offering
And with it mingle the fragrant sandal-paste of Love.

Continuing, he said: 'Longing is like the rosy dawn. After the dawn out comes the sun. Longing is followed by the vision of God.

'God reveals Himself to a devotee who feels drawn to Him by the combined force of these three attractions: the attraction of worldly possessions for the worldly man, the child's attraction for its mother, and the husband's attraction for the chaste wife. If one feels drawn to Him by the combined force of these three attractions, then through it one can attain Him.

'The point is, to love God even as the mother loves her child, the chaste wife her husband, and the worldly man his wealth. Add together these three forces of love, these three powers of attraction, and give it all to God. Then you will certainly see Him.

'It is necessary to pray to Him with a longing heart. The kitten knows only how to call its mother, crying, "Mew, mew!" It remains satisfied wherever its mother puts it. And the mother cat puts the kitten sometimes in the kitchen, sometimes on the floor, and sometimes on the bed. When it suffers it cries only, "Mew, mew!"

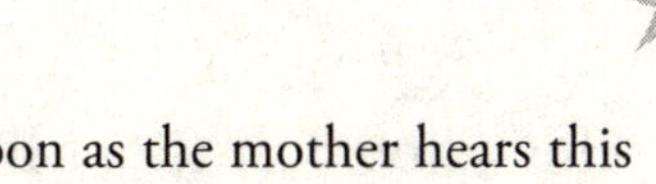

'That's all it knows. But as soon as the mother hears this cry, wherever she may be, she comes to the kitten.'

Third Visit

It was Sunday afternoon when M. came on his third visit to the Master. He had been profoundly impressed by his first two visits to this wonderful man. He had been thinking of the Master constantly, and of the utterly simple way he explained the deep truths of the spiritual life. Never before had he met such a man.

Sri Ramakrishna was sitting on the small couch. The room was filled with devotees, who had taken advantage of the holiday to come to see the Master. M. had not yet become acquainted with any of them; so he took his seat in a corner. The Master smiled as he talked with the devotees.

Narendra

He addressed his words particularly to a young man of nineteen, named Narendranath, who was a college student and frequented the Sadharan Brahmo Samaj. His eyes were bright, his words were full of spirit, and he had the look of a lover of God.

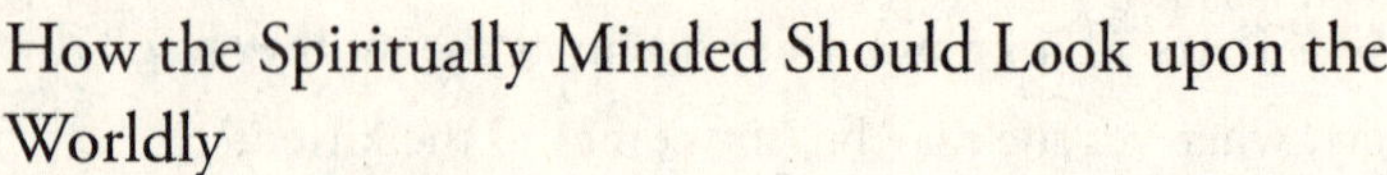

How the Spiritually Minded Should Look upon the Worldly

M. guessed that the conversation was about worldly men, who look down on those who aspire to spiritual things. The Master was talking about the great number of such people in the world, and about how to deal with them.

Master (to Narendra): 'How do you feel about it? Worldly people say all kinds of things about the spiritually minded. But look here! When an elephant moves along the street, any number of curs and other small animals may bark and cry after it; but the elephant doesn't even look back at them. If people speak ill of you, what will you think of them?'

Narendra: 'I shall think that dogs are barking at me.'

God in Every Being

Master (Smiling): 'Oh, no! You mustn't go that far, my child! (Laughter). God dwells in all beings. But you may be intimate only with good people; you must keep away from the evil-minded. God is even in the tiger; but you cannot embrace the tiger on that account. (Laughter). You may say, "Why run away from a tiger, which is also a manifestation of God?" The answer to that is: "Those who tell you to run away are also manifestations of God—and why shouldn't you listen to them?"'

Hanuman's Devotion to Rama

The conversation drifted to Hanuman, whose picture hung on the wall in the Master's room.

Sri Ramakrishna said: 'Just imagine Hanuman's state of mind. He didn't care for money, honour, creature comforts, or anything else. He longed only for God. When he was running away with the heavenly weapon that had been secreted in the crystal pillar, Mandodari began to tempt him with various fruits so that he might come down and drop the weapon. But he couldn't be tricked so easily. In reply to her persuasions, he sang this song:

Am I in need of fruit?
I have the Fruit that makes this life
Fruitful indeed. Within my heart
The Tree of Rama grows,
Bearing salvation for its fruit.

Under the Wish-fulfilling Tree
Of Rama do I sit at ease,
Plucking whatever fruit I will.
But if you speak of fruit—
No beggar, I, for common fruit.
Behold, I go,
Leaving a bitter fruit for you.'

As Sri Ramakrishna was singing the song he went into samadhi. Again the half-closed eyes and motionless body that one sees in his photograph. Just a minute before, the devotees had been making merry in his company. Now all eyes were riveted on him. Thus for the second time M. saw the Master in samadhi.

After a long time the Master came back to ordinary consciousness. His face lighted up with a smile, and his body relaxed; his senses began to function in a normal way. He shed tears of joy as he repeated the holy name of Rama. M. wondered whether this very saint was the person who a few minutes earlier had been behaving like a child of five.

The Master said to Narendra and M., 'I should like to hear you speak and argue in English.' They both laughed. But they continued to talk in their mother tongue. It was impossible for M. to argue any more before the Master. Though Ramakrishna insisted, they did not talk in English.

At five o'clock in the afternoon all the devotees except Narendra and M. took leave of the Master. As M. was walking in the temple garden, he suddenly came upon the Master talking to Narendra on the bank of the goose-pond. Sri Ramakrishna said to Narendra: 'Look here. Come a little more often. You are a new-comer. On first acquaintance people visit each other quite often, as is the case with a lover and his sweetheart. (Narendra and M. laugh.) So please come, won't you?'

Narendra, a member of the Brahmo Samaj, was very particular about his promises. He said with a smile, 'Yes, sir, I shall try.'

As they were returning to the Master's room, Sri Ramakrishna said to M.: 'When peasants go to market to buy bullocks for their ploughs, they can easily tell the good from the bad by touching their tails. On being touched there, some meekly lie down on the ground. The peasants recognize that these are without mettle and so reject them. They select only those bullocks that frisk about and show spirit when their tails are touched. Narendra is like a bullock of this latter class. He is full of spirit within.'

The Master smiled as he said this, and continued: 'There are some people who have no grit whatever. They are like flattened rice soaked in milk—soft and mushy. No inner strength!'

It was dusk. The Master was meditating on God. He said to M.: 'Go and talk to Narendra. Then tell me what you think of him.'

Evening worship was over in the temples. M. met Narendra on the bank of the Ganges and they began to converse. Narendra told M. about his studying in college, his being a member of the Brahmo Samaj, and so on.

It was now late in the evening and time for M.'s departure; but he felt reluctant to go and instead went in search of Sri Ramakrishna. He had been fascinated by the

Master's singing and wanted to hear more. At last he found the Master pacing alone in the natmandir in front of the Kali temple. A lamp was burning in the temple on either side of the image of the Divine Mother. The single lamp in the spacious natmandir blended light and darkness into a kind of mystic twilight, in which the figure of the Master could be dimly seen.

M. had been enchanted by the Master's sweet music. With some hesitation he asked him whether there would be any more singing that evening. 'No, not tonight,' said Sri Ramakrishna after a little reflection. Then, as if remembering something, he added: 'But I'm going soon to Balaram Bose's house in Calcutta. Come there and you'll hear me sing.' M. agreed to go.

Master: 'Do you know Balaram Bose?'

M: 'No, sir. I don't.'

Master: 'He lives in Bosepara.'

M: 'Well, sir, I shall find him.'

As Sri Ramakrishna walked up and down the hall with M., he said to him: 'Let me ask you something. What do you think of me?'

M. remained silent. Again Sri Ramakrishna asked: 'What do you think of me? How many annas of knowledge of God have I?'

M: 'I don't understand what you mean by "annas". But of this I am sure: I have never before seen such knowledge,

ecstatic love, faith in God, renunciation, and catholicity anywhere.'

The Master laughed.

M. bowed low before him and took his leave. He had gone as far as the main gate of the temple garden when he suddenly remembered something and came back to Sri Ramakrishna, who was still in the natmandir. In the dim light the Master, all alone, was pacing the hall, rejoicing in the Self as the lion lives and roams alone in the forest.

In silent wonder M. surveyed that great soul.

Master (to M.): 'What makes you come back?'

M: 'Perhaps the house you asked me to go to belongs to a rich man. They may not let me in. I think I had better not go. I would rather meet you here.'

Master: 'Oh, no! Why should you think that? Just mention my name. Say that you want to see me; then someone will take you to me.'

M. nodded his assent and, after saluting the Master, took his leave.

—Translated by Swami Nikhilananda

50

Rabindranath Tagore

Rabindranath Tagore (1861–1941) was a poet, novelist, playwright, essayist, composer, philosopher, educator, social reformer and painter. He was the first non-European to receive the Nobel Prize in Literature for Gitanjali*, originally written in Bengali and translated into English. He introduced the use of colloquial language in Bengali literature, which had been heavily influenced by Sanskrit until then. He wrote the national anthems for both India and Bangladesh.*

Gitanjali

1

Thou hast made me endless, such is thy pleasure. This frail vessel thou emptiest again and again, and fillest it ever with fresh life.

This little flute of a reed thou hast carried over hills and dales, and hast breathed through it melodies eternally new.

At the immortal touch of thy hands my little heart loses its limits in joy and gives birth to utterance ineffable.

Thy infinite gifts come to me only on these very small hands of mine. Ages pass, and still thou pourest, and still there is room to fill.

35

Where the mind is without fear and the head is held high;

Where knowledge is free;

Where the world has not been broken up into fragments by narrow domestic walls;

Where words come out from the depth of truth;

Where tireless striving stretches its arms towards perfection;

Where the clear stream of reason has not lost its way into the dreary desert sand of dead habit;

Where the mind is led forward by thee into ever-widening thought and action—

Into that heaven of freedom, my Father, let my country awake.

86

Death, thy servant, is at my door. He has crossed the unknown sea and brought thy call to my home.

The night is dark and my heart is fearful—yet I will take up the lamp, open my gates and bow to him my welcome. It is thy messenger who stands at my door.

I will worship him with folded hands, and with tears. I will worship him placing at his feet the treasure of my heart.

He will go back with his errand done, leaving a dark shadow on my morning; and in my desolate home only my forlorn self will remain as my last offering to thee.

93

I have got my leave. Bid me farewell, my brothers! I bow to you all and take my departure.

Here I give back the keys of my door—and I give up all claims to my house. I only ask for last kind words from you.

We were neighbours for long, but I received more than I could give. Now the day has dawned and the lamp that lit my dark corner is out. A summons has come and I am ready for my journey.

103

In one salutation to thee, my God, let all my senses spread out and touch this world at thy feet.

Like a rain-cloud of July hung low with its burden of unshed showers let all my mind bend down at thy door in one salutation to thee.

Let all my songs gather together their diverse strains into a single current and flow to a sea of silence in one salutation to thee.

Like a flock of homesick cranes flying night and day back to their mountain nests let all my life take its voyage to its eternal home in one salutation to thee.

Swami Vivekananda

Narendranath Datta (1863–1902), later known as Swami Vivekananda, was a Hindu monk, philosopher and religious teacher. He was the chief disciple of the mystic Ramakrishna Paramahamsa and remains one of the most celebrated spiritual leaders of India. A proponent of Vedanta and Yoga, he was responsible for the revival of Hindu spiritualism and established Hinduism as a revered religion on the world stage. He taught that all religions and all methods of worship lead to one and the same goal.

The World Parliament of Religion, Chicago

Response to Welcome, 11 September 1893

Sisters and Brothers of America,

It fills my heart with joy unspeakable to rise in response to the warm and cordial welcome which you have given us. I thank you in the name of the most ancient order of monks in the world; I thank you in the name of the mother of religions; and I thank you in the name of millions and millions of Hindu people of all classes and sects.

My thanks, also, to some of the speakers on this platform who, referring to the delegates from the Orient, have told you that these men from far-off nations may well claim the honour of bearing to different lands the idea of toleration. I am proud to belong to a religion which has taught the world both tolerance and universal acceptance. We believe not only in universal toleration, but we accept all religions as true. I am proud to belong to a nation which has sheltered the persecuted and the refugees of all religions and all nations of the earth. I am proud to tell you that we have gathered in our bosom the purest remnant of the Israelites, who came to Southern

India and took refuge with us in the very year in which their holy temple was shattered to pieces by Roman tyranny. I am proud to belong to the religion which has sheltered and is still fostering the remnant of the grand Zoroastrian nation. I will quote to you, brethren, a few lines from a hymn which I remember to have repeated from my earliest boyhood, which is every day repeated by millions of human beings: 'As the different streams having their sources in different places all mingle their water in the sea, so, O Lord, the different paths which men take through different tendencies, various though they appear, crooked or straight, all lead to Thee.'

The present convention, which is one of the most august assemblies ever held, is in itself a vindication, a declaration to the world of the wonderful doctrine preached in the Gita: 'Whosoever comes to Me, through whatsoever form, I reach him; all men are struggling through paths which in the end lead to Me.' Sectarianism, bigotry, and its horrible descendant, fanaticism, have long possessed this beautiful earth. They have filled the earth with violence, drenched it often and often with human blood, destroyed civilisation and sent whole nations to despair. Had it not been for these horrible demons, human society would be far more advanced than it is now. But their time is come; and I fervently hope that the bell that tolled this morning in honour of this convention may be the death-knell of all fanaticism, of all persecutions with the sword or with the pen, and of all uncharitable feelings between persons wending their way to the same goal.

Why We Disagree, 15 September 1893

I will tell you a little story. You have heard the eloquent speaker who has just finished say, 'Let us cease from abusing each other,' and he was very sorry that there should be always so much variance.

But I think I should tell you a story which would illustrate the cause of this variance. A frog lived in a well. It had lived there for a long time. It was born there and brought up there, and yet was a little, small frog. Of course, the evolutionists were not there then to tell us whether the frog lost its eyes or not, but, for our story's sake, we must take it for granted that it had its eyes, and that it every day cleansed the water of all the worms and bacilli that lived in it with an energy that would do credit to our modern bacteriologists. In this way it went on and became a little sleek and fat. Well, one day another frog that lived in the sea came and fell into the well.

'Where are you from?'

'I am from the sea.'

'The sea! How big is that? Is it as big as my well?' and he took a leap from one side of the well to the other.

'My friend,' said the frog of the sea, 'how do you compare the sea with your little well?'

Then the frog took another leap and asked, 'Is your sea so big?'

'What nonsense you speak, to compare the sea with your well!'

'Well, then,' said the frog of the well, 'nothing can be bigger than my well; there can be nothing bigger than this; this fellow is a liar, so turn him out.'

That has been the difficulty all the while.

I am a Hindu. I am sitting in my own little well and thinking that the whole world is my little well. The Christian sits in his little well and thinks the whole world is his well. The Mohammedan sits in his little well and thinks that is the whole world. I have to thank you of America for the great attempt you are making to break down the barriers of this little world of ours, and hope that, in the future, the Lord will help you to accomplish your purpose.

Paper on Hinduism, 19 September 1893

Three religions now stand in the world which have come down to us from time prehistoric—Hinduism, Zoroastrianism and Judaism. They have all received tremendous shocks, and all of them prove by their survival their internal strength. But while Judaism failed to absorb Christianity and was driven out of its place of birth by its all-conquering daughter, and a handful of Parsees is all that remains to tell the tale of their grand religion, sect after sect arose in India and seemed to shake the religion of the Vedas to its very foundations, but like the waters of the seashore in a tremendous earthquake it receded only for a while, only to return in an all-absorbing flood, a thousand times more vigorous, and when the tumult of the rush was over, these sects were all sucked in, absorbed, and assimilated into the immense body of the mother faith. From the high spiritual flights of the Vedanta philosophy, of which the latest discoveries of science seem like echoes, to the low ideas of idolatry with its multifarious mythology, the agnosticism of the Buddhists, and the atheism of the Jains, each and all have a place in the Hindu's religion.

Where then, the question arises, where is the common centre to which all these widely diverging radii converge? Where is the common basis upon which all these seemingly hopeless contradictions rest? And this is the question I shall attempt to answer.

The Hindus have received their religion through revelation, the Vedas. They hold that the Vedas are without beginning and without end. It may sound ludicrous to this audience, how a book can be without beginning or end. But by the Vedas, no books are meant. They mean the accumulated treasury of spiritual laws discovered by different persons in different times. Just as the law of gravitation existed before its discovery, and would exist if all humanity forgot it, so is it with the laws that govern the spiritual world. The moral, ethical, and spiritual relations between soul and soul and between individual spirits and the Father of all spirits, were there before their discovery, and would remain even if we forgot them.

The discoverers of these laws are called Rishis, and we honour them as perfected beings. I am glad to tell this audience that some of the very greatest of them were women. Here it may be said that these laws as laws may be without end, but they must have had a beginning. The Vedas teach us that creation is without beginning or end. Science is said to have proved that the sum total of cosmic energy is always the same. Then, if there was a time when nothing existed, where was all this manifested energy? Some say it was in a potential form in God. In that case God is sometimes potential and sometimes kinetic, which would make Him mutable. Everything mutable is a compound, and everything compound must undergo that change which is called destruction. So God would die, which is absurd. Therefore there never was a time when there was no creation.

If I may be allowed to use a simile, creation and creator are two lines, without beginning and without end, running parallel to each other. God is the ever active providence, by whose power systems after systems are being evolved out of chaos, made to run for a time and again destroyed. This is what the Brahmin boy repeats every day: 'The sun and the moon, the Lord created like the suns and moons of previous cycles.' And this agrees with modern science.

Here I stand and if I shut my eyes, and try to conceive my existence, 'I', 'I', 'I', what is the idea before me? The idea of a body. Am I, then, nothing but a combination of material substances? The Vedas declare, 'No'. I am a spirit living in a body. I am not the body. The body will die, but I shall not die. Here am I in this body; it will fall, but I shall go on living. I had also a past. The soul was not created, for creation means a combination which means a certain future dissolution. If then the soul was created, it must die. Some are born happy, enjoy perfect health, with beautiful body, mental vigour and all wants supplied. Others are born miserable, some are without hands or feet, others again are idiots and only drag on a wretched existence. Why, if they are all created, why does a just and merciful God create one happy and another unhappy, why is He so partial? Nor would it mend matters in the least to hold that those who are miserable in this life will be happy in a future one. Why should a man be miserable even here in the reign of a just and merciful God?

In the second place, the idea of a creator God does not explain the anomaly, but simply expresses the cruel fiat of an all-powerful being. There must have been causes, then, before his birth, to make a man miserable or happy and those were his past actions.

Are not all the tendencies of the mind and the body accounted for by inherited aptitude? Here are two parallel lines of existence—one of the mind, the other of matter.

If matter and its transformations answer for all that we have, there is no necessity for supposing the existence of a soul. But it cannot be proved that thought has been evolved out of matter, and if a philosophical monism is inevitable, spiritual monism is certainly logical and no less desirable than a materialistic monism; but neither of these is necessary here.

We cannot deny that bodies acquire certain tendencies from heredity, but those tendencies only mean the physical configuration, through which a peculiar mind alone can act in a peculiar way. There are other tendencies peculiar to a soul caused by its past actions. And a soul with a certain tendency would by the laws of affinity take birth in a body which is the fittest instrument for the display of that tendency. This is in accord with science, for science wants to explain everything by habit, and habit is got through repetitions. So repetitions are necessary to explain the natural habits of a new-born soul. And since they were not obtained in this present life, they must have come down from past lives.

There is another suggestion. Taking all these for granted, how is it that I do not remember anything of my past life? This can be easily explained. I am now speaking English. It is not my mother tongue, in fact no words of my mother tongue are now present in my consciousness; but let me try to bring them up, and they rush in. That shows that consciousness is only the surface of the mental ocean, and within its depths are stored up all our experiences. Try and struggle, they would come up and you would be conscious even of your past life.

This is direct and demonstrative evidence. Verification is the perfect proof of a theory, and here is the challenge thrown to the world by the Rishis. We have discovered the secret by which the very depths of the ocean of memory can be stirred up—try it and you would get a complete reminiscence of your past life.

So then the Hindu believes that he is a spirit. Him the sword cannot pierce, him the fire cannot burn, him the water cannot melt, him the air cannot dry. The Hindu believes that every soul is a circle whose circumference is nowhere, but whose centre is located in the body, and that death means the change of this centre from body to body. Nor is the soul bound by the conditions of matter. In its very essence it is free, unbounded, holy, pure, and perfect. But somehow or other it finds itself tied down to matter and thinks of itself as matter.

Why should the free, perfect, and pure being be thus under the thraldom of matter, is the next question. How can the perfect soul be deluded into the belief that it is imperfect? We have been told that the Hindus shirk the question and say that no such question can be there. Some thinkers want to answer it by positing one or more quasi-perfect beings, and use big scientific names to fill up the gap. But naming is not explaining. The question remains the same. How can the perfect become the quasi-perfect; how can the pure, the absolute, change even a microscopic particle of its nature? But the Hindu is sincere. He does not want to take shelter under sophistry. He is brave enough to face the question in a manly fashion; and his answer is: 'I do not know. I do not know how the perfect being, the soul, came to think of itself as imperfect, as joined to and conditioned by matter.' But the fact is a fact for all that. It is a fact in everybody's consciousness that one thinks of oneself as the body. The Hindu does not attempt to explain why one thinks one is the body. The answer that it is the will of God is no explanation. This is nothing more than what the Hindu says, 'I do not know.'

Well, then, the human soul is eternal and immortal, perfect and infinite, and death means only a change of centre from one body to another. The present is determined by our past actions, and the future by the present. The soul will go on evolving up or reverting back from birth to birth and death to death. But here is another question: Is man a tiny boat in a tempest, raised one moment on the foamy crest of a billow and dashed down into a yawning chasm the next, rolling to and fro at the mercy of good and bad actions—a powerless, helpless wreck in an ever-raging, ever-rushing, uncompromising current of cause and effect; a little moth placed under the wheel of causation which rolls on crushing everything in its way and waits not for the widow's tears or the orphan's cry? The heart sinks at the idea, yet this is the law of Nature. Is there no hope? Is there no escape?—was the cry that went up from the bottom of the heart of despair. It reached the throne of mercy, and words of hope and consolation came down and inspired a Vedic sage, and he stood up before the world and in trumpet voice proclaimed the glad tidings: 'Hear, ye children of immortal bliss! Even ye that reside in higher spheres! I have found the Ancient One who is beyond all darkness, all delusion: knowing Him alone you shall be saved from death over again.' 'Children of immortal bliss'—what a sweet, what a hopeful name! Allow me to call you, brethren, by that sweet name—heirs of immortal bliss—yea, the Hindu refuses to call you sinners. Ye are the Children of God, the sharers of immortal bliss, holy and perfect beings. Ye divinities on earth—sinners! It is a sin to call a man so; it is a standing libel on human nature. Come up, O lions, and shake off the delusion that you are sheep; you are souls immortal, spirits free, blest and eternal; ye are not matter, ye are not bodies; matter is your servant, not you the servant of matter.

Thus it is that the Vedas proclaim not a dreadful combination of unforgiving laws, not an endless prison of cause and effect, but that at the head of all these laws, in and through every particle of matter and force, stands One 'by whose command the wind blows, the fire burns, the clouds rain, and death stalks upon the earth.'

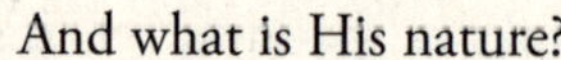

And what is His nature?

He is everywhere, the pure and formless One, the Almighty and the All-merciful. 'Thou art our father, Thou art our mother, Thou art our beloved friend, Thou art the source of all strength; give us strength. Thou art He that beareth the burdens of the universe; help me bear the little burden of this life.' Thus sang the Rishis of the Vedas. And how to worship Him? Through love. 'He is to be worshipped as the one beloved, dearer than everything in this and the next life.'

This is the doctrine of love declared in the Vedas, and let us see how it is fully developed and taught by Krishna, whom the Hindus believe to have been God incarnate on earth.

He taught that a man ought to live in this world like a lotus leaf, which grows in water but is never moistened by water; so a man ought to live in the world—his heart to God and his hands to work.

It is good to love God for hope of reward in this or the next world, but it is better to love God for love's sake, and the prayer goes: 'Lord, I do not want wealth, nor children, nor learning. If it be Thy will, I shall go from birth to birth, but grant me this, that I may love Thee without the hope of reward—love unselfishly for love's sake.' One of the disciples of Krishna, the then Emperor of India, was driven from his kingdom by his enemies and had to take shelter with his queen in a forest in the Himalayas, and there one day the queen asked him how it was that he, the most virtuous of men, should suffer so much misery. Yudhishthira answered, 'Behold, my queen, the Himalayas, how grand and beautiful they are; I love them. They do not give me anything, but my nature is to love the grand, the beautiful, therefore I love them. Similarly, I love the Lord. He is the source of all beauty, of all sublimity. He is the only object to be loved; my nature is to love Him, and therefore I love. I do not pray for anything; I do not ask for anything. Let Him place me wherever He likes. I must love Him for love's sake. I cannot trade in love.'

The Vedas teach that the soul is divine, only held in the bondage of matter; perfection will be reached when this bond will burst, and the word they use for it is therefore, Mukti—freedom, freedom from the bonds of imperfection, freedom from death and misery.

And this bondage can only fall off through the mercy of God, and this mercy comes on the pure. So purity is the condition of His mercy. How does that mercy act? He reveals Himself to the pure heart; the pure and the stainless see God, yea, even in this life; then and then only all the crookedness of the heart is made straight. Then all doubt ceases. He is no more the freak of a terrible law of causation. This is the very centre, the very vital conception of Hinduism. The Hindu does not want to live upon words and theories. If there are existences beyond the ordinary sensuous existence, he wants to come face to face with them. If there is a soul in him which is not matter, if there is an all-merciful universal Soul, he will go to Him direct. He must see Him, and that alone can destroy all doubts. So the best proof a Hindu sage gives about the soul, about God, is: 'I have seen the soul; I have seen God.' And that is the only condition of perfection. The Hindu religion does not consist in struggles and attempts to believe a certain doctrine or dogma, but in realising—not in believing, but in being and becoming.

Thus the whole object of their system is by constant struggle to become perfect, to become divine, to reach God and see God, and this reaching God, seeing God, becoming perfect even as the Father in Heaven is perfect, constitutes the religion of the Hindus.

And what becomes of a man when he attains perfection? He lives a life of bliss infinite. He enjoys infinite and perfect bliss, having obtained the only thing in which man ought to have pleasure, namely God, and enjoys the bliss with God.

So far all the Hindus are agreed. This is the common religion of all the sects of India; but, then, perfection is absolute, and the absolute cannot be two or three. It cannot have any qualities. It cannot be an individual. And so when a soul becomes perfect and absolute, it must become one with Brahman, and it would only realise the Lord as the perfection, the reality, of its own nature and existence, the existence absolute, knowledge absolute, and bliss absolute. We have often and often read this called the losing of individuality and becoming a stock or a stone.

'He jests at scars that never felt a wound.'

I tell you it is nothing of the kind. If it is happiness to enjoy the consciousness of this small body, it must be greater happiness to enjoy the consciousness of two bodies, the measure of happiness increasing with the consciousness of an increasing number of bodies, the aim, the ultimate of happiness being reached when it would become a universal consciousness.

Therefore, to gain this infinite universal individuality, this miserable little prison-individuality must go. Then alone can death cease when I am one with life, then alone can misery cease when I am one with happiness itself, then alone can all errors cease when I am one with knowledge itself; and this is the necessary scientific conclusion. Science has proved to me that physical individuality is a delusion, that really my body is one little continuously changing body in an unbroken ocean of matter; and Advaita (unity) is the necessary conclusion with my other counterpart, soul.

Science is nothing but the finding of unity. As soon as science would reach perfect unity, it would stop from further progress, because it would reach the goal. Thus Chemistry could not progress farther when it would discover one element out of which all others could be made. Physics would stop when it would be able to fulfil its services in discovering one energy of which all the others are but manifestations, and the science of religion becomes perfect when it would discover Him who is the one life in a universe of death, Him who is the constant basis of an ever-changing world. One who is the only Soul of which all souls are but delusive manifestations. Thus is it, through multiplicity and duality, that the ultimate unity is reached. Religion can go no farther. This is the goal of all science.

All science is bound to come to this conclusion in the long run. Manifestation, and not creation, is the word of science today, and the Hindu is only glad that what he has been cherishing in his bosom for ages is going to be taught in more forcible language, and with further light from the latest conclusions of science.

Descend we now from the aspirations of philosophy to the religion of the ignorant. At the very outset, I may tell you that there is no polytheism in India. In every temple, if one stands by and listens, one will find the worshippers applying all the attributes of God, including omnipresence, to the images. It is not polytheism, nor would the name henotheism explain the situation. 'The rose called by any other name would smell as sweet.' Names are not explanations.

I remember, as a boy, hearing a Christian missionary preach to a crowd in India. Among other sweet things he was telling them was that if he gave a blow to their idol with his stick, what could it do? One of his hearers sharply answered, 'If I abuse your God, what can He do?' 'You would be punished,' said the preacher, 'when you die.' 'So my idol will punish you when you die,' retorted the Hindu.

The tree is known by its fruits. When I have seen amongst them that are called idolaters, men, the like of whom in morality and spirituality and love I have never seen anywhere, I stop and ask myself, 'Can sin beget holiness?'

Superstition is a great enemy of man, but bigotry is worse. Why does a Christian go to church? Why is the cross holy? Why is the face turned toward the sky in prayer? Why are there so many images in the Catholic Church? Why are there so many images in the minds of Protestants when they pray? My brethren, we can no more think about anything without a mental image than we can live without breathing. By the law of association, the material image calls up the mental idea and vice versa. This is why the Hindu uses an external symbol when he worships. He will tell you, it helps to keep his mind fixed on the Being to whom he prays. He knows as well as you do that the image is not God, is not omnipresent. After all, how much does omnipresence mean to almost the whole world? It stands merely as a word, a symbol. Has God superficial area? If not, when we repeat that word 'omnipresent', we think of the extended sky or of space, that is all.

As we find that somehow or other, by the laws of our mental constitution, we have to associate our ideas of infinity with the image of the blue sky, or of the sea, so we naturally connect our idea of holiness with the image of a church, a mosque, or a cross. The Hindus have associated the idea of holiness, purity, truth, omnipresence, and such other ideas with different images and forms. But with this difference that while some people devote their whole lives to their idol of a church and never rise higher, because with them religion means an intellectual assent to certain doctrines and doing good to their fellows, the whole religion of the Hindu is centred in realisation. Man is to become divine by realising the divine. Idols or temples or churches or books are only the supports, the helps, of his spiritual childhood: but on and on he must progress.

He must not stop anywhere. 'External worship, material worship,' say the scriptures, 'is the lowest stage; struggling to rise high, mental prayer is the next stage, but the highest stage is when the Lord has been realised.' Mark, the same earnest man who is kneeling before the idol tells you, 'Him the sun cannot express, nor the moon, nor the stars, the lightning cannot express Him, nor what we speak of as fire; through Him they shine.' But he does not abuse any one's idol or call its worship sin. He recognises in it a necessary stage of life. 'The child is father of the man.' Would it be right for an old man to say that childhood is a sin or youth a sin?

If a man can realise his divine nature with the help of an image, would it be right to call that a sin? Nor even when he has passed that stage, should he call it an error. To the Hindu, man is not travelling from error to truth, but from truth to truth, from lower to higher truth. To him all the religions, from the lowest fetishism to the highest absolutism, mean so many attempts of the human soul to grasp and realise the Infinite, each determined by the conditions of its birth and association, and each of these marks a stage of progress; and every soul is a young eagle soaring higher and higher, gathering more and more strength, till it reaches the Glorious Sun.

Unity in variety is the plan of nature, and the Hindu has recognised it. Every other religion lays down certain fixed dogmas, and tries to force society to adopt them. It places before society only one coat which must fit Jack and John and Henry, all alike. If it does not fit John or Henry, he must go without a coat to cover his body. The Hindus have discovered that the absolute can only be realised, or thought of, or stated, through the relative, and the images, crosses, and crescents are simply so many symbols—so many pegs to hang the spiritual ideas on. It is not that this help is necessary for every one, but those that do not need it have no right to say that it is wrong. Nor is it compulsory in Hinduism.

One thing I must tell you. Idolatry in India does not mean anything horrible. It is not the mother of harlots. On the other hand, it is the attempt of undeveloped minds to grasp high spiritual truths. The Hindus have their faults, they sometimes have their exceptions; but mark this, they are always for punishing their own bodies, and never for cutting the throats of their neighbours. If the Hindu fanatic burns himself on the pyre, he never lights the fire of Inquisition. And even this cannot be laid at the door of his religion any more than the burning of witches can be laid at the door of Christianity.

To the Hindu, then, the whole world of religions is only a travelling, a coming up, of different men and women, through various conditions and circumstances, to the same goal. Every religion is only evolving a God out of the material man, and the same God is the inspirer of all of them. Why, then, are there so many contradictions? They are only apparent, says the Hindu. The contradictions come from the same truth adapting itself to the varying circumstances of different natures.

It is the same light coming through glasses of different colours. And these little variations are necessary for purposes of adaptation. But in the heart of everything the same truth reigns. The Lord has declared to the Hindu in His incarnation as Krishna, 'I am in every religion as the thread through a string of pearls. Wherever thou seest extraordinary holiness and extraordinary power raising and purifying humanity, know thou that I am there.' And what has been the result? I challenge the world to find, throughout the whole system of Sanskrit philosophy, any such expression as that the Hindu alone will be saved and not others. Says Vyasa, 'We find perfect men even beyond the pale of our caste and creed.' One thing more. How, then, can the Hindu, whose whole fabric of thought centres in God, believe in Buddhism which is agnostic, or in Jainism which is atheistic?

The Buddhists or the Jains do not depend upon God; but the whole force of their religion is directed to the great central truth in every religion, to evolve a God out of man. They have not seen the Father, but they have seen the Son. And he that hath seen the Son hath seen the Father also.

This, brethren, is a short sketch of the religious ideas of the Hindus. The Hindu may have failed to carry out all his plans, but if there is ever to be a universal religion, it must be one which will have no location in place or time; which will be infinite like the God it will preach, and whose sun will shine upon the followers of Krishna and of Christ, on saints and sinners alike; which will not be Brahminic or Buddhistic, Christian or Mohammedan, but the sum total of all these, and still have infinite space for development; which in its catholicity will embrace in its infinite arms, and find a place for, every human being, from the lowest grovelling savage not far removed from the brute, to the highest man towering by the virtues of his head and heart almost above humanity, making society stand in awe of him and doubt his human nature. It will be a religion which will have no place for persecution or intolerance in its polity, which will recognise divinity in every man and woman, and whose whole scope, whose whole force, will be created in aiding humanity to realise its own true, divine nature.

Offer such a religion, and all the nations will follow you. Asoka's council was a council of the Buddhist faith. Akbar's,

though more to the purpose, was only a parlour-meeting. It was reserved for America to proclaim to all quarters of the globe that the Lord is in every religion.

May He who is the Brahman of the Hindus, the Ahura-Mazda of the Zoroastrians, the Buddha of the Buddhists, the Jehovah of the Jews, the Father in Heaven of the Christians, give strength to you to carry out your noble idea! The star arose in the East; it travelled steadily towards the West, sometimes dimmed and sometimes effulgent, till it made a circuit of the world; and now it is again rising on the very horizon of the East, the borders of the Sanpo, a thousandfold more effulgent than it ever was before.

Hail, Columbia, motherland of liberty! It has been given to thee, who never dipped her hand in her neighbour's blood, who never found out that the shortest way of becoming rich was by robbing one's neighbours, it has been given to thee to march at the vanguard of civilisation with the flag of harmony.

Buddhism, the Fulfilment of Hinduism, 26 September 1893

I am not a Buddhist, as you have heard, and yet I am. If China, or Japan, or Ceylon follow the teachings of the Great Master, India worships him as God incarnate on earth. You have just now heard that I am going to criticise Buddhism, but by that I wish you to understand only this. Far be it from me to criticise him whom I worship as God incarnate on earth. But our views about Buddha are that he was not understood properly by his disciples. The relation between Hinduism (by Hinduism, I mean the religion of the Vedas) and what is called Buddhism at the present day is nearly the same as between Judaism and Christianity. Jesus Christ was a Jew, and Shakya Muni was a Hindu. The Jews rejected Jesus Christ, nay, crucified him, and the Hindus have accepted Shakya Muni as God and worship him. But the real difference that we Hindus want to show between modern Buddhism and what we should understand as the teachings of Lord Buddha lies principally in this: Shakya Muni came to preach nothing new. He also, like Jesus, came to fulfil and not to destroy. Only, in the case of Jesus, it was the old people, the Jews, who did not understand him, while in the case of Buddha, it was his own followers who did not realise the import of this teachings. As the Jew did not understand the fulfilment of the Old Testament, so the Buddhist did not understand the fulfilment of the truths of the Hindu religion. Again, I repeat, Shakya Muni came not to destroy, but he was the fulfilment, the logical conclusion, the logical development of the religion of the Hindus.

The religion of the Hindus is divided into two parts: the ceremonial and the spiritual. The spiritual portion is specially studied by the monks. In that there is no caste. A man from the highest caste and a man from the lowest may become a monk in India, and the two castes become equal. In religion there is no caste; caste is simply a social institution. Shakya Muni himself was a monk, and it was his glory that he had the large-heartedness to bring out the truths from the hidden Vedas and broadcast them all over the world. He was the first being in the world who brought missionarising into practice—nay, he was the first to conceive the idea of proselytising.

The great glory of the Master lay in his wonderful sympathy for everybody, especially for the ignorant and the poor. Some of his disciples were Brahmins. When Buddha was teaching, Sanskrit was no more the spoken language in India. It was then only in the books of the learned. Some of Buddha's Brahmin disciples wanted to translate his teachings into Sanskrit, but he distinctly told them, 'I am for the poor, for the people; let me speak in the tongue of the people.' And so to this day the great bulk of his teachings are in the vernacular of that day in India.

Whatever may be the position of philosophy, whatever may be the position of metaphysics, so long as there is such a thing as death in the world, so long as there is such a thing as weakness in the human heart, so long as there is a cry going out of the heart of man in his very weakness, there shall be a faith in God.

On the philosophic side the disciples of the Great Master dashed themselves against the eternal rocks of the Vedas and could not crush them, and on the other side they took away from the nation that eternal God to which every one, man or woman, clings so fondly. And the result was that Buddhism had to die a natural death in India. At the present day there is not one who calls oneself a Buddhist in India, the land of its birth.

But at the same time, Brahminism lost something—that reforming zeal, that wonderful sympathy and charity for everybody, that wonderful leaven which Buddhism had brought to the masses and which had rendered Indian society so great that a Greek historian who wrote about India of that time was led to say that no Hindu was known to tell an untruth and no Hindu woman was known to be unchaste.

Hinduism cannot live without Buddhism, nor Buddhism without Hinduism. Then realise what the separation has shown to us, that the Buddhists cannot stand without the brain and philosophy of the Brahmins, nor the Brahmin without the heart of the Buddhist. This separation between the Buddhists and the Brahmins is the cause of the downfall of India. That is why India is populated by three hundred millions of beggars, and that is why India has been the slave of conquerors for the last thousand years. Let us then join the wonderful intellect of the Brahmins with the heart, the noble soul, the wonderful humanising power of the Great Master.

Address at the Final Session, 27 September 1893

The World's Parliament of Religions has become an accomplished fact, and the merciful Father has helped those who laboured to bring it into existence, and crowned with success their most unselfish labour.

My thanks to those noble souls whose large hearts and love of truth first dreamed this wonderful dream and then realised it. My thanks to the shower of liberal sentiments that has overflowed this platform. My thanks to this enlightened audience for their uniform kindness to me and for their appreciation of every thought that tends to smooth the friction of religions. A few jarring notes were heard from time to time in this harmony. My special thanks to them, for they have, by their striking contrast, made general harmony the sweeter.

Much has been said of the common ground of religious unity. I am not going just now to venture my own theory. But if anyone here hopes that this unity will come by the triumph of any one of the religions and the destruction of the other, to him I say, 'Brother, yours is an impossible hope.' Do I wish that the Christian would become Hindu? God forbid. Do I wish that the Hindu or Buddhist would become Christian? God forbid. The seed is put in the ground, and earth and air and water are placed around it. Does the seed become the earth, or the air, or the water? No. It becomes a plant, it

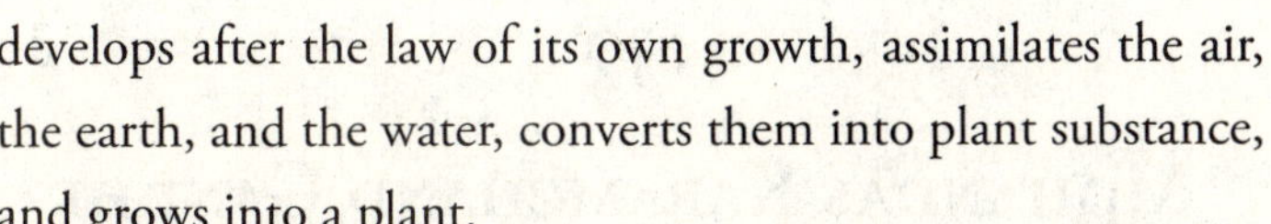

develops after the law of its own growth, assimilates the air, the earth, and the water, converts them into plant substance, and grows into a plant.

Similar is the case with religion. The Christian is not to become a Hindu or a Buddhist, nor a Hindu or a Buddhist to become a Christian. But each must assimilate the spirit of the others and yet preserve his individuality and grow according to his own law of growth.

If the Parliament of Religions has shown anything to the world it is this: It has proved to the world that holiness, purity and charity are not the exclusive possessions of any church in the world, and that every system has produced men and women of the most exalted character. In the face of this evidence, if anybody dreams of the exclusive survival of his own religion and the destruction of the others, I pity him from the bottom of my heart, and point out to him that upon the banner of every religion will soon be written, in spite of resistance: 'Help and not Fight', 'Assimilation and not Destruction', 'Harmony and Peace and not Dissension'.

52

Mohandas Karamchand Gandhi

Revered the world over for his philosophy of non-violence and passive resistance, Mohandas Karamchand Gandhi (1869–1948) was a lawyer, writer, politician, nationalist, social activist and political ethicist who became the dominant leader of the Indian Independence movement.

The Mahatma was an active proponent of three of the major revolutions of the twentieth century—the movements against colonialism, racism and caste. While best known for his role as a political leader, the driving force of his own life was Dharma or religion, not politics. For him Dharma was not about dogmas or rituals but the Vedantic ideals of self-realisation, vegetarianism and universal love.

Why Was India Lost?

Reader: You have said much about civilization—enough to make me ponder over it. I do not now know what I should adopt and what I should avoid from the nations of Europe, but one question comes to my lips immediately. If civilization is a disease and if it has attacked England, why has she been able to take India, and why is she able to retain it?

Editor: Your question is not very difficult to answer, and we shall presently be able to examine the true nature of Swaraj; for I am aware that I have still to answer that question. I will, however, take up your previous question. The English have not taken India; we have given it to them. They are not in India because of their strength, but because we keep them. Let us now see whether these propositions can be sustained. They came to our country originally for purposes of trade. Recall the Company Bahadur. Who made it Bahadur? They had not the slightest intention at the time of establishing a kingdom. Who assisted the Company's officers? Who was tempted at the sight of their silver? Who bought their goods? History testifies that we did all this. In order to become rich all at once we welcomed the Company's officers with open arms.

We assisted them. If I am in the habit of drinking bhang and a seller thereof sells it to me, am I to blame him or myself? By blaming the seller shall I be able to avoid the habit? And, if a particular retailer is driven away will not another take his place? A true servant of India will have to go to the root of the matter. If an excess of food has caused me indigestion, I shall certainly not avoid it by blaming water. He is a true physician who probes the cause of disease, and if you pose as a physician for the disease of India, you will have to find out its true cause.

The Condition of India (Continued): Railways

Reader: Be that as it may, all the disadvantages of railways are more than counterbalanced by the fact that it is due to them that we see in India the new spirit of nationalism.

Editor: I hold this to be a mistake. The English have taught us that we were not one nation before and that it will require centuries before we become one nation. This is without foundation. We were one nation before they came to India. One thought inspired us. Our mode of life was the same. It was because we were one nation that they were able to establish one kingdom. Subsequently they divided us.

Reader: This requires an explanation.

Editor: I do not wish to suggest that because we were one nation we had no differences, but it is submitted that our leading men travelled throughout India either on foot or in bullock-carts. They learned one another's languages and there was no aloofness between them. What do you think could have been the intention of those far-seeing ancestors of ours who established Setubandha (Rameshwar) in the South, Jagannath in the East and Hardwar in the North as places of pilgrimage? You will admit they were no fools. They knew that worship of God could have been performed just as well at home. They taught us that those whose hearts were aglow with righteousness had the Ganges in their own homes. But they saw that India was one undivided land so made by nature. They, therefore, argued that it must be one nation. Arguing thus, they established holy places in various parts of India, and fired the people with an idea of nationality in a manner unknown in other parts of the world. And we Indians are one as no two Englishmen are. Only you and I and others who consider ourselves civilized and superior persons imagine that we are many nations. It was after the advent of railways that we began to believe in distinctions, and you are at liberty now to say that it is through the railways that we are beginning to abolish those distinctions. An opium-eater may argue the advantage of opium eating from the fact that he began to understand the evil of the opium habit after having eaten it. I would ask you to consider well what I had said on the railways.

Reader: I will gladly do so, but one question occurs to me even now. You have described to me the India of the pre-Mahomedan period, but now we have Mahomedans, Parsis and Christians. How can they be one nation? Hindus and Mahomedans are old enemies. Our very proverbs prove it. Mahomedans turn to the West for worship, whilst Hindus turn to the East. The former look down on the Hindus as idolaters. The Hindus worship the cow, the Mahomedans kill her. The Hindus believe in the doctrine of non-killing, the Mahomedans do not. We thus meet with differences at every step. How can India be one nation?

The Condition of India (Continued): The Hindus and the Mahomedans

Editor: India cannot cease to be one nation because people belonging to different religions live in it. The introduction of foreigners does not necessarily destroy the nation, they merge in it. A country is one nation only when such a condition obtains in it. That country must have a faculty for assimilation, India has ever been such a country. In reality there are as many religions as there are individuals; but those who are conscious of the spirit of nationality do not interfere with one another's religion. If they do, they are not fit to be considered a nation. If the Hindus believe that India should be peopled only by Hindus, they are living in dreamland. The Hindus, the Mahomedans, the Parsis and the Christians who have made India their country are fellow-countrymen, and they will have to live in unity, if only for their own interest. In no part of the world are one nationality and one religion synonymous terms; nor has it ever been so in India.

Reader: But what about the inborn enmity between Hindus and Mahomedans?

Editor: That phrase has been invented by our mutual enemy. When the Hindus and Mahomedans fought against one another, they certainly spoke in that strain. They have long since ceased to fight. How, then, can there be any inborn enmity? Pray remember this too, that we did not cease to fight only after British occupation. The Hindus flourished under Moslem sovereigns and Moslems under the Hindu. Each party recognized that mutual fighting was suicidal, and that neither party would abandon its religion by force of arms. Both parties, therefore, decided to live in peace. With the English advent quarrels recommenced.

The proverbs you have quoted were coined when both were fighting; to quote them now is obviously harmful. Should we not remember that many Hindus and Mahomedans own the same ancestors and the same blood runs through their veins? Do people become enemies because they change their religion? Is the God of the Mahomedan different from the

God of the Hindu? Religions are different roads converging to the same point. What does it matter that we take different roads so long as we reach the same goal? Wherein is the cause of quarrelling?

Moreover, there are deadly proverbs as between the followers of Siva and those of Vishnu, yet nobody suggests that these two do not belong to the same nation. It is said that the Vedic religion is different from Jainism, but the followers of the respective faiths are not different nations. The fact is that we have become enslaved and, therefore, quarrel and like to have our quarrels decided by a third party. There are Hindu iconoclasts as there are Mahomedan. The more we advance in true knowledge, the better we shall understand that we need not be at war with those whose religion we may not follow.

Reader: Now I would like to know your views about cow protection.

Editor: I myself respect the cow, that is, I look upon her with affectionate reverence. The cow is the protector of India because, being an agricultural country, she is dependent on the cow. The cow is a most useful animal in hundreds of ways. Our Mahomedan brethren will admit this.

But, just as I respect the cow, so do I respect my fellow men. A man is just as useful as a cow no matter whether he be a Mahomedan or a Hindu. Am I, then, to fight with or kill a Mahomedan in order to save a cow? In doing so, I would become an enemy of the Mahomedan as well as of the cow. Therefore, the only method I know of protecting the cow is that I should approach my Mahomedan brother and urge him for the sake of the country to join me in protecting her. If he would not listen to me I should let the cow go for the simple reason that the matter is beyond my ability. If I were overfull of pity for the cow, I should sacrifice my life to save her but not take my brother's. This, I hold, is the law of our religion.

Those who do not wish to misunderstand things may read up the Koran, and they will find therein hundreds of passages acceptable to the Hindus; and the Bhagavad Gita contains passages to which not a Mahomedan can take exception. Am I to dislike a Mahomedan because there are passages in the Koran I do not understand or like? It takes two to make a quarrel. If I do not want to quarrel with a Mahomedan, the latter will be powerless to foist a quarrel on me; and, similarly, I should be powerless if a Mahomedan refuses his assistance to quarrel with me. An arm striking the air will become disjointed. If everyone will try to understand the core of his own religion and adhere to it, and will not allow false teachers to dictate to him, there will be no room left for quarrelling.

Reader: But will the English ever allow the two bodies to join hands?

Editor: This question arises out of your timidity. It betrays our shallowness. If two brothers want to live in peace, is it possible for a third party to separate them? If they were to listen to evil counsels we would consider them to be foolish. Similarly, we Hindus and Mahomedans would have to blame our folly rather than the English, if we allowed them to put us asunder. A clay pot would break through impact, if not with one stone, then with another. The way to save the pot is not to keep it away from the danger point but to bake it so that no stone would break it. We have then to make our hearts of perfectly baked clay. Then we shall be steeled against all danger.

—From *Hind Swaraj*

Face to Face with Ahimsa

My object was to inquire into the condition of the Champaran agriculturists and understand their grievances against the indigo planters. For this purpose it was necessary that I should meet thousands of the ryots. But I deemed it essential, before starting on my inquiry, to know the planters' side of the case and see the Commissioner of the Division. I sought and was granted appointments with both.

The Secretary of the Planters' Association told me plainly that I was an outsider and that I had no business to come between the planters and their tenants, but if I had any representation to make, I might submit it in writing. I politely told him that I did not regard myself as an outsider, and that I had every right to inquire into the condition of the tenants if they desired me to do so.

The Commissioner, on whom I called, proceeded to bully me, and advised me forthwith to leave Tirhut.

I acquainted my co-workers with all this, and told them that there was a likelihood of Government stopping me from proceeding further, and that I might have to go to jail earlier than I had expected, and that, if I was to be arrested, it would be best that the arrest should take place in Motihari or if possible in Bettiah. It was advisable, therefore, that I should go to those places as early as possible.

Champaran is a district of the Tirhut division and Motihari is its headquarters. Rajkumar Shukla's place was in the vicinity of Bettiah, and the tenants belonging to the kothis in its neighbourhood were the poorest in the district. Rajkumar Shukla wanted me to see them and I was equally anxious to do so.

So I started with my co-workers for Motihari the same day. Babu Gorakh Prasad harboured us in his home, which became a caravanserai. It could hardly contain us all. The very same day we heard that about five miles from Motihari a tenant had been ill-treated. It was decided that, in company with Babu Dharanidhar Prasad, I should go and see him the next morning, and we accordingly set off for the place on elephant's back. An elephant, by the way, is about as common in Champaran as a bullock-cart in Gujarat. We had scarcely gone half way when a messenger from the Police Superintendent overtook us and said that the latter had sent his compliments. I saw what he meant. Having left Dharanidhar babu to proceed to the original destination, I got into the hired carriage which the messenger had brought. He then served on me a notice to leave Champaran, and drove me to my place. On his asking me to acknowledge the service of the notice, I wrote to the effect that I did not propose to comply with it and leave Champaran till my inquiry was finished. Thereupon I received a summons to take my trial the next day for disobeying the order to leave Champaran.

I kept awake that whole night writing letters and giving necessary instructions to Babu Brajkishore Prasad.

The news of the notice and the summons spread like wildfire, and I was told that Motihari that day witnessed unprecedented scenes. Gorakh babu's house and the court house overflowed with men. Fortunately I had finished all my work during the night and so was able to cope with the crowds. My companions proved the greatest help. They occupied themselves with regulating the crowds, for the latter followed me wherever I went.

A sort of friendliness sprang up between the officials—Collector, Magistrate, Police Superintendent—and myself. I might have legally resisted the notices served on me. Instead I accepted them all, and my conduct towards the officials was correct. They thus saw that I did not want to offend them personally, but that I wanted to offer civil resistance to their orders. In this way they were put at ease, and instead of harassing me they gladly availed themselves of my and my co-workers' co-operation in regulating the crowds. But it was an ocular demonstration to them of the fact that their authority was shaken. The people had for the moment lost all fear of punishment and yielded obedience to the power of love which their new friend exercised.

It should be remembered that no one knew me in Champaran. The peasants were all ignorant. Champaran, being far up north of the Ganges, and right at the foot of the Himalayas in close proximity to Nepal, was cut off from the rest of India. The Congress was practically unknown in those parts. Even those who had heard the name of the Congress shrank from joining it or even mentioning it. And now the Congress and its members had entered this land, though not in the name of the Congress, yet in a far more real sense.

In consultation with my co-workers I had decided that nothing should be done in the name of the Congress. What we wanted was work and not name, substance and not shadow. For the name of the Congress was the *bête noire* of the Government and their controllers—the planters. To them the Congress was a byword for lawyer's wrangles, evasion of law through legal loopholes, a byword for bombs and anarchical crime and for diplomacy and hypocrisy. We had to disillusion them both. Therefore we had decided not to mention the name of the Congress and not to acquaint the peasants with the organization called the Congress. It was enough, we thought, if they understood and followed the spirit of the Congress instead of its letter.

No emissaries had therefore been sent there, openly or secretly, on behalf of the Congress to prepare the ground for our arrival. Rajkumar Shukla was incapable of reaching the thousands of peasants. No political work had yet been done amongst them. The world outside Champaran was not known to them. And yet they received me as though we had been age-long friends. It is no exaggeration, but the literal truth, to say that in this meeting with the peasants I was face to face with God, *Ahimsa* and Truth.

When I come to examine my title to this realization, I find nothing but my love for the people. And this in turn is nothing but an expression of my unshakable faith in *Ahimsa*.

That day in Champaran was an unforgettable event in my life and a red-letter day for the peasants and for me.

According to the law, I was to be on my trial, but truly speaking Government was to be on its trial. The Commissioner only succeeded in trapping Government in the net which he had spread for me.

Case Withdrawn

The trial began. The Government pleader, the Magistrate and other officials were on tenterhooks. They were at a loss to know what to do. The Government pleader was pressing the Magistrate to postpone the case. But I interfered and requested the Magistrate not to postpone the case, as I wanted to plead guilty to having disobeyed the order to leave Champaran, and read a brief statement as follows:

'With the permission of the Court I would like to make a brief statement showing why I have taken the very serious step of seemingly disobeying the order passed under Section 144 of Cr. P. C. In my humble opinion it is a question of difference of opinion between the Local Administration and myself. I have entered the country with motives of rendering humanitarian and national service. I have done so in response to a pressing invitation to come and help the ryots, who urge they are not being fairly treated by the indigo planters. I could not render any help without studying the problem. I have, therefore, come to study it with the assistance, if possible, of the Administration and the planters. I have no other motive, and cannot believe that my coming can in any way disturb public peace and cause loss of life. I claim to have considerable experience in such matters. The Administration, however, have thought differently. I fully appreciate their difficulty, and I admit too that they can only proceed upon information they received. As a law-abiding citizen my first instinct would be, as it was, to obey the order served upon me. But I could not do so without doing violence to my sense of duty to those for whom I have come. I feel that I could just now serve them only by remaining in their midst. I could not, therefore, voluntarily retire. Amid this conflict of duties I could only throw the responsibility of removing me from them on the Administration. I am fully conscious of the fact that a person, holding, in the public life of India, a position such as I do, has to be most careful in setting an example. It is my firm belief that in the complex constitution under which we are living, the only safe and honourable course for a self-respecting man is, in the circumstances such as face me, to do what I have decided to do, that is, to submit without protest to the penalty of disobedience.

'I venture to make this statement not in any way in extenuation of the penalty to be awarded against me, but to show that I have disregarded the order served upon me not for want of respect for lawful authority, but in obedience to the higher law of our being, the voice of conscience.'

There was now no occasion to postpone the hearing, but as both the Magistrate and the Government pleader had been taken by surprise, the Magistrate postponed judgment. Meanwhile I had wired full details to the Viceroy, to Patna friends, as also to Pandit Madan Mohan Malaviya and others.

Before I could appear before the Court to receive the sentence, the Magistrate sent a written message that the Lieutenant Governor had ordered the case against me to be withdrawn, and the Collector wrote to me saying that I was at liberty to conduct the proposed inquiry, and that I might count on whatever help I needed from the officials. None of us was prepared for this prompt and happy issue.

I called on the Collector, Mr Heycock. He seemed to be a good man, anxious to do justice. He told me that I might ask for whatever papers I desired to see, and that I was at liberty to see him whenever I liked.

The country thus had its first direct object lesson in Civil Disobedience. The affair was freely discussed both locally and in the press, and my inquiry got unexpected publicity.

Methods of Work

At least five to seven volunteers were required to take down statements, and even then some people had to go away in the evening without being able to make their statements. All these statements were not essential, many of them being repetitions, but the people could not be satisfied otherwise, and I appreciated their feeling in the matter.

Those who took down the statements had to observe certain rules. Each peasant had to be closely cross-examined, and whoever failed to satisfy the test was rejected. This entailed a lot of extra time, but most of the statements were thus rendered incontrovertible.

An officer from the CID would always be present when these statements were recorded. We might have prevented him, but we had decided from the very beginning not only not to mind the presence of CID officers, but to treat them with courtesy and to give them all the information that it was possible to give them. This was far from doing us any harm. On the contrary, the very fact that the statements were taken down in the presence of the CID officers made the peasants more fearless.

Companions

As I gained more experience of Bihar, I became convinced that work of a permanent nature was impossible without proper village education. The ryots' ignorance was pathetic. They either allowed their children to roam about, or made them toil on indigo plantations from morning to night for a couple of coppers a day. In those days a male labourer's wage did not exceed ten pice, a female's did not exceed six, and a child's three. He who succeeded in earning four annas a day was considered most fortunate.

In consultation with my companions I decided to open primary schools in six villages. One of our conditions with the villagers was that they should provide the teachers with board and lodging while we would see to the other expenses.

But I did not want to stop at providing for primary education. The villages were insanitary, the lanes full of filth, the wells surrounded by mud and stink and the courtyards unbearably untidy. The elder people badly needed education in cleanliness. They were all suffering from various skin diseases. So it was decided to do as much sanitary work as possible and to penetrate every department of their lives.

Penetrating the Villages

Medical relief was a very simple affair. Castor oil, quinine and sulphur ointment were the only drugs provided to the volunteers. If the patient showed a furred tongue or complained of constipation, castor oil was administered, in case of fever quinine was given after an opening dose of castor oil, and the sulphur ointment was applied in case of boils and itch after thoroughly washing the affected parts. No patient was permitted to take home any medicine. Wherever there was some complication Dr Dev was consulted. Dr Dev used to visit each centre on certain fixed days in the week.

When a Governor Is Good

Whilst on the one hand social service work of the kind I have described in the foregoing chapters was being carried out, on the other the work of recording statements of the ryots' grievances was progressing apace. Thousands of such statements were taken, and they could not but have their effect. The ever growing number of ryots coming to make their statements increased the planters' wrath, and they moved heaven and earth to counteract my inquiry.

One day I received a letter from the Bihar Government to the following effect: 'Your inquiry has been sufficiently prolonged, should you not now bring it to an end and leave Bihar?' The letter was couched in polite language, but its meaning was obvious.

I wrote in reply that the inquiry was bound to be prolonged, and unless and until it resulted in bringing relief to the people, I had no intention of leaving Bihar. I pointed out that it was open to Government to terminate my inquiry by accepting the ryots' grievances as genuine and redressing them, or by recognizing that the ryots had made out a *prima facie* case for an official inquiry which should be immediately instituted.

Sir Edward Gait, the Lieutenant Governor, asked me to see him, expressed his willingness to appoint an inquiry and invited me to be a member of the Committee. I ascertained the names of the other members, and after consultation with my co-workers agreed to serve on the Committee, on condition that I should be free to confer with my co-workers during the progress of the inquiry, that Government should recognize that, by being a member of the Committee, I did not cease to be the ryots' advocate, and that in case the result of the inquiry failed to give me satisfaction, I should be free to guide and advise the ryots as to what line of action they should take.

Sir Edward Gait accepted the condition as just and proper and announced the inquiry. The late Sir Frank Sly was appointed Chairman of the Committee.

The Committee found in favour of the ryots, and recommended that the planters should refund a portion of the exactions made by them which the Committee had found to be unlawful, and that the *tinkathia* system should be abolished by law.

The *tinkathia* system which had been in existence for about a century was thus abolished, and with it the planters' raj came to an end. The ryots, who had all along remained crushed, now somewhat came into their own, and the superstition that the stain of indigo could never be washed out was exploded.

—From *My Experiments with Truth*

Sri Aurobindo

Aurobindo Ackroyd Ghose (1872–1950), later known as Sri Aurobindo, was a philosopher and a yogi. He joined the movement for independence from British colonial rule, was imprisoned, and quit politics upon release. He became a spiritual reformer and moved to Pondicherry (Puducherry), then a French territory and outside British control. He rejected the ancient Indian concept of achieving liberation from the cycle of death and rebirth. He advocated a philosophy of divine life on earth through internal yoga and spiritual evolution.

15 August 1947

15 August 1947 is the birthday of free India. It marks for her the end of an old era, the beginning of a new age. But we can also make it by our life and acts as a free nation an important date in a new age opening for the whole world, for the political, social, cultural and spiritual future of humanity.

15 August is my own birthday and it is naturally gratifying to me that it should have assumed this vast significance. I take this coincidence, not as a fortuitous accident, but as the sanction and seal of the Divine Force that guides my steps on the work with which I began life, the beginning of its full fruition. Indeed, on this day I can watch almost all the world-movements which I hoped to see fulfilled in my lifetime, though then they looked like impracticable dreams, arriving at fruition or on their way to achievement. In all these movements free India may well play a large part and take a leading position.

The first of these dreams was a revolutionary movement which would create a free and united India. India today is free but she has not achieved unity. At one moment it almost seemed as if in the very act of liberation she would fall back into the chaos of separate States which preceded the British conquest. But fortunately it now seems probable that this danger will be averted and a large and powerful, though not yet a complete union will be established. Also, the wisely drastic policy of the Constituent Assembly has made it probable that the problem of the depressed classes will be solved without schism or fissure. But the old communal division into Hindus and Muslims seems now to have hardened into a permanent political division of the country. It is to be hoped that this settled fact will not be accepted as settled for ever or as anything more than a temporary expedient. For if it lasts, India may be seriously weakened, even crippled: civil strife may remain always possible, possible even a new invasion and foreign conquest. India's internal development and prosperity may be impeded, her position among the nations weakened, her destiny impaired or even frustrated. This must not be; the partition must go. Let us hope that that may come about naturally, by an increasing recognition of the necessity not only of peace and concord but of common action, by the practice of common action and the creation of means for that purpose. In this way unity may finally come about under whatever form—the exact form may have a pragmatic but not a fundamental importance. But by whatever means, in whatever way, the division must go; unity must and will be achieved, for it is necessary for the greatness of India's future.

Another dream was for the resurgence and liberation of the peoples of Asia and her return to her great role in the progress of human civilisation. Asia has arisen; large parts are now quite free or are at this moment being liberated: its other still subject or partly subject parts are moving through whatever struggles towards freedom. Only a little has to be done and that will be done today or tomorrow. There India has her part to play and has begun to play it with an energy and ability which already indicate the measure of her possibilities and the place she can take in the council of the nations.

The third dream was a world-union forming the outer basis of a fairer, brighter and nobler life for all mankind. That unification of the human world is under way; there is an imperfect initiation organised but struggling against tremendous difficulties. But the momentum is there and it must inevitably increase and conquer. Here too India has begun to play a prominent part and, if she can develop that larger statesmanship which is not limited by the present facts and immediate possibilities but looks into the future and brings it nearer, her presence may make all the difference between a slow and timid and a bold and swift development. A catastrophe may intervene and interrupt or destroy what is being done, but even then the final result is sure. For unification is a necessity of Nature, an inevitable movement. Its necessity for the nations is also clear, for without it the freedom of the small nations may be at any moment in peril and the life even of the large and powerful nations insecure. The unification is therefore to the interests of all, and only human imbecility and stupid selfishness can prevent it; but these cannot stand for ever against the necessity of Nature and the Divine Will. But an outward basis is not enough; there must grow up an international spirit and outlook, international forms and institutions must appear, perhaps such developments as dual or multilateral citizenship, willed interchange or voluntary fusion of cultures. Nationalism will have fulfilled itself and lost its militancy and would no longer find these things incompatible with self-preservation and the integrality of its outlook. A new spirit of oneness will take hold of the human race.

Another dream, the spiritual gift of India to the world has already begun. India's spirituality is entering Europe and America in an ever-increasing measure. That movement will grow; amid the disasters of the time more and more eyes are turning towards her with hope and there is even an increasing resort not only to her teachings, but to her psychic and spiritual practice.

The final dream was a step in evolution which would raise man to a higher and larger consciousness and begin the solution of the problems which have perplexed and vexed him since he first began to think and to dream of individual perfection and a perfect society. This is still a personal hope and an idea, an ideal which has begun to take hold both in India and in the West on forward-looking minds. The difficulties in the way are more formidable than in any other field of endeavour, but difficulties were made to be overcome and if the Supreme Will is there, they will be overcome. Here too, if this evolution is to take place, since it must proceed through a growth of the spirit and the inner consciousness, the initiative can come from India and, although the scope must be universal, the central movement may be hers.

Such is the content which I put into this date of India's liberation; whether or how far this hope will be justified depends upon the new and free India.

54

Sardar Vallabhbhai Patel

Vallabhbhai Jhaverbhai Patel (1875–1950), popularly known as Sardar Vallabhbhai Patel, was one of the most venerated leaders of India, admired by friends and foes alike. He was a barrister and a statesman and among the leaders of the Indian National Congress during the struggle for independence. He served as deputy prime minister, home minister, minister of information and minister of states in newly independent India.

The geographical entity that we know as India today is the result of Sardar Patel's statesmanship, as he worked to achieve peaceful integration of the princely states into the Indian Union and brought about the political unification of India.

Speech at Island Grounds, Madras, 23 February 1949

You want me to talk to you in English. I shall obey your command; but take it from me that it will not be long before you yourselves will have to speak in our national language. If you do not do that, you will drag the country backward. We have to exert our maximum effort to go forward. Unless you do that, I am afraid, you will suffer.

After a prolonged struggle the country has secured freedom, but it is not freedom of the kind that we wanted.

It is not freedom of the kind that the deliverer of the country expected, and to our shame we have to confess that by our folly we have lost him. Now after his going we must do penance and try our best to deserve the freedom that he obtained for us.

Free India is only a child of a year and a half. It has yet to learn to walk; it has to grow, to be strong, and its future depends upon how we build today. Therefore, we have to nurse it carefully; we have to feed, clothe and strengthen it properly. It is our great good fortune that we have here a rare opportunity to build our own country in our own fashion. History will record what we are doing today.

The first requisite for building a strong, free India is unity and peace. If there is no unity in the country, it is bound to go down. Therefore, we must first of all adjust our differences and behave in such a manner that there is complete harmony and peace in the country. You cannot expect the government continuously to maintain peace by force. It would be an evil day when in this country the Government has to use repressive measures permanently. Today we are passing through a period of crisis and our young men have, in their impatience, not realised that the freedom which has been obtained with great difficulty is likely to be lost or likely to give no benefit, no advantage, if we do not appreciate that our present duty is to unite and consolidate our freedom.

We lost our leader because we forgot the very first lesson. If we do not realise even after his going that in unity lies our strength, then greater misfortune will befall us.

For unity, we must forget differences of caste and creed and remember that we are all Indians, and all equal. There can be no distinction between man and man in a free country. All must have equal opportunities, equal rights and equal responsibilities. This is difficult of achievement in practice, but we must continuously strive towards that end.

There is one other thing that we have to do to maintain peace and order in this country. For a few years at least, till we are able to stand on our own legs, we must forget that we can every now and then threaten the government. We cannot function if the Government is to be challenged day after day by groups of people who want to have their own way. What they want may be, according to their own honest thinking, very good; but Gandhiji has put before us the ideal of obtaining what we want by peaceful methods and through truth and non-violence. If people begin to threaten and challenge Government's authority and try to overthrow it to gain their objectives by force, the latter would not be able to do anything constructive. Forces are existing in this country which would create chaos and disorder, which would weaken the country instead of strengthening it.

We in the government have been dealing with the R.S.S. movement. They want that Hindu Rajya or Hindu culture should be imposed by force. No government can tolerate this. There are almost as many Muslims in this country as in the part that has been partitioned away. We are not going to drive them away. It would be an evil day if we started that game, in spite of partition and whatever happens. We must understand that they are going to stay here and it is our obligation and our responsibility to make them feel that this is their country. It is, of course, their responsibility, on the other hand, to discharge their duties as citizens of this country.

We must all understand that partition is behind us. It has come to stay. I honestly believe that it is good for both the new nations to be rid of a perpetual source of trouble and quarrels. In two hundred years of slavery, the administration

created a situation in which we began to drift away from each other. It is good that we have agreed to partition in spite of all its evils; I have never repented my agreeing to partition. From the experience of one year of joint administration when we had not agreed to partition, I know we would have erred grievously and repented if we had not agreed. It would have resulted in a partition not into two countries but into several bits. Therefore, whatever some people may say, I am convinced and I remain convinced that our having agreed to partition has been for the good of the country.

After partition, we had a huge problem; those who partitioned the country with our concurrence had mental reservations; they thought that partition into two is not the last word and they started their game immediately after partition. They went to Junagadh in the midst of the Kathiawar States, where nearly half the number of princely states are located. From the middle of that group, they took Junagadh and secured its accession to Pakistan. It was the first danger sign, the signal for dividing India again. Fortunately for us, we woke up in time and those who tried that game saw that we are not sleeping. Simultaneously, there was trouble in Kashmir. Although there were many difficulties, the Government of India, despite all the impediments, got the situation under control rapidly. I should say we enhanced our reputation by sending there our army, which, in spite of its complete Indianisation, has proved its mettle and proved its worth. It is a great thing that immediately after the partition of the army and the partition of the country, our army, manned absolutely by our own people, showed by their strategy, their valour and their organising ability that it can stand comparison with any army in the world. It is a great gain.

Then our neighbour gave us long sleepless nights. Often, people were angry with us and thought we were neglecting the South. They hardly knew our difficulties and our plans. These plans cannot be revealed. What would happen if Hyderabad was invaded from the outside or if Hyderabad attacked us. We had to make preparations all over India. You know now by the results that we have kept our promise to perform the operation in such a manner that there is the least possible bleeding. This is what we have to show for the first year of our freedom.

People are impatient; they want more wages for labour. Do they think we want to starve labour? Are we foreigners? Some people say we are capitalist agents. One thing I learnt from Mahatma Gandhi is that a public man should not have any property and I can challenge any Socialist or any Communist to play this game with me. But my quarrel is with those who, contrary to the second part of Mahatmaji's advice to us, want to use violence. There should be no terrorism amongst ourselves. So long as people were playing that game when we were under a foreign power, we made allowance for it; we are paying for it also, because an evil once tolerated grows. That is what we see in Hyderabad.

Why are these Communists creating trouble there? How did they grow? It was because the Hyderabad Government was foolish enough to allow them to grow for its own ends and we had no control over them then to be able to suppress them. And what is it that we see there now? In three or four months' time, 200 or more young Congressmen, their own brothers, have been murdered. Is it a sign of freedom that in the first year of freedom you have 200 Congressmen killed in cold blood in a small area? Once these terrorists are driven out from that area, where will they go? Inside your border. They will harass you; they will play the same game with you. To the Communists, my appeal may be in vain, because they do not listen. I told them immediately after my release from jail last time that I was prepared to take all the Communists into the Congress, to forget the past and keep the doors open provided they give up violence and cease to draw their inspiration from foreign countries. Even now our offer is open, but if terrorism is the only method they want to employ, because they cannot defeat us at the polls and separate us from the masses of India, then it is our misfortune that we have to put our own dear young men and women into prison or to drive them underground.

That is one section of the people with whom we have to deal; the other is the R.S.S. I have made them an open offer: 'Change your plans, give up secrecy, eschew communal conflict, respect the Constitution of India, show your loyalty to the Flag and make us believe that we can trust your words.' To say one thing and to do another is a game which will not do. In one year of freedom we have experienced many things and learnt many lessons. Whether they are friends or foes, whether they are our own dear young children, we are not going to allow them to play with fire, so that the house is not set on fire. It would be criminal to allow young men to indulge in acts of violence and destruction, to let the lessons that our neighbouring countries have learnt be wasted on us.

Thus, I have spoken to the R.S.S. and to the Communists. Then you have our Sikh friends. Some of them have also begun to threaten us and throw challenges. They are the only community in India which is allowed, with the unanimous voice of the Constituent Assembly, to keep arms. No other community is allowed to keep a sword or a kirpan. Why did we do this? Not in order that they might threaten the government with the use of force. Government is prepared to hand over power to anybody who can take the people with him. But if anybody is going to play false and threaten the popular government, the latter will not fail the people.

These are some of the many forces we are handling simultaneously in the first or second year of our freedom. We know that we have your affection, your love, your confidence, but that is not enough. You have seen our friends in the railways threaten us. They say there is going to be a strike in the railways if we do not meet their demands. We are willing to do so if we can. We would be most anxious to do so. But I must point out to those who are in charge of the railway union that there are millions in this country who do not get as much as the railwaymen get; let them not create forces which they will not be able to control; let the railwaymen understand that it is also their duty to share the misfortunes of the people in a period of trouble. Let us tide over the difficulty first. After all, the railway is a nationalised concern; it is not a private company. Imagine the consequences, in this period of trouble, if railwaymen do not play their part. If there is a strike on the railways and we have to move the army from one place to another with railway communications cut off, what will happen? We continuously need to move food from one place to another swiftly, as we are faced with the threatened famine. If during such a period the South Indian railway, which has threatened to strike, goes on strike, who will starve, and what would be the consequences? When the Railway Federation suspended its strike threat and kept it in abeyance, the other group called them capitalist agents. Now these other people have called for a strike; they know that they are in a minority and they will not succeed in making the railwaymen go on strike. So, their only weapon is terrorism, sabotage, dislocation and disorder.

The Provincial Governments naturally have to tackle these people and immediately the Federation comes in with a statement that it is a wrong policy. I would like to know what is the right policy. When a house is on fire, is it the right policy to throw petrol or kerosene on it, or water? We are living in very difficult times; yet the heart of the country is sound. The whole country knows that we are carrying an unbearable burden. Yet if anyone wants to see what the country thinks, let him come to the polls; I am prepared to accept the challenge. I am prepared to vacate as many seats as you like and have a trial of strength. And if you are able to take the country with you, we shall bless you, because the country is not going to follow any path which is foreign to Indian culture and civilisation and the path that Mahatma Gandhi has shown. But I want to ask you why a few people round about the border of Hyderabad are terrorising the people in Krishna district? It is the fault of Congressmen. Are they united? Why are they quarrelling? Why do they not understand their responsibility? We made all kinds of sacrifices all our lives. Why did we make these sacrifices? Let not South India lose its good name and reputation. I appeal to you to realise what is happening. Did you ever imagine that Gandhiji would hear of a Congressman murdering a Congressman, or a Congressman instigating or helping a Communist to murder another Congressman? If the South Indian Railway is threatened, or if those railwaymen who work in South India are asked to go on strike, have you no responsibility? Everyone in India has to realise that, as a free citizen of India, he must shoulder graver and greater responsibility if India is to take its proper place amongst the nations of the world.

Yesterday, I was presented an address by the Chambers of Commerce. It was in fact a catalogue of grievances. I had to tell them the unpleasant truth that unless everybody in this country, that is businessmen, labourers, industrialists, students and government, all combine and co-operate, we are not going to make progress. We have not yet put democracy on a sound basis. In a democracy, of course, it is the will of the people that prevails, but the people must have experience to make their own free will felt and must have the responsibility to see that everyone is going to fulfil his obligations.

In this country, the greatest need of the hour is food. We import millions of tons of food into our country. We have not got the ships to bring the food that we want. So we pay crores of rupees as freight charges simply to bring the food here. We have not enough boats even to catch fish. We have no mercantile marine. We have nothing left in this country; for the last 200 years it has been bled white; during the war years in particular, every ounce of blood has been taken out. Our railway system has been completely disorganised. The Transport Member makes tremendous efforts to set it right. But the railways are like a decrepit old widow. Railway sleepers and rails were taken out and sent to various theatres of war. We cannot replace the wagons which have been overused for so many years. We cannot get locomotives. We cannot make them here; we have yet to establish factories for meeting the requirements of our country.

We must have a good mercantile marine; so, we are building a fine port at Vishakhapatnam. But it is only a beginning. A small country like Portugal has got pockets on our soil; we also have French colonies. Our friends in these areas who are fighting for freedom along with us ask us to first settle this question; others talk of the wages for labour; and still others want us to deal with the businessmen first and to give them their due. The businessmen are frightened of the talk of nationalisation. They say: 'Unless you give us conditions in which industry can thrive, we cannot invest money or we cannot get money.' So production has been at a standstill. We cannot produce more wealth in this country. The Communists and the Socialists say: let us first divide whatever is left and be all poor. But if you do not produce anything, then neither you nor any other section of the people will have anything. Therefore, so far as food is concerned, I have a grievance against Congressmen and against those people who were in the Congress and today are preaching to peasants not to help this government in procurement and to ask for more money. They are no better than the other people who say: 'Do not work, stop work, go slow, ask for more wages.' Because if there is no procurement, then the only course open to us is to import more and more, and importing more is nothing but economic ruin of this country.

If we in this country realize our responsibility, there will be no dearth of food. Of course, there is scarcity to a certain extent; the shortage of food according to our statistics is 7 per cent; in a vast country like this, if we act up to our responsibilities, this is negligible. Many people waste their food and cook more than they should. Those people should put a stop to this wastage. Then we should produce more food. Every inch of land that is available should be used for growing vegetables, fruit and other food. Wherever there is waste land which can be reclaimed, it would be the duty of government, local bodies, zamindars, and every citizen of India to use all his resources in the immediate task of growing more food on it. Thirdly, whatever surplus you have got, give it to the Government. When your neighbours are starving, do not be selfish. That is not the way which Gandhiji showed us. That is not our culture. Let not our neighbour starve; we must share his misery. Educate the peasants; tell them it is a religious duty to give all their surplus for government procurement, so that Government can decrease the imports that are being made.

There are many Congressmen who are indifferent to this matter. They think that elections are coming and they will be unpopular if they ask for procurement. A greater crime is committed by those who teach the peasants to ask for higher prices and not to give crops for procurement.

That is a crime against humanity. A real Congressman would say: 'My friends, our neighbours are dying; our country is being ruined; let us share the suffering of our brothers.' I am saying hard things to Congressmen because they have a greater responsibility, greater influence and a greater hold on the people.

Let us all put our heads as well as our hands together, tighten up our belts and be prepared to share the sufferings for a while. It is only for a while, because I assure you that the economy of the country is sound; the heart of the country is sound; there is immense wealth in the country. The country is full of mineral resources and wealth. We have simply to use our brains and our resources to take them out and use them. But it will take time; it is not an easy thing. We shall require experts, machinery and capital goods. If we tide over this short period, India will be flowing with milk and honey.

I am extremely touched by the affection that you have shown me. I have said some things which may be harsh, but however bitter they may be, they are a dose of medicine. In return for your affection, I can only ask you to forgive me if I have said anything harsh; take it as a piece of advice which comes from an honest and humble servant.

55

PERIYAR

Erode Venkatappa Ramasamy (1879–1973), commonly known as Periyar, was a radical social activist and politician. He is known as the Father of the Dravidian Movement. He started the Self-Respect Movement and Dravidar Kazhagam and promoted rationalism. He aggressively opposed Brahminical dominance and gender and caste inequalities. He advocated for an independent Dravida Nadu as the land of the Dravidians, comprising those speaking Tamil, Malayalam, Telugu and Kannada. He was a very influential orator, and it would not be wrong to say that every prominent change in Tamil politics and society in the twentieth century was initiated through the reforms he introduced.

Why Do We Criticise and Deny God?

I make this submission to your reason: You are humans. You are capable of thinking. Think about what I say. I ask you to accept only those things that you consider to be proper and to reject the rest. We remain fools because we have been blindly accepting whatever is said by every Tom, Dick and Harry. That is why I appeal to you to put to the test of reasoning whatever you hear or read before accepting it.

We are now entering into a new world. We have to take to new things. We have to live in new surroundings. Living amidst new surroundings requires knowledge and reasoning very much.

Man's belief in God is only nominal. One who conceptualised God has assigned certain attributes to him. No one believes in God having those attributes. It is said that God is omnipotent and it is he who activates everything. But no one acts according to this belief, no one leaves anything to be done by God.

To make people foolish, dishonest persons have built temples, churches and mosques. Using the services of Sankaracharis, Friars, Mullahs, heads of Mutts, priests, narrators of mythological stories and all sorts of religious propagandists, they have propagated the idea of God, and people have accepted that idea and remain fools.

While being sick no devotee of God or propagandist of God, no bishop or mullah, no Sankarachari or mutt head or clergyman thinks that he has fallen ill due to God's mercy. None of them abstains from consulting the doctor; they seek and get medical help. If their faith is true, they should go to the temple and pray. Why do they go to the hospitals? Do such people really believe that God is all powerful? Please think it over.

The changes that have been taking place during these 150 years have not happened before that period. Why is it? We are still steeped in the superstition of believing in God. Other people in the world do not give primary place to faith in God. They give importance to knowledge and wisdom, and think about the why and how of the phenomena. So they are making progress in science and technology.

We have thousands of Gods and temples, persons possessing divine power and mahatmas. Nevertheless, we have not invented anything wonderful in science. Think about the reason for our failure in this sphere.

It is said that God is compassionate and he treats all on equal terms. If it is so, then why did he make Brahmins, who constitute just three per cent of our population and do no work, high caste people, and the remaining 97 percent toiling masses, Sudras, who are described in the Sastras (scriptures) as the sons of concubines of Brahmins?

If God really exists, should he not be the one and the same all over the world? Why should the attributes of God differ from country to country, from religion to religion? Please think about the reason for the differences.

Why do we talk about God? What benefit do we derive by denying his existence? We know that most of the people are believers. Yet we criticise the concept of God. You should understand why we do so.

He who conceived and propagated God has composed songs that say: 'A non-believer is a dishonest person. He should be got rid of. The chastity of his wife should be violated.' The theists had killed the atheists by impaling them on sharp stakes. They have tortured people to make them accept the existence of God. (*Here, the reference is to the cruel and inhuman treatment meted out to the Jains by the Saivities in southern part of Tamil Nadu in the medieval times—translator.*)

You should know why we want to exterminate the idea of God and the religion imposed on us by such cruel means. This religion and God have made the 97 per cent of the population, people of low caste. We have thus become Sudras, Chandalas, Paraiahs, Chakkilis, etc. By whom have we been degraded in this manner? By the Brahmins who migrated into this country seeking their livelihood.

Being fools we have been acquiescing to the degrading social status for the past 2000 years. So far no one had endeavoured to eradicate this indignity. On the contrary, the saints and sages, the monks and mahatmas had only endeavoured to strengthen our low status. When they introduced God and made it an object of worship, when they introduced religious scriptures to be adopted in life, they had also sown the seeds of ignorance and superstition to grow among the people.

It is not enough merely to speak about the eradication of caste. The root cause of caste should be found out and rooted out. Then only caste can be annihilated. As God, religion and scriptures form the basis of caste, we want to get rid of them. Wherever they are abolished there will be no discrimination.

—Translated by Aasaan

56

Vinayak Damodar Savarkar

Vinayak Damodar Savarkar (1883–1966) is revered by some as a great revolutionary of the Indian freedom struggle, while others call him a communalist. He popularised Chandranath Basu's term 'Hindutva' to establish a collective Hindu identity as an essence of Bharat (India).

Savarkar claimed to be an atheist but practised Hindu philosophy as he considered Hinduism a political and cultural identity and not merely a religion. He was a fierce critic of Mahatma Gandhi and the Indian National Congress.

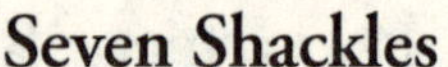

Seven Shackles

According to Savarkar, the Hindu society was bound by seven shackles (*bandi*) viz. prohibition of touch (*sparshabandi*) of certain castes, prohibition of interdining (*rotibandi*) with certain castes, prohibition of intercaste marriages (*betibandi*), prohibition of pursuing certain occupations (*vyavasayabandi*), prohibition of seafaring (*sindhubandi*), prohibition of rites sanctioned by the Vedas (*vedoktabandi*), prohibition of reconversion (*shuddhibandi*) to the Hindu fold. Given below is an English translation of Savarkar's assorted thoughts on six shackles. The seventh shackle viz. prohibition of reconversion (*shuddhibandi*) has been dealt with separately. Some of these shackles may seem unbelievable, even laughable to the reader today. The remarkable social reform that has taken place in the last 100 years is due to the tireless efforts of social reformers like Savarkar.

Eating and Drinking

What to eat and drink is a medical issue, not a religious one. One may eat and drink as per individual preference and digestive capacity under specific circumstances.

(1937, *Samagra Savarkar Vangmaya*, vol.3, p.652)

Hinduism Does Not Die by Partaking of Food Cooked by Other Religionists

If the Muslim or Christian does not become a Hindu by eating food cooked by a Hindu and remains a Muslim or Christian after digesting that food, then why should your religion be flushed out by partaking of food cooked by a Muslim? How come the digestive power of your religion has become so weak? ... Now brothers, eat and digest food cooked by anyone in the world and yet remain Hindu! Only then is there hope (for survival).

(1927, 'Maajhi Janmathep' or My Transportation for Life, *Samagra Savarkar Vangmaya*, vol.1, p.495)

Interdining Does Not Destroy Religion and Caste

There is no harm in eating what is medically permissible with any medically fit individual, not in a common plate but as a common meal. It is insane to believe that caste changes forever simply by sitting and eating next to an individual from a different caste.

Be it a Hindu or a Muslim or an Andamanese—eating and drinking with any one destroys neither caste nor religion.

(1935, 'Hindutvache Panchapran' or The Spirit of Hindutva, *Samagra Savarkar Vangmaya*, vol.3, p.83)

Other Shackles Break with Interdining

Just as there was a regulation in the past that at least one Brahmin should dine in a Ganesh Chaturthi meal, there should be a now be a regulation that there should be at least one Chamar–Mahar–Bhangi (*Balmiki) brother to dine in the Ganeshotsav meal.

The poisonous fang of scripture-based caste distinction will be uprooted once the prohibition of interdining is violated! The breaking of this prohibition automatically loosens the shackles of prohibition of touch, seafaring, re-conversion, conducting Vedic rites and pursuing certain occupations!

(1935, *Kirloskar* monthly, September)

Interdining Is a Litmus Test of Reformism

Many Chamar, Mahar brethren gladly break bread with Brahmins and Marathas but become Brahmins and Kshatriyas themselves and claim caste privilege when Bhangi (*Balmiki) or Maatang brethren seek to break bread with them. Their reformism should also be put to test. Hence in every common meal, there should be at least one or two Bhangi or Maatang brothers in addition to Mahars and Chamars.

(1935, *Maharashtra Sharada* periodical, November)

How Will Caste Distinction Go?

Interdining is the magic sorcerer that will bury the demon of caste distinction! Caste distinction will not die with sterile arguments. Nor is it easy or even desirable to kill it by force … Oh reformer, violate the prohibition of interdining at this very instant. How easy it is; Brahmins and Mahars may together gorge themselves with sweets and you may be certain that caste distinction will vanish! The impregnable fort of caste distinction has been cursed such that while it will not fall to volleys of cannon balls, it will crumble under the onslaught of sweet balls!

(1935, 'Hindutvache Panchapran' or The Spirit of Hindutva, *Samagra Savarkar Vangmaya*, vol.3, p.87)

How Should the Prohibition of Intermarriages Be Broken?

Breaking the prohibition of intermarriage does not imply forcibly marrying off girls of one caste into another caste. What it means is that if a Hindu with desirable qualities such as love, character, and capacity to beget healthy offspring chooses a spouse from another caste, then such an alliance should not be condemned simply because their castes are different. Such a couple should not be considered as unworthy of cohabitation.

Permission for such mixed marriages is extremely desirable not only for the removal of birth-based caste distinction but also for the success of the re-conversion movement. It is both beneficial and essential for the consolidation of the Hindu nation.

(1935, 'Hindutvache Panchapran' or The Spirit of Hindutva, *Samagra Savarkar Vangmaya*, vol.3, p.85)

When Does Reason Strike Those Who Advocate Compulsory Intermarriages?

If a hundred Brahmin–Bania girls are to be forcibly married off to Mahar–Chamar boys, then applying the same rule, a hundred Mahar or Chamar girls should be forcibly married off to Bhangi–Dhend boys. Confronted with this argument, those Mahar or Chamar hotheads who make demands on behalf of their community develop cold feet and begin to see reason.

(1935, 'Hindutvache Panchapran' or The Spirit of Hindutva, *Samagra Savarkar Vangmaya*, vol.3, p.85)

A Limitation of Intermarriages

In the present stage of human progress and the current peculiar situation in the Hindu Nation, one limit should be followed without exception as far as intermarriages are concerned. While there is no cause for concern if Hindus marry amongst themselves without any caste considerations no one should cross the ambit of Hindutva and marry Muslims, Christians and the like. So long as the Muslim desires to remain a Muslim, the Hindu too must remain a Hindu. It is extremely harmful to our Hindu nation if a Hindu marries a non-Hindu without bringing that girl or boy into the Hindu fold. It is only when the adamant non-Hindus swear by humanism and merge their Muslim identity into humanism that the Hindu too will abide by humanism and leaving aside considerations of caste, religion and country shall follow the ties of humanism only. But it will be against humanism if Hindus show such misplaced generosity at this point in time.

(1935, 'Hindutvache Panchapran' or The Spirit of Hindutva, *Samagra Savarkar Vangmaya*, vol.3, p.86)

The Notion of 'Ritual Impurity'

Most customs that have been responsible for our social and national decline have their seeds in one notion—that of 'ritual impurity'.

(1927, 'Maajhi Janmathep' or My Transportation for Life, *Samagra Savarkar Vangmaya*, vol.1, p.495)

How to Break the Prohibition of Touch

Oh, organizer of Hindus! Rise and irrespective whether others do it or not, take a pledge at this very instant that I shall use the hand with which I touch my cat and dog to touch my untouchable brother in dharma, failing which I shall go hungry. Say, I will touch! And by publicly touching some untouchable brother, show the world that as far as you are concerned, you have acquired the boon of freeing the Hindu race from the sin of untouchability! Throw your house open to the untouchable to the extent you do for the caste Hindu. Those who have houses to rent should do so to untouchables and caste Hindus alike; those who own wells should throw them open to untouchables and caste Hindus alike ... in short, let not a day pass without you publicly behaving with an untouchable as you would with a caste Hindu. The 'untouchable' reformist should follow the same custom and publicly give the right of touchability at least once a day to an untouchable who belongs to a 'lower' caste—the Chamar to the Dhend, the Mahar to the Bhangi (*Balmiki)!

(1935, 'Hindutvache Panchapran' or The Spirit of Hindutva, *Samagra Savarkar Vangmaya*, vol.3, p.81)

57

S. Radhakrishnan

Sarvepalli Radhakrishnan (1888–1975) was India's first vice president and subsequently its second president. He was one of the most influential scholars of comparative religion and philosophy. He identified his religion as Hinduism, Vedanta and the religion of the Spirit. He had an extraordinary ability to represent both Indian and Western philosophical ideas, skilfully incorporating insights from both into his writings. His birth anniversary is celebrated as 'Teacher's Day' across the country.

Philosophical Development

Throughout the history of Indian thought, the ideal of a world behind the ordinary world of human strivings, more real and more intangible, which is the true home of the spirit, has been haunting the Indian race. Man's never-ceasing effort to read the riddle of the sphinx and raise himself above the level of the beast to a moral and spiritual height finds a striking illustration in India. We can watch the struggle for four millenniums (or longer, if the recent archaeological finds in Sind and the Punjab, which are withdrawing the shroud that hid the remote past, are to be taken into account). The naïve belief that the world is ruled by the gods of Sun and Sky, who watch from on high the conduct of men, whether it is straight or crooked; the faith that the gods who can be persuaded by prayer or compelled by rites to grant our requests, are only the forms of the one Supreme; the firm conviction that the pure stainless spirit, to know whom is life eternal, is one with the innermost soul of man; the rise of materialism, scepticism and fatalism, and their supersession by the ethical systems of Buddhism and Jainism, with their central doctrine that one can free one-self from all ill only by refraining from all evil, in thought, word and deed—God or no God; the liberal theism of the Bhagavadgita, which endows the all-soul with ethical in addition to metaphysical perfections; the logical scheme of the Nyaya, which furnishes the principal categories of the world of knowledge which are in use even today; the Vaisesika interpretation of nature; the Samkhya speculations in science and psychology; the Yoga scheme of the pathway to perfection; the ethical and social regulations of the Mimamsa and the religious interpretations of the Supreme reality, as put forward by Samkara, Ramanuja, Madhva and Nimbarka, Vallabha and Jiva Gosvami, form a remarkable record of philosophical development in the history of the human race. Type succeeds type, school follows on school, in logical sequence. The life of the Indian was ever on the move, shaping itself as it grew, and changing from time to time in relation to its physical, social and cultural contexts. In the early stages the ancient Indians were doing everything for the first time. They had practically no wisdom of the past to fall back upon. They had, moreover, enormous difficulties to contend with, which are now almost things of the past. In spite of these, their achievement in the realm of thought and practice is a considerable one. But the cycle is not complete, and the range of possible forms is not exhausted; for the sphinx still smiles. Philosophy is yet in its infancy.

The survey of Indian thought, as of all thought, impresses one with the mystery and the immensity of existence as well as the beauty and persistence of the human effort to understand it. The long procession of thinkers struggled hard to add some small piece to the temple of human wisdom, some fresh fragment to the ever incomplete sum of human knowledge. But human speculation falls short of the ideal, which it can neither abandon nor attain. We are far more conscious of the depth of the surrounding darkness than of the power to dispel it possessed by the flickering torches that we have the privilege to carry as the inheritors of a great past. After all the attempts of philosophers, we stand today in relation to the ultimate problems very near where we stood far away in the ages—where perhaps we shall ever stand as long as we are human, bound Prometheus-like to the rock of mystery by the chains of our finite mind.[65] The pursuit of philosophy is not, however, a vain endeavour. It helps us to feel the grip and the clanging of the chains. It sharpens the consciousness of human imperfection, and thus deepens the sense of perfection in us, which reveals the imperfection of our passing lives. That the world is not so transparent to our intellects as we could wish is not to be wondered at, for the philosopher is only the lover of wisdom and not its possessor. It is not the end of the voyage that matters, but the voyage itself. To travel is a better thing than to arrive.

At the end of our course, we may ask whether the known facts of history support a belief in progress. Is the march of human thought a forward movement, or is it one of retrogression? The sequence is not capricious and unmeaning. India believes in progress, for, as we have already said, the cycles are bound together by an organic tie. The inner thread of continuity is never cut. Even the revolutions that threaten to engulf the past help to restore it. Backward eddies serve rather to strengthen than retard the current. Epochs of decadence, like the recent past of his country, are in truth periods of transition from an old life to a new. The two currents of progress and decline are intermingled. At one stage the forces of progress press forward with a persistent sweep, at another the line sways to and fro, and sometimes the forces of retrogression seem to overwhelm those of progress, but on the whole the record is one of advance. It would be idle to deny that much has perished in the process. But few things are more futile than to rail against the course which the historical past has taken or weep over it. In any case, some other kind of development would have been worse. The important thing is the future. We are able to see further than our predecessors, since we can climb on their shoulders. Instead of resting content with the foundations nobly laid in the past, we must build a greater edifice in harmony with ancient endeavour as well as the modern outlook.

The Unity of All Systems

The twin strands which in one shape or another run through all the efforts of the Indian thinkers are loyalty to tradition and devotion to truth. Every thinker recognises that the principles of his predecessors are stones built into the spiritual fabric, and, if they are traduced, one's own culture is defamed. A progressive people with a rich tradition cannot afford to neglect it, though it may contain elements which are not edifying. The thinkers try hard to explain, allegorise, alter and expurgate the traditional lore, since men's emotions are centred round it. The later Indian thinkers justify the different philosophical interpretations of the universe advanced by the earlier ones, and regard them as varying approximations to the truth as a whole. The different views are not looked upon as unrelated adventures of the human mind into the realm of the unknown or a collection of philosophical curiosities. They are regarded as the expression of a single mind, which has built up the great temple, though it is divided into numerous walls and vestibules, passages and pillars.

Logic and science, philosophy and religion are related organically. Every fresh epoch in the progress of thought has been inaugurated by a reform in logic. The problem of method, involving as it does an insight into the nature of human thought, is of great value. The Nyaya points out that no stable philosophy can be built except on the foundations of logic. The Vaisesika warns us that all fruitful philosophy must take into account the constitution of physical nature. We cannot build in the clouds. Though physics and metaphysics are clearly distinct and cannot be blended, still a philosophic scheme must be in harmony with the results of natural science. But to extend to the universe at large what is true of the physical world would be to commit the fallacy of scientific metaphysics, and the Samkhya asks us to beware of that danger. The resources of nature cannot generate consciousness. We cannot reduce nature and consciousness the one to the other, as scientific and psychological metaphysics attempt to do. Reality appears not only in science and in human life, but in religious experience, which is the subject matter of the Yoga system. The Purva Mimamsa and the Vedanta lay stress on ethics and religion. The relation between nature and mind is the supreme problem of philosophy which the Vedanta takes up. The saying, that the saints do not contradict one another, is true of philosophies also. The Nyaya-Vaisesika realism, the Samkhya-Yoga dualism and the Vedanta monism do not differ as true and false but as more or less true.[66] They are adapted to the needs of the slow-witted (mandadhikari), the average intellect (madhyamadhikari) and the strong-minded (uttamadhikari) respectively. The different views are hewn out of one stone and belong to one whole, integral, entire and self-contained. No scheme of the universe can be regarded as complete, if it has not the different sides of logic and physics, psychology and ethics, metaphysics and religion. Every system of thought developed in India offered its own theory of knowledge, interpretation of nature and mind, ethics and religion. Our knowledge of the universe has grown enormously under the guidance of the natural sciences, and we cannot afford to be satisfied with any restricted outlook on life. The future attempts at philosophic construction will have to relate themselves to the recent advances of natural science and psychology.

The Decline of Philosophy in the Recent Past

The evidence brought together in this work does not support the general criticism that the Indian mind has a fear of thinking. We cannot dismiss the whole progress of Indian thought with a sapient reference to the oriental mind, which is not sufficiently dry and virile to rise above grotesque imagination and puerile mythology. Yet there is much in the thought history of the last three or four centuries to lend countenance to this charge. India is no longer playing her historic role as the vanguard of higher knowledge in Asia.[67] It seems to some that the river that has flowed down the centuries so strong and full is likely to end in a stagnant waste of waters. The philosophers, or rather the writers on philosophy of this period of decadence, profess to be votaries of truth, though they understand by it merely the pious sophistries or the sacrosanct hair-splittings of this or that school of dogmatics. These professional dialecticians imagine that the small brook by their side, trickling away in the sand or evaporating in the fog, is the broad river of Indian philosophy.

A variety of causes have contributed to this result. The political changes brought about by the establishment of the Mohammadan supremacy turned men's minds into conservative moulds. In an age when individual self-assertion and private judgment threatened at every point to dissolve into anarchy the old social order and all stable conviction, the need for authoritative control was urgently felt. The Mohammadan conquest, with its propagandist work, and later the Christian missionary movement, attempted to shake the stability of Hindu society, and in an age deeply conscious of instability, authority naturally became the rock on which alone it seemed that social safety and ethical order could be reared. The Hindu, in the face of the clash of cultures, fortified himself with conventions and barred all entry to invading ideas. His society, mistrusting reason and weary of argument, flung itself passionately into the arms of an authority which stamped all free questioning as sin. Since then it has failed in loyalty to its mission. There were no longer any thinkers, but only scholars who refused to strike new notes, and were content to raise echoes of the old call. For some centuries they succeeded in deceiving themselves with a supposedly final theory. Philosophy became confused with the history of philosophy when the creative spirit had left her. It abdicated its function and remained wrapped up in its illusions. When it ceased to be the guide and the guardian of the general reason, it did a great wrong to itself. Many believed that their race had travelled long and far towards a goal at which it had at length arrived. They felt rather tired and inclined to rest. Even those who knew that they had not arrived, and saw the large

tract of the country stretching into the future, were afraid of the unknown and its ordeals. The silences and the eternities cannot be questioned without peril by the weak of heart. The dizziness of the inquiry into the infinite is a vertigo which even mighty minds try to avoid, if they can. The strongest of human forces are subject to intervals of lethargy, and the philosophic impulse has had in these three or four centuries an attack of lethargy.

The Present Situation

Today the great religions of the world and the different currents of thought have met on Indian soil. The contact with the spirit of the West has disturbed the placid contentment of recent times. The assimilation of a different culture has led to the impression that there are no official answers to ultimate problems. It has shaken the faith in the traditional solutions, and has, in some degree, helped to a larger freedom and flexibility of thought. Tradition has become fluid again, and while some thinkers are busy rebuilding the house on ancient foundations, others want to remove the foundations altogether. The present age of transition is as full of interest as of anxiety.

During the recent past, India was comfortably moored in a backwater outside the full current of contemporary thought, but she is no longer isolated from the rest of the world. The

historian of three or four centuries hence may have much to say on the issues of the intercourse between India and Europe, but as yet they lie hidden from our view. So far as India is concerned, we notice the broadening of men's range of experience, the growth of the critical temper and a sort of distaste for mere speculation.

But there is another side to the picture. In the field of thought, as well as in that of action, the spirit of man is doomed to decay as much in anarchy as in bondage. There is not much to choose between the two, so far as culture and civilisation are concerned. Anarchy may mean material discomfort, economic ruin and social danger and bondage material comfort, economic stability and social peace. But it would be incorrect to confuse the standards of civilisation with economic welfare and maintenance of social order. It is easy to understand the feeling of the Indians of the beginning of the nineteenth century, who after generations of public strife and private suffering welcomed the British rule as the dawn of a golden age; but it should be equally easy to sympathise with the Indian feeling of the present day that the spirit of man craves, not comfort, but happiness, not peace and order, but life and liberty, not economic stability or equitable administration, but the right to work out one's own salvation even at the cost of infinite toil and tribulation. Even non-political virtues do not thrive in the absence of political autonomy. British rule has given India peace and security, but they are not ends in themselves. If we are to put first things first, then we must admit that economic stability and political security are only means, however valuable and necessary, to spiritual freedom. A bureaucratic despotism which forgets the spiritual ends, for all its integrity and enlightenment, cannot invigorate the peoples beneath her sway, and cannot therefore evoke any living response in them. When the founts of life are drying up, when the ideals for which the race stood for millenniums, the glow of consciousness, the free exercise of faculty, the play of life, the pleasure of mind and the fulness of peace, pranaramam, mana-anandam, santi-samrddham, are decaying, it is no wonder that the Indian is conscious only of the crushing burden and not of the lifted weight. It is no use speaking to him of the magnitude of Britain's work, for the verdict of history is passed on the spiritual quality of the achievement. If the leaders of recent generations have been content to be mere echoes of the past and not independent voices, if they have been intellectual middlemen and not original thinkers, this sterility is to no small extent due to the shock of the Western spirit and the shame of subjection. The British are aware of the deep-rooted causes of the present attitude of India, whatever it may be called, unrest, revolt or challenge. They tried to bring their civilisation, which they naturally regard as higher, to touch the Indians, and they felt that they should press on in the task of enlightenment and education, good in themselves, without any hesitation or cessation of effort. But India has no sympathy with this policy of cultural imperialism. She tenaciously clings to her ancient customs which helped her to check the swell of passion, the blindness of temper and the thrust of desire. One who is acquainted with the history of her past can sympathise with her anxiety to dwell in her own spiritual house, for 'each man is the master of his own house.'[68] Political subjection which interferes with this inner freedom is felt as a gross humiliation. The cry for swaraj is the other expression of the anxiety to preserve the provinces of the soul.

Yet the future is full of promise. If India gains freedom within, then the Western spirit will be a great help to the Indian mind. Hindu thought never developed a Monroe doctrine in matters of culture. Even in the ancient times when India grew enough spiritual food to satisfy her own people, there is no recorded age when she was not ready and eager to appreciate the products of other people's imagination. In her great days India conformed to the wisdom of the Athenians, of whom Pericles said: 'We listen gladly to the opinions of others and do not turn sour faces on those who disagree with us.' Our fear of outside influence is proportioned to our own weakness and want of faith in ourselves. Today, it is true, we bear lines of sorrow in our face and our hair is grey with age. The thoughtful among us have a brooding uneasiness of soul, some are even steeped in pessimism, and so have become intellectual hermits. The non-co-operation with Western culture is a passing episode due to unnatural circumstances. In spite of it, there are attempts to understand and appreciate the spirit of Western culture. If India assimilates the valuable elements in the Western civilisation, it will be only a repetition of parallel processes which happened a number of times in the history of Indian thought.

Those who are untouched by the Western influence are for a large part intellectual and moral aristocrats, who are indifferent to political issues, and adopt a gospel not of confident hope but of resignation and detachment. They think that they have little to learn or to unlearn, and that they do their duty with their gaze fixed on the eternal dharma of the past. They realise that other forces are at work, which they cannot check or control, and ask us to face the storms and disillusionment of life with the unruffled calm of self-respect. This was the class which in better times was more elastic and was ever renewing the attempts to reconcile rational philosophy with revealed religion. It had always explained and defended the faith in the face of heretics and unbelievers, and had recourse to the allegorical method as the instrument of theological interpretation. Religion, for it, embraced within its scope the whole nature of man, his intelligence as much as his practical and emotional aspirations. If today the representatives of the ancient learning had the inspiration of the past, they would, instead of non-co-operating with other forces, build a fresh scheme with originality and freedom and in the strength of the legacy of ancient wisdom. But they have an exaggerated respect for authority in thought and action, in things spiritual and things secular, and have thus exposed themselves to the charges of mental servility and obscurantism. While, in pre-Mohammadan times, appeal to authority was no bar to intellectual independence, and while men were able and ready to offer rational grounds for allegiance to the authorities of their choice, be they the Vedas or the Agamas, and while authority was made to speak in the voice of reason by means of a critical selection and philosophical interpretation, now reverence for authority has become the imprisonment of the human spirit. To question the belief of the scriptures is to question the authority of the great dead. To accept them is a sign of loyalty. Inquiry and doubt are silenced by the citation of ancient texts, scientific truths are slighted, if they cannot be fitted into the procrustean bed of established belief. Passivity, docility and acquiescence become the primary intellectual virtues. No wonder the philosophical writings of recent times are far below the level of the best work of the past ages. If thought had been less strained, it would have been more spacious.

The thinkers of India are the inheritors of the great tradition of faith in reason. The ancient seers desired not to copy but to create. They were ever anxious to win fresh fields for truth and answer the riddles of experience, which is ever changing and therefore new. The richness of the inheritance never served to enslave their minds. We cannot simply copy the solutions of the past, for history never repeats itself. What they did in their generation need not be done over again. We have to keep our eyes open, find out our problems and seek the inspiration of the past in solving them. The spirit of truth never clings to its forms but ever renews them. Even the old phrases are used in a new way. The philosophy of the present will be relevant to the present and not to the past. It will be as original in its form and its content as the life which it interprets. As the present is continuous with the past, so there will be no breach of continuity with the past.

One of the arguments of the conservatives is that truth is not affected by time. It cannot be superseded, any more than the beauty of the sunset or a mother's love for a child. Truth may be immutable, but the form in which it is embodied consists of elements which admit of change. We may take our spirit from the past, for the germinal ideas are yet vital, but the body and the pulse must be from the present. It is forgotten that religion, as it is today, is itself the product of ages of change; and there is no reason why its forms should not undergo fresh changes so long as the spirit demands it. It is possible to remain faithful to the letter and yet pervert the whole spirit. If the Hindu leaders of two thousand years ago, who had less learning and more light, could come on earth again after all these centuries, they would seldom find their true followers among those who have never deviated from the most literal interpretations of their views.[69] Today a great mass of accretions have accumulated, which are choking up the stream and the free life of spirit. To say that the dead forms, which have no vital truth to them, are too ancient and venerable to be tampered with, only prolongs the suffering of the patient who is ailing from the poison generated by the putrid waste of the past. The conservative mind must open itself to the necessity of change. Since it is not sufficiently alive to this need, we find in the realm of philosophy a strange mixture of penetrating sagacity and unphilosophical confusion. The chief energies of the thinking Indians should be thrown into the problems of how to disentangle the old faith from its temporary accretions, how to bring religion into line with the spirit of science, how to meet and interpret the claims of temperament and individuality, how to organise the divergent influences on the basis of the ancient faith. But, unfortunately, some of the parisads are engaged not with these problems but those suited for the society of Antiquarians. It has become the tilting-ground of the specialists. The religious education of the nation is not undertaken on broad lines. It is not seen that the spiritual inheritance cannot be any longer the monopoly of a favoured few. Ideas are forces, and they must be broadcasted, if the present ageing to death is to be averted. It would be indeed strange if the spirit of the Upanisads, the Gita and the Dialogues of Buddha, that could touch the mind to such fine issues, should have lost its power over man. If, before it is too late, there is a reorganisation of national life, there is a future for Indian thought; and one cannot tell what flowers may yet bloom, what fruits may yet ripen on the hardy old trees.

While those who have not yet been subjected to the influence of Western culture are conservatives in all matters of thought and practice, there are those educated in Western ways of thinking who adopt a despairing philosophy of naturalistic rationalism and ask us to get rid of the weight of the past. These are intolerant of tradition and suspicious of the alleged wisdom of age. This attitude of the 'progressives' is easily understood. The spiritual heritage of the race has not protected India from the invader and the spoiler. It seems to have played her false and betrayed her into the present state of subjection. These patriots are eager to imitate the material achievements of Western states, and tear up the roots of the ancient civilisation, so as to make room for the novelties imported from the West. Till the other day Indian thought was not a subject of study in the Indian Universities, and even now its place in the philosophical curricula of the Universities is insignificant. Suggestions of the inferiority of Indian culture permeate the whole educational atmosphere. The policy inaugurated by Macaulay, with all its cultural value, is loaded on one side. While it is so careful as not to make us forget the force and vitality of Western culture, it has not helped us to love our own culture and refine it where necessary. In some cases, Macaulay's wish is fulfilled, and we have educated Indians who are 'more English than the English themselves,' to quote his well-known words. Naturally some of these are not behind the hostile foreign critic in their estimate of the history of Indian culture. They look upon India's cultural evolution as one dreary scene of discord, folly and superstition. One of their number recently declared that, if India is to thrive and flourish, England must be her 'spiritual mother' and Greece her 'spiritual grandmother'. Albeit, since he has no faith in religion, he does not propose the displacement of Hinduism by Christianity. These victims of the present age of disillusion and defeat tell us that the love of Indian thought is a nationalist foible, if not a pose of the highbrows.

It is a bewildering phenomenon that, just when India is ceasing to appear grotesque to Western eyes, she is beginning to appear so to the eyes of some of her own sons. The West tried its best to persuade India that its philosophy is absurd, its art puerile, its poetry uninspired, its religion grotesque and its ethics barbarous. Now that the West is feeling that its judgment is not quite correct, some of us are insisting that it was wholly right. While it is true that it is difficult in an age of reflection to push men back into an earlier stage of culture and save them from the dangers of doubt and the disturbing power of dialectic, we should not forget that we can build better on foundations already laid than by attempting to substitute a completely new structure of morality, of life and of ethics. We cannot cut ourselves off from the springs of our life. Philosophical schemes, unlike geometrical constructions, are the products of life. The heritage of our history is the food that we have to absorb on pain of inanition.

The conservatives are convinced of the glory of the ancient heritage and the godlessness of modern culture; the radicals are equally certain of the futility of the ancient heritage and the value of naturalistic rationalism. There is much to be said for these views; but the history of Indian thought, when rightly studied, will lead us to regard the two as equally defective. Those who condemn Indian culture as useless are ignorant of it, while those who commend it as perfect are ignorant of any other. The radicals and the conservatives, who stand for the new hope and the old learning, must come closer and understand each other. We cannot live by ourselves in a world where aircraft and steamships, railways and telegraphs are linking all men together into a living whole. Our system of thought must act and react on the world progress. Stagnant systems, like pools, breed obnoxious growths, while flowing rivers constantly renew their waters from fresh springs of inspiration. There is nothing wrong in absorbing the culture of other peoples; only we must enhance, raise and purify the elements we take over, fuse them with the best in our own. The right procedure regarding the fusing together of the different elements tossed from outside into the national crucible, is indicated roughly in the writings of Gandhi and Tagore, Aurobindo Ghosh and Bhagavan Das. In them we see the faint promise of a great future, some signs of a triumph over scholasticism, as well as a response to the discovery of a great culture. While drawing upon the fountains of humanist idealism in India's past, they show a keen appreciation of Western thought. They are anxious to re-seek the ancient fountain-head and direct its waters to irrigate, through pure and uncontaminated conduits, lands which hunger and thirst. But the future which we wish to see is practically non-existent. With the slackening of the political excitement, which is absorbing the energies of some of the best minds of India, with the increasing insistence on the study of Indian thought in the new Universities, which the old ones are following most reluctantly, the dawn may break. The forces of the conservatism, which prefers the life that was to the life that will be, are not likely to gain any strength in the days to come.

The problem facing Indian Philosophy today is whether it is to be reduced to a cult, restricted in scope and with no application to the present facts, or whether it is to be made alive and real, so as to become what it should be, one of the great formative elements in human progress, by relating the immensely increased knowledge of modern science to the ancient ideals of India's philosophers. All signs indicate that the future is bound up with the latter alternative. Loyalty to the spirit of the previous systems of thought, as well as the mission of philosophy, requires us to possess an outlook that always broadens. Indian philosophy acquires a meaning and a justification for the present only if it advances and ennobles life. The past course of Indian philosophic development encourages us in our hope. The great thinkers Yajnavalkya and Gargi, Buddha and Mahavira, Gautama and Kapila, Samkara and Ramanuja, Madhva and Vallabha, and scores of others are India's grandest title to existence, a clear testimony of her dignity as a nation with a soul, the proof that she may yet rise above herself and the pledge of this supreme possibility.

—From *Indian Philosophy*

58

Maulana Abul Kalam Azad

Abul Kalam Azad (1888–1958) was a journalist and educationist. An Islamic theologian and a senior leader of the Indian National Congress, he often spoke up against the radicalising policies of other prominent Muslims leaders during the freedom struggle. In 1947, he became the first education minister and shaped the education policy of independent India. He championed the right to free education for children up to the age of fourteen. His birth anniversary is celebrated as 'National Education Day'.

Speech at the Constituent Assembly of India (Legislative), 11 March 1948

Adult Education, Technical Education and Language Policy

There is no doubt that the problem of adult education is as important as that of child education. The adult education has far greater aims than merely teaching adults how to read and write. It is our duty to impart to adults an education which should develop their thinking faculty so that they are enlightened and enabled to take due interest in the affairs of a democratic state and society. In no walk of our national life can we progress without the considered and judicious co-operation of millions of our countrymen. Anyhow, nobody would deny the extreme importance of this work. What we have to see is how best this work can be accomplished in the shortest time.

The report submitted by the Central Advisory Board in the year 1944 contained also a scheme for adult education. But this scheme could not be enforced. It was after the last general elections, when the Congress Ministries were re-established in the provinces, that attention was paid to this thing. Work was taken in hand but on too small a scale to meet the demands of the day. After my assumption of office as Education Minister last year the first task that confronted me was the Basic Education and Adult Education schemes. But the political condition of our country at that time was such that no time could be spared for attending to the task of education. Government was over head and ears engrossed with other affairs. I wanted to convene a meeting of the provincial education ministers and representatives of the Universities. Twice a date was fixed but every time it had to be postponed because conditions at that time made it impossible for men to assemble for a conference. Opportunity offered itself at last, and in January meetings of the Educational Conference and the Central Advisory Committee were held. I placed before them a new scheme for Adult Education; and you know that it was approved by both of these bodies. The report of the sub-committee appointed for this purpose by the Standing Committee of the Central Advisory Board was presented and accepted with some modifications. Our scheme is ready now. Its one branch concerns literary education and the other with the development of mental faculties. The latter provides besides oral lectures, the media of radio, films and modern methods of open-air dramas. Efforts are being made to secure the best equipment. For this very reason this year money has been earmarked for a film library. Production of educational films is being undertaken. A separate section has been started under the ministry for the purpose of helping in the preparation of necessary literature. The sub-committee appointed by the Advisory Board had stressed the inclusion of certain amount of technical education in this scheme because a majority of the adults receiving education under this scheme would be connected with some profession or art. This suggestion has therefore also been incorporated in the scheme. Opinions of the Provincial Governments have been invited in this connection. We intend to introduce this scheme in such a way as should enable the schools of Basic Education to become centres of all activities of the Adult Education as well. In this way we want to create a new intellectual atmosphere in this country.

So far I have told you the story of Adult Education. But mere paper scheme does not do. It requires material and for material the question of money comes first. The House is familiar with the attitude the Central Government have hitherto been adopting in this connection. Government proceeds up to a certain point beyond which it cannot proceed. I wish we could cross these old limits and move along new lines.

I wanted to have double the present grant but due to the emphasis laid by the Ministry of Finance on our limitations for the year I had to content myself with it. The political conditions and especially the misfortunes of the Punjab, have suddenly burdened the finances of the Central Government; and due to this we have been forced to proceed slowly. Nevertheless I admit that other things can afford to wait but not education. It is necessary that somehow or other provision for money for this work must be made. This was also one of the fundamental questions which were raised in the Educational Conference which met on 16th January. The Conference has appointed a committee to go into this question and to make its recommendation. I hope Government will receive their recommendation by June and we will be able to arrange sufficient funds for carrying out essential schemes of education.

In moving the second cut motion the Honourable Shri Deshmukh has drawn the attention of Government to the necessity for technical education. I may assure him that Government have been doing everything possible in this connection and in our plan for the next year's Budget we have tried to move quickly. If the Honourable Members had glanced through the statement circulated to them, this cut-motion would probably have not been necessary. I will briefly tell the House what has been done in this connection.

The Government of India have decided to open four Higher Technical Institutions on the model of American Institutes; of these, two will be located near Calcutta and Bombay and work has to be started at once. From the files I find that this matter has been under consideration for the last two years, but so far neither any site has been selected nor any progress made in pushing through the work. I tried to remedy this state of affairs, and to enforce the scheme as soon as possible. The site has now been selected and arrangements for the staff are being made. Each of the four institutes would cost rupees three crores as capital expenditure and rupees forty-four lakhs as recurring expenditure and will provide for the training of 3,000 students—2,000 undergraduates and 1,000 postgraduates. The whole scheme is expected to be completed within two or three years.

Four years' development plan for the Indian Institute of Science, Bangalore, has been sanctioned, and the power engineering department is being opened.

Three years' development plan for the Delhi Polytechnic has been sanctioned and the work is being started.

The All-India Council for Technical Education recommended to give from the Centre a grant to the existing technical institutions in the country. Accordingly, the grant has been sanctioned for five years and it is being given.

The House might be aware of the fact that an Overseas Scholarship scheme was passed by the Central Government in 1944 and scholars from India were being sent abroad for training. When the new Government assumed office, it was felt that this scheme was not followed properly. Therefore, the first thing was to try to raise the status of the existing institutions to a level so as to train students with much higher qualifications, and then to determine according to the plan the subjects for the study of which scholars should be sent abroad and then to grant scholarship for those subjects only. Accordingly with this object in view a committee called the Scientific Manpower Committee was set up to investigate into the country's immediate scientific requirements and to prepare a plan.

The committee is still functioning. It has submitted its interim report and Government gave their immediate attention to it and have accepted most of its recommendations. The recommendations stressed the need for giving fresh grants to the country's Universities and institutions to enable them to augment their resources for imparting educational facilities in scientific and technical subjects. We have started giving grants from this year, and allotment of funds has been made for the three Central Universities.

In addition to these activities of the Central Government the technical education work is also being generally accelerated in all the provinces. The Central Government have this year given handsome amounts to the Provincial Governments to enable them to implement their development schemes quickly.

Accordingly, 29 Junior Technical Institutions are being reorganised, and their scope of instructions is being enlarged, 4 Technical High Schools are being opened; 11 Senior Technical Institutions; 140 Junior Technical Schools; 38 Technical High Schools; 16 Polytechnics; 4 Senior Technical Institutions, will soon begin to function.

These statistics relate to the general Post-War Development Plan.

In moving the third cut motion, the Honourable Mrs Hansa Mehta has drawn our attention to the fact that no rules have yet been prescribed for grants to the Universities. And it is necessary that the Central Government should elucidate its policy in this respect. I feel that no such question arises. The practice followed by the previous Government was to give grants to the three Central Universities only and with a view to give these grants, a committee called the University Grants Committee was constituted. The present Government felt that if it was desired to raise the standard of education of the entire country to the same level, then the scope of Central Government's help should not be confined to the three Universities only. It should be further expanded. In other words, we should open its doors for the distribution of grants to other Universities also. With this object the University Grants Committee was constituted *de novo* and its terms of reference have been framed in such a manner so as to fully conform to this new policy. All the applications which are now received by the Ministry will be passed on to the University Grants Committee. The Government will carefully consider the recommendations made by the Committee in this respect.

Mrs Hansa Mehta has also referred in her speech to the existence of communal institutions and has stressed the point as why the word 'Hindu' and 'Muslim' should at all be associated with the names of Benares and Aligarh Universities? I fully agree with the views expressed by her. I do not only agree but welcome this idea. I extend a hearty welcome to this. No one else than myself will be happier if the words 'Hindu' and 'Muslim' are eliminated from the names of those two Universities. But it is clear that legislation establishing these Universities was passed by this House and until the Acts are amended we cannot make any change. ... The Government are also in full agreement with the point stressed by Shrimati Mehta. Any Honourable Member of the House can move for an amendment of the Act. In any case this change must be made.

The Government are also in full agreement with the point stressed by Shrimati G. Durga Bai. Nothing can retard more the growth of our national life than the encouragement of 'community', 'religion' and 'caste' in the educational sphere and placing of such limitations as would separate one class of people from the other. When we oppose this, it is not our intention that the backward classes should not be provided with facilities for advancement. On the contrary they should be helped in every walk of life and there is no doubt education is the high-road for their advancement. If they have been left behind in the sphere of progress it is not their fault. The society is to be blamed for this. It is all the more necessary therefore that the society which has not until now placed them on an equal footing, should help in their advancement. Take the case of our Harijan brethren. If seats can be reserved for them in some institutions it does not mean that they are accorded discriminatory treatment over other classes. The reason is that if such a course is not adopted there is danger that they would be lost and will not be able to receive the benefit of education according to their share. The Government quite agree with the view that there should be no distinction of caste or creed in the sphere of education and whatever policy the Government and Universities of the provinces have so far followed in this respect they should now adopt the national policy of the Central Government.

The last motion was moved by the Honourable Mr Frank Anthony, pointing out that the Government should have a uniform policy regarding language. If any change has to be introduced it should be done slowly and gradually after full consideration. The change from English to an Indian language should not be sudden as this will disturb the standard of education and will result in harassment to people. I can assure the Honourable Member that this is the policy of the Government who have advised the Provincial Governments to move cautiously and slowly in this matter. It must be known to the Honourable Members that I was first to raise my voice and warn the people against taking hasty steps and to move slowly. In my convocation address at the Patna University, I first expressed my view that we should substitute the language in the course of five years and though we should start the process now the English language should continue for five years. This opinion applies not only to matters of education but also to matters of administration. Later on in the month of January when the Central Advisory Board and the Educational Conference met, I placed the same view before them and laid emphasis on the point that English should be replaced gradually and after due consideration. I am glad the Central Advisory Board and the Educational Conference both agreed to this view, and I can say with confidence that the general policy of the Government in this connection will be as was indicated by me. Thus, the Central Government have, so far as they are concerned, laid down a definite and clear policy on this subject and as medium of instruction English will be replaced by one or more Indian languages. We do not want a sudden change but the change should be effected step by step. Our plan is that this should be accomplished in five years and in such a manner that in the sixth year the need for English should vanish.

To put it succinctly the Government policy can be described as follows:

So far as the primary and secondary stage is concerned it has been decided that the medium of instruction will be the mother tongue, and this is being put into practice by all the provinces.

For the University stage, it has been decided that English cannot continue as the medium of instruction but this change we should bring about in five years so that in the sixth year English will be fully replaced.

This then is the policy of the Government on the language question and the representatives of the Provinces who came to attend the Educational Conference also agreed to it. It is, therefore, not correct to say that the Government have no uniform policy in this matter.

As I have already said it has been decided that the medium of instruction even in the University will be the national language. But we have not decided yet whether we are going to have one or more national languages. The All India Educational Conference which I convened in January last has appointed a committee to go into this matter and we are awaiting the recommendations of this Committee.

The Honourable Member has specially mentioned the U.P. Government. I cannot say what exactly his point is? In November last I saw a press report to the effect that the U.P. Government will stop printing the U.P. Government Gazette in English from the new year. I immediately wrote a letter to the U.P. Premier suggesting that it will not be proper to do away with English so suddenly. In his reply to my letter, he assured me that his Government was not in favour of making sudden changes and that he fully concurred in my opinion expressed in my address at the Patna University. Now

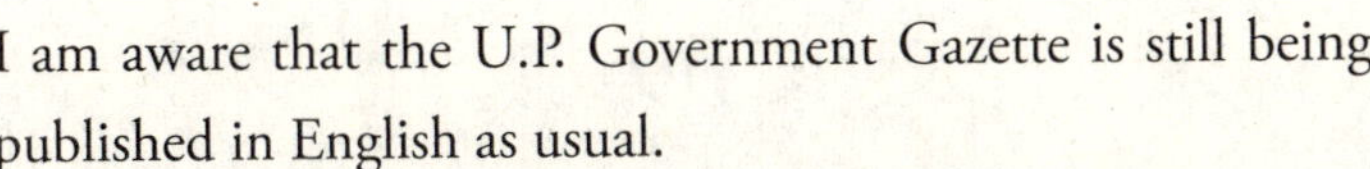

I am aware that the U.P. Government Gazette is still being published in English as usual.

I will also tell the House that it is welcome to make as many requests as it pleases regarding matters educational and I will welcome all such requests but it should not forget that I am only a Minister of Education and not an Officer-in-charge of paradise, nor have I a magician's basket with me to produce a full-grown tree at a moment's notice.

59
Jawaharlal Nehru

Jawaharlal Nehru (1889–1964) was the first prime minister of independent India and the founder of the modern Indian state. He was an ardent follower of Mahatma Gandhi, who, in turn, supported him wholeheartedly. Nehru was a firm believer in parliamentary democracy and secularism, and these became the ideological pillars of the new nation he led. He followed an independent foreign policy during the Cold War and was one of the founders of the Non-Aligned Movement.

A Tryst with Destiny, 14 August 1947

Long years ago we made a tryst with destiny, and now the time comes when we shall redeem our pledge, not wholly or in full measure, but very substantially. At the stroke of the midnight hour, when the world sleeps, India will awake to life and freedom. A moment comes, which comes but rarely in history, when we step out from the old to the new, when an age ends, and when the soul of a nation, long suppressed, finds utterance. It is fitting that at this solemn moment, we take the pledge of dedication to the service of India and her people and to the still larger cause of humanity.

At the dawn of history, India started on her unending quest, and trackless centuries are filled with her striving and the grandeur of her successes and her failures. Through good and ill fortune alike, she has never lost sight of that quest or forgotten the ideals which gave her strength. We end today a period of misfortunes and India discovers herself again. The achievement we celebrate today is but a step, an opening of opportunity to the greater triumphs and achievements that await us. Are we brave enough and wise enough to grasp this opportunity and accept the challenge of the future?

JAWAHARLAL NEHRU

Freedom and power bring responsibility. That responsibility rests upon this Assembly, a sovereign body representing the sovereign people of India. Before the birth of freedom, we have endured all the pains of labour and our hearts are heavy with the memory of this sorrow. Some of those pains continue even now. Nevertheless, the past is over and it is the future that beckons to us now.

That future is not one of ease or resting but of incessant striving so that we might fulfil the pledges we have so often taken and the one we shall take today. The service of India means the service of the millions who suffer. It means the ending of poverty and ignorance and disease and inequality of opportunity. The ambition of the greatest men of our generation has been to wipe every tear from every eye. That may be beyond us, but so long as there are tears and suffering, so long our work will not be over.

And so we have to labour and to work, and work hard, to give reality to our dreams. Those dreams are for India, but they are also for the world, for all the nations and peoples are too closely knit together today for any one of them to imagine that it can live apart. Peace has been said to be indivisible, so is freedom, so is prosperity now, and also is disaster in this one world that can no longer be split into isolated fragments.

To the people of India, whose representatives we are, we make appeal to join us with faith and confidence in this great adventure. This is no time for petty and destructive criticism, no time for ill-will or blaming others. We have to build the noble mansion of free India where all her children may dwell.

The appointed day has come—the day appointed by destiny—and India stands forth again, after long slumber and struggle, awake, vital, free and independent. The past clings on to us still in some measure and we have to do much before we redeem the pledges we have so often taken. Yet the turning-point is past, and history begins anew for us, the history which we shall live and act and others will write about.

It is a fateful moment for us in India, for all Asia and for the world. A new star rises, the star of freedom in the East, a new hope comes into being, a vision long cherished materialises. May the star never set and that hope never be betrayed!

We rejoice in that freedom, even though clouds surround us, and many of our people are sorrow-stricken and difficult problems encompass us. But freedom brings responsibilities and burdens and we have to face them in the spirit of a free and disciplined people.

On this day our first thoughts go to the architect of this freedom, the Father of our Nation, who, embodying the old spirit of India, held aloft the torch of freedom and lighted up the darkness that surrounded us. We have often been unworthy followers of his and have strayed from his message, but not only we but succeeding generations will remember this message and bear the imprint in their hearts of this great son of India, magnificent in his faith and strength and courage and humility. We shall never allow that torch of freedom to be blown out, however high the wind or stormy the tempest.

Our next thoughts must be of the unknown volunteers and soldiers of freedom who, without praise or reward, have served India even unto death.

We think also of our brothers and sisters who have been cut off from us by political boundaries and who unhappily cannot share at present in the freedom that has come. They are of us and will remain of us whatever may happen, and we shall be sharers in their good and ill fortune alike.

The future beckons to us. Whither do we go and what shall be our endeavour? To bring freedom and opportunity to the common man, to the peasants and workers of India; to fight and end poverty and ignorance and disease; to build up a prosperous, democratic and progressive nation, and to create social, economic and political institutions which will ensure justice and fullness of life to every man and woman.

We have hard work ahead. There is no resting for any one of us till we redeem our pledge in full, till we make all the people of India what destiny intended them to be. We are citizens of a great country on the verge of bold advance, and we have to live up to that high standard. All of us, to whatever religion we may belong, are equally the children of India with equal rights, privileges and obligations. We cannot encourage communalism or narrow-mindedness, for no nation can be great whose people are narrow in thought or in action.

To the nations and peoples of the world we send greetings and pledge ourselves to cooperate with them in furthering peace, freedom and democracy.

And to India, our much-loved motherland, the ancient, the eternal and the ever-new, we pay our reverent homage and we bind ourselves afresh to her service.

Jai Hind.

The Quest

The Panorama of India's Past

During these years of thought and activity my mind has been full of India, trying to understand her and to analyse my own reactions towards her. I went back to my childhood days and tried to remember what I felt like then, what vague shape this conception took in my growing mind, and how it was moulded by fresh experience. Sometimes it receded into the background, but it was always there, slowly changing, a queer mixture derived from old story and legend and modern fact. It produced a sensation of pride in me as well as that of shame, for I was ashamed of much that I saw around me, of superstitious practices, of outworn ideas, and, above all, our subject and poverty-stricken state.

As I grew up and became engaged in activities which promised to lead to India's freedom, I became obsessed with the thought of India. What was this India that possessed me and beckoned to me continually, urging me to action so that we might realize some vague but deeply-felt desire of our hearts? The initial urge came to me, I suppose, through pride, both individual and national, and the desire, common to all men, to resist another's domination and have the freedom to live the life of our choice. It seemed monstrous to me that a great country like India, with a rich and immemorial past, should be bound hand and foot to a far-away island which imposed its will upon her. It was still more monstrous that this forcible union had resulted in poverty and degradation beyond measure. That was reason enough for me and for others to act.

But it was not enough to satisfy the questioning that arose within me. What is this India, apart from her physical and geographical aspects? What did she represent in the past? What gave strength to her then? How did she lose that old strength? And has she lost it completely? Does she represent anything vital now, apart from being the home of a vast number of human beings? How does she fit into the modern world?

This wider international aspect of the problem grew upon me as I realized more and more how isolation was both undesirable and impossible. The future that took shape in my mind was one of intimate co-operation politically, economically, and culturally, between India and the other countries of the world. But before the future came there was the present, and behind the present lay the long and tangled past, out of which the present had grown. So to the past I looked for understanding.

India was in my blood and there was much in her that instinctively thrilled me. And yet I approached her almost as an alien critic, full of dislike for the present as well as for many of the relics of the past that I saw. To some extent I came to her via the West, and looked at her as a friendly Westerner might have done. I was eager and anxious to change her outlook and appearance and give her the garb of modernity. And yet doubts arose within me. Did I know India?—I who presumed to scrap much of her past heritage? There was a great deal that had to be scrapped, that must be scrapped; but surely India could not have been what she undoubtedly was, and could not have continued a cultured existence for thousands of years, if she had not possessed something very vital and enduring, something that was worthwhile. What was this something?

I stood on a mound of Mohenjo-Daro in the Indus Valley in the north-west of India, and all around me lay the houses and streets of this ancient city that is said to have existed over five thousand years ago; and even then it was an old and well-developed civilization. 'The Indus civilization,' writes Professor Childe, 'represents a very prefect adjustment of human life to a specific environment that can only have resulted from years of patient effort. And it has endured; it is already specifically Indian and forms the basis of modern Indian culture.' Astonishing thought: that any culture or civilization should have this continuity for five or six thousand years or more; and not in a static, unchanging sense, for India was changing and progressing all the time. She was coming into intimate contact with the Persians, the Egyptians, the Greeks, the Chinese, the Arabs, the Central Asians, and the peoples of the Mediterranean. But though she influenced them and was influenced by them, her cultural basis was strong enough to endure. What was the secret of this strength? Where did it come from?

I read her history and read also a part of her abundant ancient literature, and was powerfully impressed by the vigour of the thought, the clarity of the language, and the richness of the mind that lay behind it. I journeyed through India in the company of mighty travellers from China and Western and Central Asia who came here in the remote past and left records of their travels. I thought of what India had accomplished in Eastern Asia, in Angkor, Borobudur, and many other places. I wandered over the Himalayas, which are closely connected with old myth and legend, and which have influenced so much of our thought and literature. My love of the mountains and my kinship with Kashmir especially drew me to them, and I saw there not only the life and vigour and beauty of the present, but also the memorised loveliness of ages past. The mighty rivers of India that flow from this great mountain barrier into the plains of India attracted me and reminded me of innumerable phases of our history. The Indus or *Sindhu*, from which our country came to be called India and Hindustan, and across which races and tribes and caravans and armies have come for thousands of years; the Brahmaputra, rather cut off from the main current of history, but living in old stories, forcing its way into India through deep chasms cut in the heart of the northeastern mountains, and then flowing calmly in a gracious sweep between mountain and wooded plain; the Jumna, round which cluster so many legends of dance and fun and play; and the Ganges, above all the river of India, which has held India's heart captive and drawn uncounted millions to her banks since the dawn of history. The story of the Ganges, from her source to the sea, from old times to new, is the story of India's civilization and culture, of the rise and fall of empires, of great and proud cities, of the adventure of man and the quest of the mind which has so occupied India's thinkers, of the richness and fulfilment of life as well as its denial and renunciation, of ups and downs, of growth and decay, of life and death.

I visited old monuments and ruins and ancient sculptures and frescoes—Ajanta, Ellora, the Elephanta Caves, and other places—and I also saw the lovely buildings of a later age in Agra and Delhi, where every stone told its story of India's past.

In my own city of Allahabad or in Hardwar I would go to the great bathing festivals, the *Kumbh Mela*, and see hundreds of thousands of people come, as their forebears had come for thousands of years from all over India, to bathe in the Ganges. I would remember descriptions of these festivals written thirteen hundred years ago by Chinese pilgrims and others, and even then these *melas* were ancient and lost in an unknown antiquity. What was the tremendous faith, I wondered, that had drawn our people for untold generations to this famous river of India?

These journeys and visits of mine, with the background of my reading, gave me an insight into the past. To a somewhat bare intellectual understanding was added an emotional appreciation, and gradually a sense of reality began to creep into my mental picture of India, and the land of my forefathers became peopled with living beings, who laughed and wept, loved and suffered; and among them were men who seemed to know life and understand it, and out of their wisdom they had built a structure which gave India a cultural stability which lasted for thousands of years. Hundreds of vivid pictures of this past filled my mind, and they would stand out as soon as I visited a particular place associated with them. At Sarnath, near Benares, I would almost see the Buddha preaching his first sermon, and some of his recorded words would come like a distant echo to me through two thousand five hundred years. Ashoka's pillars of stone with their inscriptions would speak to me in their magnificent language and tell me of a man who, though an emperor, was greater than any king or emperor. At Fatehpur-Sikri, Akbar, forgetful of his empire, was seated holding converse and debate with the learned of all faiths, curious to learn something new and seeking an answer to the eternal problem of man.

Thus slowly the long panorama of India's history unfolded itself before me, with its ups and downs, its triumphs and defeats. There seemed to me something unique about the continuity of a cultural tradition through five thousand years of history, of invasion and upheaval, a tradition which was widespread among the masses and powerfully influenced them. Only China has had such a continuity of tradition and cultural life. And this panorama of the past gradually merged into the unhappy present, when India, for all her past greatness and stability, was a slave country, an appendage of Britain, and all over the world terrible and devastating war was raging and brutalizing humanity. But that vision of five thousand years gave me a new perspective, and the burden of the present seemed to grow lighter.

The hundred and eighty years of British rule in India were just one of the unhappy interludes in her long story; she would find herself again; already the last page of this chapter was being written. The world also will survive the horror of today and build itself anew on fresh foundations.

—From *The Discovery of India*

60

B.R. Ambedkar

Bhimrao Ramji Ambedkar (1891–1956), or Babasaheb as he was popularly called, is best known as the principal architect of the Indian Constitution and a staunch champion of Dalit rights. He advocated for greater equality and rights for the poor and for women. He was a social reformer, jurist, economist, and scholar of comparative religion. He is also credited with the establishment of the Reserve Bank of India and a central banking system in India.

Caste Destroys Public Spirit, Public Opinion, and Public Charity

The effect of caste on the ethics of the Hindus is simply deplorable. Caste has killed public spirit. Caste has destroyed the sense of public charity. Caste has made public opinion impossible. A Hindu's public is his caste. His responsibility is only to his caste. His loyalty is restricted only to his caste. Virtue has become caste-ridden, and morality has become caste-bound. There is no sympathy for the deserving. There is no appreciation of the meritorious. There is no charity to the needy. Suffering as such calls for no response. There is charity, but it begins with the caste and ends with the caste. There is sympathy, but not for men of other castes.

Would a Hindu acknowledge and follow the leadership of a great and good man? The case of a Mahatma apart, the answer must be that he will follow a leader if he is a man of his caste. A Brahmin will follow a leader only if he is a Brahmin, a Kayastha if he is a Kayastha, and so on. The capacity to appreciate merits in a man, apart from his caste, does not exist in a Hindu. There is appreciation of virtue, but only when the man is a fellow caste-man. The whole morality is as bad as tribal morality. My caste-man, right or wrong; my caste-man, good or bad. It is not a case of standing by virtue or not standing by vice. It is a case of standing by, or not standing by, the caste. Have not Hindus committed treason against their country in the interests of their caste?

My Ideal: A Society Based on Liberty, Equality, and Fraternity

I would not be surprised if some of you have grown weary listening to this tiresome tale of the sad effects which caste has produced. There is nothing new in it. I will therefore turn to the constructive side of the problem. What is your ideal society if you do not want caste, is a question that is bound to be asked of you. If you ask me, my ideal would be a society based on Liberty, Equality, and Fraternity. And why not?

What objection can there be to Fraternity? I cannot imagine any. An ideal society should be mobile, should be full of channels for conveying a change taking place in one part to other parts. In an ideal society there should be many interests consciously communicated and shared. There should be varied and free points of contact with other modes of association. In other words there must be social endosmosis. This is fraternity, which is only another name for democracy. Democracy is not merely a form of government. It is primarily a mode of associated living, of conjoint communicated experience. It is essentially an attitude of respect and reverence towards one's fellow men.

Any objection to Liberty? Few object to liberty in the sense of a right to free movement, in the sense of a right to life and limb. There is no objection to liberty in the sense of a right to property, tools, and materials, as being necessary for earning a living, to keep the body in a due state of health. Why not allow a person the liberty to benefit from an effective and competent use of a person's powers? The supporters of Caste who would allow liberty in the sense of a right to life, limb, and property, would not readily consent to liberty in this sense, inasmuch as it involves liberty to choose one's profession.

But to object to this kind of liberty is to perpetuate slavery. For slavery does not merely mean a legalized form of subjection. It means a state of society in which some men are forced to accept from others the purposes which control their conduct. This condition obtains even where there is no slavery in the legal sense. It is found where, as in the Caste System, some persons are compelled to carry on certain prescribed callings which are not of their choice.

Any objection to equality? This has obviously been the most contentious part of the slogan of the French Revolution. The objections to equality may be sound, and one may have to admit that all men are not equal. But what of that? Equality may be a fiction, but nonetheless one must accept it as the governing principle. A man's power is dependent upon (1) physical heredity; (2) social inheritance or endowment in the form of parental care, education, accumulation of scientific knowledge, everything which enables him to be more efficient than the savage; and finally, (3) on his own efforts. In all these three respects men are undoubtedly unequal. But the question is, shall we treat them as unequal because they are unequal? This is a question which the opponents of equality must answer.

From the standpoint of the individualist, it may be just to treat men unequally so far as their efforts are unequal. It may be desirable to give as much incentive as possible to the full development of everyone's powers. But what would happen if men were treated as unequally as they are unequal in the first two respects? It is obvious that those individuals also in whose favour there is birth, education, family name, business connections, and inherited wealth, would be selected in the race. But selection under such circumstances would not be a selection of the able. It would be the selection of the privileged. The reason, therefore, which requires that in the third respect we should treat men unequally, demands that in the first two respects we should treat men as equally as possible.

On the other hand, it can be urged that if it is good for the social body to get the most out of its members, it can get the most out of them only by making them equal as far as possible at the very start of the race. That is one reason why we cannot escape equality. But there is another reason why we must accept equality. A statesman is concerned with vast numbers of people. He has neither the time nor the knowledge to draw fine distinctions and to treat each one equitably, i.e. according to need or according to capacity. However desirable or reasonable an equitable treatment of men may be, humanity is not capable of assortment and classification. The statesman, therefore, must follow some rough and ready rule, and that rough and ready rule is to treat all men alike, not because they are alike but because classification and assortment is impossible. The doctrine of equality is glaringly fallacious but, taking all in all, it is the only way a statesman can proceed in politics—which is a severely practical affair and which demands a severely practical test.

If Hindu Society Is to Progress, Its Traditions Must Be Able to Evolve

I have kept you too long. It is time I brought this address to a close. This would have been a convenient point for me to have stopped. But this would probably be my last address to a Hindu audience, on a subject vitally concerning the Hindus. I would therefore like, before I close, to place before the

Hindus, if they will allow me, some questions which I regard as vital, and invite them seriously to consider the same.

In the first place, the Hindus must consider whether it is sufficient to take the placid view of the anthropologist that there is nothing to be said about the beliefs, habits, morals, and outlooks on life which obtain among the different peoples of the world, except that they often differ; or whether it is not necessary to make an attempt to find out what kind of morality, beliefs, habits, and outlook have worked best and have enabled those who possessed them to flourish, to grow strong, to people the earth and to have dominion over it. As is observed by Prof. Carver,

> Morality and religion, as the organised expression of moral approval and disapproval, must be regarded as factors in the struggle for existence as truly as are weapons for offence and defence, teeth and claws, horns and hoofs, furs and feathers. The social group, community, tribe, or nation, which develops an unworkable scheme of morality or within which those social acts which weaken it and make it unfit it for survival, habitually create the sentiment of approval, while those which would strengthen and enable it to be expanded habitually create the sentiment of disapproval, will eventually be eliminated. It is its habits of approval or disapproval (these are the results

> of religion and morality) that handicap it, as really as the possession of two wings on one side with none on the other will handicap the colony of flies. It would be as futile in the one case as in the other to argue, that one system is just as good as another.

Morality and religion, therefore, are not mere matters of likes and dislikes. You may dislike exceedingly a scheme of morality which, if universally practised within a nation, would make that nation the strongest nation on the face of the earth. Yet in spite of your dislike, such a nation will become strong. You may like exceedingly a scheme of morality and an ideal of justice which, if universally practised within a nation, would make it unable to hold its own in the struggle with other nations. Yet in spite of your admiration, this nation will eventually disappear. The Hindus must, therefore, examine their religion and their morality in terms of their survival value.

Secondly, the Hindus must consider whether they should conserve the whole of their social heritage, or select what is helpful and transmit to future generations only that much and no more. Prof. John Dewey, who was my teacher and to whom I owe so much, has said: 'Every society gets encumbered with what is trivial, with dead wood from the past, and with what is positively perverse … As a society becomes more enlightened, it realizes that it is responsible not to conserve and transmit the whole of its existing achievements, but only such as make for a better future society.' Even Burke, in spite of the vehemence with which he opposed the principle of change embodied in the French Revolution, was compelled to admit that 'a State without the means of some change is without the means of its conservation. Without such means it might even risk the loss of that part of the constitution which it wished the most religiously to preserve.' What Burke said of a State applies equally to a society.

Thirdly, the Hindus must consider whether they must not cease to worship the past as supplying their ideals. The baneful effects of this worship of the past are best summed up by Prof. Dewey when he says:

> An individual can live only in the present. The present is not just something which comes after the past; much less something produced by it. It is what life is in leaving the past behind it. The study of past products will not help us to understand the present. A knowledge of the past and its heritage is of great significance when it enters into the present, but not otherwise. And the mistake of making the records and remains of the past the main material of education is that it tends to make the past a rival of the present and the present a more or less futile imitation of the past.

The principle which makes little of the present act of living and growing, naturally looks upon the present as empty and upon the future as remote. Such a principle is inimical to progress, and is a hindrance to a strong and a steady current of life.

Fourthly, the Hindus must consider whether the time has not come for them to recognize that there is nothing fixed, nothing eternal, nothing *sanatan;* that everything is changing, that change is the law of life for individuals as well as for society. In a changing society, there must be a constant revolution of old values; and the Hindus must realize that if there must be standards to measure the acts of men, there must also be a readiness to revise those standards.

—From *Annihilation of Caste*

Concluding Remarks in the Constituent Assembly on Constitution, 25 November 1949

… The first charge of centralization defeating federalism must therefore fall.

The second charge is that the Centre has been given the power to override the States. This charge must be admitted. But before condemning the Constitution for containing such overriding powers, certain considerations must be borne in mind. The first is that these overriding powers do not form the normal feature of the constitution. Their use and operation are expressly confined to emergencies only. The second consideration is: Could we avoid giving overriding powers to the Centre when an emergency has arisen? Those who do not admit the justification for such overriding powers to the Centre even in an emergency, do not seem to have a clear idea of the problem which lies at the root of the matter. The problem is so clearly set out by a writer in that well-known magazine *The Round Table* in its issue of December 1935 that I offer no apology for quoting the following extract from it. Says the writer:

> Political systems are a complex of rights and duties resting ultimately on the question, to whom, or to what authority, does the citizen owe allegiance. In normal affairs the question is not present, for the law works smoothly, and a man goes about his business obeying one authority in this set of matters and another authority in that. But in a moment of crisis, a conflict of claims may arise, and it is then apparent that ultimate allegiance cannot be divided. The issue

> of allegiance cannot be determined in the last resort by a juristic interpretation of statutes.
>
> The law must conform to the facts or so much the worse for the law. When all formalism is stripped away, the bare question is, what authority commands the residual loyalty of the citizen. Is it the Centre or the Constituent State?

The solution of this problem depends upon one's answer to this question which is the crux of the problem. There can be no doubt that in the opinion of the vast majority of the people, the residual loyalty of the citizen in an emergency must be to the Centre and not to the Constituent States. For it is only the Centre which can work for a common end and for the general interests of the country as a whole. Herein lies the justification for giving to the Centre certain overriding powers to be used in an emergency. And after all what is the obligation imposed upon the Constituent States by these emergency powers? No more than this—that in an emergency, they should take into consideration alongside their own local interests, the opinions and interests of the nation as a whole. Only those who have not understood the problem can complain against it.

Here I could have ended. But my mind is so full of the future of our country that I feel I ought to take this occasion to give expression to some of my reflections thereon. On

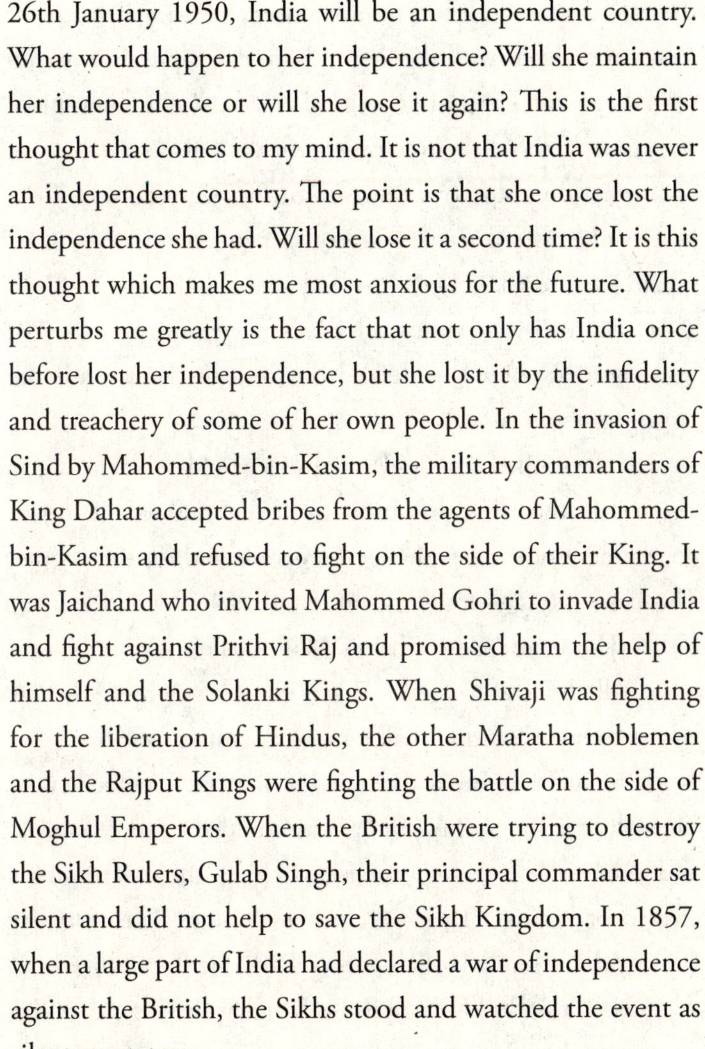

26th January 1950, India will be an independent country. What would happen to her independence? Will she maintain her independence or will she lose it again? This is the first thought that comes to my mind. It is not that India was never an independent country. The point is that she once lost the independence she had. Will she lose it a second time? It is this thought which makes me most anxious for the future. What perturbs me greatly is the fact that not only has India once before lost her independence, but she lost it by the infidelity and treachery of some of her own people. In the invasion of Sind by Mahommed-bin-Kasim, the military commanders of King Dahar accepted bribes from the agents of Mahommed-bin-Kasim and refused to fight on the side of their King. It was Jaichand who invited Mahommed Gohri to invade India and fight against Prithvi Raj and promised him the help of himself and the Solanki Kings. When Shivaji was fighting for the liberation of Hindus, the other Maratha noblemen and the Rajput Kings were fighting the battle on the side of Moghul Emperors. When the British were trying to destroy the Sikh Rulers, Gulab Singh, their principal commander sat silent and did not help to save the Sikh Kingdom. In 1857, when a large part of India had declared a war of independence against the British, the Sikhs stood and watched the event as silent spectators.

Will history repeat itself? It is this thought which fills me with anxiety. This anxiety is deepened by the realization of the fact that in addition to our old enemies in the form of castes and creeds we are going to have many political parties with diverse and opposing political creeds. Will Indians place the country above their creed or will they place creed above country? I do not know. But this much is certain, that if the parties place creed above country, our independence will be put in jeopardy a second time and probably be lost for ever. This eventuality we must all resolutely guard against. We must be determined to defend our independence with the last drop of our blood.

On the 26th of January 1950, India would be a democratic country in the sense that India from that day would have a government of the people, by the people and for the people. The same thought comes to my mind. What would happen to her democratic Constitution? Will she be able to maintain it or will she lose it again? This is the second thought that comes to my mind and makes me as anxious as the first.

It is not that India did not know what Democracy is. There was a time when India was studded with republics, and even where there were monarchies, they were either elected or limited. They were never absolute. It is not that India did not know Parliaments or Parliamentary Procedure. A study of the Buddhist Bhikshu Sanghas discloses that not only were there Parliaments—for the Sanghas were nothing but Parliaments—but the Sanghas knew and observed all the rules of Parliamentary Procedure known to modern times. They had rules regarding seating arrangements, rules regarding Motions, Resolutions, Quorum, Whip, Counting of Votes, Voting by Ballot, Censure Motion, Regularization, Res Judicata, etc. Although these rules of Parliamentary Procedure were applied by the Buddha to the meetings of the Sanghas, he must have borrowed them from the rules of the Political Assemblies functioning in the country in his time.

This democratic system India lost. Will she lose it a second time? I do not know. But it is quite possible in a country like India—where democracy from its long disuse must be regarded as something quite new—there is danger of democracy giving place to dictatorship. It is quite possible for this new born democracy to retain its form but give place to dictatorship in fact. If there is a landslide, the danger of the second possibility becoming actuality is much greater.

If we wish to maintain democracy not merely in form, but also in fact, what must we do? The first thing in my judgment we must do is to hold fast to constitutional methods of achieving our social and economic objectives. It means we must abandon the bloody methods of revolution. It means that we must abandon the method of civil disobedience, non-cooperation and satyagraha. When there was no way left for constitutional methods for achieving economic and social objectives, there was a great deal of justification for unconstitutional methods. But where constitutional methods are open, there can be no justification for these unconstitutional methods. These methods are nothing but the Grammar of Anarchy and the sooner they are abandoned, the better for us.

The second thing we must do is to observe the caution which John Stuart Mill has given to all who are interested in the maintenance of democracy, namely, not 'to lay their liberties at the feet of even a great man, or to trust him with powers which enable him to subvert their institutions'. There is nothing wrong in being grateful to great men who have rendered life-long services to the country. But there are limits to gratefulness. As has been well said by the Irish Patriot Daniel O'Connell, no man can be grateful at the cost of his honour, no woman can be grateful at the cost of her chastity and no nation can be grateful at the cost of its liberty. This caution is far more necessary in the case of India than in the case of any other country. For in India, Bhakti or what may be called the path of devotion or hero-worship, plays a part in its politics unequalled in magnitude by the part it plays in the politics of any other country in the world. Bhakti in religion may be a road to the salvation of the soul. But in politics, Bhakti or hero-worship is a sure road to degradation and to eventual dictatorship.

The third thing we must do is not to be content with mere political democracy. We must make our political democracy a social democracy as well. Political democracy cannot last unless there lies at the base of it social democracy.

What does social democracy mean? It means a way of life which recognizes liberty, equality and fraternity as the principles of life. These principles of liberty, equality and fraternity are not to be treated as separate items in a trinity. They form a union of trinity in the sense that to divorce one from the other is to defeat the very purpose of democracy. Liberty cannot be divorced from equality, equality cannot be divorced from liberty. Nor can liberty and equality be divorced from fraternity. Without equality, liberty would produce the supremacy of the few over the many. Equality without liberty would kill individual initiative. Without fraternity, liberty and equality could not become a natural course of things. It would require a constable to enforce them. We must begin by acknowledging the fact that there is complete absence of two things in Indian society. One of these is equality. On the social plane, we have in India a society based on the principle of graded inequality with elevation for some and degradation for others. On the economic plane, we have a society in which there are some who have immense wealth as against many who live in abject poverty. On the 26th of January 1950, we are going to enter into a life of contradictions. In politics we will have equality and in social and economic life we will have inequality. In politics we will be recognizing the principle of one man one vote and one vote one value. In our social and economic life, we shall, by reason of our social and economic structure, continue to deny the principle of one man one value. How long shall we continue to live this life of contradictions? How long shall we continue to deny equality in our social and economic life? If we continue to deny it for long, we will do so only by putting our political democracy in peril. We must remove this contradiction at the earliest possible moment or else those who suffer from inequality will blow up the structure of political democracy which this Assembly has laboriously built up.

The second thing we are wanting in is recognition of the principle of fraternity. What does fraternity mean? Fraternity means a sense of common brotherhood of all Indians—of Indians being one people. It is the principle which gives unity and solidarity to social life. It is a difficult thing to achieve. How difficult it is, can be realized from the story related by James Bryce in his volume on American Commonwealth about the United States of America.

The story is—I propose to recount it in the words of Bryce himself—that:

> Some years ago the American Protestant Episcopal Church was occupied at its triennial Convention in revising its liturgy. It was thought desirable to introduce among the short sentence prayers a prayer for the whole people, and an eminent New England divine proposed the words `O Lord, bless our

> nation'. Accepted one afternoon, on the spur of the moment, the sentence was brought up next day for reconsideration, when so many objections were raised by the laity to the word 'nation' as importing too definite a recognition of national unity, that it was dropped, and instead there were adopted the words 'O Lord, bless these United States.'

There was so little solidarity in the U.S.A. at the time when this incident occurred that the people of America did not think that they were a nation. If the people of the United States could not feel that they were a nation, how difficult it is for Indians to think that they are a nation. I remember the days when politically-minded Indians resented the expression 'the people of India'. They preferred the expression 'the Indian nation'. I am of opinion that in believing that we are a nation, we are cherishing a great delusion. How can people divided into several thousands of castes be a nation? The sooner we realize that we are not as yet a nation in the social and psychological sense of the world, the better for us. For then only we shall realize the necessity of becoming a nation and seriously think of ways and means of realizing the goal. The realization of this goal is going to be very difficult—far more difficult than it has been in the United States. The United States has no caste problem. In India there are castes. The castes are anti-national. In the first place because they bring about separation in social life. They are anti-national also because they generate jealousy and antipathy between caste and caste. But we must overcome all these difficulties if we wish to become a nation in reality. For fraternity can be a fact only when there is a nation. Without fraternity, equality and liberty will be no deeper than coats of paint.

These are my reflections about the tasks that lie ahead of us. They may not be very pleasant to some. But there can be no gainsaying that political power in this country has too long been the monopoly of a few and the many are not only beasts of burden, but also beasts of prey. This monopoly has not merely deprived them of their chance of betterment, it has sapped them of what may be called the significance of life. These down-trodden classes are tired of being governed. They are impatient to govern themselves. This urge for self-realization in the down-trodden classes must not be allowed to devolve into a class struggle or class war. It would lead to a division of the House. That would indeed be a day of disaster. For, as has been well said by Abraham Lincoln, a House divided against itself cannot stand very long. Therefore, the sooner room is made for the realization of their aspiration, the better for the few, the better for the country, the better for the maintenance of its independence and the better for the continuance of its democratic structure. This can only be done by the establishment of equality and fraternity in all spheres of life. That is why I have laid so much stress on them.

I do not wish to weary the House any further. Independence is no doubt a matter of joy. But let us not forget that this independence has thrown on us great responsibilities. By independence, we have lost the excuse of blaming the British for anything going wrong. If hereafter things go wrong, we will have nobody to blame except ourselves. There is great danger of things going wrong. Times are fast changing. People including our own are being moved by new ideologies. They are getting tired of Government by the people. They are prepared to have Governments for the people and are indifferent whether it is Government of the people and by the people. If we wish to preserve the Constitution in which we have sought to enshrine the principle of Government of the people, for the people and by the people, let us resolve not to be tardy in the recognition of the evils that lie across our path and which induce people to prefer Government for the people to Government by the people, nor to be weak in our initiative to remove them. That is the only way to serve the country. I know of no better.

61

J. Krishnamurti

Jiddu Krishnamurti (1895–1986) was an Indian philosopher, speaker, writer and spiritual figure. He attained fame through his presentation of a unique version of Indian philosophy and mysticism, and taught a philosophy that bordered on atheism. Krishnamurti asserted that 'truth is a pathless land' and advised against following any sort of dogma, doctrine, creed, discipline, ritual, priest, teacher, guru or authority, including himself. He said that truth cannot be found through any philosophical knowledge or psychological technique. It can only be found through an understanding of the contents of one's own mind and through observation.

The Purpose of Life

As the shadows were awakening and a scent of the morn was carried on the breeze, I saw an eagle descending from the mountain-tops. It came down without a flutter of the wings into the valley, and there disappeared among the shadows of the black mountains. At the end of the day I saw it return again to its abode among the mountain peaks, far away from the strife, the struggle and the jostle of the world.

So is the man who has seen the vision of the Truth, who has, during his strife in the world, established for himself the eternal goal. Though he may wander among the transient things, and lose himself among the shadows, yet all his life will be guided by that goal. As the eagle soars to its abode, so will he soar beyond all sorrows, beyond all fleeting pleasures and passing joys.

The establishment of that eternal goal is of primary importance for one who desires to disentangle himself from all the complications of life—not the goal of another, nor the vision of another, but the goal that is born of his own experience, his own sorrow, suffering, and understanding. Such a goal, when once it is established, will throw light on

the confusion of all thought, and thereby make clear the purpose of life.

As a ship that is lost at sea without a compass, so the man without the perception of the goal which is constant and eternal is lost in this world of confusion. As the captain of a ship establishes the destination of his vessel and by the compass is able to guide his course through stormy nights and dark waters, so the man who has knowledge of his goal can guide his life by that compass of understanding.

Because the individual does not know his purpose, he is in a state of uncertainty and chaos. Because the individual has not solved his own problem, the problem of the world has not been solved. The individual problem is the world problem. If an individual is unhappy, discontented, dissatisfied, then the world around him is in sorrow, discontent and ignorance. If the individual has not found his goal, the world will not find its goal. You cannot separate the individual from the world. The world and the individual are one. If the individual problem can be solved by understanding, so can the problem of the world be solved. Before you can give understanding to others you have first to understand for yourself. When you establish the Truth in your heart and mind, there it will abide eternally.

One day in Benares I was going in a boat down the sacred Ganges, watching the people on the river banks worshiping God in search of happiness, in search of their goal and the

way of its attainment. I saw one man in deep meditation, forgetting everything around him, holding but the one thought in his mind—to find and to attain the goal. I saw another performing rites required by his system of yoga. I saw another repeating chants, lost to the world and to himself. They were all seeking what you are seeking, what everyone in the world is seeking in moments of deep thought, and of great desire.

As the boat is carried down the stream by the current, so is every one carried away by his desires, by his passions and longings, because not one has found or established his purpose. Because the goal has not been established, because the path that leads to that goal has not been found, there is confusion and chaos, there is questioning and doubt in the mind. As long as there is doubt in the mind there is no peace, nor certainty and ecstasy of purpose.

This condition exists throughout the world, but everywhere there is a heart beating and a mind capable of thought. Man everywhere is unconsciously seeking a way to free himself from his narrowness, his pettiness. The end of this search is freedom and eternal happiness. He experiments along many paths, and every path leads to complications. From life to life he wanders, from shrine to shrine, from one creed to another—gathering experience, accepting, rejecting, and again accepting—thus he goes forward towards that goal which awaits him as it awaits all men.

In the process of accumulation and rejection, he does not know which way to turn for comfort, and when he seeks comfort through any particular channel he is enmeshed and entangled. Because there are many interpreters of the Truth, because there are many conflicting paths, beliefs and religions, man is lost in their complexities. As a butterfly that knocks against the windowpane, struggling to escape into the fresh air and the open sky, so do men struggle when they have not caught a glimpse of the goal—but it is not hard to establish. It is because they are in darkness that the goal seems far away.

As the potter moulds the clay to the delight of his imagination, so can man mould his life through the desire of his heart. As the earthen vessels are fashioned into beautiful or ugly forms, so life can be made beautiful or ugly according to the purpose which you have established for yourself.

I would help you to that goal which you are seeking, which you desire to attain—the goal which awaits all the peoples of the world, whatever their experiences, thoughts or feelings. Then you will be able to guide yourself through the darkness of the world as a man guides himself through a dark night by the stars.

If you once establish such a goal—which is happiness and hence freedom—life becomes simple. There is no longer confusion, and time, and the complications of time disappear. It is because you have not established your goal that the present is as the mountain when the sun has set—the light fails and the darkness of the mountain overshadows the valley. Time is only a binder of life and the moment you are free you are beyond time.

Then you can guide yourself without depending upon any authority. Then you will no longer have fear. Then for you there will be no conflict of good and evil. When you have set life free you will find happiness, which is the only goal, the only absolute Truth.

Happiness and Desire

Because man has forgotten that the true purpose of his being is to cultivate happiness within himself and in those around him, there is confusion and chaos, and his actions but add to that chaos.

What is it for which everyone in the world is craving and longing? To find happiness. True happiness is neither selfish, nor negative. It is intelligence, the accumulation of all experience; it is Truth which is eternal. No cloud can hide it nor can any sorrow lessen it. It is such happiness that every one desires. It is such happiness that I have always desired. I have seen people weighed down with labour, performing great works, accumulating knowledge, struggling to be spiritual and yet they had forgotten the one thing—happiness—which alone gives life to the mind and nourishment to the heart. There can be no health except in happiness. He who has not found it will never find Truth, will never bring life to its fulfilment, will never have tranquillity in this world of travail.

If you desire to establish that happiness within yourself, you must make it your goal and then your life will be as the flame which soars heavenwards.

People in search of happiness resort to many things—they will worship at temples and churches, they will gather from books the knowledge of others, they will perform religious rites in the hope of establishing in their minds peace and tranquillity. The desire for happiness is ever gnawing at their hearts.

In the great continent of America they are making the physical predominant in search for happiness. They say that without physical comfort, without a body that is strong and healthy, there cannot be a right development of the emotions. But in trying to establish perfect physical conditions they are losing sight of other essential things. In India, they go to the opposite extreme and in search for happiness they neglect altogether the physical.

Look where you will, every human being is seeking happiness. He begins his search in the mere pleasures which come from physical excitement. Then discovering that this excitement does not satisfy his craving for the lasting happiness, he experiments with other experiences, mental and emotional.

Life is a process of accumulating and discarding, of gathering and setting aside. What you gather you reject, and the more you reject the nearer you are to liberation. By setting aside what you have gained, you acquire the knowledge which will give you strength to shape your purpose, which will give you power ultimately to reach the Kingdom of Happiness which each one of you seeks.

As there is sap in the tree which brings forth foliage for the glory of its being, so in each man there is the spark of divinity which through sorrow, through ecstasy, through struggle, through all the processes of life, grows to perfection, to that state of eternal happiness which is the goal for all, which is the truest spirituality—the greatest gift that anyone can give to another.

You will find this undying, unalterable happiness when you are liberated from the tyrannies of the self—its desires and longings. This is not a goal imposed upon you by another. It is the longing of every human soul, of every individual who is striving, who is in sorrow, who is seeking. It is the spark of this desire which grows into a flame and becomes part of the Eternal Flame, and when you are able to lose yourself in that Flame, then you are in the Kingdom of Happiness.

Each must discover his own way of attainment. There is no other truth or other god but that goal which each one has established for himself, which cannot be destroyed by the breath of man or by the passing whims of any god.

In what way can you attain this goal and hold this happiness eternally in your heart? If you are a thoughtful person, you will recognize that in every one there are three different beings: the mind, the emotions and the body. And if you observe you will find that each of these beings has a separate existence of its own and tries to create and to act independently of the others, thus causing disharmony. Absolute happiness comes from the establishment of harmony between these three. If you are driving three horses—each desiring to run independently of the other two—unless you are able to control them and drive them all together, you will not reach your destination.

The mind must have a goal of its own, but it must be a goal created by you yourself; otherwise it will lead to superstition.

What is the ultimate goal for the mind?

It is the purification of the self, which means the development of individual uniqueness.

As the seed is forced by the life within it to break through the heavy earth and come into light, so if you are urged by the desire to find freedom, you will break through all limitations which bind you. To gain freedom, great desire is needed. People are afraid of desire, thinking that it is something evil which must be destroyed. But this is a mistaken attitude. Desire is the motive power behind all action. If you would light a great fire to warm and comfort you, you must give fuel to it, feed it with great logs of wood. So if you would fulfil life you must have great desires, for desire brings experience and experience leads to knowledge. If a man knows how to use desire it will bring him to the freedom for which he longs. If desire is killed or suppressed, there is no possibility of freedom. Most people in the world have intense, burning, vital desires but instead of utilizing them and training them, they either suppress them or are controlled by them. Without desire there can be no creative work. If you kill desire you become like a piece of dead wood, or else you become an automaton, a machine. Machines have been invented to minimize human labour. Physical problems perhaps may be solved in this way, but mental and emotional problems are more difficult to solve, and because the way to solve these problems is so little understood, religions, creeds, and dogmas have been invented.

If desire gives life it should be encouraged. If desire creates sorrow, through understanding that sorrow must be overcome. Because man does not want to be free, he kills his desires; because he does not want to attain true liberation, he is making of himself a machine. Use desire as a stepping-stone to kindle greater desires, to awaken greater delight and longing.

But intelligence is necessary in order to develop your individual uniqueness, to purify your desires, to realize that self which is the self of all—that absolute union with all things which brings to an end the sense of separation. It is necessary for the mind to be simple, but simplicity does not mean crudeness. We should not turn our back upon the results of progress and evolution, but on the contrary we should utilize them.

A mind that is simple will understand perfection because it is part of perfection itself. A mind that is crooked cannot understand the Truth. A mind that is complicated, that is full of the knowledge of books—though they have their value—is apt to become crystallised. In all great architecture, painting and sculpture, in all the greatest forms of beauty, there is simplicity and there is restraint. Simplicity of the mind is the greatest and most difficult thing to acquire, but in order to be simple you must have had great experience. Simplicity of the truest kind is the highest form of spirituality.

What is the ultimate goal for the emotions?

It is affectionate detachment. To be able to love and yet not be attached to anyone or anything is the absolute perfection of emotion.

As a barren tree in winter without leaf or flower to give scent to the morning air, so is a man without love. Those who would attain to Truth must cultivate—as the gardener cultivates his garden—this flower of affection, which is to give delight, which is to be a source of comfort in disappointment and sorrow. Love—however envious, jealous, tyrannical, selfish it may be at first—is a bud that will grow into great glory and give the scent of its perfection to every passer-by.

Without love man is as a desert of dry sand, as the river in the summer time, without water to nourish its banks. Those who would attain the perfection of happiness, the beauty that is hidden from the human eye, must cultivate this quality of love. You must love all and yet be detached from all, for love is necessary to the unfoldment of life. To cultivate it you must learn to observe, you must gather experience—vicariously, or through your own treading of the sorrowful paths of experience. It is through experience that you know sympathy, that you are able to give affection to those who desire it, for if you have never experienced sorrow then your heart is incapable of sympathy and understanding.

This does not mean that you should taste of everything. There are many ways of acquiring experience—one is by living in the life of everyone, looking through the eyes of every passer-by and experiencing in imagination his sorrow, his transient pleasures. When you see a drunken man in the street, it should be sufficient to give you the experience of drunkenness; if you see a man in tears, that should give you the experience of grief; if you see a man in joy and ecstasy, that should give you the experience of joy. We need not all follow one road of knowledge. We give and take from each other. We can gather knowledge from the experience of the whole world and that is sufficient for progress, for culture and refinement. If you would attain to the fulfilment of life, you must have this accumulation of experience, for without experience you cannot arrive at the goal, you cannot unite the beginning and the end. While there is separation, there is pain, and it is only in the union with the goal that there is happiness, that you establish lasting Truth within yourself. To do that, you must from the very beginning gather experience as a man gathers the grain of the field.

If you have no sympathy, no affection, you can never achieve, you can never identify yourself with the goal. A mind that is contented and satisfied will never acquire sympathy or affection or give understanding to others. I have watched people who have greatly desired to help others but they do not know how to help. They are incapable of putting themselves into the place of another and so envisaging his point of view.

Those who would understand the life around them, who would see the goal and thereby establish the Beloved in their hearts, must develop great love and yet be detached from the bondage of that love. They must have great sympathy and yet not be bound by that sympathy. They must have great desires and yet not be slaves of those desires.

What is the ultimate goal for the body?

Everyone in the world is seeking for beauty but they seek without understanding. It is essential for the body to be beautiful, but it must not be a mere shell of beauty without beautiful thought and feeling. Restraint is necessary for the body—control without suppression.

These are the essentials for the absolute harmony of the three beings in each of us.

The desire for freedom, the desire to escape from all things, or rather to transcend all things, is necessary for the attainment of perfection. You can only free yourself if your mind and heart have determined their purpose in life and are continually struggling towards it, never yielding to those things which create barriers between yourself and your goal.

To attain perfection, to walk towards the goal of Truth which is eternal happiness for all, at whatever stage of evolution you may be, it is necessary to be rid of the binding narrow traditions that are born out of blind belief and have no touch with life.

As, when the rains come, only those who have prepared their fields and removed the weeds will have the full produce of their labour, the full benefit of the rain, so, if you would have the Beloved always with you, you must remove from your mind and heart the complicated ideas, traditions, and narrow points of view, which are as weeds that kill true understanding. For without understanding there can be no cooperation with life.

—From *Life in Freedom*

Subhas Chandra Bose

Subhas Chandra Bose (1897–1945), popularly called Netaji, is one of the most celebrated freedom fighters of India. He was a leader of the Indian National Congress before moving away from it due to differences in ideology. He founded and led the Indian National Army (INA) and—controversially—sought assistance from Nazi Germany and Imperial Japan during the Second World War to overthrow the British in India. The INA's slogan 'Jai Hind' still resonates across India, long after his death.

To Delhi, to Delhi!

Soldiers of India's Army of Liberation! Today is the proudest day of my life. Today it has pleased Providence to give me the unique privilege and honour of announcing to the whole world that India's Army of Liberation has come into being. This army has now been drawn up in military formation on the battlefield of Singapore—which was once the bulwark of the British Empire. This is not only the Army that will emancipate India from the British yoke, it is also the Army that will hereafter create the future national army of free India. Every Indian must feel proud that this Army—his own army—has been organized entirely under Indian leadership and that when the historic moment arrives, under Indian leadership it will go to battle.

There are people who thought at one time that the Empire on which the sun did not set was an everlasting Empire. No such thought ever troubled me. History had taught me that every Empire has its inevitable decline and collapse. Moreover I had seen, with my own eyes, cities and fortresses that were once the bulwarks but which became the graveyards of bygone empires. Standing today on the graveyard of the

British Empire, even a child is convinced that the almighty British Empire is already a thing of the past.

... Comrades! Soldiers! Let your battle-cry be—'To Delhi, to Delhi!' How many of us will individually survive this war of freedom, I do not know. But I do know this, that we shall ultimately win and our task will not end until our surviving heroes hold the victory parade on another graveyard of the British Empire—the Lal Quila or Red Fortress of ancient Delhi.

Throughout my public career, I have always felt that though India is otherwise ripe for independence in every way, she has lacked one thing, namely an army of liberation. George Washington of America could fight and win freedom, because he had his army. Garibaldi could liberate Italy, because he had his armed volunteers behind him. It is your privilege and honour to be the first to come forward and organize India's national army. By doing so, you have removed the last obstacle in our path to freedom. Be happy and proud that you are the pioneers, the vanguard, in such a noble cause.

Let me remind you that you have a two-fold task to perform. With the force of arms and at the cost of your blood you will have to win liberty. Then, when India is free, you will have to organize the permanent army of free India, whose task it will be to preserve our liberty for all time. We must build up our national defence on such an unshakable foundation that never again in our history shall we lose our freedom.

As soldiers, you will always have to cherish and live up to the three ideals of faithfulness, duty and sacrifice. Soldiers who always remain faithful to their nation, who are always prepared to sacrifice their lives, are invincible. If you, too, want to be invincible, engrave these three ideals in the innermost core of your hearts.

A true soldier needs both military and spiritual training. You must, all of you, so train yourselves and your comrades that every soldier will have unbounded confidence in himself, will be conscious of being immensely superior to the enemy, will be fearless of death and will have sufficient initiative to act on his own in any critical situation should the need arise. During the course of the present war, you have seen with your own eyes what wonders scientific training, coupled with courage, fearlessness and dynamism, can achieve. Learn all that you can from this example and build up for Mother India an absolutely first-class modern army.

To those of you who are officers, I should like to say that your responsibility is a heavy one. Though the responsibility of an officer in every army in this world is indeed great, it is far greater in your case. Because of our political enslavement, we have no tradition like that of Mukden, Port Arthur or Sedan to inspire us. We have to unlearn some of the things that the British taught us and we have to learn much that they did not teach. Nevertheless, I am confident that you will rise to the occasion and fulfil the task that your countrymen have thrown on your brave shoulders. Remember always that officers can make or unmake an army. Remember too that the British have suffered defeats on so many fronts largely because of worthless officers. And remember also that out of your ranks will be born the future General Staff of the Army of free India.

To all of you I should like to say that in the course of this war you will have to acquire the experience and achieve the success which alone can build up a national tradition for our Army. An army that has no tradition of courage, fearlessness and invincibility cannot hold its own in a struggle with a powerful enemy.

Comrades! You have voluntarily accepted a mission that is the noblest that the human mind can conceive of. For the fulfilment of such a mission no sacrifice is too great, not even the sacrifice of one's life. You are today the custodians of India's national honour and the embodiment of India's hopes and aspirations. So conduct yourself in such a way that your countrymen may bless you and posterity may be proud of you.

I have said that today is the proudest day of my life. For an enslaved people, there can be no greater pride, no higher honour, than to be the first soldier in the army of liberation. But this honour carries with it a corresponding responsibility and I am deeply conscious of it. I assure you that I shall be with you in darkness and in sunshine, in sorrow and in joy, in suffering and in victory. For the present, I can offer you nothing except hunger, thirst, privation, forced marches and death. But if you follow me in life and in death, as I am confident you will, I shall lead you to victory and freedom. It does not matter who among us will live to see India free. It is enough that India shall be free and that we shall give our all to make her free. May God now bless our Army and grant us victory in the coming fight!

Inquilab Zindabad! Azad Hind Zindabad!

63

Ram Manohar Lohia

Ram Manohar Lohia (1910–1967), a prominent socialist leader, played a key role in the struggle for India's independence. He was a great orator and advocated several sociopolitical reforms, including the abolition of the caste system. He believed in democratic socialism and supported non-violent struggles against social, economic and political injustices.

Guilty Men of India's Partition

At the bottom of all of India's ills is the almost complete loss of identification between the rulers and the ruled, the middle class and the masses. The absence of identification has been over the centuries documented as total divorce in the shape of castes. The right word to use is not divorce but a state of total unrelatedness. India's masses have been totally unrelated to her ruling classes, the vast sea of the mass to the tiny ruling minority among the high caste. Mahatma Gandhi did not create this situation. He was heir to it. It was something which several thousand years of Indian history had given him. It is something nobody can escape. It is, I believe, the prime causation of much that has happened in recent years in our country, certainly of its partition. That is not to say that events in India are iron bound by this phenomenon and that they must take place precisely in the way they do.

The absence of identification between the rulers among high castes and the vast masses is the most important, the most stubborn and the most deciding single factor of the current Indian situation. The consequences of this factor are highly uncertain. That would depend on whether the factor is submitted to or overcome or partly submitted to or partly overcome, and a hundred different combinations of the process. But the factor must produce consequences, one way or another or in a hundred different ways.

Did Mahatma Gandhi succeed in overcoming, or even seeking fully to overcome, this state of total unrelatedness between India's masses and their rulers? On the surface, it would appear that he did. He swung numberless masses of men and women into action as few other men have done in the country's history. But there was something wrong with the activising somewhere; it appeared to be much more universal than it actually was. A great error of observation of happenings in India arises because of her teeming millions. An activity, though not spread over the people as a whole, but which has moved some numerically important sections, would appear to be more universal than it actually was.

Gandhiji does not seem to have been aware of the full implications of the caste system right up to a few years before his death. He started with some kind of a romantic idealisation of it. He tried to shear it of its evils as though the thing was not evil in itself. It was only sometime around the last great struggle for freedom, the Open Rebellion of 1942, that he recognised the inherent evil of the caste system. It is true that he had all along tried to remove untouchability. That was a reformer's act, and not a revolutionary's. He had for a long time wanted to maintain the caste system, but to reform it of its dross. He changed his position only a few years before his death when he became a revolutionary also in respect of caste. Then, it was too late. The weakness of his earlier position had already caused a basic anaemia in the nationalist movement.

The first question with regard to restoration of normalcy is a little bit more difficult to answer. The system of castes has given to the Indian character certain extraordinary virtues and vices. The virtues are obvious. Indian character, moulded as it is by the caste system, does not easily take to change, which it inspects over and over again before acceptance and, more often than not, which it strangulates by a surface acquiescence and basic rejection. In times of prosperity and strength, such a character strives for an odd kind of justice and, at all times, it strives for stability and maintenance of identity. The vices are much more numerous and deep-going. Indian character has become the most split in all the world. The total loss of identification between higher and lower castes has produced a situation of great unreality, of lying and double-dealing, of tensions that have become a normal part of the mind, of readiness to whine and wheedle and cajole in the moment immediately before or after, threatening, bullying or assaulting, of great bravery without tenacity and cowardice without total submission, of a ruling class unparallelled in all the world for its duration or its ability to adjust alongside of its stubbornness to maintain its identity.

It is often said that India's susceptibility to invasions and her frequent submission to them is the result of situations of disunity. Even if we assume that such disunities have from time to time affected the people, the question arises why the Indian people, more than any other, have been subject to them. Actually, however, that is not the issue at all. The people have not figured in India's wars or at best only secondarily.

The Indian people gave the job of governing and of fighting wars and of thinking about such matters or providing for them to certain selected castes. The mass of the people had nothing whatever to do with this business. Long disuse of a limb atrophies it. The system of caste has atrophied the Indian people for political purposes. When people talk of disunity as the prime factor behind India's submissiveness to foreign invasions, they do so because of their ruling class or high caste angle. Disunity among whom? Obviously among the ruling classes. Disunity among the people in terms of India's history means precious little, for the people were not politically active. Again, this disunity among ruling castes would not have caused the damage that it did, if the mass of the people had not been afflicted by the curse of caste into a non-political existence. Not disunity, but caste has been the prime factor behind India's susceptibility to invasions and her frequent submission to them.

—From *Guilty Men of India's Partition*

64

Indira Gandhi

Indira Gandhi (1917–1984), the first (and only) female prime minister of India, ruled for three consecutive terms (1966–1977) and for a fourth term from 1980 until her assassination in 1984. As prime minister, she continued her father's policies of industrialisation, promoting the public sector and socialism. She led India's Green Revolution that resulted in self-sufficiency in foodgrain production. She supported the creation of Bangladesh in 1971 after the atrocities committed there by Pakistan.

As prime minister, she was known for her centralisation of power and political ruthlessness. She declared a state of emergency in India from 1975 to 1977, but returned to power after the general elections of 1980. She was assassinated in 1984, a few months after she ordered Operation Blue Star in Punjab.

Speech at the United Nations, 14 October 1968

Mr President, Mr Secretary-General, distinguished representatives, I am grateful to you for according me the high honour of addressing this great Assembly. May I take this opportunity to congratulate you, Sir, on your election to the distinguished office of President of the General Assembly. It is a fitting tribute to Guatemala and to your own personal qualities. I wish you success.

I have just come from an instructive and stimulating visit to a number of countries in Latin America and the Caribbean. This enabled me to see the earnest strivings of the peoples of that great continent for social progress and better standards of living.

I should like to pay a special tribute to the Secretary-General. Where others might have been overwhelmed by heart-break, U Thant has persevered, undaunted, in his great work with rare faith, devotion and detachment. It is up to all of us to give him our fullest support.

The United Nations is the trustee of the world's peace and represents the hopes of mankind. Its very existence gives a feeling of assurance that the justice of true causes can be brought fearlessly before the world. This Assembly and the agencies of the United Nations should, in all that they do sustain those hopes and promote the causes of peace.

Seven years ago, India's first Prime Minister Jawaharlal Nehru, addressed this Assembly. He was a believer in seeking areas of agreement and co-operation, and in enlarging them. He advocated before this Assembly a 'new approach to co-operation and the furtherance of the co-operative effort'. The Assembly accepted his suggestion of an International Co-operation Year. The United Nations also launched a development decade to promote greater economic co-operation between the rich and the poor nations. Two major international conferences on trade and development were held.

The interest shown by Member States in these moves aroused great expectations among the developing countries. We did not seek to share the power of the big Powers. We did not ask that they deny any of their own people their needs in order to fulfil ours. We, who have had twenty years or less of freedom to work for our progress, did not expect miracles of sudden transformation. Only too well do we know how long and hard is the path of development. What we do expect is understanding of the intangible yearnings of people who have long been under foreign domination.

Unfortunately, economic co-operation has little progress to show. Nor has there been any notable advance in international co-operation in the political sphere. The reasons for this failure are obvious and many: Economic and military power continue to dominate politics. The carving out of spheres of influence still motivates policies and action. The desire to mould other nations in the image of one's own inspires propaganda, sowing seeds of mistrust. Nations continue to place national ends above the larger purposes of peace and universal security.

In India, we have been powerfully conditioned by Mahatma Gandhi. We believe that the evolution of individuals and societies depends on the extent to which they exercise self-restraint and abjure the use of force. Jawaharlal Nehru, who combined in himself modern political thought and the basic teaching of Mahatma Gandhi, strove to bring about a new system of relations among nations. He was tireless in advocating peaceful coexistence. He believed that in a world rent by conflict, freedom not fear, faith not doubt, confidence not suspicion would lead to friendship amongst nations.

The concept was evoking some response among statesmen and nations, and there was a growing recognition that, howsoever difficult it might seem, peaceful coexistence alone could enable the post-war world to solve its disputes rationally. But this trend has received severe jolts.

Every now and then violence erupts. Sheer power seemingly prevails over principles, seeking obedience and demanding respect instead of commanding it. Indeed, those who have attempted to eschew the use of force have had to pay the price of restraint. And yet, the world is changing. Implicit faith in the efficacy of and unquestioning dependence on military alliances, as well as the rigidities of the bipolar world, are in a state of flux. Every nation, regardless of size, is endeavouring to establish its own identity. This encourages the hope that despite obstacles the United Nations will be able to help all nations to live in peace and independence.

While there is search for a more equitable and humane world order, force continues to be used to attain political ends and to promote national or global interests. It is not my intention to deal with specific issues. Our views have been stated in this Assembly and elsewhere. But there are some which cannot be ignored. The continuance of the tragic conflict in Viet-Nam is source of constant anxiety. We fervently hope that conditions will be created to enable the discussions to become more purposeful. The Viet-Namese people must be assured of their inherent right to shape their destiny peacefully and without outside interference. We believe that the key to the next step still lies in the total cessation of the bombing of North Viet-Nam. In advocating this we are not actuated by a partisan spirit but by our sincere desire for peace and stability.

Another source of anxiety, the west Asian crisis, also needs to be resolved by political means. There is every opportunity for doing so, if it is recognized that the security, sovereignty and territorial integrity of the States in this part of the world cannot be based on the redrawing of State frontiers by force or on the basis of permanent hostility.

Essential for a peaceful settlement is the withdrawal of foreign forces from all Arab territories occupied in June last year. The process of the restoration of peace can begin and Ambassador Jarring's mission be fruitful only with the clear affirmation of this.

Equally explosive is the continued denial of basic human rights on grounds of race. The consciousness of the world community must be aroused not only against South Africa where racial discrimination has been elevated to the level of State policy, but against the emergence of racialism in any form in other areas. We must also firmly resist the last vestiges of colonialism. Our freedom and independence will not be complete so long as the people of South West Africa, Angola, Mozambique and Portuguese Guinea are denied theirs.

Recent events in Czechoslovakia have cast yet another shadow on the fragile structure for a new world order. The principles of non-interference by one State in the internal affairs of another, of scrupulous respect for the sovereignty, territorial integrity and political independence of all States are essential to the principle of peaceful coexistence. It is of the utmost importance that normal conditions should be restored without delay in Czechoslovakia.

If the use of force in international affairs is not renounced, and the rights of nations and the equality of races are not respected, how can tensions be reduced or the dangers of conflicts avoided? The world is caught in a vicious circle, because of which any viable international machinery to regulate relations between States is being progressively undermined and faces the danger of eventual collapse.

Nuclear weapons today represent the ultimate in force. Thus any attempt to eliminate force as the determining factor in international relations must begin with practical steps towards disarmament. But the nuclear menace has become an accepted fact of life and the world has developed a certain insensitivity to the nature of this threat. Despite every solemn resolution adopted by the Assembly, States continue to enlarge their capacity for nuclear war. The arms race and the search for more sophisticated weapons have rendered meaningless the concept of balance of power. Yet, every advance in military technology is accompanied by an effort to maintain a balance of terror. This encourages local wars and undermines the established political authority in States which are struggling to protect their freedom.

It is by restricting, reducing and eventually eliminating the growing nuclear menace that firm foundations of peace can be laid. The limited achievement of the parties' test-ban Treaty has been offset by the refusal of States to halt the testing of nuclear weapons. The problems of insecurity cannot be solved by imposing arbitrary restrictions on those who do not possess nuclear weapons, without any corresponding steps to deal with the basic problem of limiting stockpiles in the hands of a few Powers. How can the urge to acquire nuclear status be controlled so long as this imbalance persists? Unless the Powers which possess these weapons are prepared to exercise some self-restraint, collective efforts to rid the world of the nuclear menace cannot bear fruit.

We yearn for peace, not merely because it is good in itself, but because, without peace, there can be no improvement in the lives of the vast majority of the world's peoples. Development must receive the first priority and must be based on self-reliance. Our peoples expect their governments to build, in a generation, the apparatus of production and distribution which took the present advanced nations many centuries to install. Progress in technology and the acceleration of the processes of history will certainly help the developing nations to telescope the stages of their economic growth. But this acceleration works even more dramatically in favor of the affluent. The chasm between the rich and the poor nations, which is already a source of tension and bitterness in the world, is not decreasing but growing. This situation is fraught with danger for the future well-being of our world. It is natural that we in the developing countries should be more aware of the peril than those who live in the

affluent countries. The peril is on our doorstep, but it is not too far from theirs.

The world has changed, the membership of the United Nations has changed, but attitudes of mind have not. The representatives who are gathered here come from countries with distinct personalities. They have had great civilisations in the past—some known and some yet to be discovered. In the old colonial days, history, geography, culture and civilisation were all viewed from a particular perspective. Even today to be civilized is held to be synonymous with being westernized. Advanced countries devote large resources to formulating and spreading ideas and doctrines and they tend to impose on the developing nations their own norms and methods. The pattern of the classical acquisitive society with its deliberate multiplication of wants not only is unsuited to conditions in our countries but is positively harmful.

Developing nations have their special problems, and there is much scope for co-operation amongst themselves. Some problems are common, but the conditions in each country differ, and the same remedy cannot be prescribed for all. Those who seek to advise us seldom realize that we need new and different answers to our problems. We need solutions which are suited to our conditions, not imitative theories or techniques grafted from outside. We must make our own analysis of developments and how to deal with them. International forums such as this Assembly and the

specialized agencies of the United Nations give us the opportunity to place our views before the world. But of what avail is this if we cannot forge the solidarity which would command attention?

Our problems are such as did not confront the advanced nations when they were at a similar stage of economic development. Freedom awakens hope. It generates consciousness of economic, social and political rights. As literacy spreads, as modern communications and close contacts grow with affluent countries, new expectations and tensions are created.

In India, our effort has been to build democracy and to develop a technologically mature society. Each in itself is a formidable endeavour in a country of our size. Demands grow much faster than the means to fulfill them, but changes do not come about easily. Every step forward meets with impediments created by the forces of the status quo. Every step forward, even though intended to end inequality, leads to a phase where inequality becomes more obvious or new equalities come into existence. Let me give an example. We have introduced universal primary education and expanded higher education. We have done so because education is the key to the ending of existing disparities; because it is the greatest influence for modernisation and because it gives full scope to the flowering of the human personality. However, certain groups and regions which are already comparatively better off are able to take greater advantage of the new facilities: for example, the urban areas more than the rural, the rich farmers more than the poor peasants.

The affluence of the industrialised nations itself attracts and exerts a certain pull on the more fortunate sections in the developing countries, further sharpening the difference between aspirations and their fulfilment. This in turn leads to the alienation of the elite from the rest of society, because they are attracted by the glamour of catching up with their opposites in the advanced countries, while their own society cries out for bread.

We are not unaware of the important developments taking shape within the affluent countries themselves, where increasing numbers have begun to question the purpose of their lives. Poverty and want must be eradicated for they degrade the human personality. On the other hand, the affluent society, as it has emerged, seems to have become entangled in its instruments. Dazzled by its own glitter, it has lost sight of the goals it set out to achieve. It is natural, therefore, that societies which have stressed the importance of material possessions should anxiously seek a balance between spiritual and material values.

This is still an intellectual groping which lacks articulation, but one can sense it in the restlessness of younger people and students, in the various forms of protest against traditional or established authority. There is a desire to assert individuality in technological societies which are becoming more uniform and more impersonal. Abundance without commitment to ideals will sow the seeds of discontent and invite its own disruption. Prosperity must be integrated with a higher purpose, and it should be the endeavour of all nations—it certainly is ours in India—to achieve harmony between progress and the timeless values of the spirit. We are human and do not always succeed; but, as Mahatma Gandhi said, 'Satisfaction lies in the effort, not in the attainment.'

The individual is no longer content to entrust to others the shaping of his destiny; he wants to be the master of his fate. So also with nations, which, while co-operating with others, wish to develop and progress according to their own genius and tradition. The question is vital for developing nations, which still have time to chart their purse. The methods they use, the directions they take, will determine their goals.

We welcome any genuine form of international co-operation for the development of under-developed areas. At its best, foreign aid represents such an endeavour.

But can it not also be legitimately described as a form of enlightened self-interest on the part of aid-giving countries, especially when it is tied with the purchase of equipment and of know-how from donor countries? In India, aid accounts for only a fifth of our total investment in development. Economic progress is not possible without investment.

Not all the investment for Europe's progress came from the sweated labour of European workers and farmers. It came also from the people of Asia, Africa and South America who were denied a fair return for their work and their produce. Empires have ended, but the colonial pattern of economy remains with us in one form or another. As exporters of primary agricultural produce and minerals, we know to our cost how the terms of trade have steadily gone against us. Aid is only partial recompense for what the superior economic power of the advanced countries denies us through trade. Trade has the further advantage of placing greater responsibility on the developing nations, leading them towards self-reliance. I urge the nations assembled here to give their fullest support to the work initiated by the two United Nations Conferences on Trade and Development and to persuade the strong to dismantle the economic walls which they have built to defend themselves from the weak. In so doing they will be fortifying the defences of peace before it is too late.

These are the factors which cause tensions and bitterness, which divide society and lead it away from co-operation and the paths of peace. Fear grips large parts of the world. Sages in my land exhorted us to be free from that which made us afraid, anticipating by thirty centuries those famous words of our own times, that there is nothing to fear but fear itself. No people were so cowed down as my countrymen before Mahatma Gandhi came on the scene. India was able to

wrest freedom because he taught us to overcome fear and hatred and to be absorbed in a cause which was greater than ourselves.

We in India are attuned to the idea that the paths to truth are many and various. An attempt to remake the world in any one image will not be countenanced by the majority of mankind. Our age has been called the Space Age, but I would call it the Age of the People. Revolutionaries, liberators and political leaders have always talked of the people, but for the first time now, 'we the people' does not mean a few representing the many, but the masses themselves, each one of whom is seeking to assert his rights and to voice his demands.

Through the ages, man has struggled against vastly superior forces. The one constant has been his indomitable spirit. He has pitted his puny frame against nature. He has fought against tremendous odds for freedom, for his beliefs, for an idea or an ideal. Endowed with such a spirit, will man abdicate in favour of the machine or bow to the dominance of tyranny in new garbs? Men have been tortured, men have been killed, but the idea has prevailed.

Two years hence, in 1970, the United Nations will complete twenty-five years. Can we make it a year of peace? A starting point of a united endeavour to give mankind the blessings of a durable peace? To this end let us devote ourselves.

One of our ancient prayers says:

'Common be your prayer;
Common be your end;
Common be your purpose;
Common be your deliberation;
Common be your desires;
Unified be your hearts;
Unified be your intentions;
Perfect be the union among you.'

65

Atal Bihari Vajpayee

Atal Bihari Vajpayee (1924–2018) served three terms as the prime minister of India—the first for thirteen days in 1996, the second for thirteen months in 1998–1999 and the third a full five-year term between 1999 and 2004. A member of the Indian Parliament for over five decades, he was the first non-Congress prime minister to serve a full term. He was one of the co-founders of the Bharatiya Janata Party, the successor of the erstwhile Jana Sangh, and also a member of the RSS.

Motion of Confidence in the Council of Ministers, 27 May 1996

Before I move a motion of confidence on the floor of the House, I would like to pay my humble tributes to Pandit Jawahar Lal Nehru whose death anniversary is falling today.

When I was first elected to this House, Pandit Nehru was the Prime Minister of India. I had seen him at work for several years. In those days I used to sit on that side. I have not forgotten that side even now. But I used to sit far behind because our number was very small. Today, a change has taken place and BJP has gradually increased its strength and influence and thus first became the main opposition party and now it has emerged as the single largest party in this election. This change did not take place all of a sudden. It reflects the changing process of history.

In the elections held recently, the people have given their mandate. It is high time that we ponder over the mandate seriously. We have emerged as the largest party. We should keep in mind the position obtained by other political parties as well. The Congress party had 260 members in the House when the Lok Sabha was dissolved. Now their number has gone down to 136. This is due to the mandate given by the people. This mandate should be accepted gracefully. It needs some introspection. Their strength has come down to half. The strength of Left Front has also come down from 57 to 52. In West Bengal their strength has dwindled in terms of votes in the Lok Sabha as well as Legislative Assembly seats. Their strength has also gone down in Bihar. The strength of Janata Dal in the previous Lok Sabha was 56 from Bihar which has been reduced to 44 now.

The BJP contested Lok Sabha elections in Bihar in alliance with Samta Party and it has got massive success. On the other hand, the strength of Congress has gone down not only in Lok Sabha but in several other states also where they have lost people's faith. Other parties have formed their Governments in those states. Why has this change taken place? What does it indicate?

It should also be noticed that the parties which are united together to express lack of confidence against my Government today, had contested the elections on different planks. They contested against one another. They contested the election by levelling serious allegations against one another. There was no alliance among these parties before the election.

What is the basis of your alliance? What is its conceptual basis? This controversy is going on for so many days as to why the President has invited me to form the Government. It has disturbed the sleep of so many people. Some people have uttered such words for the President as should not have been used. But what else could the President do in the post election scenario? Should he have called the Congress, which was defeated in the elections and lost the mandate and whose rule the people had rejected? Should he have called a weird assortment of heterogenous elements which had not come into existence till then?

If the President has invited the BJP as the largest single party, he has acted according to constitutional propriety and democratic norms.

Democracy rests on moral values. Basically, it is a morality based system. The previous Government had the option of entering into alliance honestly. There was no need to split opposition parties. There was no need to overstep the anti-defection law. The alliance should have been formed honestly and transparently. If political parties propose to come together with authentic transparency, they should do so but on the basis of a common programme and not on the basis of their share of participation in the Government. They should not deposit lakhs of rupees in the banks for this purpose. If the country has really entered into the phase of coalition Governments, then the old experiences of 1977 or 1989 should not be repeated. Is that not the demand of the hour? Should we not resolve this?

It has been the history of the Congress that first they extend their support, then soon after they withdraw it. This is the sequence which has been coming down from Travancore days. If there is a change in the ideology of the Congress, then we will welcome it. But its history till date tells a different story. Coalition Governments collapse on such issues that have no bearing on the national life. At the moment we need to learn the art of working together. This does not apply only when different political parties come together. This applies within the party as well. I do not know what curse lies on this country. I do not know what is plaguing us today. Whenever there is a crisis in the country, people unitedly face it but as soon as it is over, they indulge in fighting one another and create unnecessary and irrelevant issues to undermine others.

I am not an exception to this. My party is also not an exception. This is work which no single party can do. We tried to do it, but we did not succeed. This is for all of us to decide collectively. I do not know what political configuration the nation will acquire tomorrow onwards. But one thing is clear, that the Government should follow the middle path, irrespective of whether there is a one-party rule or multiparty rule. The Government should be dedicated to the cause of people. Each and every conduct of the Government should be marked by transparency and authencity. This did not take place. This did not happen during the last five years. Why? Are we sure that this will happen in the future?

If the United Front comes forward with a programme and assures us that because of political ambition and obsession for power no bitter experiences of the past will be allowed to repeat, only then people may feel a bit reassured. Otherwise, people are very unhappy. There is an apprehension of instability looming large. There is a concern for the future of India. On 29 May 1964, as a member of the Rajya Sabha, I made a speech while paying my tributes to Panditji. I would like to quote. I had said that Pandit Nehru was a fighter for the cause of freedom and was its saviour. Today, that freedom is in peril. We will have to protect it with all our might. The national unity and integrity which he championed stands endangered today. We will have to maintain it at all costs. Today, apprehensions are being raised about the future of Indian democracy which was established and made a great success of by Pandit Nehru. We have to make democracy successful by maintaining our unity, discipline and self-confidence. That leader has gone, leaving behind his followers. The sun has set. We will have to make our way in the starry nights. This is the period of great test. If we all manage to dedicate ourselves to a noble cause that could make a strong, capable and prosperous nation and contribute with a sense of pride to the restoration of world peace, then we will be able to pay our real tributes to that great soul. And here I conclude this part of the quotation from my speech.

During the last fifty years we have made enormous progress. Nobody can deny it. During the election campaign I had enough materials to launch a tirade against the policies of the previous Government. But everywhere I had said that I was not one of those who deny the achievements of the last fifty years. To do so would be tantamount to nullifying the achievements of our nation. That would be injustice to our farmers and our labourers and in fact it would not be a good gesture towards the common man of this country. At this moment, when fifty years have already elapsed since independence and we are going to celebrate the golden jubilee of our independence, the question that arises in our mind, and that should indeed arise, is about the condition of this country—and why we have lagged behind. Those countries which came into existence after us, have left us far behind in the race of development. Today we are regarded as one of the poorest countries in the world. Here more than twenty per cent of the people live below the poverty line. The President's address refers to the villages where there is no drinking water available. We have not been able to make compulsory primary education. Women's education is being neglected. To this day the birth of a female child in the family is considered to be a curse in this country. Is it not possible that the Government take steps to mobilise public opinion and create an awakening in society? This is the work which has no room for party politics. We cannot change the course of our nation. There is no dearth of resources in our country and if at all there is, then it can be mobilised properly. We can add to our resources. The revenue collected by imposing taxes on the people is not utilised for the benefit of the common man. But whatever resources are available with us they are also not being utilised properly. Where does that money go? Who pockets it? Into whose lockers does this money go? Why is money being deposited in foreign banks even now? What steps have been taken to check this? We are making efforts for getting foreign investment. Foreign capital is welcome. If the foreign capital is for bringing better technology, infrastructure and for promoting export-import, then we will have no objection to it. I am sure that our communist friends will also not object to it. But the point is whether we are making the optimum utilisation of indigenous resources available in the country. Is it not a fact that the menace of corruption has assumed a national dimension? I remember the late Rajiv Gandhi had said that when he sent one rupee from Delhi, only nineteen paise reached the people who were meant to get this money. I asked him how this miracle was taking place. He laughed and said that when the rupee begins to trickle, it passes through a process. And in that process, it continues to get smaller. Then it becomes difficult to identify it. Also, it may disappear. The present condition of the rupee is not very good. On the one hand, the governmental expenditure has gone up, and that trend continues unabated. We need the support of all the parties for curtailing governmental expenditure. No particular party can do it. Yes, had our former Prime

Minister Narsimha Rao ji, having achieved stability of his Government, made some efforts in this direction, then we would have definitely succeeded in this mission. But he was engaged in such activities that these problems failed to draw his attention.

Our foreign trade has gone down. At the beginning of the century, it was 10 per cent, then it came down to 2.5 per cent, and now it stands at 0.5 per cent. This is the factual position. This is not for the sake of criticism. The people of the world do not look at us as different political entities. Our neighbouring countries do not make any distinction among us. Whenever we fail, the world laughs at us. Our neighbours pass comments on us. There is no objection if we fight sometimes. One must fight. It has been said that '*Munde munde mattir bhinna*'. All the people have their different lines of thinking. But we should express our views fearlessly. Yet, there are some values of life that cannot be compromised. One such value is the honesty of politicians. We need impeccable leadership. Do you know the extent to which this corruption has permeated? There has been a fodder scandal in Bihar. I do not want to go into it as the matter is under investigation. But there is no end to it.

Just now, a Chief Minister told me that when he was going to appoint the Chairman of a State Electricity Board, some officers came to him who wanted to grab the post of Chairman by offering me one crore, two crore, five crore. I did not ask him whom he selected for this post. But I have faith in his statement. Today, there is a shortage of electricity in the country. We are inviting foreign capital, and we are signing agreements, but we are not able to produce the electricity required in this country.

I was told that a meeting of the Chief Ministers was convened but they could not arrive at a consensus, apparently because of excessive political rivalry. As a result, the interests of the country have taken a back seat in the field of power generation. We had fixed a target of 33,000 megawatt. But the data that we have got reveals that we have been able to add only 13,000 megawatts to the existing capacity. Uttar Pradesh is complaining of power shortage. When I visited Bihar on an election campaign, the people of that state and Mr Nitish Kumar told me that the state remains without power four days in a week. I do not know why. Our ancestors used to pray '*Tamaso ma jyotirgamaya*', lead me from darkness to light. But their able successors are preparing to take the people from light to darkness. Does this not strike at the core of our heart? Does it call for party-based politics?

We have not done anything during the last ten days that would invite criticism against us and if we are given a five-year tenure, we will provide a spotless administration. But there is a question of bringing about orderliness in the system of administration that we have inherited. The President's address says that we will take up the work of electoral reforms that has been pending for the last many years. How will the expenses for the elections be met? If black money is accepted for contesting elections, then one cannot get out of the web of black money even after elections. This tendency of accepting black money needs to be changed.

The Goswami Committee was constituted. It decided upon the issue of state funding and made recommendations to that effect. During the last session of the previous Lok Sabha, the Minister of Home Affairs of the erstwhile Government, Shri Chavan had stated in a meeting of the leaders of the opposition parties that the Government had, in principle, accepted the proposal regarding state funding and that it was under consideration of the Cabinet and the same would be implemented prior to the ensuing elections. It is not known what fate that proposal met with and whether the meeting of the Cabinet was held or not. It was not a recommendation of large magnitude. I do not claim that it would have plugged all the loopholes of the electoral system. There are many aspects to it. But a step should have been taken in this direction. At times, some friends seem to be in favour of status quo in the present corrupt and costly system in order to serve their vested interests. This should not happen. Stringent measures should be taken to curb the use of black money in elections. We are ready to lend our support in this direction. You, too, should be ready to co-operate if we initiate the steps. The Lok Pal Bill has been gathering dust for several years. Is the Prime Minister above the law? Which door should one knock on when one has a grievance against the Prime Minister or allegations are levelled against him? The issue whether the Prime Minister should be brought under the purview of the Lok Pal Bill or not has been discussed for years together.

Shri Narasimha Rao had stated that he had given his clearance to bring the Prime Minister under the purview of the Bill. When I asked about the Bill, I did not get a response. After the adjournment of the House, the Government was ready to promulgate ordinances on matters which could have inflated its vote bank but not with regard to Lok Pal. An ordinance could have been promulgated in this regard, but it did not happen. The other day, my friends were complaining about excessive interference of the courts of law. Perhaps Comrade Indrajit Gupta talked about judicial activism that day. If the Prime Minister does not discharge his duties, the Executive does not take decisions and keeps matters in limbo and when in reply to a question asked about his indecisiveness, the Prime Minister says that not taking a decision is also a decision, then it does not augur well. I am saying so on the basis of newspaper reports. If the news reports are not correct, he can intimate the correct position. When not taking a decision is considered a decision it is a state of culmination of Karmyoga. The country can be administered without taking decisions. At times the Government banked upon procrastination in order to avoid new areas of dispute and left everything to the judgment of the courts. Now the

courts have started giving verdicts in matters which ought to have been decided by the Executive and the Parliament. Why can't the Parliament discharge its duties and take on the responsibilities of the Executive? In order to achieve this, the Executive should be honest and vibrant and it should not delay matters. But it has not been so. We want to work in this direction. Any Government that comes to power will have to achieve that end. Otherwise, one Government may last for twelve days and another for six months. That will be a great injustice to the people of this country. People have performed their duty. The electorate is not responsible for a hung Parliament. We could not probably convey to the voter our message in a proper manner. Sometimes, the poor turn-out of voters caused concern as to whether democracy has lost credibility in the eyes of the people. They think that things will go on like this, whosoever forms the Government. Manthara had said, '*Koyi nrip hoye, hamein ka hani.*' These words of Manthara will not be quoted throughout the country. Governments will not be formed on the basis of horse-trading and defections. The Government should be based on programmes and an assurance should be given that injustice will not be done to the people. Now people will have their say against injustice. The Honourable President invited us because we emerged as the single largest party on the basis of our ideology, programmes and policies. Some of our policies have found mention in the President's Address.

Mamata ji objected to only one point and I hope she agrees to the rest of the Address. I would also like to know from my other friends if there is anything objectionable in the Address. Is it not the need of the hour to take unanimous decisions, run the Government on minimum common programmes and strive to concentrate on them, leaving aside most other issues? Yet, certain issues need to be deliberated upon.

The biggest allegation levelled against us is that we are a communal party and we lack secular credentials, so all the guardians of so-called secularism must unite and vote the BJP out of power. Democracy is a game of numbers which is not in our favour. Yet we have got the largest popular mandate.

Mr Speaker, Sir, the time has come when we should view our old values in the context of the changing situation. Communalism is not of one kind. If one kind of communalism is stirred up, then another kind of communalism will rise. This fact has not been realised to this day.

No call for oppressing people on the basis of religion and ideological differences has ever been made in this country, and will never be made, and should not be made, and if it is made then we will oppose it to the hilt. We want to give you this assurance. India should remain a secular state. We will never make our country a theocratic state like our neighbouring countries. But does this mean that we do not have our own roots of civilisation? Does it mean that we have no values? We have inherited this ancient civilisation and culture which are 5000 years old. We are proud of it. This civilisation and culture have moulded our life. But in what direction is our life headed nowadays?

I recall those days when Pandit Jawahar Lal Nehru went to Aligarh University to deliver a speech after the unfortunate partition of the country. It was a convocation function; I would quote a portion of his speech before you:

> I have said that I am proud of my inheritance and our ancestors who gave an intellectual and cultural pre-eminence to India. How do you feel about this past? Do you feel that we are sharers in it and inheritors in it and, therefore, proud of something that belongs to you as much as to me or do you feel alien to it? Was it without understanding that strange thrill which comes from the realisation that we are the trustees and inheritors of this vast treasure? You are a Muslim and I am a Hindu. We may adhere to different religious faiths or even to none but that does not take away that inheritance, that is yours as well as mine. The past holds us together whilst the present or the future divides us in a split.

These are the views of Nehruji.

There is a need to again go through whatever Nehru had written in his last document and which has become part of our curriculum. No one can brand Nehru as orthodox. Nehru had mentioned that inheritance which we have got through centuries. He praised our open-mindedness. But he also said that we are strong enough to stay firm on our feet. Is this sort of common inheritance and cultural inheritance feasible? Can we be proud of this past?

Several foreigners came here. They were accepted and admitted to our fold. We did not close our doors to those who were innocent and were uprooted. We accommodated everyone. Those who were victims of oppression in their own countries found shelter here. The first mosque was built in Kerala with the permission of the Hindu king. The first church was also built in Kerala, with permission. This is in our blood. This is in our system. There should not be discrimination on religious grounds. Everyone should have religious freedom. Everyone should be treated equally. But this is not happening. Therefore, our problems are rising and people are becoming apprehensive. You will not remove these apprehensions, as you are interested in vote politics. But I want to say that there is a need to arrive at a consensus on these matters. The Supreme Court gave its verdict on the Shah Bano case. Consensus could have been arrived at and steps towards this could have been taken. But this was not done.

Mr Speaker, Sir, there is another aspect to this problem. We are committed to social justice. Justice should be done to those who have been denied it so far, and at a faster pace. Discrimination should end in society. The help of the law has been sought for this. While doing away with disparities, it is essential that social ill-will should not be fermented and casteism should not be encouraged. Today, the country seems to be divided on the issue of casteism. This poison of casteism is spreading in all classes of society. So much so that it cannot be said with certainty that the Services remain unaffected by casteism. This situation is worrisome for all. The nation is already beset with communal problems and if we do not take care of this problem, then a new problem will arise, which will harm the social structure and create problems in the villages, i.e., in every corner of the country. We need social equality and social harmony.

We took steps to institute and develop Panchayati Raj institutions, ensured participation of all, specially gave the women their rights. If best results are to be achieved, then along with that, a change in outlook is also essential.

I am sure that the House would also pay attention to this question. And a unanimous policy in this regard would be formulated, which would strengthen social justice without disturbing social harmony. Harmony does not imply that social evils should be tolerated. Nor does it mean that the backward and oppressed should be maltreated. Harmony means that, as we are all the sons and daughters of mother India, we have to solve our problems amicably. We should feel the pain of others and respect their sentiments. Any reform bereft of inherent mercy or sentiment can be effective only partially. It cannot bring about permanent change in society. And the need is for steps to be taken to usher in permanent change in society.

Mr Speaker, Sir, an allegation has been levelled against me that I have a lust for power and whatever I did during the last ten days was only because of my lust for power. This allegation has hurt me deep in my heart. Just now I said that I have been in Parliament for forty years. The Honourable Members have seen my behaviour and my conduct. I had been in the Government with my friends in the Janata Dal. I have never done anything wrong in pursuit of power. Shri Sharad Pawar is sitting here. He was not present in the House when Shri Jaswant Singh was speaking. He said in his speech that Shri Pawar had caused a split in his party to form the Government with our support. Whether he formed the Government for the sake of power or for the good of Maharashtra is a different matter. But the fact remains that he caused a split in his party and cooperated with us. But I did nothing of this sort. During the course of this debate, a remark has been made repeatedly that personally Vajpayee is a good leader but his party is not good. Then what do you intend to do for a good Vajpayee?

Mr Speaker, Sir, I won't name anybody. I did not want to name even Sharad ji. If I am offered power with a new alliance at the cost of a split in my party, I would be the last person even to remotely entertain such an idea.

'*Na bhito maranadasmi kewalam dusthito yash.*' Lord Rama has said that 'I do not fear death, if at all I fear, I fear a bad name, I fear public odium.' My political career spanning forty years has been an open book. But when the electorate voted us as the single largest party, should we have rejected their mandate? When the Honourable President invited me to form the Government and told me that the oath of the Council of Minsters would take place the next day and the majority should be proved by the 31st, should I have run away from shouldering the responsibility? When I initiated the discussion, I had clarified this point too. Isn't it a fact that we have emerged as the single largest party?

Now I shall come to the other arguments that are being given in this regard. On being invited to form the Government, should I have asked the Honourable President to give me some time so that I may have consultations within the party?

When the President told me that the oath ceremony would take place the next day and I was given time up to 31st May '96 to prove majority, I offered to make best use of the time being given to me by talking to other parties in a bid to garner their support and try to create an atmosphere conducive to moving ahead on the basis of a common programme. What is objectionable in that? How does it indicate our greed for power? Moreover, the decision to form the Government was not just mine, it was that of the party.

Mr Speaker, once the date, i.e., 31st May was fixed for a trial of strength, it could take place only on the floor of the House. We never subscribed to the view that this trial of strength should take place either in the Rashtrapati Bhawan or the Raj Bhawan—it therefore became necessary to summon the House and once the House is summoned, the President's Address is a Constitutional obligation. We could have listed some other business too for the sitting, at least we could have moved a Motion of Thanks on the President's Address, but neither did the Opposition benches permit it, nor did I insist on it lest it create any doubts. We looked for the earliest opportunity for the trial of strength. Hence the Motion of Confidence was brought on 27th May and today is 28th May and the matter will be decided. We could have insisted that we have been given time up to 31st May and we will remain in power. Mr Speaker, Sir, one should not be hit below the belt or be put under a cloud. I never played this game nor will I ever play such a game in the future. Democracy is a system. Now they are making a count of the percentage of votes we got. Under the Westminster model of parliamentary system that our country has adopted, the number of votes or the percentage thereof which a party gets is not taken into account. What counts is the number of seats that a party wins. This system cannot serve the twin

objective, i.e., percentage of votes as well as number of seats. Our country has not adopted the List System of proportional representation. I, for one, have always been pointing out the defects of the Westminster system in which, at times, it is quite possible that a party getting lesser number of votes on an aggregate may corner a disproportionately large number of seats or vice-versa. In Kerala a coalition Government has come to power with just one per cent margin of votes, dislodging the party in power. The difference in votes was of just one per cent but this difference which we have presently has to be recognised. And now the total number of votes you got are being counted but I can make a count of your percentage of votes, which would be only to your disadvantage. They now say that they are uniting. Are they uniting for the explicit purpose of providing a stable and responsible Government in the country? I do not want to repeat, they have not chalked out a programme so far, nor have they approached the electorate with a common programme. The mandate received and the vote percentage obtained about which they are now talking is for different states and for divergent reasons. In Tamil Nadu it was the Congress that was fighting against DMK and not our party. The same situation obtained in Andhra Pradesh where we were nowhere in the picture. How can they say the mandate is against us when it was the Congress that they were fighting against and not us? What sort of a mandate is this? Say explicitly what you are murmuring. Say openly that you will not let us come to power at any cost. It is proper to speak in such a vein? The spirit behind this speech is even more despicable. A bogey is being created in this House that India is moving towards a Hitler type of dictatorship and fascism is raising its head in the country. This sort of fear is being created. The debutants in this House are quite unaware of even the dignity of the house. I have been in Parliament for forty years now. We have been working as a party here on democratic lines and have been contesting elections.

The mandate is against the Congress. The strength of the Congress in the House stands reduced to just half of its previous strength. The people have given their verdict differently in different states, disregarding which, all the other parties are now uniting and enlisting Congress support and the latter is willing to extend its unqualified support to them. I do not want to reiterate what my friend Mr George Fernandes said yesterday. The stand taken by the other parties seems to be that irrespective of whatever invectives they might have hurled at each other, now they should unite and ensure the BJP does not form the Government. If this is your collective decision, I will not say anything. Nonetheless, such a decision would be negative, reactionary, with the sole purpose of preventing us from coming to power and hardly conducive to the health of democracy.

I want to caution them today that, on our part, we are ready to sit in the opposition. Mr Speaker, Sir, when I joined

politics, I never dreamt of becoming an MP. I was a journalist. I am not keen on the type of politics being practised today. I wish to renounce politics. But politics itself refuses to part company with me.

I became the leader of the opposition. Today, I am the Prime Minister and after some time I shall cease to be so. I was not overjoyed when I became the Prime Minister, nor shall I have any qualms when I demit the office. However, I would like to raise some issues.

Today a number of fresh allegations are being levelled against us that we have not included certain important issues in the President's Address. The President's Address makes no mention of the Ram Temple, Article 370 and the Uniform Civil Code; in fact, the Swadeshi slogan has also been jettisoned. All this is being said in a tone that suggests they are very much aggrieved on account of our putting aside these issues, whereas these are the same people who have all along been criticising us for these issues. They have been holding us guilty because we intend to construct the Ram Temple and want abrogation of Article 370 of the Constitution and ask us how we can keep the unity of the country intact. Even though it is written in the Constitution, and the Supreme Court has also vindicated this view point that there should be a Uniform Civil Code, but we cannot say this? And if we do, we are branded as subverters of the unity of the country. But what we are saying is that these

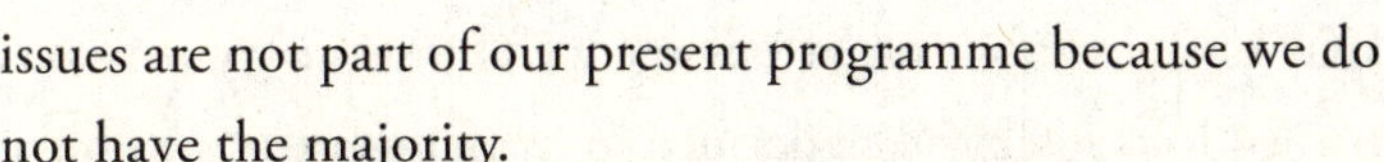

issues are not part of our present programme because we do not have the majority.

We are fighting for a majority. If the people's mandate is not in your favour, they have not fully accepted us either, and with the mandate we have received now, we are not in a position to implement all the programmes. We wanted a majority but we could not get it. We have emerged as the single largest party and our endeavour is to evolve a workable system through consensus and that is why we did not touch upon the disputed issues. What objection do you have over that?

Now, the United Front is being formed. It is good if it has been formed but its programme is yet to be chalked out. If that has been done, then have they assimilated the philosophy and the programmes of the Marxist party in it, in totality? If they have done so, then why has the Marxist Party been keeping a distance from the Government?

When a United Front is formed, a number of parties come together. When different political parties come together, every party has to give up some of its programmes. In 1977 also we were supporting the demand for abrogation of Article 370 of the Constitution. Shri Ram Vilas Paswan, who is present here, was with us at that time. In 1977 we were in favour of making the atom bomb also, but when we realised that democracy was in danger and there was a need to save it, we kept aside many of our party programmes.

Due to the imposition of Emergency, the entire country was turned into a jail. We all decided to work together to stop the authoritarianism. At that time, no one asked us why we were not pressing for the demand of abrogation of Article 370. In a way, it was right. Now, you are forming a United Front, so each one of you will have to forgo some of your party programmes. The Honourable President has given us time up to 31st because he knew that we were not in majority. But the Honourable President called us to form the Government because we were the single largest party in the House. He gave us time up to 31st May so that we could talk to other political parties and make efforts to form a stable Government. Such things are happening in other countries also. It has also been done here.

Mr Speaker, Sir, I would like to reply to one more point which came up during the course of discussion. It has been said that the BJP did not receive wide support from the people. It was said that we got support from the cow-belt. It is improper to refer to this entire region as the cow-belt in the House. We won in Haryana. We received support in Karnataka. It is correct that we are not that strong in Kerala and Tamil Nadu. But we have our organisation there. We have also received a little less than ten per cent votes in West Bengal. If you talk of votes, then talk of ten per cent votes. In this House individual Members constitute a party and they are trying to dislodge us by mobilising people against us.

They have every right to do so. Each of them has come alone from his constituency and become united here in Delhi. Why have they united? Is it for the well-being of the country? If so, they are welcome. We are also serving the nation in our own way. Are we not patriots and rendering selfless service to the country by carving a niche for ourselves in politics? We have been sincerely making efforts for the last forty years to reach this position. It is not a sudden mandate. It was not a miracle. We worked hard. We went to people; we have struggled. Ours is a party which functions round the year. Ours is not like the parties which mushroom during the elections. Today we are unnecessarily being put in an embarrassing position just because we could not get a few more seats. We do admit that is our weakness. We should have got a majority. The President gave us an opportunity and we tried to avail of it. It is another matter that we did not succeed. But do not forget that even then we are going to sit in the House as the largest party in the Opposition and they have to run the House with our cooperation. l would like to assure them that we will extend our fullest cooperation to them in conducting the business of the House. But I do not know what type of Government they will form, on what programmes it would be formed and how it would be run.

So far as Dalits are concerned, out of the total of seventy-seven Scheduled Caste Members, twenty-nine belong to BJP, while five members are from CPI(M), one from CPI, fifteen from the Congress Party, and seven from Janata Dal. We have the maximum number. Similarly, there are as many as eleven Members belonging to Scheduled Tribes in the BJP out of the total of forty-one Members. Please don't say that we do not have a popular base, we do not have wide support from people. They may think that they can form the Government without us and that Government will last, but I do not see any such possibility. First of all, it will be difficult for the Government to come into being. And it is hardly possible that it will survive. The question is, how is this Government, surrounded by internal squabbles, going to benefit the country? For each and everything they have to approach the Congress party. I cannot say this about the present, but earlier there was some talk that the Congress party has laid down certain conditions. Then there was a tale that a Cabinet Coordinating Committee will be formed. They should also have coordination on the floor of the House. Without that the business of the House cannot be conducted. It is very good that they want to govern the country. Our good wishes are with them. We shall continue to serve the country. We bow before the numerical strength and we assure you that we will not rest until we achieve the national objective.

Mr Speaker, Sir, I am going to submit my resignation to the President.

66

Osho

Rajneesh (1931–1990), born Chandra Mohan Jain, was also known as Acharya Rajneesh, Bhagwan Shree Rajneesh, and later as Osho. He preached an eclectic doctrine of Eastern mysticism, individual devotion and sexual freedom. He rejected traditional religions saying that spiritual experience could not be organised into any one system of religious dogma. He promoted dynamic meditation and encouraged his followers to live life fully, but without attachment.

The Art of Celebration

We train a child to focus his mind, to concentrate, because without concentration he will not be able to cope with life. Life requires it; the mind must be able to concentrate. But the moment the mind becomes able to concentrate, it becomes less aware. Awareness means a mind that is conscious but not focused. Awareness is a consciousness of all that is happening.

Concentration is a choice. It excludes all except its object of concentration; it is a narrowing. If you are walking on the street, you will have to narrow your consciousness in order to walk. You cannot ordinarily be aware of all that is happening because if you are aware of everything that is happening you will become unfocused. So concentration is a need. Concentration of the mind is a need in order to live—to survive and exist. That is why every culture, in its own way, tries to narrow the mind of the child.

Children, as they are, are never focused; their consciousness is open from all sides. Everything is coming in, nothing is being excluded. The child is open to every sensation, every sensation is included in his consciousness. And so much is coming in! That is why he is so wavering, so unstable. A child's unconditioned mind is a flux—a flux of sensations—but he will not be able to survive with this type of mind. He must learn how to narrow his mind, to concentrate.

The moment you narrow the mind you become particularly conscious of one thing and simultaneously unconscious of so many other things. The more narrowed the mind is, the more successful it will be. You will become a specialist, you will become an expert, but the whole thing will consist of knowing more and more about less and less.

The narrowing is an existential necessity; no one is responsible for it. As life exists, it is needed, but it is not enough. It is utilitarian, but just to survive is not enough; just to be utilitarian is not enough. So when you become utilitarian and the consciousness is narrowed, you deny your mind much of which it was capable. You are not using the total mind, you are using a very small part of it. And the remaining—the major portion—will become unconscious.

In fact, there is no boundary between conscious and unconscious. These are not two minds. 'Conscious mind' means that part of the mind that has been used in the narrowing process. 'Unconscious mind' means that portion that has been neglected, ignored, closed. This creates a division, a split. The greater portion of your mind becomes alien to you. You become alienated from your own self; you become a stranger to your own totality.

A small part is being identified as yourself and the rest is lost. But the remaining unconscious part is always there as unused potentiality, unused possibilities, unlived adventures. This unconscious mind—this potential, this unused mind—will always be in a fight with the conscious mind; that is why there is always a conflict within. Everyone is in conflict because of this split between the unconscious and the conscious. But only if the potential, the unconscious, is allowed to flower can you feel the bliss of existence; otherwise not.

If the major portion of your potentialities remains unfulfilled, your life will be a frustration. That is why the more utilitarian a person is, the less he is fulfilled, the less he is blissful. The more utilitarian the approach—the more one is in business life—the less he is living, the less he is ecstatic. The part of the mind that cannot be made useful in the utilitarian world has been denied.

The utilitarian life is necessary but at a great cost: you have lost the festivity of life. Life becomes a festivity, a celebration, if all your potentialities come to a flowering; then life is a ceremony. That is why I always say that religion means transforming life into a celebration. The dimension of religion is the dimension of the festive, the nonutilitarian.

The utilitarian mind must not be taken as the whole. The remaining, the greater—the whole mind—should not be sacrificed to it. The utilitarian mind must not become the end. It will have to remain there, but as a means. The other—

the remaining, the greater, the potential—must become the end. That is what I mean by a religious approach.

With a nonreligious approach, the businesslike mind, the utilitarian, becomes the end. When this becomes the end, there is no possibility of the unconscious actualizing the potential; the unconscious will be denied. If the utilitarian becomes the end, it means that the servant is playing the role of the master.

Intelligence, the narrowing of the mind, is a means toward survival, but not toward life. Survival is not life. Survival is a necessity—to exist in the material world is a necessity—but the end is always to come to a flowering of the potential, of all that is meant by you. If you are fulfilled completely, if nothing remains inside in seed form, if everything becomes actual, if you are a flowering, then and only then can you feel the bliss, the ecstasy of life.

The denied part of you, the unconscious part, can become active and creative only if you add a new dimension to your life—the dimension of the festive, the dimension of play. So meditation is not a work, it is a play. Praying is not a business, it is a play. Meditation is not something to be done to achieve some goal—peace, bliss—but something to be enjoyed as an end in itself.

The festive dimension is the most important thing to be understood—and we have lost it totally. By festive, I mean the capacity to enjoy, moment to moment, all that comes to you.

We have become so conditioned and habits have become so mechanical that even when there is no business to be done, our minds are businesslike. When no narrowing is needed, you are narrowed. Even when you are playing, you are not playing, you are not enjoying it. Even when you are playing cards, you are not enjoying it. You play for the victory and then the play becomes a work; then what is going on is not important, only the result.

In business the result is important. In festivity, the act is important. If you can make any act significant in itself, then you become festive and you can celebrate it. Whenever you are in celebration, the limits, the narrowing limits are broken. They are not needed, they are thrown. You come out of your straitjacket, the narrowing jacket of concentration. Now you are not choosing; everything that comes, you allow. And the moment you allow the total existence to come in, you become one with it. There is a communion.

This communion—this celebration, this choiceless awareness, this non businesslike attitude—I call meditation. The festivity is in the moment, in the act, not in the bothering about the results, not in achieving something. There is nothing to be achieved, so you can enjoy that which is here and now.

You can explain it in this way: I am talking to you; if I am concerned about the result, then the talk becomes a business, it becomes a work. But if I talk to you without any expectations, without any desire about the result, then the talk becomes a play. The very act, in itself, is the end. Then narrowing is not needed. I can play with the words, I can play with the thoughts. I can play with your question, I can play with my answer; then it is not serious, then it is light hearted.

And if you are listening to me without thinking about getting something out of it, then you can be relaxed; then you can allow me to be in communion with you and your consciousness will not be narrowed. Then it is open—playing, enjoying.

Any moment can be a business moment, any moment can be a meditative moment; the difference is in the attitude. If it is choiceless, if you are playing with it, it is meditative.

There are social needs and there are existential needs that are to be fulfilled. I will not say, 'Do not condition children.' If you leave them totally unconditioned, they will be barbaric. They will not be able to exist. Survival needs conditioning but survival is not the end, so you must be able to put your conditioning on and take it off—just like clothes. You can put them on, go out and do your business, and then come home and take them off. Then you *are*.

If you are not identified with your clothes, with your conditioning, if you do not say, for example, 'I am my mind,' it is not difficult; then you can change easily. But you become identified with your conditioning. You say, 'My conditioning is me,' and all that is not your conditioning is denied. You think, 'All that is not conditioned is not me, the unconscious is not me; I am the conscious, the focused mind.' This identification is dangerous. This should not be. A proper education is not conditioned, but is conditioned with the condition that conditioning is a utilitarian need; you must be able to take it on and off. When it is needed you put it on, and when you do not need it you can take it off. Until it is possible to educate human beings so that they do not become identified with their conditionings, human beings are not really human beings. They are robots—conditioned, narrowed.

To understand this is to become aware of that part of the mind, the greater part, which has been denied light. And to become aware of it is to become aware that you are not the conscious mind. The conscious mind is just a part. 'I' am both, and the greater part is unconditioned. But it is always there, waiting.

My definition of meditation is that it is simply an effort to jump into the unconscious. You cannot jump by calculation because all calculation is of the conscious and the conscious mind will not allow it. It will caution: 'You will go mad. Do not do it.'

The conscious mind is always afraid of the unconscious because if the unconscious emerges, all that is calm and clear in the conscious will be swept away. Then everything will be dark, as in a forest.

It is like this: you have made a garden, a garden with a boundary. Very little ground has been cleared, but you have planted some flowers and everything is okay—ordered, clear.

Only, the forest is always nearby. It is unruly, uncontrollable, and the garden is in constant fear of it. At any moment the forest can enter and then the garden will disappear.

In the same way, you have cultivated a part of your mind. You have made everything clear. But the unconscious is always around, and the conscious mind is always in fear of it. The conscious mind says, 'Don't go into the unconscious. Don't look at it, don't think about it.'

The path of the unconscious is dark and unknown. To reason, it will look irrational; to logic, it will look illogical. So if you *think* in order to go into meditation, you will never go because the thinking part will not allow you to.

This becomes a dilemma. You cannot do anything without thinking, and with thinking you cannot go into meditation. What to do? Even if you think, 'I am not going to think,' this is also thinking. It is the thinking part of the mind that is saying, 'I shall not allow thinking.'

Meditation cannot be done by thinking; this is the dilemma—the greatest dilemma. Every seeker will have to come to this dilemma; somewhere, sometime, the dilemma will be there. Those who know say, 'Jump! Do not think!' But you cannot do anything without thinking. That is why unnecessary devices have been created—I say unnecessary devices, because if you jump without thinking, no device is needed. But you *cannot* jump without thinking, so a device is needed.

You can think about the device, your thinking mind can be put at ease about the device, but not about meditation. Meditation will be a jump into the unknown. You can work with a device and the device will automatically push you into the unknown. The device is necessary only because of the training of the mind; otherwise, it is not needed.

Once you have jumped you will say, 'The device was not necessary, it was not needed.' But this is a retrospective knowing; you will know afterward that the device was not needed. That is what Krishnamurti is saying: 'No device is needed; no method is needed.' The Zen teachers are saying, 'No effort is needed; it is effortless.' But this is absurd for one who has not crossed the barrier. And one is mainly talking with those who have not crossed the barrier.

So I say that a device is artificial. It is just a trick to put your rational mind at ease so that you can be pushed into the unknown.

That is why I use vigorous methods. The more vigorous the method, the less your calculative mind will be needed. The more vigorous it becomes, the more total, because vitality is not only of the mind—it is of the body, of the emotions. It is of your full being.

Sufi dervishes have used dance as a technique, as a device. If you go into dance, you cannot remain intellectual, because dance is an arduous phenomenon; your whole being is needed in it. And a moment is bound to come when dance will become mindless. The more vital, the more vigorous, the more you are in it, the less reason will be there. So dance was devised as a technique to push. At some point you will not be dancing, but the dance will take over, will take you over; you will be swept away to the unknown source.

Zen teachers have used the koan method. Koans are puzzles that by their very nature are absurd. They cannot be solved by reason; you cannot think about them. Ostensibly, it looks as if something can be thought about them; that is the catch. It seems as if something can be thought about koans, so you begin to think. Your rational mind is put at ease; something has been given to it to be solved. But the thing given to it is something that cannot be solved. The very nature of it is such that it cannot be solved because the very nature of it is absurd.

There are hundreds of puzzles. The teacher will say, 'Think about a soundless sound.' Verbally, it seems as though it can be thought about. If you try hard, somehow, somewhere, a soundless sound can be found; it *may* be possible. Then, at a certain point—and that point cannot be predicted; it is not the same for everyone—the mind just goes flat. It is not there. You are, but the mind, with all its conditioning, is gone. You are just like a child. Conditioning is not there, you are just conscious; the narrowing concentration is not there. Now you know that the device was not necessary—but this is an afterthought, it should not be said beforehand.

No method is causal; no method is the cause of meditation. That is why so many methods are possible. Every method is just a device, but every religion says that its method is the way and no other method will do. They all think in terms of causality.

By heating water, the water evaporates. Heat is the cause: without the heat, the water will not evaporate. This is causal. Heat is a necessity that must precede evaporation. But meditation is not causal, so any method is possible. Every method is just a device; it is just creating a situation for the happening; it is not causing it.

For example, beyond the boundary of this room is the unbound, open sky. You have never seen it. I can talk with you about the sky, about the freshness, about the sea, about all that is beyond this room, but you have not seen it. You do not know about it. You just laugh; you think I am making it up. You say, 'It is all fantastic. You are a dreamer.' I cannot convince you to go outside because everything that I can talk about is meaningless to you.

Then I say, 'The house is on fire!' This is meaningful to you; this is something that you can understand.

Now I do not have to give you any explanations. I just run; you follow me. The house is not on fire, but the moment you are outside you don't have to ask me why I lied. The meaning is there; the sky is there. Now you thank me. Any lie will do. The lie was just a device; it was just a device to bring you outside. It did not cause the outside to be there.

Every religion is based on a lie device. All methods are lies; they just create a situation, they are not causal. New devices can be created, new religions can be created. Old devices become flat, an old lie becomes flat, and new ones are needed. You have been told so many times that the house is on fire when it is not, that the lie has become useless. Now someone has to create a new device.

If something is the cause of something else, it is never useless. But an old device is always useless; new devices are needed. That is why every new prophet will have to struggle with the old prophets. He is doing the same work that they are doing, but he will have to oppose their teachings because he will have to deny old devices that have become flat and meaningless.

All the great ones—Buddha, Christ, Mahavira—have, out of compassion, created great lies just to push you out of the house. If you can be pushed out of your mind through any device, that is all that is needed. Your mind is the imprisonment, your mind is fatal; it is the slavery.

As I have said, this dilemma is bound to happen—the nature of life is such. You will have to learn to narrow the mind. This narrowing will be helpful when you move outward, but it will be fatal inside. It will be utilitarian with others; it will be suicidal with oneself.

You have to exist with others and with yourself. Any life that is one-sided is crippled. You must exist among others with a conditioned mind, but you must exist with yourself with a totally unconditioned consciousness. Society creates a narrowed consciousness, but consciousness itself means expansion; it is unlimited. Both are needs, and both should be fulfilled.

I call a person wise who can fulfil both needs. Either extreme is unwise; either extreme is harmful. So live in the world with the mind, with your conditioning, but live with yourself without mind, without training. Use your mind as a means, do not make it an end; come out of it the moment you have the opportunity. The moment you are alone, come out of it, take it off. Then celebrate the moment; celebrate the existence itself, being itself.

Just to *be* is such a great celebration if you know how to take the conditioning off. This 'taking off' you will learn through Dynamic Meditation. It will not be caused; it will come to you uncaused. Meditation will create a situation in which you will come to the unknown; by and by you will be pushed from your habitual, mechanical, robotlike personality. Be courageous: practice Dynamic Meditation vigorously and all else will follow. It will not be your doing, it will be a happening.

You cannot bring the divine, but you can hinder its coming. You cannot bring the sun into the house, but you can close the door. Negatively, mind can do much; positively, nothing. Everything positive is a gift, everything positive is a blessing; it comes to you, while everything negative is your own doing.

Meditation, and all meditation devices, can do one thing: push you away from your negative hindrances. It can bring you out of the imprisonment that is the mind, and when you have come out you will laugh. It was so easy to come out, it was right there. Only one step was needed. But we go on in a circle and the one step is always missed … the one step that can bring you to the center.

You go on in a circle on the periphery, repeating the same thing; somewhere the continuity must be broken. That is all that can be done by any meditation method. If the continuity is broken, if you become discontinuous with your past, then that very moment is the explosion! In that very moment you are centered, centered in your being, and then you know all that has always been yours, all that has just been awaiting you.

A.P.J. Abdul Kalam

Dr Avul Pakir Jainulabdeen Abdul Kalam (1931–2015) was the eleventh president of India. He played a leading role in the development of India's missile and nuclear weapons programmes as well as the civilian space programme.

His unfussy and non-heirarchial public demeanour and his ability to connect with young minds allied with his groundbreaking achievements made Dr Kalam a role model and an inspiration, especially for students. His autobiography remains one of the most popular books of our time.

Emancipators

On Republic Day 1990, the nation celebrated the success of its missile programme. I was conferred the Padma Vibhushan along with Dr Arunachalam. Two of my other colleagues—J.C. Bhattacharya and R.N. Agarwal—were also decorated with the Padma Shree awards. It was the first time in the history of free India that so many scientists affiliated to the same organization found their names on the awards list. Memories of the Padma Bhushan awarded a decade ago came alive. I still lived more or less as I had lived then—in a room ten feet wide and twelve feet long, furnished mainly with books, papers and a few pieces of hired furniture. The only difference was at that time, my room was in Trivandrum and now it was in Hyderabad. The mess bearer brought me my breakfast of idlis and buttermilk and smiled in silent congratulation for the award. I was touched by the recognition bestowed on me by my countrymen. A large number of scientists and engineers leave this country at the first opportunity to earn more money abroad. It is true that they definitely get greater monetary benefits, but could anything compensate for this love and respect from one's own countrymen?

I sat alone for a while in silent contemplation. The sand and shells of Rameswaram, the care of Iyadurai Solomon in Ramanathapuram, the guidance of Rev. Father Sequeira in Trichi and Prof. Pandalai in Madras, the encouragement of Dr Mediratta in Bangalore, the hovercraft ride with Prof. Menon, the pre-dawn visit to the Tilpat Range with Prof. Sarabhai, the healing touch of Dr Brahm Prakash on the day of the SLV-3 failure, the national jubilation on the SLV-3 launch, Madam Gandhi's appreciative smile, the post-SLV-3 simmering at VSSC, Dr Ramanna's faith in inviting me to DRDO, the IGMDP, the creation of RCI, Prithvi, Agni … a flood of memories swept over me. Where were all these men now? My father, Prof. Sarabhai, Dr Brahm Prakash? I wished I could meet them and share my joy with them. I felt the paternal forces of heaven and the maternal and cosmic forces of nature embrace me as parents would hug their long-lost child. I scribbled in my diary:

Away! fond thoughts, and vex my soul no more!
Work claimed my wakeful nights, my busy days
Albeit brought memories of Rameswaram shore
Yet haunt my dreaming gaze!

A fortnight later, Iyer and his team celebrated the awards for the missile programme with the maiden flight of Nag. They repeated the feat again on the very next day, thus testing twice over the first Indian all-composite airframe and the propulsion system. These tests also proved the worth of the indigenous thermal batteries.

India had achieved the status of having a third generation anti-tank missile system with 'fire-and-forget' capability—on par with any state-of-the-art technology in the world. Indigenous composite technology had achieved a major milestone. The success of Nag also confirmed the efficacy of the consortium approach, which had led to the successful development of Agni.

Nag uses two key technologies—an Imaging Infra Red (IIR) system and a Millimetric Wave (MMW) seeker radar as its guiding eye. No single laboratory in the country possessed the capability of developing these highly advanced systems. But the urge to succeed existed, which resulted in a very effective joint effort. The Semi Conductor Complex at Chandigarh developed the Charge Coupled Devices (CCD) array. The Solid Physics Laboratory, Delhi, made the matching Mercury Cadmium Telluride (MCT) detectors. The Defence Science Centre (DSC), Delhi, put together an indigenous cooling system based on the Joules Thomson effect. The transmitter receiver front end was devised at the Defence Electronics Application Laboratory (DEAL), Dehra Dun.

The special gallium arsenide gun, Schottky barrier mixer diodes, compact comparator for antenna system—India was banned from buying any one of these high technology devices, but innovation cannot be suppressed by international restrictions.

I went to Madurai Kamaraj University the same month to deliver their convocation address. When I reached Madurai, I asked after my high school teacher Iyadurai Solomon, who was by now a Reverend and eighty years old. I was told that he lived in a suburb of Madurai, so I took a taxi and looked for his house. Rev. Solomon knew that I was going to give the convocation address that day. However, he had no way of getting there. There was a touching reunion between teacher and pupil. Dr P.C. Alexander, the Governor of Tamil Nadu, who was presiding over the function, was deeply moved on seeing the elderly teacher who had not forgotten his pupil of long ago, and requested him to share the dais.

'Every convocation day of every University is like opening the floodgates of energy which, once harnessed by institutions, organizations and industry, aids in nation-building,' I told the young graduates. Somehow I felt I was echoing Rev. Solomon's words, spoken about half a century ago. After my lecture, I bowed down before my teacher. 'Great dreams of great dreamers are always transcended,' I told Rev. Solomon. 'You have not only reached my goals, Kalam! You have eclipsed them,' he told me in a voice choked with emotion.

The next month, I happened to be in Trichi and used that opportunity to visit St. Joseph's College. I did not find Rev. Father Sequeira, Rev. Father Erhart, Prof. Subramanyam,

Prof. Iyyamperumal Konar, or Prof. Thothathri Iyengar there, but it seemed to me that the stones of the St. Joseph's building still carried the imprint of the wisdom of those great people. I shared with the young students my memories of St. Joseph's and paid tribute to the teachers who had moulded me.

We celebrated the nation's forty-fourth Independence Day with the test firing of Akash. Prahlada and his team evaluated a new solid propellant booster system based on a composite modified double base propellant. This propellant with its unprecedented high energy properties was crucial in assuring the long-range surface-to-air missiles. The country had taken an important step in ground-based air defence of vulnerable areas.

Towards the end of 1990, Jadavpur University conferred on me the honour of Doctor of Science at a special convocation. I was a little embarrassed at finding my name mentioned along with that of the legendary Nelson Mandela, who was also honoured at the same convocation. What could I possibly have in common with a legend like Mandela? Perhaps it was our persistence in our missions. My mission of advancing rocketry in my country was perhaps nothing when compared with Mandela's mission of achieving dignity for a great mass of humanity; but there was no difference in the intensity of our passions. 'Be more dedicated to making solid achievements than in running after swift but synthetic happiness,' was my advice to the young audience.

The Missile Council declared 1991 the Year of Initiative for DRDL and RCI. When we chose the route of concurrent engineering in IGMDP, we selected a rough track. With the completion of developmental trials on Prithvi and Trishul, our choice was on test now. I exhorted my colleagues to commence user trials within the year. I knew that it was going to be a tough task, but that was not going to discourage us.

Rear Admiral Mohan retired and his deputy, Kapoor, was to take over Trishul. I had always admired Mohan's understanding of missile command guidance. This sailor-teacher-scientist could outwit any other expert in the country in this field. I will always remember his candid exposition of various aspects of the Command Line of Sight (CLOS) guidance system during the Trishul meetings. Once, he showed me a verse that he had composed to highlight the woes of an IGMDP Project Director. It was a good way of letting off steam:

Impossible timeframes,
PERT charts to boot
Are driving me almost crazy as a coot;
Presentations to MC add to one's woes,
If they solve anything, Heaven only knows.
Meetings on holidays, even at night,
The family is fed up,
And all ready to fight.

My hands are itching
To tear my hair—
But alas! I haven't any more to tear ...

I told him, 'I have handed over all my problems to my best teams in DRDL, RCI, and other participating labs. That has given me a full head of hair.'

The year 1991 began on a very ominous note. On the night of 15 January 1991, the Gulf War broke out between Iraq and the Allied Forces led by the USA. In one stroke, thanks to satellite television invading Indian skies by that time, rockets and missiles captured the imagination of the entire nation. People started discussing Scuds and Patriots in coffee houses and tea shops. Children began flying paper kites shaped like missiles, and playing war games along the lines of what they saw on American television networks. The successful test firing of Prithvi and Trishul during the course of the Gulf War was enough to make an anxious nation relax. The newspaper reports of the programmable trajectory capability of the Prithvi and Trishul guidance system, using microwave frequencies in virtually unjammable bands, created widespread awareness. The nation was quick to draw parallels between the missiles operational in the Gulf War and our own warhead carriers. A common query I encountered was whether Prithvi was superior to a Scud, whether Akash could perform like a Patriot, and so on. Hearing a 'Yes' or a

'Why not?' from me, people's faces would light up with pride and satisfaction.

The Allied Forces had a marked technological edge, as they were fielding systems built using the technologies of the eighties and nineties. Iraq was fighting with the by-and-large vintage weapon systems of the sixties and seventies.

Now, this is where the key to the modern world order lies—superiority through technology. Deprive the opponent of the latest technology and then dictate your terms in an unequal contest. When the Chinese war philosopher Sun Tzu ruminated over 2000 years ago that what matters in war is not decimating the enemy army physically but breaking his will so as to make him concede defeat in the mind, he seems to have visualized the domination of technology in the twentieth century theatres of war. The missile force coupled with the electronic warfare used in the Gulf War was a feast for military strategic experts. It acted as a curtain-raiser for the twenty-first century war scenario with missiles and electronics and information warfare playing the lead roles.

In India, even today, the term technology, for most people, conjures up images of smoky steel mills or clanking machines. This is a rather inadequate conception of what technology denotes. The invention of the horse collar in the Middle Ages led to major changes in agricultural methods, and was as much a technological advance as the invention of the Bessemer furnace centuries later. Moreover, technology includes techniques as well as the machines that may or may not be necessary to apply them. It includes ways to make chemical reactions occur, ways to breed fish, eradicate weeds, light theatres, treat patients, teach history, fight wars, or even prevent them.

Today, most advanced technological processes are carried out far from assembly lines or open hearths. Indeed, in electronics, in space technology, in most of the new industries, relative silence and clean surroundings are characteristic, even essential. The assembly line, with the organization of armies of men to carry out simple, routine functions is an anachronism. Our symbols of technology must change before we can keep pace with changes in technology itself. We should never forget that technology feeds on itself. Technology makes more technology possible. In fact, technological innovation consists of three stages linked together in a self-reinforcing cycle. First, there is the creative stage, with the blueprint of a feasible idea. This is made real by its practical application, and this finally ends in its diffusion through society. The process is then complete; the loop is closed when the diffusion of technology embodying the new idea in its turn helps generate new creative ideas. Today, all over the developed world, the time gap between each of the steps in this cycle has been shortened. In India, we are just progressing towards that stage—closing the loop.

After the Gulf War concluded with the victory of the technologically superior Allied Forces, over 500 scientists of DRDL and RCI gathered to discuss issues that had emerged. I posed a question before the assembly: was technology or weapon symmetry with other nations feasible, and if so, should it be attempted? The discussion led to many more serious questions, such as, how to establish effective electronic warfare support? How to make missile development proceed apace with the development of equally necessary systems like the LCA; and what were the key areas where a push would bring progress?

At the end of a lively discussion spread over three hours, the consensus emerged that there was no way to redress asymmetry in military capability except to have the same capability in specific areas as your potential opponent. The scientists vowed to achieve a reduced CEP in the accuracy of Prithvi's delivery, perfecting the Ka band guidance system for Trishul and realising all carbon-carbon re-entry control surfaces for Agni by the end of the year. The vow was later fulfilled. The year also saw tube-launched Nag flights, and the manoeuvre of Trishul at seven metres above sea level, at speeds which exceeded three times the speed of sound. The latter was a breakthrough in the development of an indigenous ship-launched anti-sea-skimmer missile.

The same year, I received an honorary degree of Doctor of Science from the IIT, Bombay. In the citation read by Prof. B. Nag on the occasion, I was described as 'an inspiration behind the creation of a solid technological base from which India's future aerospace programmes can be launched to meet the challenges of the twenty-first century'. Well, perhaps Prof. Nag was only being polite, but I do believe that India will enter the next century with its own satellite in geo-stationary orbit 36,000 km away in space, positioned by its own launch vehicle. India will also become a missile power. Ours is a country with tremendous vitality. Even though the world may not see its full potential or feel its full power, no one dare ignore it any more.

On 15 October, I turned sixty. I looked forward to retirement and planned to open a school for the less privileged children. My friend, Prof. P Rama Rao, who was heading the Department of Science and Technology in the Government of India, even struck up a partnership with me to establish what he called the Rao–Kalam school. We were unanimous in our opinion that carrying out certain missions and reaching certain milestones, however important they may be or however impressive they might appear to be, is not all there is to life. But we had to postpone our plan as neither of us was relieved from our post by the Government of India.

It was during this period that I decided to put down my memoirs and express my observations and opinions on certain issues.

The biggest problem Indian youth faced, I felt, was a lack of clarity of vision, a lack of direction. It was then that I decided to write about the circumstances and people who made me what I am today; the idea was not merely to pay tribute to some individuals or highlight certain aspects of my life. What I wanted to say was that no one, however poor, underprivileged or small, need feel disheartened about life. Problems are a part of life. Suffering is the essence of success. As someone said:

God has not promised
Skies always blue,
Flower-strewn pathways
All our life through;
God has not promised
Sun without rain,
Joy without sorrow,
Peace without pain.

I will not be presumptuous enough to say that my life can be a role model for anybody; but some poor child living in an obscure place, in an underprivileged social setting may find a little solace in the way my destiny has been shaped.

It could perhaps help such children liberate themselves from the bondage of their illusory backwardness and hopelessness. Irrespective of where they are right now, they should be aware that God is with them and when He is with them, who can be against them?

But God has promised
Strength for the day,
Rest for the labour
Light for the way.

It has been my observation that most Indians suffer unnecessary misery all their lives because they do not know how to manage their emotions. They are paralysed by some sort of a psychological inertia. Phrases like 'the next best alternative', 'the only feasible option or solution', and 'till things take a turn for the better' are commonplace in our business conversations. Why not write about the deep-rooted character traits which manifest themselves in such widespread, self-defeatist thought patterns and negative behaviour? I have worked with many people and organizations and have had to deal with people who were so full of their own limitations that they had no other way to prove their self-worth than by intimidating me. Why not write about the victimization which is a hallmark of the tragedy of Indian science and technology? And about the

pathways to organizational success? Let the latent fire in the heart of every Indian acquire wings, and the glory of this great country light up the sky.

—From *Wings of Fire*

Notes

1 F.E. Pargiter, *Encyclopaedia of Religion and Ethics*, X, p. 448.
2 *Journal of the Behar and Orissa Research Society*, p. 329.
3 *Journal of the University of Bombay*, X, pp. 148–155.
4 *Encyclopaedia of Religions and Ethics*, X, p. 448.
5 J.N. Farquhar, *Outline of the Religious Literature of India*, p. 139.
6 *Annals of the Bhandarkar Oriental Research Institute*, XXI, p. 49n.
7 *Indian Historical Quarterly*, VIII, p. 766.
8 *Journal of the Behar and Orissa Research Society*, XIV, pp. 330–337.
9 *Journal of the Behar and Orissa Research Society*, p. 336.
10 Hermann Oldenberg, *Buddha: His Life, His Doctrine, His Order* (Williams and Norgate, 1882), p. 127.
11 T. Suzuki (tr.), *The Awakening of Faith in the Mahayana* (The Open Court Publishing Company, 1900), pp. 111–112.
12 T. Richard (tr.), *The Awakening of Faith in the Mahayana* (1907), p. 26.
13 K.M. Sen, *Hinduism* (Penguin Books, 1961), p. 80.
14 P.D. Devanandan, *The Concept of Maya* (YMCA Publishing House, 1954), p. 91.
15 Shankara Bhashya on the Brahman Sutra.
16 Shankara Bhashya on the Brahman Sutra, quoted in S. Radhakrishnan, *Indian Philosophy, vol. 2* (Oxford University Press, 1923), p. 450.
17 Kokileshwar Shastri, *An Introduction to Adwaita Philsophy* (University of Calcutta, 1926), p. 15–16.
18 Radhakrishnan, *Indian Philosophy, vol. 2*, p. 536.
19 Radhakrishnan, *Indian Philosophy, vol. 2*, p. 59.

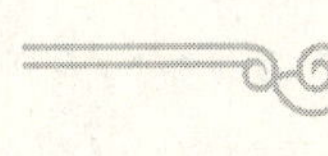

20 Radhakrishnan, *Indian Philosophy, vol. 2*, p. 536.
21 Shankara Bhashya, cited in Radhakrishnan, *Indian Philosophy, vol. 2*, p. 540.
22 P.D. Devanandan, cited in Radhakrishnan, *Indian Philosophy, vol. 2*, p. 110.
23 Shankara Bhashya, cited in Radhakrishnan, *Indian Philosophy, vol. 2*, p. 540.
24 Stella Kramrisch, *The Art of India: Traditions of Indian Sculpture Painting and Architecture* (The Phaidon Press, 1954), p. 14.
25 Kapila Vatsyayan, *The Square and the Circle of the Indian Arts* (Roli Books, 1997), pp. 3, 53.
26 Shakti Maira, *Towards Ananda: Rethinking Indian Art and Aesthetics* (Penguin Books, 2006), p. 4.
27 Harsha V. Dehejia, *The Beautifully Indian Hindu Mind* (D.K. Printworld, 2020), p. 48.
28 Kramrisch, *The Art of India*, pp. 26–27.
29 Vatsyayan, *The Square and the Circle of the Indian Arts*, p. 57.
30 Vatsyayan, *The Square and the Circle of the Indian Arts*, p. 39.
31 Stella Kramrisch, *The Art of India*, p. 9.
32 Vatsyayan, *The Square and the Circle of the Indian Arts*, pp. 39, 60.
33 Kapila Vatsyayan, 'From Interior Landscapes into Cyber Space: Fluidity and Dynamics of Tradition', in Kamala Ganesh and Usha Thakkar (eds), *Culture and the Making of Identity in Contemporary India* (Sage, 2005), p. 40.
34 M. Hiriyana, *Outlines of Indian Philosophy* (George, Allen & Unwin, Mumbai, 1973), p. 386.
35 Hiriyana, *Outlines of Indian Philosophy*, p. 387.
36 Radhakrishnan, *Indian Philosophy, vol. 2*, p. 638.
37 A.J. Appasamy (ed.), *Temple Bells: Readings from Hindu Religious Literature* (Association Press, 1930).
38 J.T.F. Jordens, 'Medieval Hindu Devotionalism', in A.L. Basham (ed.), *A Cultural History of India* (Clarendon Press, 1975), p. 269.

39 Appasamy (ed.), *Temple Bells*, p. 63.
40 Deben Bhattacharya (trans.), *Love Songs of Chandidas, the Rebel Poet–Priest of Bengal* (George Allen & Unwin, 1967), p. 57.
41 Bihari Lal, *The Satasai*, translated by K.P. Bahadur (Penguin Books/ UNESCO, 1992), p. 46.
42 J.S. Hawley, Surdas, Poet, Singer, Saint (Oxford University Press, 1984), p. 65.
43 Jordens, 'Medieval Hindu Devotionalism', p. 274.
44 Rabindranath Tagore (trans.), *One Hundred Poems of Kabir* (Macmillan, 1962).
45 Tagore (trans.), *One Hundred Poems of Kabir*, Poem number XLII.
46 Tagore (trans.), *One Hundred Poems of Kabir*, Poem No II.
47 A.K. Ramanujan (trans.), 'Basavanna' in *Speaking of Shiva* (Penguin Books, 1973), p. 19.
48 Ramanujan (trans.), 'Basavanna', p. 28
49 A.K. Ramanujan (trans.), 'Allama Prabhu', in *Speaking of Shiva*, p. 147.
50 L.D. Barnett (trans.), 'Nannaya', in *The Heart of India: Sketches in the History of Hindu Religion and Morals* (Wisdom of the East series, 1913), pp. 111–112.
51 Friedhelm Hardy, *Viraha-Bhakti: The Early History of Krishna Devotion in South India* (Oxford University Press, 1973), p. 420.
52 Rana Fulop-Miller, *Saints That Moved the World* (Thomas Y. Crowell, 1945), p. 175.
53 Fulop-Miller, *Saints That Moved the World*, Pp. 424–425.
54 A.J. Alston (trans.), *The Devotional Poems of Mirabai* (Motilal Banarasidass, 1980).
55 Alston (trans.), *The Devotional Poems of Mirabai.*
56 Alston (trans.), *The Devotional Poems of Mirabai.*
57 Norman Cutler (trans.), 'Karaikkalammaiyar', in *Songs of Experience: The Poetics of Tamil Devotion* (Indiana University Press, 1987), p. 121.

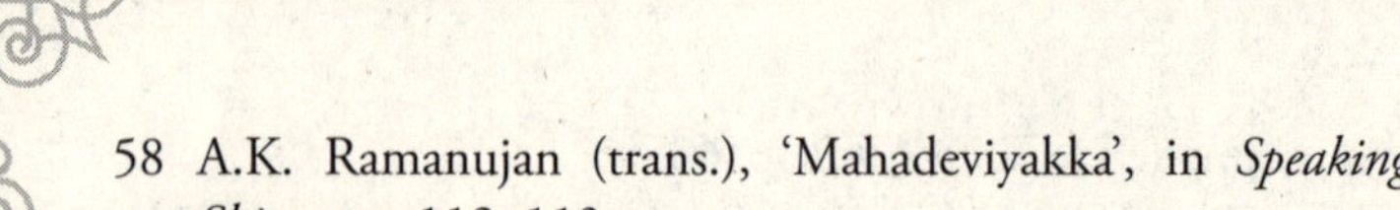

58 A.K. Ramanujan (trans.), 'Mahadeviyakka', in *Speaking of Shiva*, pp. 112–113.
59 Ramanujan (trans.), 'Mahadeviyakka', in *Speaking of Shiva*, p. 116.
60 Ramanujan (trans.), 'Mahadeviyakka', in *Speaking of Shiva*, pp. 48–49.
61 'Introduction' in Alston (trans.), *The Devotional Poems of Mirabai*, p. 25.
62 Milton Singer (ed.), *Krishna: Myths, Rites, and Attitudes* (East-West Centre Press, 1966), p. 133.
63 Chaturvedi Badrinath, *Dharma: Hinduism and Religions in India* (Penguin Books, 2019), p. 88.
64 Vinay Dharwadkar (ed.), *The Collected Essays of A.K. Ramanujan* (Oxford University Press, 2004), p. 271.
65 'No one,' exclaims Xenophanes, 'has attained complete certainty in respect to the gods and to that which I call universal nature, will nor anyone ever attain it. Nay, even if a man happened to light on the truth, he would not know that he did so, for appearance is spread over all things' (Theodor Gomperz, *Greek Thinkers: A History of Ancient Philosophy*, vol. I (J. Murray, 1901), p. 164).
66 Mādhava S.D.S.; Madhusudana Sarasvati's *Prasthānabheda*; Vijñānabhikṣu's Introduction to S.P.B. Cp. Kant: 'We are in a way maintaining the honour of human reason when we reconcile it with itself in the different persons of acute thinkers and discover the truth, which is never entirely missed by men of such thoroughness, even if they directly contradict each other' (quoted in James Ward, *A Study of Kant* (Cambridge University Press, 1922), p. 11n1).
67 Regarding China's debt to India, Professor Liang Chi Cho says: 'India taught us to embrace the idea of absolute freedom, that fundamental freedom of mind, which enables it to shake off all the fetters of past tradition and habit as well as the present customs of a particular age—that spiritual freedom which casts

off the enslaving forces of material existence. ... India also taught us the idea of absolute love, that pure love towards all living beings which eliminates all obsessions of jealousy, anger, impatience, disgust and emulation, which expresses itself in deep pity and sympathy for the foolish, the wicked and the sinful-that absolute love which recognises the inseparability between all beings.' He goes on to explain the contributions of India to Chinese literature and art, music and architecture, painting and sculpture, drama, poetry and fiction, astronomy and medicine, educational method and social organisations. See *Viśvabharati Quarterly*, October 1924. The influence of India on Burma and Ceylon, Japan and Corea, is well known.

68 *Sarvas sve sve gṛhe rājā.* Every man is the lord in his own house.

69 Aurobindo Ghosh: 'If an ancient Indian of the time of the Upanishad of the Buddha, or the later classical age were to be set down in modern India ... he would see his race clinging to forms and shells and rags of the past and missing nine-tenths of its nobler meaning ... he would be amazed by the extent of the mental poverty, the immobility, the static repetition, the cessation of science, the long sterility of art, the comparative feebleness of the creative intuition' (Arya, v. p. 424).

Copyright Acknowledgements

- **Nasadiya Sukta of Rigveda:** 'Anuvaka XI', in *Rig-Veda-Sanhita*, vol. VI, translated by H.H. Wilson (Ashtekar & Co., 1928).
- **Isha Upanishad:** *Isha Upanishad*, translated by Sri Aurobindo, in *The Complete Works of Sri Aurobindo*, vol. 17 (Sri Aurobindo Ashram Publication Department, 2003).
- **Mundaka Upanishad:** Karan Singh (trans.), *Mundaka Upanishad: The Bridge of Immortality* (Bharatiya Vidya Bhavan, Mumbai, 1987).
- **Mahabharata: Yaksha Prashna and Shanti Parva:** K.M. Ganguli, *The Mahabharata of Krishna-Dwaipayana Vyasa*.
- **Bhagavad Gita:** Annie Besant and Bhagavan Das (trans.), *The Bhagavad-Gîtâ* (Theosophical Publishing Society, 1905).
- **Bhumi Sukta of Atharvaveda:** 'Cosmogonic and Theosophic Hymns', in *Hymns of the Atharva-Veda*, translated by Maurice Bloomfield, in F. Max Müller (ed.), *Sacred Books of the East*, vol. 42 (Clarendon Press, 1897).
- **Puranas:** 'Introduction', in A.D. Pusalker, *Studies in the Epics and Puranas* (Bharatiya Vidya Bhavan, Mumbai, 1955).

- **Kama Sutra of Vatsyayana:** The Hindoo Kama Shastra Society (trans.), *The Kama Sutra of Vatsyayana* (The Society of the Friends of India Benaras, 1883–1925).
- **Arthashastra of Kautilya:** Dr. R. Shamasastry (trans.), *Kautilya's Arthashastra* (Mysore Printing and Publishing House, 1929).
- **Teachings of the Buddha:** Chandradhar Sharma, *Indian Philosophy: A Critical Survey* (Barnes & Noble, Inc., 1962).
- **Nagarjuna:** Kenneth K. Inada (trans.), *Nagarjuna: A Translation of His Mulamadhyamakakarika*, Bibliotheca Indo-Buddhica Series No. 127 (Sri Satguru Publications, 1993).
- **The Jain Texts:** 'Syadvada' in Chandradhar Sharma, *Indian Philosophy: A Critical Survey* (Barnes & Noble, Inc., 1962) and *The Naladiyar or Four Hundred Quatrains in Tamil*, translated by U.G. Pope.
- **Six Systems of Indian Philosophy:** 'The Canvas Before', in Pavan K. Varma, *Adi Shankaracharya: Hinduism's Greatest Thinker* (Westland Books, 2022).
- **Adi Shankaracharya and His Doctrine of Advaita:** Pavan K. Varma, *Adi Shankaracharya: Hinduism's Greatest Thinker* (Westland Books, 2022).
- **Brahma Sutra of Badarayana:** Swami Vireswarananda (trans.), *Brahma-Sutras* (Swami Vireswaranda, Advaita Ashrama, 1936).
- **Thirukkural of Thiruvalluvar:** M. Rajaram (trans.), *Thirukkural: Pearls of Inspiration* (Rupa Publications, 2009).

- **Dharmashastras:** Ganganatha Jha (trans.), *Manu-Smriti: The Laws of Manu with the Bhasya of Medhatithi*, vol. 1 (University of Calcutta, 1920).
- **Natyashastra of Bharat Muni:** 'The Realm of Ideas', in Pavan K. Varma, *The Great Hindu Civilisation* (Westland Books, 2024).
- **Shatakas of Bhartrihari:** Rev. B. Hale Wortham (trans.) *The Śatakas of Bhartṛihari* (Trubner & Co., 1886).
- **Sri Nimbarkacharya and His Doctrine of Dvaitadvaita:** 'Sri Nimbarkacharya', in Dr Swami Satya Prasad Dasji, *Indian Philosophy* (Sadguru Mahant Swami Sri Dharmanandan Dasji, Shri Swaminarayan Mandir, 2010).
- **Sri Ramanujacharya and His Doctrine of Vishishtadvaita:** 'Epilogue: The Legacy', in Pavan K. Varma, *Adi Shankaracharya: Hinduism's Greatest Thinker* (Westland Books, 2022).
- **Sri Madhvacharya and His Doctrine of Dvaita Philosophy:** 'Sri Madhvacharya', in Dr Swami Satya Prasad Dasji, *Indian Philosophy* (Sadguru Mahant Swami Sri Dharmanandan Dasji, Shri Swaminarayan Mandir, 2010).
- **Sri Vallabhacharya and His Doctrine of Shuddhadvaita:** 'Sri Nimbarkacharya', in Dr Swami Satya Prasad Dasji, *Indian Philosophy* (Sadguru Mahant Swami Sri Dharmanandan Dasji, Shri Swaminarayan Mandir, 2010).

- **Sri Chaitanya Mahaprabhu and His Doctrine of Achintyabhedabheda:** 'Shri Chaitanya Mahaprabhu', in Dr Swami Satya Prasad Dasji, *Indian Philosophy* (Sadguru Mahant Swami Sri Dharmanandan Dasji, Shri Swaminarayan Mandir, 2010).
- **Sri Ramcharitmanas:** Pavan K. Varma, *The Greatest Ode to Lord Ram: Tulsidas's Ramcharitmanas; Selections & Commentaries* (Westland Books, 2023).
- **The Bhakti Movement:** Pavan K. Varma, *The Great Hindu Civilisation* (Westland Books, 2024).
- **Narsinh Mehta:** *Vaishnav Jan To Tene Kahiye Je*, translation courtesy https://www.indembassybern.gov.in/docs/Lyrics%20of%20Vaishnav%20Jan%20To%20bhajan_23052018_111927.pdf.
- **The Japji and the Rehras:** Copyright © Naina Dayal.
- **Amir Khusrau Dehlavi:** 'Amir Khusaro Poems', translation courtesy https://www.poemhunter.com/amir-khusro/.
- **Baba Bulleh Shah:** 'Bulleh Shah Poems', translation courtesy https://www.poemhunter.com/poem/bulla-i-know-not-who-i-am/.
- **Din-i-Ilahi:** Makhanlal Roychoudhury, *The Din-i-Ilahi or The Religion of Akbar* (University of Calcutta, 1941).
- **Mir Taqi Mir:** 'All plans have gone amiss …', in K.C. Kanda (trans.), *Masterpieces of Urdu Ghazals: From the 17th to the 20th Century* (Sterling Pub Private Ltd, 1990).

- **Bahadur Shah Zafar:** 'I am not the apple of any eye …', in K.C. Kanda (trans.), *Masterpieces of Urdu Ghazals: From the 17th to the 20th Century* (Sterling Pub Private Ltd, 1990).
- **Mohammed Ibrahim Zauq:** 'Commissioned by life we come …', in K.C. Kanda (trans.), *Masterpieces of Urdu Ghazals: From the 17th to the 20th Century* (Sterling Pub Private Ltd, 1990).
- **Asadullah Khan Ghalib:** 'To have met my friend …', in K.C. Kanda (trans.), *Masterpieces of Urdu Ghazals: From the 17th to the 20th Century* (Sterling Pub Private Ltd, 1990).
- **Suryakant Tripathi 'Nirala'**: 'Breaking Stones', translated by Arvind Krishna Mehrotra, in A.K. Mehrotra, *Collected Poems (1969–2014)* (Penguin Random House, 2014). Reproduced with permission of the translator.
- **Maithili Sharan Gupt:** 'Panchavati, An Introduction', translated by Paddy Raghunathan, translation courtesy https://classicalpoets.org/2023/07/15/excerpt-from-panchavati-by-maithili-sharan-gupt-translated-by-paddy-raghunathan/.
- **Ramdhari Singh 'Dinkar':** 'Parichay', translation courtesy 'Reading and Rambling', https://sigma_sm.blogspot.com/2007/07/parichay.html.
- **Amrita Pritam:** 'To Waris Shah', translated by Amrita Pritam, in *Selected Poems of Amrita Pritam* (Dialogue Calcutta Publications).

- **Sahir Ludhianvi:** 'Taj Mahal', in K.C. Kanda (trans.), *Masterpieces of Urdu Nazm* (Sterling Pub Private Ltd, 2009).
- **Gopaldas Neeraj:** 'Let Us Have a Different Religion', translated by Ravindra Kumar Karnani, https://rkkblog1951.wordpress.com/tag/gopaldas-niraj/.
- **Dushyant Kumar:** 'Ghazal', translated by Harish Trivedi. Reproduced with permission of the translator.
- **Namdeo Dhasal:** 'Tree of Violence', translated by Dilip Chitre, in *A Current of Blood* (Navayana, 2011).
- **Gulzar:** 'Old Woman', translated by Pavan K. Varma. Reproduced with permission of the translator.
- **Raja Rammohun Roy:** *Selected Works of Raja Rammohun Roy* (Publication Division, Ministry of Information and Broadcasting, Government of India, 1977).
- **Ishwar Chandra Vidyasagar:** *Marriage of Hindu Widows* (The Sanskrit Press, 1864).
- **Dadabhai Naoroji:** *Poverty and Un-British Rule in India* (Swan Sonnenschein & Co., 1901).
- **Jyotirao Govindrao Phule:** P.G. Patil (trans.), *Selections: Collected Works of Mahatma Jotirao Phule, Vol. II* (Education Department, Government of Maharashtra, 1991).
- **Ramakrishna Paramahamsa:** Mahendranath Gupta, *The Gospel of Sri Ramakrishna*, translated by Swami Nikhilananda (Ramkrishna Math and Ramakrishna Mission).

- **Rabindranath Tagore:** *Gitanjali: Song Offerings* (Macmillan and Co. Limited, 1913).
- **Swami Vivekananda:** 'Swami Vivekananda's Speech at World Parliament of Religion, Chicago', https://arunshanbhag.wordpress.com/wp-content/uploads/2009/07/vivekananda_chicagospeech.pdf.
- **Mohandas Karamchand Gandhi:** *Hind Swaraj* (Navajivan Trust); *The Story of My Experiments with Truth*, translated by Mahadev Desai (Navajivan Trust).
- **Sri Aurobindo:** '1947, August 15th Message', Sri Aurobindo Society, https://aurosociety.org/society/index/1947%2C-August-15th-Message.
- **Sardar Vallabhbhai Patel:** *For a United India, Speeches of Sardar Patel 1947–1950* (Publications Division, Ministry of Information and Broadcasting, Government of India, 1949).
- **Periyar:** *Thoughts of Periyar*, compiled by Dr K. Veeramani (Dravidar Kazhagam Publications, Chennai, 2012).
- **Vinayak Damodar Savarkar:** 'Seven Shackles', https://savarkar.org/en/encyc/2017/5/22/Seven-shackles.html.
- **S. Radhakrishnan:** *Indian Philosophy*, vol. 2 (Oxford University Press, 2008).
- **Maulana Abul Kalam Azad:** Subhash C. Kashyap (ed.), *Maulana Abul Kalam Azad* (National Publishing House, 1989).
- **Jawaharlal Nehru:** 'A Tryst with Destiny: Indian Prime Minister Jawaharlal Nehru's Inaugural Address', https://

www.files.ethz.ch/isn/125396/1154_trystnehru.pdf.; *The Discovery of India* (Jawaharlal Nehru Memorial Fund, 1997).

- **B.R. Ambedkar:** *Dr. Babasaheb Ambedkar Writings and Speeches* (Dr. Ambedkar Foundation, Ministry of Social Justice & Empowerment, Government of India).
- **J. Krishnamurti:** *Life in Freedom* (The Star Publishing Trust, 1928).
- **Subhas Chandra Bose:** Dr R.C. Bhardwaj (ed.), *Netaji and the INA* (Lok Sabha Secretariat, New Delhi, 1994).
- **Ram Manohar Lohia:** *Guilty Men of India's Partition* (B.R. Publishing Corporation, 2020).
- **Indira Gandhi:** '23rd Session, 169th Plenary Meeting, 14th October, 1968, Speech by Mrs. Indira Gandhi, Prime Minister of India', https://pminewyork.gov.in/pdf/uploadpdf/79878lms20.pdf.
- **Atal Bihari Vajpayee:** 'Motion of Confidence in the Council of Ministers', in Digital library, Lok Sabha, Parliament of India, https://eparlib.nic.in/bitstream/123456789/5985/1/11_I_28061996_p11_p51_t4.pdf.
- **Osho:** *Meditation: Chapter 1 in The Art of Ecstasy* (OSHO International, 2006).
- **A.P.J. Abdul Kalam:** A.P.J. Kalam with Arun Tiwari, *Wings of Fire: An Autobiography* (Universities Press, 1999).